International African Seminars
New Series, No. 6

TRANSFORMING SETTLEMENT IN SOUTHERN AFRICA

TRANSFORMING SETTLEMENT IN SOUTHERN AFRICA

EDITED BY
Chris de Wet and **Roddy Fox**

Edinburgh University Press
for the
INTERNATIONAL AFRICAN INSTITUTE

© International African Institute, 2001

Edinburgh University Press Ltd
22 George Square, Edinburgh

Reprinted 2003

Typeset in Plantin
by Koinonia, Bury, and
printed and bound in Great Britain by
Biddles Ltd, Guildford

A CIP record for this book is available
from the British Library

ISBN 0 7486 1465 6 (hardback)

CONTENTS

LIST OF TABLES

LIST OF FIGURES

PREFACE

The International African Seminar series was inaugurated in the 1950s, when a conference on *Urbanization in Africa* was mounted in Kampala. Since then, further conferences have been convened in other university towns across Africa on a variety of topics concerned with problems of change and adaptation throughout the region. However, this discourse did not extend to South Africa, because the policy of apartheid isolated the academic community from the wider debate until 1990, when the foundations were laid for a more democratic and liberal society. It was in the context of this opening up in South Africa that a conference on changing patterns of settlement was first conceived. This seminar was convened in 1996 at Rhodes University in collaboration with the International African Institute, leading to the production of this latest volume in the series. This serves to celebrate the formal recognition of those who have been particularly concerned with the impact of change within South Africa over the years, initiating a wider, regional debate.

Fitting the occasion, the topic of this work and the way it is handled are bracing and draw attention to the sheer complexity of political and economic upheaval, extending beyond South Africa to the whole sub-continent. The drift towards towns has been exacerbated by movement within urban areas, and across ethnic groupings and international boundaries, even by the uprooting of whole populations. This challenges the relevance of prevailing assumptions concerning sedentary populations and traditional communities that are tied to their ancestral homelands. The contemporary world is characterized by movement, displacement, and shifting populations, and not by stable communities, which are the exception rather than the norm.

In approaching this fluid situation, the editors outline the debate on models that can be applied, and they develop a comprehensive argument, setting the tone for the remainder of the work. The emphasis here is on the present and not the past, and the regional setting facilitates a comprehensive grasp of the processes involved as part of a wider pattern. The range of examples in the successive chapters testifies to the sheer scope of this process and the cumulative implications of mobility. The chapters themselves progress from a range of local studies to more theoretical contributions that seek to set the problem in a global context.

This volume provides an important and disquieting contribution to the discourse shared among those who are concerned with the dilemmas facing Africa in the twenty-first century. We are very grateful to the editors for taking the initiative in its production and to all those who have contributed to it, making this series more representatiave of Africa as a whole and advancing our appreciation of a critical topic.

The editors and the International African Institute record with sadness the death of Malefane Maema, one of the contributors to this volume. He was tragically killed in a car accident in 1996.

Paul Spencer
Honorary Director, International African Institute

CONTRIBUTORS

Leslie Bank is an anthropologist working for the Institute of Social and Economic Research at Rhodes University, East London campus, South Africa. He has worked extensively on rural and urban research projects in the Eastern Cape and has recently completed a longitudinal study of energy use in low income households in the metropolitan areas in the Eastern Cape.

Per Bertilsson is with the Lesotho Highlands Water Authority, in Maseru, Lesotho.

Michael M. Cernea recently retired after fifteen years as the World Bank's Senior Advisor on Social Policy and Sociology in Washington. His work, research and publications focus on the application of social perspectives to a range of development issues, including population settlement. He has been responsible for defining the content of many World Bank policies in this regard, and has received the Solon T. Kimball Prize and the Bronislaw Malinowski Award for his contributions to development and policy formulation.

Luís António Covane lectured in History at the Eduardo Mondlane University in Maputo, Mozambique. He has conducted extensive research into labour migration and refugee issues in Mozambique. He is currently Mozambican Deputy Minister of Culture.

Catherine Cross is Head of the Rural–Urban Studies Programme, a research group devoted to policy studies, at the Centre for Social and Development Studies, University of Natal, Durban, South Africa. She has published extensively in the fields of rural development, migration studies, land reform, environment and the household economy, and has consulted for a range of South African and international organisations.

David Dewar holds the BP Chair in Urban and Regional Planning in the School of Architecture and Planning, University of Cape Town. He is author or co-author of seven books and over 170 monographs and articles on urban and regional development in southern Africa.

Chris de Wet is Professor in Anthropology at Rhodes University, Grahamstown, South Africa. His research and publications relate to resettlement, land reform and rural development.

Roddy Fox is Associate Professor in the Department of Geography at Rhodes University, Grahamstown, South Africa. He has published widely on aspects of urban, regional and political development in Kenya and South Africa.

Thando Gwintsa is with the Lesotho Highlands Water Authority, in Maseru, Lesotho.

Art Hansen is Associate Professor and Graduate Coordinator of Anthropology at the University of Florida at Gainesville. He has been President of the International Association for the Study of Forced Migration and co-director of the University of Florida's Displacement and Resettlement Studies Program. He has conducted long-term research on Angolan refugees in Zambia. His most recent activities are in post-war reconstruction and reconciliation in Angola, Eritrea and Liberia. He is currently Chair of the Department of International Affairs and Development, Clark Atlanta University.

Anthony Lemon, Lecturer in Geography at Oxford University and Fellow of Mansfield College, has written two and edited three books on South Africa, the latest being *The Geography of Change in South Africa* (Wiley 1995). His interests include urban segregation, local government, elections, education, regional relations and foreign policy.

Malefane Maema, who was tragically killed in a car accident in 1996, was, at the time of his death, with the School of Rural Community Development, at the University of Natal in Pietermaritzburg, South Africa. Before that he had been with the Lesotho Highlands Water Authority. His research and publications had concentrated on the Lesotho Highlands Water Project.

Brij Maharaj is Professor in the Department of Geography at the University of Natal, Pietermaritzburg. He has published over thirty-five articles on various issues relating to urban politics.

Mampho Molaoa is with the Lesotho Highlands Water Authority, in Maseru, Lesotho.

Naison Mutizwa-Mangiza is in the Research and Development Division of the United Nations Centre for Human Settlements (Habitat), Nairobi. He has published widely on local government and planning; settlement systems and planning; rural development planning; and urban planning.

Hopolang Phororo is Research Fellow at the Institute of Southern African Studies at the National University of Lesotho. Her recent research has been on urban gardening.

Tsebang Putsoane is with the Lesotho Highlands Water Authority, in Maseru, Lesotho.

Graeme Rodgers is currently lecturing in the Department of Social Anthropology, University of the Witwatersrand, Johannesburg, South Africa. His current research interests include transnational settlement practices between Mozambique and South Africa.

Thayer Scudder is Professor of Anthropology at the California Institute of Technology (USA) and is one of three founding directors of the Institute for Development Anthropology. For the past forty years his research and consulting has concentrated on the impacts of large-scale river basin development projects on local people, including the Kariba and Lesotho Highlands Water schemes in southern Africa.

Keketso Sefeane is with the Lesotho Highlands Water Authority, in Maseru, Lesotho.

Linda Semu lectures in Sociology at Chancellor College, Malawi. Her research, publications and consultancies relate to settlement formation, and to the interface between development and the environment.

Robson Silitshena was formerly Head of the Department of Environmental Science at the University of Botswana. He has published widely on settlement issues in Botswana.

David Simon is Professor in Development Geography and Director of the Centre for Developing Areas Research at Royal Holloway, University of London. He is author and editor of four books on Africa, including *South Africa in Southern Africa: Reconfiguring the Region* (James Currey 1998).

Carel van Aardt is Professor in Sociology at the University of Pretoria, South Africa. His teaching, research and publications focus on population and development issues.

Kadmiel Wekwete is Urban Management Advisor and Co-ordinator, Urban Poverty Research (Southern and Eastern Africa), at the United Nations Centre for Human Settlement (Habitat), Nairobi.

Lovemore M. Zinyama was Professor of Geography at the University of Zimbabwe, Harare, where he taught from 1979. He has written extensively on rural development and agriculture change in the smallholder farming sector in Zimbabwe. Environmental change in southern Africa is his other area of interest.

INTRODUCTION:
TRANSFORMING SETTLEMENT IN
SOUTHERN AFRICA

This volume is the outcome of a seminar on issues relating to changing patterns of population mobility and settlement in southern Africa. The seminar was held in January 1996 at the Grahamstown campus of Rhodes University in South Africa, and was arranged jointly by the Institute for Social and Economic Research at Rhodes University and the International African Institute. We have organised the order of the chapters in the book, as well as our discussion of them, in terms of the broad thematic sequence of population mobility, settlement and policy implications.

THE NEED FOR A NEW APPROACH

'It is now widely conceded that human movement is definitive of social life more often than it is exceptional in the contemporary world' (Appadurai 1995: 215). One might add that this is especially so in what is broadly known as the Third World, where political instability and its correlate of weak states often result in governments resorting to violence to achieve obedience from their citizens (Migdal 1988: ch. 1). In addition to wide-spread circular labour migration, urbanisation and movement within urban areas, in Africa as a whole, over the last half century or so, more than fifty million people have been uprooted, as shown in Table 1.1.

In southern Africa, such widespread human movement has been occasioned by economic forces (including widespread migrant labour to the mines and the urban areas), environmental pressures (such as the harsh droughts of the 1980s), political policies (notably apartheid in South Africa, socialist-based villagisation policies in Mozambique, and security villages in Angola and the then Rhodesia during the wars of decolonisation) and flight from the oppression and civil war in Angola, Mozambique, Namibia, South Africa and Zimbabwe. Some of the more prominent instances of population movement in southern Africa have been:

ANGOLA. Between 1961 and 1972 approximately 700,000 people were moved into concentrated settlements for purposes of military security during the

Table 1.1 Population displacement in Africa since World War II

External refugees (i.e. who have fled their country)	at least 6.2 million
Internal refugees/internally displaced people (i.e. who have remained within their country)	10 to 20 million
Dam-related displacement	at least 400,000
Agricultural projects displacement	at least 1 million
Villagisation projects displacement	at least 25 million
Political displacement	at least 4 million
Repatriation of refugees	at least 6 million

Sources: de Wet 1995: 1–2; Hampton 1998: 89ff.; UNHCR 1997: 23.

Angolan war of liberation against the Portuguese (Niddrie 1974: 56–7, 76). During the period 1961 to 1992 the average number of Angolan refugees in Zaire was 315,932, peaking at 620,000 in 1978, while during the period 1966 to 1992 the average number of Angolan refugees in Zambia was 48,604, peaking at 102,500 in 1991 (Hansen this volume). In addition, more than twenty years of civil war since independence have generated up to 3.7 million Angolans internally displaced within their country (Hampton 1998: 90).

MOZAMBIQUE. Upward of 1.8 million people were moved into rural socialist villages in the years following independence (Hampton 1998: 94), while 'by 1991 the war in Mozambique had generated almost two million refugees in the neighbouring countries, about half of whom are in Malawi. There were a further 1.9 million officially "internally displaced" within the country living in camps around Frelimo garrisons ... there are [also] large "displaced" populations in areas outside the control of the government, and ... in many but not all Renamo controlled zones people are living a highly precarious existence ... many [people] have been displaced several times during the course of the war' (Wilson and Nunes 1994: 169–70).

RHODESIA/ZIMBABWE. In the then Rhodesia some 200,000 refugees fled into the neighbouring countries (Makanya 1994: 121), while between 750,000 and one million people were internally displaced (Jackson 1994: 129) and 250,000 rural people were moved into security villages during the war of liberation (Weinrich 1977: 207, 217).

SOUTH AFRICA. From the 1950s onwards at least 3 million people were moved into concentrated villages as part of the government's 'betterment' programme (de Wet 1995: 28), while some 3.5 million people were relocated as a result of the apartheid policy (Surplus People Project 1983: Vol. 1: 1).

DEVELOPMENT-INDUCED RESETTLEMENT. The construction of development infrastructure has led to the forced resettlement of people in a number of instances in southern Africa. Possibly the best-known case of this has been the construction of the Kariba Dam on the Zambezi River, which led to the forced resettlement of some 57,000 people in (what are now) Zambia and Zimbabwe in the late 1950s (Scudder 1973: 206).

REPATRIATION IN SOUTHERN AFRICA. During the period 1971 to 1990, 730,995 refugees were recorded as having repatriated to Angola, Mozambique, Namibia and Zimbabwe, and 177,886 to Zaire, principally from Angola (calculated from Rogge 1994: 16–17). After the 1992 peace accord between Frelimo and Renamo, 'some 1.7 million Mozambican refugees returned to their homeland from six countries of asylum, of whom more than 375,000 were provided with transport and reception facilities by UNHCR' (Crisp 1996: 1).

Together with some contemporary social analysts (Appadurai 1995; Hastrup and Olwig 1997; Malkki 1995; 1997), such widespread movement leads us to question the appropriateness of much of social theory, which has tended to assume permanent and stable settlement as the norm, or as the desired state of affairs. Urban geographers, for example, have long assumed that there will be a symbiotic relationship, expressed through flows of goods and services, between urban centres and their rural hinterlands. The kind of movement to which we have been referring, has usually been seen as the exception, as the result of unusual circumstances, rather than the norm – and has been explained accordingly. In this vein, migrant labour in southern Africa has been analysed in terms of the artificial urbanisation patterns arising out of the segregation of the races during the colonial and apartheid eras. Similarly for what Colin Murray (1987) calls 'displaced urbanisation', the sprawling shack settlements in essentially rural areas like the Winterveld and Onverwacht are only understandable in the context of apartheid's attempts to move black South Africans out of what were seen as 'white' urban areas to the (then) homelands. In these areas there is no close tie between the displaced urban population and their adjacent rural areas. Refugee movements have likewise been seen as the product of abnormal situations, such as civil war, political persecution or famine. Refugees are seen as atypical in another sense: they have been driven from their home area as well as their home country, or patria. Rodgers and Hansen both raise this issue in their chapters in this book on Mozambican and Angolan refugees respectively, when they discuss the issue of repatriation. For most governments and aid agencies, but not necessarily for all refugees, repatriation is regarded as the desirable and even the natural resolution of the 'refugee problem'.

The fact that much of social theory has subscribed to such assumptions about 'home', place and permanency has led to an emphasis on continuity, coherence, the 'normal', and to a broadly functionalist orientation. Where that (possibly hypothetical) state of affairs is disrupted, the focus has been on how people seek to recover that coherence, continuity, stability.

But, as Malkki, who is concerned with the situation of Hutu refugees in Tanzania, asks: what happens if the phenomena we are studying are of a 'transitory, deterritorialised, unfixed, processual character' – and hence potentially 'unrepresentative' of the kinds of social phenomena that social theory is accustomed to deal with? (Malkki 1997: 86). The kinds of population movement, with which a number of chapters in this volume are concerned, would in significant measure appear to be so widespread that they can hardly be seen as atypical. The kinds of events that give rise to them, such as economic instability, civil war or natural disasters, and the inability to deal with them, are increasingly becoming more and more part of the norm, rather than the exception. The implication of this is that such population movement is increasingly becoming part of the 'normal' situation that we have to confront in the analysis of settlement formation, and, indeed, as a central problem in social theory, challenging our assumptions about stability and continuity. We are not trying to suggest that the field of population movement and settlement formation is totally random but that a central problem confronting scholars and practitioners in the field should be: How can we usefully identify trends and patterns within this essentially fluid situation in order to be able to arrive at the generalisations necessary for theory construction and policy formation? This Introduction, and the chapters in this volume, will hopefully make some suggestions in this regard.

RECONSIDERING POPULATION MOBILITY

'While "sedentarism" (staying in one place) is the taken-for-granted condition of human existence, movement is problematic – both for researchers who want to "explain" it and governments who often want to stop it' (Allen and Turton 1996: 11). The assumption of sedentarism, together with its corollary, that 'a given population has its own proper place, territory or homeland' (10) has strongly influenced the way in which both academics and policy makers have thought about population mobility. This applies to refugees, as well as to those displaced by development, and to people who live in informal settlements in urban areas. Not being sedentary, refugees 'are no longer [seen as being] unproblematically citizens or native informants. They can no longer satisfy as "representatives" of a particular local culture' (Malkki 1995: 7). They are accordingly seen as constituting a 'problem', as having a 'refugee mentality' or a 'refugee psychology' (8). If not problems, then they are seen as 'victims' (Mazur 1991: 6).

In spite of recent concern with what have become known as Internally Displaced People (Davies 1998), the refugee regime is still largely concerned with external refugees, i.e. refugees who have fled across a national border. If refugees are regarded as abnormal, then the desired condition of rootedness, permanence, belonging can only be re-achieved by returning them to where they 'really belong', i.e. to their country of origin. Hence the natural and durable solution, is seen as repatriation. Indeed, the UNHCR has tended to see settlement programmes in host countries as 'temporary solutions pending a repatriation; programmes specifically aimed at the permanent integration and absorption of refugees in their country of first asylum have been few and far between' (Rogge 1994: 20).

Because the 'refugee condition' is seen as one of abnormality and suffering, its resolution is to be found in repatriation. While this should ideally be voluntary, pressures to repatriate have been building up in host countries leading to a 'growing risk that some repatriations may become less than completely voluntary' (20).

The refugee experience is thus seen as consisting of two kinds of movement: flight into exile, suffering and social disruption; and the resolution of that unhappy and unnatural condition by return 'home' – where 'home' is one's native land. It is therefore not surprising that officials and aid workers tend to treat 'returnees' as a single, undifferentiated mass (Allen and Morsink 1994: 8).

Such views of normality and of 'home' have several problematic aspects. For many people in the world, mobility, rather than sedentarism and identification with one place as home, would appear to be the predominant experience, and hence the 'normal' condition. This applies to voluntary, as well as involuntary movement (see Table 1.1). For people such as pastoralists, 'geographical mobility and wide-ranging networks are a normal rather than a pathological aspect of life' (Allen and Turton 1996: 5). Indeed, attempts to sedentarise pastoralists have given rise to what to them may be abnormal and pathological conditions (Galaty and Bonte 1991: 269–70). Peoples who straddle international borders frequently move back and forth across them, as is evidenced by Luvale people moving between Angola and Zambia (Hansen this volume) and pre-refugee movement between Malawi and Mozambique (Wilson and Nunes 1994: 177).

Displacement and deterritorialisation are thus becoming increasingly 'normal' for significant numbers of people (Malkki 1995: 1). Such mobility, together with the accompanying movement of people between groups, leads us to 'the further questioning of the anthropological concepts of culture, society and community as bounded, territorialised concepts ... [and of] ... the notion of identity as a historical essence rooted in particular places' (2).

Refugees

This has direct implications for the way in which we conceptualise the movement of people classified as refugees. Their movement across borders during times of threat may be a continuation of pre-refugee patterns of movement (Wilson and Nunes 1994: 184). Angolan refugees, while crossing international borders, had not left what they perceived as their own territory (Hansen 1991). People whom analysts and officials see as refugees may thus not see themselves in that way at all. And accordingly, 'the distinction between "refugees" and "returnees" may have no meaning for the people themselves (except as identities to be assumed in order to obtain access to relief)' (Allen and Turton 1996: 5). Refugees may move across borders on an ongoing basis, moving 'back home' as things improve in their home country and then away again as trouble flares in their country of origin. Refugee flows 'are thus not single events but part of a long-term process' (6)

Rodgers (this volume) shows us how Mozambican refugees in South Africa made instrumental use of the UNHCR voluntary repatriation pro-gramme to transport family members and goods between the two countries, helping them to keep a foot in both camps. Such refugees clearly do not see themselves as the 'victims' (Mazur 1991: 7) or as the undifferentiated mass (Allen and Morsink 1994: 8) that many aid workers and officials would have them be.

Indeed, if ongoing, and instrumentally motivated, movement is part of the refugee experience, then the idea of 'returnees' as people going home – and wanting to go home – with a view to staying at home, becomes problematic (7). The two-stage model of refugee movement, i.e. into exile and then home, is clearly often inappropriate. But if the concept of returnee is problematised by developments on the ground, then so is the very concept and process of repatriation itself. It is not necessarily the return to stable sedentarism hoped for by many aid workers and policy makers.

This may partly be a result of the wishes of the refugees. As Kibreab (1996: ch6) shows us in the context of Eritrean refugees in Sudan, not every one wants to go 'home', as they have established themselves economically and socially in the host country. Moreover, as Allen and Morsink (1994: 7) caution us, there may not be a common conception of a homeland and of shared values among a potential 'returnee' population. Wilson and Nunes (1994: 203) tell us that 'a good number of [Mozambican] refugees in the border camps are keeping their options open: they use land and other resources in Mozambique, but they maintain their residence in Malawi', and have 'complex attitudes towards repatriation' (213). The Zimbabwean refugees were almost unanimously enthusiastic about coming home in 1979–80 with independence, whereas the Ndebele refugees who had fled political conflict in the 1980s were much more wary about coming home (Jackson 1994: 160).

The fact that repatriation is not necessarily a return to stable sedentarism may also be a result of the repatriation process itself, which may work against the very stability and sedentarism it seeks to establish. Mass repatri-ation tends to aggravate problems of reconstruction faced by countries emerging from war situations (Allen and Turton 1996: 2), as it puts additional strain on already pressured resources and personnel in these countries – in the same way that refugee flows into host countries divert resources from existing priorities. Refugees coming 'home' also make for potential conflict and competition between such returnees and local host communities, who may not even be the same communities the refugees left behind years ago.

The pressures to repatriate that seem to be building up in aid and UNHCR circles, to which Rodgers refers in his chapter in this volume, lead to what may be 'less than completely voluntary' repatriation. As a result, refugees may be returned to 'areas ill-prepared or incapable of receiving them' and where home governments see the welfare of such refugees as a liability, rather than a priority (Rogge 1994: 20). The response of agencies also affects the way in which the repatriation process unfolds. The decision by Medecins Sans Frontières to discontinue food aid to the Mozambican refugees in Hlupekani camp in the (then) Gazankulu homeland in South Africa was in support of the UNHCR Voluntary Repatriation Programme (Rodgers, this volume). On the other hand, some aid organisations may be unwilling to lose those refugees dependent upon their services as this may affect their access to international funding support (Rogge 1994: 33).

Another factor complicating the pursuit of repatriation as a return to a stable and sedentary situation, is the return of the internally displaced, who remained within their own country (15). Their return also creates pressure on scarce resources and potential conflict with host communities, but they do not count as external refugees and therefore are not always provided for in the same way.

Part of our uncertainty on conceptualising repatriation is that the literature on what happens to returnees is 'thin and limited in scope' (Allen and Turton 1996: 2). Unlike refugees in delineable camps, returnees become dispersed among the rest of their compatriots and the socio-economic implications need to be studied over a number of years, and not in a short term survey. Moreover, 'many mass return movements occur in highly unstable situations, sometimes ones of full-scale war. Independent research in these circumstances is likely to be dangerous or impossible' (2).

These variables suggest that we should delineate different kinds of processes for different kinds of refugee experience. We need to examine the differences between self-settled refugees in a host community, refugees settled on official schemes in host countries, self-repatriating refugees, refugees repatriated through an agency, such as UNHCR, and internal refugees, who may have become self-settled, or have gone home, with or without official assistance.

The potential problem is that the idea of a process implies a regularity, a set of stages with a beginning and an end, with the added assumption that the end is broadly characterised by equilibrium and stability. Yet, the way in which we have been looking at population mobility would seem to bring such assumptions into question. How are we to reconcile the analytical requirements of identifying regularity in the phenomena under study with the 'transitory, deterritorialised, unfixed, processual character' (Malkki 1997: 86) of those phenomena? To give just one example, Hansen (1991) raises a key conceptual issue concerning how refugee status may end and when it may be held to have done so. We seem to need a model of the refugee process in order to be able to delineate the refugee status, and vice-versa.

Comparing refugees and development-induced displacement

One possible way to examine refugee experience is to compare it with another kind of movement and settlement and consider parallels or pointers to the refugee condition. We refer here to involuntary resettlement following some development initiative such as the construction of a dam, a transport development project, or urban renewal. Such initiatives could also include politically motivated resettlement, such as Group Areas removals in South Africa (see Maharaj, this volume) or villagisation schemes (de Wet 1991; 1995) which have occurred across southern Africa.

It is necessary here to distinguish between

1. Development-Induced Displacement and Resettlement (DIDR), which is planned at each stage by the authorities and implementing agencies; and
2. Development-Induced Displacement (DID), where the removal may or may not be planned. In some cases, people may simply be expelled from the area and left to their own devices.

Attempts to conceptualise displacement in a systematic fashion have made most headway in relation to DIDR situations, and the most influential approaches have been those of Scudder on the one hand, and Cernea on the other. Scudder argues that we should see successful resettlement as a process in which relocatees pass through various socio-economic stages as they respond to the experience of being resettled (Scudder 1993a; 1997a, b, c; Scudder and Colson 1982). The first stage (that of Planning and Recruitment) involves mainly officials rather than the relocatees themselves. Thereafter relocatees have to adjust to the impact of the resettlement experience, and tend to adopt passive attitudes and avoid risks (the stage of Transition or of Physical Removal and Initial Adaptation). After a few years they re-establish themselves socially and economically (the stage of Community Formation and Economic Development). They then develop the capacity to take over responsibility from resettlement agencies for administering their new situation, and as they become economically and politically adjusted they are 'able to compete successfully with other districts and regions for scarce national resources' (the stage of Incorporation and Handing Over) (Scudder 1993a: 134).

Successful resettlement thus involves the creation of new communities (129) and is a multi-stage process in which resettlement becomes sustainable settlement. This dynamic process takes a minimum of two generations (130) as it is really only when the second generation is able and willing to take over the resettlement scheme that it can be regarded as a success. As we shall discuss below, many schemes have problems reaching and sustaining the latter two stages of the process, and the question therefore arises: can a model that is predicated upon success be applied to 'unsuccessful' situations?

Cernea has a somewhat different view of the resettlement process. He sees the risk of economic and social impoverishment as a key factor in the resettlement process, and argues that measures to counteract this should be our central concern (Cernea 1990, 1996b, and this volume). Rather than explicitly seeing the resettlement process as a series of stages, Cernea identifies eight key sub-processes in which resettlement makes for impoverishment, arguing that a focus on these tendencies will enable us to convert potential impoverishment into development.

Both Scudder and Cernea seek to find a pattern in the resettlement phenomenon. Both acknowledge that in many cases resettlement is a failure. This is, *inter alia*, due to poor planning and implementation, lack of political will, and the inherent complexity of the resettlement process. Both Scudder and Cernea adopt a systems approach, seeking to identify the variables that affect the outcome of the process. While moving beyond equilibrium analysis, they both still seem to regard permanence of settlement as part of what characterises successful resettlement.

Scudder acknowledges that his model applies only to successful cases, and that 'the ... framework does not deal with the longer term implications' of situations where 'a majority of those relocated are unable to proceed ... [to the stage of Community Formation and Economic Development] ... or if they do, are unable to sustain the development process during the first generation let alone pass it on to their children' (Scudder 1993a: 135). As Scudder himself (1997c: 16) asks: do a majority of resettlers slip back into a Transition/Initial Adaptation stage, or do distinctly different sets of responses occur?

This suggests that we need to allow Scudder's model to develop in two directions: one for successful situations, and one for unsuccessful ones. For the latter, we need to accept that, while relocatees may not attain the stage of Economic Development, they are clearly no longer in a state of Transition or Initial Adaptation, as they may achieve Community Formation, and Handing Over, and possibly even Incorporation. This would provide a more open-ended post-Transition/Initial Adaptation stage, which may have different details and combinations in terms of its economic, social and administrative aspects. We need to try to outline a structure and process of involuntary relocation that allows for settlement in the absence of permanence or successful resettlement.

This also raises the issue that much displacement does not take place in a planned DIDR type context. In many situations, people are moved to a place and left to fend for themselves, or are simply ordered to leave and have to find a place for themselves.

Thus, in the 1960s and 1970s, over one million farm labourers and their families were either turned off farms in South Africa or fled from worsening terms of employment. The apartheid bantustan of Qwaqwa became a dumping ground and effective refugee camp for Africans not permitted to reside in 'white' South Africa. Qwaqwa's population rocketed from about 25,000 in 1970 to over 400,000 in 1983 (Sharp 1982: 13) and its authorities were simply unable to cater for such vast numbers of people, who had to make do with absolutely minimal services and employment opportunities. Such expulsion would seem to have more in common with refugee situations than planned resettlement, and is perhaps better analysed with this in mind. A number of scholars have in recent years been arguing for combining insights derived from the study of resettlement and of refugees (Cernea 1996d; de Jongh 1994; Lassailly-Jacob 1996b; Scudder 1993a).

We need to revisit the ethnography in order to see to what extent it is feasible to discern an orderly pattern of stages in the phenomenon of relocation, incorporating others affected by projects besides the relocatees, and also those who leave resettlement schemes to strike off on their own (Scudder 1993a: 146; 1997a). One way of proceeding would be from Cernea's model of multidimensional impoverishment and of the possibilities of inverting the risks into opportunities for development. While his deconstruction of the concept of impoverishment needs to be more rigorously systematised so that the relationship between the different subprocesses of impoverishment become clearer, his approach allows us to refine our understanding of the dynamics of resettlement. It has the potential to contribute towards a much more detailed analysis and understanding of what happens in the various stages of the resettlement process. In this way, Scudder (personal communication) suggests that Cernea's account of impoverishment risks provides a framework for focusing on the Transition/Initial Adaptation stage of his own (Scudder's) model. Similarly, we suggest that the inversion of the impoverishment risks into opportunities for development (or 'reconstruction') provides us with a framework to do the same for the stage of Community Formation and Economic Development. Looking at the impoverishment risks that had not been converted into development opportunities would pinpoint more clearly the issues involved.

Most of the theoretical analysis of resettlement has been developed from a rural context. However, resettlement is increasingly becoming an urban issue also (Cernea 1993), and a systematic comparison of its dynamics in urban and rural settings would enable us to sharpen our understanding of the interplay between the analytical moments of impoverishment and process.

While the resettlement of development relocatees is planned and, to an extent, provided for by the authorities, the movement of refugees is a much more ad hoc process, as it is individuals, families or small groups of people that decide to flee at a given moment, rather than being ordered to move as communities. The numbers of refugees crossing a border, and their times and directions of movement, are therefore much less predictable, and much more difficult to plan for, than in the case of development relocatees. If there is something akin to Scudder's stage of Planning and Recruitment in the case of refugees, it will be much more provisional, and very different in the way it affects subsequent stages of the movement and settlement process. The linkage between the stages is also made much more provisional by the fact that it is stretched across two countries and is more tenuous. Most host countries regard repatriation as the desired and even natural outcome of the refugee process, and therefore are unlikely to commit resources to the long-term development of people who are seen as short-term guests benefiting from their goodwill and charity.

The repatriation of refugees is widely regarded as the desired – although in many cases not the actual – outcome. With this in mind, we need to ask ourselves whether it makes more sense to look at two separate, or at one multi-component, process(es) of movement and settling down – one relating to essentially unplanned flight and then settlement in the host country, and a second process relating to planned or unplanned resettlement in the refugee's home country. From the refugee's perspective these might be seen as parts of a single, multi-component, process. However, from the perspective of the host and home countries, there is not likely to be that kind of continuity. Refugees would not by choice flee to a country sympathetic to the government from which they are seeking to escape. Indeed, there often is open hostility between neighbouring countries which support guerillas fighting against their neighbours. Such conditions are hardly likely to make for a coordinated approach towards planning and provision for the refugees moving between the two countries. This suggests that there is likely to be discontinuity in the refugee process, initiated when refugees cross over into the host country and again when they return to their home country.

Not all refugees repatriate. Some operate through official channels in the host country, allowing them to settle in refugee camps and to be repatriated later on, while others take their destiny into their own hands, establishing themselves as self-settled refugees in the host country and, if they do go 'home' again, doing so on own initiative.

If we take the flight and refuge stage of the refugee experience as a process in its own right, then obviously, whether refugees are self- or officially settled will make a difference to the manner in which it is useful to speak of a stage similar to Scudder's Community Formation and Economic Development. Self-settled refugees will not be in isolatable refugee camps, separated from the surrounding communities (Hansen 1991).

Inasmuch as refugee camps are usually regarded as temporary phenomena, Scudder's Handing Over stage does not apply, although there may be something similar to his Incorporation as the last stage for those refugees who become integrated into the regional economic system within the host country. Again for those refugees who take matters into their own hands in returning to their home country and for those who are repatriated through official channels, one would need to look for very different parallels with Scudder's stages of Community Formation and Economic Development, and Handing Over and Incorporation.

Yet another set of dynamics would seem to apply to those refugees who are beyond the official spotlight in almost every sense: internal refugees, who, in many instances, are not even defined as refugees in the first place. They may have become successfully self-settled elsewhere in their own country, or may seek to return to their original home area, or move to a town or city after hostilities die down. Wilson and Nunes (1994: 169) tell us that in 1991 in Mozambique there were 'probably more than a million rural people dwelling in new shanty camps around cities where they were uncounted'. Covane (this volume) also draws attention to such urbanisation resulting from internal displacement during the war. While aid programmes, both state and private, sought to assist IDPs in Mozambique (Wilson and Nunes 1994: 227) and in Zimbabwe (Jackson 1994: 134–5), in Zimbabwe such IDPs 'simply fell outside of the UNHCR mandate in 1980' (129) and were 'uncounted' in urban areas of Mozambique. Many IDPs have therefore been operating without the knowledge or support of the authorities or aid agencies.

The refugee experience thus seems to be much more diverse than that of development relocatees in resettlement schemes. This again suggests that we need to develop a more open-ended approach following Physical Removal (or Flight) and Initial Adaptation. We may well need to generate a model which is more directly geared towards the particularities of the refugee situation if it is not to become so general as to be of only rather limited analytical value. As we develop a more detailed set of models specific to the refugee situation, we can then return to those focusing on DIDR in a search for common ground.

Population mobility within urban areas
Patterns of population mobility are interrelated, and what have usually been regarded as the more atypical and unrepresentative types of movement (such as refugees and resettlement) interact with what are usually seen as more conventional types of movement, such as circular migration and urbanisation.

The violence, upheaval and political instability associated with the civil-war-type situations, result in population movement within the rural areas, and from rural to urban areas (cf. Wilson and Nunes 1994: 168). Covane (this volume) tells of the movement of refugees to Mozambican towns such as Xai-Xai. Hansen (this volume) refers to UNHCR reports linking the 'flight from the land' to the towns and cities in Angola, *inter alia*, to 'the marginal quality of agricultural land because of soil erosion, which was accentuated by the large refugee population'. In South Africa, an unofficial low-level civil war in the KwaZulu-Natal province over the last decade or so has resulted in many smaller-scale and shorter-distance flights and returns, as well as more permanent urban migration, to escape from the violence, which has been prominently brought to our attention by the Truth and Reconciliation Commission (Krog 1998).

Where civil war has coincided with natural disasters such as floods, drought, crop failures and losses of livestock, as in Mozambique, the effect has been even more pronounced. Such natural disasters may by themselves drive people to cities in search of a livelihood. They may leave the rural areas of their own volition, but may also be compelled to do so, as in the case of displaced farm workers in South Africa who have been turned off the land in the wake of such disasters and rising costs (Manona, Bank and Higginbottom 1996: 58–9)

A combination of factors originating outside as well as inside urban areas is currently making for a high degree of urban mobility. The lives of many people are characterised by a condition of ongoing movement, such that they do not stay in one household or settlement on anything like a permanent basis. Those refugees and development relocatees who chose to escape to town themselves to establish a foothold, contribute towards the scale of this movement.

Indeed, it is not only that people seem to be constantly moving between households, but that even physical shelters themselves do not necessarily stay in one place for any great length of time in shanty settlements in South Africa (Spiegel 1996). The far-reaching nature and social implications of this mobility is captured by Jones' (1993) and Ramphele's (1993) documentation of the itinerant lives of women and children in South Africa, in a context which for years has been premissed upon male migrant labour.

It is this ongoing movement, at all levels, that should be our starting point in understanding contemporary settlement patterns in southern Africa, rather than the more customary push–pull urbanisation models which assume broadly enduring settlements and domestic units enjoying, or working towards, structural stability and a continuity in their composition. It has become clear over the last number of years that the vast recent growth in informal settlements in southern Africa has been attributable, not only to people immigrating from the rural areas, but also to people seeking to escape overcrowding in existing urban-housing areas and to achieve some autonomy away from parental homes (Cross, this volume; Manona, Bank and Higginbottom 1996: 50). This suggests that we need to revise the way we conceptualise the nature and growth of urban settlements.

Migration and settlement patterns will always reflect opportunities for improvement of income levels and general quality of life. However, it is precisely the increasingly precarious nature of urban economies and local government (whether official or informal) that tends to make for fluctuations in levels of income, service delivery, entitlements and law and order (and therefore of violence) – and hence of human movement. People trade these various goods off against each other and move or stay accordingly. Cross (this volume) and Spiegel (1996), Jones (1993) and Ramphele (1993) show us how people from the rural areas move back and forth and spread their household members, economic and social commitments and resources between rural and urban areas as they struggle to optimise the balance of these factors.

One of the key factors making for the precarious nature of urban life in southern Africa, and which impacts directly upon movement and settlement, is the seeming inability of the state, particularly at the local level, to impose its will upon the people or to deliver the level of services that would evoke compliance. This is shown in the failure to control the urban settlement process, and in the resulting proliferation of informal settlements/ shack areas (see Tripp 1997: 139 for the case of Dar es Salaam, and the contributions of Bank, Cross, Maharaj and Phororo in this volume). An estimated 8 million people live in shack settlements in and around urban areas in South Africa alone. Yet again, we seem to be pushed to let go of another of the assumptions we have held about the nature of settlements: i.e. that they are (fairly viable) units of administration, revenue generation and service provision, and hence of stable and potentially permanent habitation and household composition.

Case studies

Let us now turn to a discussion of those case studies in this volume that address the issue of population mobility. Figure 1.1 locates these case studies geographically. The theme of settlement in these chapters emerges in a re-active sense, as a response to movement under duress rather than the result of pro-active government settlement policy at national level. We have arranged the mobility-focused case studies into two groups:

1. those which are located outside South Africa, and show the impact of external forces on patterns of mobility and settlement. We have included Rodger's study of a United Nations-sponsored voluntary repatriation programme designed for Mozambican refugees in South Africa as part of this group as it relates to an international programme;
2. those cases which are located inside South Africa and show the impact of apartheid, and more recently of the decline of state control over patterns of mobility and settlement.

1. Non South African cases

Hansen suggests 'Since the early 1960s settlement patterns throughout the southern African region have been profoundly affected by forced displacement caused by widespread warfare and politically related governmental

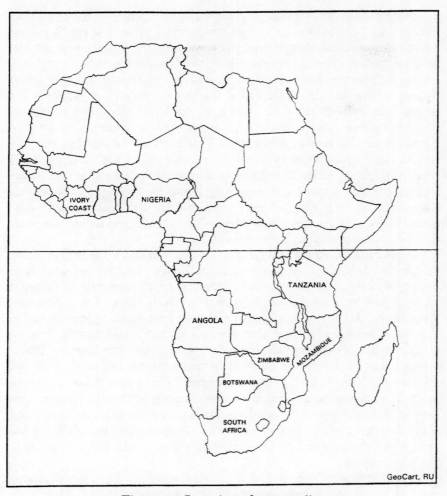

Figure 1.1 Location of case studies

programmes.' Millions of people have been displaced in Angola, Mozambique, Namibia and Zimbabwe, as well as by apartheid policies in South Africa, with the Angolan and Mozambican civil wars giving rise to millions of external refugees. Both warfare and its cessation involve changes in settlement patterns.

Hansen provides detailed long-term statistics for flows of refugees out of Angola to (the former) Zaire and to Zambia on an annual basis, for the period from 1961 to 1992, i.e. during the colonial period, with the war of liberation before independence in 1974, and then for the civil war up to the period of the Bicesse Accord in 1992. This is, to our knowledge, the only such detailed compilation of refugee flows over such a sustained period of time for southern Africa. It suggests that in situations where neither adversary has the clear upper hand (as in Angola and Mozambique), the fighting drags on, as do the flows of refugees – the 1994 Angolan peace accord is now a dead letter. Hansen shows how waves of flight and of self-repatriation vary with political and military developments.

Another major element affecting refugee movement, is the way in which refugees see themselves – and this relates, in Hansen's analysis, to the response of people in the host country, rather than to events in the home country. Many Angolans have historically lived on both sides of the Angolan/Zambian border as labour migrants and have long-standing kinship ties in Zambia. They have become Zambians in all but name, having become integrated into local Zambian communities. Mozambicans have, in similar fashion, treated the border between Mozambique and Malawi as porous (Wilson and Nunes 1994) over a long period. Where repatriation does take place in significant numbers, particularly among long-term refugees, we need to look, not only to the relative balance of opportunities in the host and home countries, but also to ways in which refugees have been incorporated or kept at a distance and under control by communities and authorities in the host country.

Covane traces the ways in which a combination of environmental, economic and political factors originating in Mozambique and South Africa have disrupted patterns of mobility and settlement in the southern provinces of Mozambique over the last twenty or so years. These areas have a long-standing dependence upon income earned by migrant labourers working in South Africa. The rise in wages paid by the South African mines in the 1970s served to make such migrancy more desirable, while the reductions in the numbers of foreign mine workers saw those miners with jobs being able to diversify economically and to accumulate wealth and status in Mozambique.

These changes in the mining industry coincided with the independence of Mozambique. Devastating floods in 1977 forced people to break their mining contracts to re-establish their homesteads and accelerated Frelimo's socialist villagisation programme as people had to abandon the flooded areas and move into villages – again threatening their labour contracts. The early 1980s saw the combined onslaught of drought and civil war in the region, with South Africa's hand again making itself felt in its support for Renamo. Thousands of displaced people sought refuge and livelihood in the towns and cities, as they fled violence and were cut off from their agricultural base. After the war there have been mixed responses to people returning to the countryside as the state has had limited resources for rural reconstruction and a number of refugees had developed commitments in the towns. The failure of the socialist programme, the impact of the war and natural disasters have, if anything, intensified dependency upon labour migrancy, while South Africa has been rethinking its position on immigration and the status of refugees.

Rodgers highlights the movement of Mozambican refugees in South Africa in the context of a Voluntary Repatriation Programme (VRP) launched by the United Nations High Commissioner for Refugees (UNHCR) in 1994. UNHCR clearly espoused the conventional view of repatriation to one's native land as the natural solution for refugees, and assumed that refugees themselves would also subscribe to this view. With a longstanding tradition of movement across the South African–Mozambican border, and with important links in South Africa, the refugees (like the Angolans that Hansen studied in Zambia) had their own view of whether they were in fact refugees, and of how they saw repatriation. As a result, only 32,000 out of a UNHCR guesstimate of 250,000 refugees responded to the offer of assisted repatriation to Mozambique.

The 'refugees' saw the refugee camps, as well as the VRP, as resources with which to reconstruct their homesteads in Mozambique which had been destroyed by the civil war. The camps provided sources of food aid, as well as springboards for legal or illegal sources of income, while the VRP trucks provided a (literal) vehicle with which to ferry physical homestead structures and other goods to Mozambique, keeping social ties intact.

Rodgers makes the telling point that there is 'the potential for countries, homes and other socially defined places to be creatively imaged in diverse ways'. He shows how this creativity affects the definitions of borders and of refugees themselves, and how the coming together of UNHCR and of Mozambican definitions gave rise to the way in which the VRP unfolded in practice. The future of cross-border movements remains an open question, following the termination of the VRP and of the 'refugee status' of Mozambicans remaining in South Africa.

Maema and his colleagues show us how wider international forces have not only been responsible for interventions that have given rise to resettlement in the first place, but have also influenced the process of resettlement. The Lesotho Highlands Water Project (LHWP) is a joint venture between Lesotho and South Africa, with increasing the water supply to Gauteng Province, the industrial heartland of South Africa, as one of its principal aims. The financial involvement of the World Bank in this project has led to the removal of households affected by the construction of the Katse Dam being 'switched from relocation to resettlement, i.e. relocation plus rehabilitation'. The chapter traces the various ways in which the Lesotho Highlands Development Authority is seeking to 'make resettlement a community development project'. This emphasis is still too recent to be able to evaluate its impact, and the chapter focuses more on means and management, and initial activities, rather than on consequences.

Linda Semu traces the way in which the Mozambican civil war has interacted with local factors in Malawi affecting the development of the settlement of Chiweta. On the delta of two rivers, Chiweta has access to good agricultural soil, as well as to Lake Malawi for fishing. The proximity of Livingstonia Mission has contributed to the development of the area as migrants educated there send back remittance and resources to invest in the settlement.

These local level factors received a boost from the Mozambican civil war which effectively closed the usual transport route to the ports of Beira and Nacala in Mozambique. This led to increased use of the Northern Corridor, running through the Chiweta area to the Tanzanian port of Mbeya, and to increased economic activity and growth in Chiweta.

The local and external factors favouring Chiweta may, however, hold threats to the sustainability of the settlement. The war in Mozambique is now over, which may lead to a decline in the importance of the Northern Corridor road; the fish in Lake Malawi are a finite resource; there is not much room for agricultural expansion to cater for population growth; and the Malawian economy is able to provide only limited employment opportunities for Chiweta's educated citizens. Without inputs such as irrigation and electricity, which would require assistance from an already extended Malawian government, Chiweta may well have to face a decline in numbers to achieve sustainability under these less favourable conditions – at the price of a significant proportion of its population seeking their fortunes in the urban areas.

This urban exodus is what Hopolang Phororo takes up in looking at Maseru, in Lesotho, which has two mainstays to its predominantly rurally based economy: agriculture and remittances from migrant labour in South Africa. Rising population has created land scarcity in the mountainous rural areas, and Basotho workers have recently been retrenched in increasing numbers from South African mines and other places of employment, in part due to policies aimed at stabilising the labour force. The only formal alternative is to move to towns in Lesotho – notably Maseru. Phororo looks at the resort to urban cultivation in Maseru and at its increasing role in providing a source of supplementary subsistence, as the movement to town makes for increasing subdivision of sites, with areas for urban cultivation becoming too small to generate sufficient produce for sale on the market.

2. South African cases

The South African case studies in this volume are somewhat different, as they see patterns of population mobility and settlement dynamics largely in terms of the workings of the apartheid system – both in its implementation and in its decline. While the chapters by Leslie Bank and by Brij Maharaj focus on specific settlements, that by Catherine Cross takes a wider perspective, looking at the greater Durban area, and its hinterland. Cross argues that, as the state's control over black settlement weakened in the 1980s, and as influx control was abolished, a mushrooming of new black informal settlements occurred. This resulted both from a 'decompression' of existing black settlements (as younger married couples and singles were able to move out of their parents' homes, and start their own), as well as from a movement in from the rural areas. This latter movement has perhaps not been as dramatic as some commentators suppose, for a range of reasons which include the high levels of unemployment and of violence in urban KwaZulu-Natal. At the more local level, as elsewhere in Africa, the traditional land tenure system is increasingly unable to serve as a filter to keep strangers out of a community's territory, with land-holding becoming increasingly individualised through informal sales as people move into the peri-urban areas, from where they commute to town.

With neither the state nor local authority systems policing boundaries strictly, population movement is becoming increasingly determined by economic considerations, such as access to resources, income and services. The 1980s, with prolonged drought, saw heavy pressure on the rural natural-resource base. Where the resource base is still viable, the peri-urban areas offer an effective combination of rural and urban benefits in terms of access to rural resources and lifestyle, and increasingly to urban services and work opportunities.

The increasingly limited capacity of the rural, and particularly the peri-urban, resource base suggests that future migration flows in the province will revolve around the affordability of urban-style services. This focus, rather than (lack of) access to arable land, will characterise the nature of any urban–rural divide.

Still in KwaZulu-Natal, Brij Maharaj focuses on the settlement of Cato Manor, five kilometres from the Durban Central Business District. Initially occupied by Indians, it became a mixed area as Indian 'shacklords' took in black South Africans as tenants, who in turn became 'tenant-landlords', with population, poverty and socio-economic tension building up in an area, which Maharaj suggests, 'remained a chronically neglected area in terms of services and facilities for some years'.

The story of Cato Manor after the Second World War encapsulates the increasing concern of government to organise the use of space along racial lines – with the inevitable waves of removals and resistance as Cato Manor was zoned first for Indian, then for white, and then again partly for Indian ownership and occupation. Both Indians and blacks were compelled to move out to other, racially designated areas. Large parts of Cato Manor had remained vacant and underdeveloped for almost twenty years. As the state's control of settlement and spatial politics loosened in the 1980s, so blacks started returning to Cato Manor, with both land and house invasions increasing as the new democratic system in South Africa has been getting under way.

Attempts made by local groupings to transform Cato Manor into a non-racial area have been faced by the problems that have characterised the settlement since its inception: competition for land, inadequate services, political rivalry, ineffective local government and tensions between Indian and black residents. The nature of these problems has been significantly modified by the impact of apartheid. The way in which they develop and possibly are resolved will hinge on the balance that is struck between 'orderly and planned development and the rapid expansion of uncontrolled informal settlements. Hence Cato Manor remains today, as it was in the 1940s, a politically contested terrain.'

Leslie Bank considers the ways in which patterns of movement within informal settlements affect, and are affected by, the 'increasing frequency and severity of shack fires in metropolitan areas'. His focus is on the township area of Duncan Village in the city of East London. With easy access to the city centre, it has long been an attractive destination for the region's black work seekers, and has experienced an ongoing population influx.

Yet again, the state's weakening control in the 1980s has had a significant impact upon settlement politics and dynamics. The state-approved Gompo Town Council was ousted by a civic body, the Duncan Village Residents' Association, which allowed more than 18,000 new shacks to be built between 1986 and 1996. The combination of high residential densities, highly inflammable materials in shack construction, and a high dependence upon paraffin as a domestic fuel, have led to a dramatic increase in the number of dwellings destroyed by accidental fire. This has led to the fragmentation of groups as established male household heads have been able to assert their claims for space and materials to rebuild their shacks, while younger, and female-headed, households have found themselves pushed further out into new shack areas.

The phenomenon of shack fires provides a very fitting metaphor for the way in which the state's capacity to administer and service settlements has weakened, while patterns of interaction within informal settlements appear to take on a life of their own.

RECONSIDERING SETTLEMENT

The sections above have discussed the need to reconceptualise population settlement, since movement rather than stability appears to be the dominant process operating in southern Africa. It follows that most of the geographic research into settlement size and distribution in this region needs to be re-assessed since most authors have assumed that the number of people in a settlement is linked to the quality of functions to be found there, dating back to the work of Christaller in the late 1930s (Christaller 1966).

In the late 1960s, research into South Africa's urban system followed positivistic Central Place Theory lines. This identified hierarchies of urban centres in South Africa through examining their functional complexities. Beavon (1972) was more interested in intra-urban functional complexity, but together with Davies (1967) and Cook (Davies and Cook 1968), he relied heavily on a positivistic stance. There is order and structure in South Africa's urban system, which can be understood through the principles developed by Christaller (1966) and Lösch (1940). We can now see that this approach would have problems in handling situations of rapid population movement.

Since the early 1970s there has been very little detailed research into the urban systems of southern Africa. Elsewhere, Vance's mercantile model (1970) shifted attention to external linkages between a region and the world economy; the wholesaling ventures which articulated this, initially extractive, system, were located in urban centres and focused on external communications in locations peripheral to national space. Subsequently, Johnston (1984) and Christopher (1982) showed in a fairly general way how colonial urban systems developed following Vance's ideas. In southern Africa, however, no detailed work could compare with Slater's (1975) study of Tanzanian urban development, which viewed urban and rural settlement as the product of the process of underdevelopment. Administrative, extractive and transportation functions would be developed in urban and rural service centres to facilitate the extraction of a surplus to be exported to the colonial powers or core nations of the world economy.

From this point of view, circular migration can be related to recruitment from administrative towns operating in underdeveloped black rural areas and with subsequent movement to mining, industrial or commercial centres in the white core urban areas of the colonial space economy. Thus urban centres, as a whole, would have fewer permanent people resident in them than 'should' be the case, and thus they would appear to be overprovided with goods and services. Black rural areas would, as a corollary, exhibit an underprovision of service centres. The urban system as a whole would be providing goods and services to a population that was both permanent and semi-permanent.

Some more recent work has attempted to merge some of the ideas mentioned above with the principles of Central Place Theory within a broad political-economy type of framework. Fox (1991) based his regionalisation of Kenya's urban hierarchy on the colonially divided urban system. The major urban centres and rural service centres were located in European scheduled areas and provided goods and services to a white settler community already provided with access to road and rail transportation. We can now understand, additionally, that these urban centres were smaller in population size than they otherwise should have been through the operation of influx control and the circular migration system. The black rural areas were grossly underprovided with urban and rural centres and agriculture was underdeveloped until the late colonial period, when commercially oriented black agriculture emerged. The post-colonial period has witnessed the mushrooming of small service centres in black and former white rural areas (Fox 1992). These new and rapidly growing centres grew to service the people who moved from black to white rural areas in either planned or spontaneous population movements.

The Whitsun Foundation (1980) produced some extremely detailed work on Zimbabwe, which showed broad comparisons with Kenya in that there was a gross lack of rural service centres and urban areas in the communal areas at independence and a much greater number of functionally diverse urban centres serving the white commercial-farming sector. Elsewhere in this volume Zinyama shows that Zimbabwe's current settlement patterns reflect post-colonial population movements and also government-induced attempts at resettlement. Wekwete (this volume) also demonstrates how growth centre policies have been used in Zimbabwe to redress the patterns of regional inequality discussed above.

A good deal of work has been undertaken, however, examining how government policies have been used over the last two decades to promote the economic development of rural and urban areas in underdeveloped regions. Policies have usually attempted to set up growth centres through the promotion of industry or commerce/administration (see Wekwete, this volume) or attempted to build a network of rural service centres through Central Place principles or using the 'Urban Functions for Rural Development' approach (Mutizwa-Mangiza, this volume; Silitshena, this volume). In most cases, the policies have been attempting to promote regional development, aimed at redressing the inequalities which have come about through the colonial or apartheid development process, rather than at coping with rapid population movements that do not affect major urban areas.

Case studies

Rural settlements in Zimbabwe (Zinyama, this volume) have been influenced by land division since the early twentieth century and by rapid population growth. The former provided an initial template which has become increasingly modified through population movements since Zimbabwe's independence and is associated with the land redistribution programme and the rural service centre strategy. Thus, new settlement patterns come to be super-imposed on the old.

Kadmiel Wekwete's chapter has been fundamentally influenced by a political-economy perspective and so he calls for an examination of historical and behavioural factors, rather than for a neo-classical locational analysis of urban settlement in Zimbabwe. He examines the key policies that impacted on Zimbabwe's urban development from 1890 onwards. In particular, he chronicles the state's intervention through the 1930s and 1980s as Marketing Acts, Meat and Electricity Commissions, and the Iron and Steel Act set up a framework to benefit white industrial towns. He is therefore looking at the impact of sectoral policies on urban development in the colonial period. After independence, policies have attempted to redress this regional imbalance, and designated district centres, land resettlement and growth centres have all been tried. Critically, each instrument had depended on public sector investment and direction. He sees the policy reversals inherent in structural adjustment and also recurrent drought as major obstacles to these programmes which are aimed at redressing urban imbalances. There is thus an implicit assumption that a more 'ideal' state is desirable/attainable.

In Botswana, Silitshena shows how 'traditional' rural settlement patterns have been modified by government policy. He shows that policy in a pastorally-based society has attempted to both stem rural–urban migration and overcome the service provision problems that occur with a low density, highly scattered population. Cultural factors have come under threat and been weakened, for example the chiefly powers that bound together the agro-town settlements, also hunter–gatherers are now increasingly restricted in their range as colonial and post-colonial governments have removed their access to land. Policies have attempted to regroup villages in areas of high dispersion and provide a package of services.

More recently a comprehensive National Settlement Policy has been drawn up in an attempt to control the whole nature of settlement in Botswana in the light of the spontaneous changes that previous sectoral agricultural and administrative policies have produced, planning services for new and rapid settlement at cattle posts, on lands far from agro-towns and in the remote area settlements. The hierarchy he describes for the National Settlement Policy appears to be strongly derived from Central Place Theory and so is unlikely a priori to provide a solution to the patterns of change in Botswana.

Naison Mutizwa-Mangiza takes the post-colonial period as the starting point for a multi-national comparison of rural service centre strategies in Côte d'Ivoire, Malawi, Nigeria and Tanzania. The commonalities are that rural service centres all must offer basic commercial, administrative and transport services and some may also have rural industries. In Côte d'Ivoire small centres were promoted to counteract the perceived excessive size and dominance of Abidjan over the rest of the urban hierarchy; a typical example of national-level planning attempting to redress regional inequality between core and periphery. Such primacy is itself the result of spontaneous migration and was therefore seen as undesirable, while regional centres and small towns were seen as necessary to address such inequality. Malawi's National Physical Development Plan explicitly attempts to impose a Christaller-devised six-tier Central Place hierarchy to promote regional development, administrative decentralisation and integrated development. Again, we need to comment that this is unlikely to match large-scale population movements. By way of a contrast, Nigeria's rural service centres and associated traditional authorities have evolved over a long period and onto this 'natural' relationship have been grafted basic infrastructure – water, electricity, feeder roads, etc; a far more 'organic' and workable pattern. Finally, Tanzania has explicit plans for service centre provision, again based on hierarchical and spatial principles, with a growth centre strategy running in parallel. A multiplicity of other policies, such as villagisation, is also found in Tanzania.

Mutizwa-Mangiza shows that the top–down nature of such planning has been a major problem throughout. Furthermore, the rural–urban imbalances aimed at through these policies have not been achieved. We would maintain that such policies are unlikely to succeed as they are based on inappropriate conceptions of the relationship between population and settlement.

Anthony Lemon gives an overview of settlement strategies before tackling the role of secondary cities and small towns in South Africa. He reiterates Dewar's insightful point that 'it may well be the case that spatially uneven development and atypical settlement hierarchy result from economic and political policy'. We would agree with this view and take it a step further, arguing that an 'atypical' hierarchy may well be typical and often expected in southern Africa. Lemon's chapter argues for the strengthening of existing small centres rather than for a grandiose national physical plan intent on developing large numbers of new centres (as was the case in Malawi, Tanzania and Côte d'Ivoire). Such strengthening would need to come from local innovation (such as Local Economic Development) within a national facilitating framework.

David Dewar gives a summary of the 'long history of interference with settlement patterns in South Africa' before examining international trends and turning to the role of settlement policies and planning in South Africa today. He starts from the premise that urbanisation in southern Africa has been consciously manipulated to serve political-economic ends and so cannot expect to display 'natural' relationships to indigenous economic pressures and responses. Influx control, betterment programmes, industrial decentralisation, homelands development and the Group Areas Act have all played a role here. He argues for a synergy of economic and settlement policies and a move away from 'static blue-print approaches to settlement planning' that take no account of the reflexive relationship between an urban centre and its hinterland. Dewar agrees with Lemon that bottom–up initiatives stand a better chance of success and that there is a need for a national small-towns programme.

POLICY IMPLICATIONS

Post-modernism and policy do not usually sit well together. The concerns and issues that we have raised in this Introduction are in a sense post-modern inasmuch as we have indicated our unease with the modernist, generalisation-seeking, system-oriented way in which much of social theory and policy has approached issues of population mobility and settlement.

Policy makers are in the difficult position that they need to be able to achieve the kind of generalisations that will allow them to make the predictions necessary to be able to devise and apply policies at national or regional/provincial level. This constraint would seem to incline them to make theory and research the servants of policy, and to read/look for system and coherence in the data and analysis more readily than would scholars who have the privilege of detachment. This in turn tends to give rise to the well-known top–down kind of approach, in the interests of tidiness, efficiency and control. The case studies in this volume show all too clearly that this approach does not work, as it imposes a uniformity on diverse situations and assumes a coherence, continuity and stability which we have suggested is dubious.

Generalised policy instruments should ideally be formulated and applied in an open-ended manner, with a flexible time-frame. This is because the phenomena relating to mobility and settlement do not readily lend themselves to systematisation, and flexibility allows for interaction between national-level policy and local-level situations, leading to adaptations.

Various factors seem to be working respectively *against* such an open-ended approach to policy. These are:

1. governments have particular visions and specific goals that they wish to achieve;
2. governments are under time pressure, because they need to be seen to be doing something, both by international funders, and by their electorates;
3. governments often do not have the resources, in terms of finance, personnel and skills, to allow for such flexibility;
4. Scudder and Cernea show that poorly planned and implemented resettlement – and, by extension, settlement – limits the way in which such projects develop by closing off options and making for a widespread and fairly uniform pattern of failure, instead of creating options and making for a diversity in patterns of success. This is in considerable measure because of the shortages of resources mentioned above, and because of inadequate re/settlement policy instruments and guidelines at national level.

However, a number of factors also seem to be working *in favour of* the desired open-ended approach. These are:

1. pressures being brought to bear on borrower countries by international donors/lenders, and by the growing international human-rights culture, to conform to internationally acceptable guidelines in relation to resettlement practice, with its emphasis on consultation and participation;
2. the fact that this international pressure reinforces the new democratic culture which is finding its feet in southern Africa;
3. the fact that in most southern African countries, government control over patterns of population mobility and settlement is limited, and cannot impose a uniform policy across the nation. As the South African case studies show, local political groupings are increasingly able to influence the manner and the pace of developments at the local level.
4. the fact that the shortages of resources mentioned earlier work not only against, but also in some ways in favour of, an open-ended approach – precisely because these shortages make for the inability of government to impose a blanket policy at national level.

This open-endedness would seem to have both positive and negative aspects. On the one hand, international and internal political pressures may make for an openness resulting from dialogue and participation in the context of international guidelines. On the other hand, the openness resulting from weak states short on resources and legitimacy, is more of an openness by default, and not as a result of conscious policy initiatives.

In their chapters in this volume, Cernea and Scudder both seek to use their understanding of the re/settlement process and potential patterns in it in order to find ways of counteracting the problems arising from the default position and from poor planning and implementation, and to suggest policy initiatives that will generate options in a positive and potentially sustainable manner.

Cernea argues that a number of mutually reinforcing factors interact, so as to trap affected people in a downward spiral of socio-economic impoverishment. One process of limitations (poorly planned, top–down projects) sets in motion a further process of limitations (eight related sub-processes of impoverishment, which Cernea discusses in detail in his chapter). While Cernea presents what is essentially a system-oriented analysis, in which a number of variables influence each other, it is open-ended in the sense that one can enter his 'matrix' from the direction of any one of the eight sub-processes which separately and cumulatively make for socio-economic impoverishment. Planners can thus select the risk of landlessness arising out of re/settlement, and consciously incorporate plans to counteract that risk. Similarly for homelessness, joblessness, ill-health, marginalisation, etc. In this way, Cernea argues, we can invert the set of risks inherent in re/settlement, and turn them into opportunities for increasing people's socio-economic welfare. The fact that one can enter the impoverishment/development matrix from a number of points also enables planners and implementers to take account of specific situations where, for example, landlessness may not be an important risk, but marginalisation may be, etc.

Cernea's matrix thus provides an adjunct to policy formation, as it is concerned more with how policies should be planned for and implemented, rather than with the content of policies, such as what kind of settlement pattern should be implemented, within what time span, etc. These concerns with the 'how' will nevertheless feed back into the 'what' of re/settlement policy, as certain approaches to, for example, size of plots, type of tenure, speed of implementation, nature of compensation, will clearly be more likely to realise the risks, rather than the opportunities, and vice versa. Cernea quotes D'Souza (1990) in arguing that there is a need to focus on the fulfilment of human needs and the elimination of glaring inequalities in society as the yardstick for success in planning. His analysis is geared towards facilitating such an approach towards policy, which is increasingly being taken up in the re/settlement guidelines of international funding agencies. It must, however, be added that these organisations are still struggling to get the borrower countries to comply with such guidelines, and that many private-sector funders do not have such guidelines in the first place. National and private-sector political will seemingly remain fairly obdurate.

Scudder's chapter also seeks to introduce flexibility into the policy process. In contrast to Cernea's approach, which is universal in its potential application, Scudder focuses on southern Africa. Scudder moves away from his long-standing concern with understanding the generally delineable stages of the resettlement/new land settlement process, to a focus on household production systems as a means of helping people move from the stage of Transition/Initial Adaptation to that of sustainable Economic Development. People rapidly develop entrepreneurial and social initiative, and we need to cater for this through policies that enhance opportunities for household income generation. Scudder sees small-scale irrigation schemes and household gardens as a key factor in this regard, and argues that the supply of water to Black peri-urban and urban households is central in this regard. Opportunity beckons from the water transfer systems from the Orange, Vaal, Tugela and Komati Rivers in South Africa.

Scudder argues that, up to now, water policy in South Africa has done little to go beyond the facilitation of water supply for the domestic use of the low income majority. There is a need for pricing mechanisms to finance future water-supply projects which will correct the favourable imbalance currently enjoyed by commercial farmers, to allow for the development of market gardening in South Africa. This should not be a financial impossibility, when one takes the successes of such ventures in poorer cities such as Harare, Maputo and Maseru into account.

As with Cernea's approach, Scudder's suggestions for income generation will also have implications for the content of settlement policies, as household plots will need to be of a minimum size, certain tenurial arrangements will need to be secured if people are to agree to pay for water for cultivation, local water committees will need to be established, etc. Policy makers will, however, need to guard against the temptation to impose uniform conditions on all participants in the interests of ease of administration, but rather strive to facilitate as much flexibility as possible so as not to shut out precisely those people whom they are trying to reach. Support will also be needed in terms of assistance with access to markets, so as to prevent more powerful interests monopolising developments.

Scudder's suggestions for income generation (which go beyond market gardening) not only serve to make for potentially more viable settlements, but also feed directly into Cernea's concerns with turning the risks of impoverishment into opportunities for development – a theme which is reflected in Maema and his colleagues' account (this volume) of the attempt at Katse Dam in Lesotho to turn resettlement into positive rehabilitation by making it into a community development project.

Both Carel van Aardt and David Simon highlight some of the complex policy implications of two interrelated issues which have been central to our approach to population mobility and settlement in this Introduction. These are, firstly, that human movement, rather than stable settlement, has, in Appadurai's words (1995: 25), become 'definitive of social life more often than it is exceptional in the contemporary world'; and secondly, that, in southern Africa in particular, governments have become increasingly unable, and even politically unwilling, to be the primary controller of such movement.

Van Aardt argues for less governmental control over population processes – both in terms of growth and of movement. He contends that the state's appropriate role is perhaps more one of development and facilitation. Patterns of settlement and migration do, however, have unintended and undesired consequences when they lead to land invasions and uncontrolled peri-urban development. It is not only a question of finding the correct policy, but of finding how to make it work – and here again, the 'what' and the 'how' of policy remain inextricably intertwined. As van Aardt forcefully reminds us, it remains very difficult to find the appropriate policy mix of 'control, facilitation, development and infrastructural redistribution', since control may be an appropriate short-term measure, whilst development is a more important long-term strategy. The elusiveness of that mix, and of the balancing of short- and long-term considerations, has been a refrain throughout most of the case-studies in this volume.

David Simon grapples with another of the tensions that has emerged throughout this volume: that between, on the one hand, rapid population growth and movement, both into and within urban centres, together with the state's limited ability to plan for and cope with such dynamics, and on the other hand, the need for sustainable urbanisation in the future southern Africa. Sustainability should, however, be seen, not only in terms of ecological and financial 'bottom line' scenarios, but should also be socio-politically sustainable. This calls for policies which directly address and promote social, political and economic equitability. Simon calls for the need to *relink* people to a political, social and economic functionality of place, that will require fundamentally restructured urban centres. Such centres will need to be managed and designed sustainably, with equitable resource use as a central part of the urban development process which will have to square that need for equitability with the increasingly fluid population and settlement patterns which characterise our cities and societies in southern Africa.

Like the constituencies it seeks to address, settlement policy is itself becoming a moving target. Like the members of those constituencies, policy makers are going to have to become risk-taking, entrepreneurial and innovative if they are to steer settlement policy and formation through the transitions, adaptions and developments necessary for success in contemporary, post-project, southern Africa.

ANGOLAN REFUGEE DISPLACEMENT AND SETTLEMENT IN ZAIRE[1] AND ZAMBIA

Since the early 1960s settlement patterns throughout the southern African region have been profoundly affected by forced displacement caused by widespread warfare and politically related governmental programmes. Millions of refugees fled wars in Angola, Mozambique, Namibia and Zimbabwe to crowd border villages, designated rural settlement areas, small towns and cities in neighbouring countries. Even more people were internally displaced within Angola, Mozambique, Namibia and Zimbabwe by warfare and by official villagisation (or *concentracao*) programmes that were instituted to contain anti-colonial forces. Additional millions of people were forcibly displaced within the Republic of South Africa by its programmes to channel or stop political change by territorially separating racial and ethnic categories.

The Mozambican, Namibian, and Zimbabwean wars are over, and the long-anticipated political transformation within South Africa is underway. The last remaining major war in southern Africa, the civil war in Angola, appeared to have ended, but flares up intermittently. The cessation of warfare is also associated with widespread changes in settlement patterns. All of the countries in southern Africa are experiencing some form of demilitarisation, postwar population movement, reconstruction and reshuffling of priorities. Postwar population movements include the demobilisation of soldiers and the return of many refugees and internally displaced people.

Policy makers and scholars are turning their attention to the problems and features of these new movements. This is a good time to try to understand some of the lessons learned from the study of the earlier flight into exile of millions of refugees in southern Africa. This chapter addresses these lessons by focusing on the flow of refugees out of Angola from 1961 to 1992 and the settlement of these refugees in the host countries of Zaire and Zambia. After documenting the waves of refugees, where they went, and how they settled, the chapter analyses the general structural characteristics of refugee populations, the relevance of examining the concept of refugee, and the varying attractiveness of repatriation to long-term refugees.

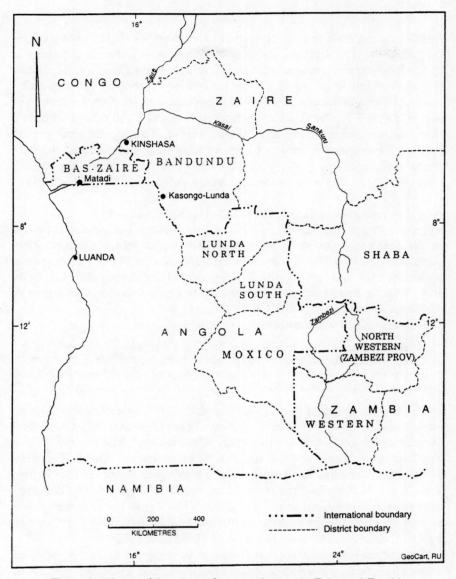

Figure 2.1 Areas of Angolan refugee settlement in Zaire and Zambia

DATA

Annual reports from the Office of the United Nations High Commissioner for Refugees (UNHCR) are the primary source of statistics in this chapter on the long-term movements of Angolan refugees into Zaire and Zambia as they are the only sources with the necessary time depth. This section is subdivided by two host countries and time periods, and the data are summarised in Table 2.1. The first time period ends in 1974 and takes account of refugee movements during the colonial period. The second time period (1975–92) recognises refugee movements during the first (pre-Bicesse Accord) phase of the civil war (1975–94). This chapter does not cover the second phase (1992–4) that ended with the Lusaka Protocol of November 1994.

Angolan refugees in Zaire, 1961–1974 (colonial period)

Angolan refugees began moving into Zaire over thirty-five years ago (1961). In the first year, almost 150,000 Angolans sought refuge in Zaire. This population grew to 400,000 by 1969 and 450,000 by 1974. The Angolans constituted the vast majority of all refugees in Zaire throughout the 1960s and 1970s, and Angolans in Zaire were the largest population of refugees in Africa for several years (UNHCR 1970b: 16).

Refugee statistics are notoriously unreliable:

> No precise figures of the total number [of Angolan refugees] now [1967] in the Congo [Zaire] are available, and estimates vary between 300,000 and 600,000. A conservative figure of 350,000 refugees at the end of 1967 is the UNHCR estimate. (UNHCR 1968a: 25)

The basic features of the refugee population, its settlement and the responses of local hosts were established during the first years. Most Angolans lived in southwestern Zaire (between Kinshasa and Matadi and in the Bas-Zaire Province) and along the border toward Shaba Province (concentrated around Kasongo-Lunda in Bandundu Province) (see Figure 2.1). The UN described the refugees as mostly belonging to the Bakongo tribe (historically known as the Kingdom of the Kongo), whose traditional territory included areas in three countries: Angola (including the Cabinda enclave), Zaire, and Congo (Brazzaville) (UNHCR 1962: 5).

Most of the refugees dispersed themselves among the Zairian population rather than being clumped together and segregated in camps (UNHCR 1966a: 22; 1967a: 31).

Recurring themes in UNHCR reports were the affinity between refugees and their local hosts, and the generosity with which hosts shared their resources with refugees. Consistently through the years, only a small minority of the refugees received official assistance. Most Angolan refugees were self-sufficient in their food supply within one year, 'largely through spontaneous integration'. Official assistance was provided mainly to newly arriving refugees (UNHCR 1967a: 32–3).

Table 2.1 Angolan refugees in Zaire and Zambia, 1961–1992

End of year	Refugees in Zaire		Refugees in Zambia	
	From Angola	Total	From Angola	Total
1961	148,000	No Data	No Data	No Data
1962	158,000–168,000	No Data	No Data	No Data
1963	No Data	No Data	No Data	No Data
1964	150,000	236,000	No Data	No Data
1965	270,000	317,000	No Data	No Data
1966	300,000	387,000	3,800	6,300
1967	350,000	435,000	6,200	10,740
1968	370,000	475,000	7,900	12,800
1969	400,000	500,000	8,200	12,700
1970	400,000	490,000	9,900	16,000
1971	400,000	No Data	11,000	17,000
1972	400,000	500,000	17,000	25,000
1973	400,000	460,000	22,000	36,000
1974	450,000	500,000	25,000	40,000
1975	460,000	510,000	30,000	36,000
1976	470,000	515,000	28,000	33,600
1977	500,000	530,000	30,000	64,000
1978	620,000	653,000	26,000	80,000
1979	*215,000	*299,000	26,000	57,000
1980	215,000	350,000	28,000	36,000
1981	215,000	365,000	37,000	50,100
1982	215,000	301,200	71,400	89,000
1983	215,000	300,000	83,100	103,000
1984	262,700	317,000	75,000	96,500
1985	240,500	No Data	77,000	103,600
1986	261,000	301,000	94,300	138,300
1987	298,700	320,000	97,100	146,100
1988	310,085	340,675	97,100	146,100
1989	310,092	340,689	98,000	137,100
1990	308,242	416,435	99,000	138,044
1991	278,580	482,959	102,500	140,672
1992	197,954	400,000	101,779	142,108

Key: * Refugees arriving in Zaire before 11 November 1975 were de-classified as refugees.
Source: Data from UNHCR documents (see references see Bibliography).

A series of problems were noted. Periodic serious local food shortages were reported, affecting both refugees and hosts. Many refugees did not want 'to become re-settled elsewhere or even to accept employment' (UNHCR 1963: 5). Other problems were caused by the impact of such a large population (UNHCR 1972: 66–8). Rural–urban migration, or 'flight from the land,' was attributed to several factors, including the marginal quality of agricultural land because of soil erosion, which was accentuated by the large refugee population (UNHCR 1968a: 25).

The April 1974 military coup in Portugal seemed to mark the end of the war, which would be followed by the consequent repatriation of the Angolan refugees (UNHCR 1974: 60). Some 450,000 Angolan refugees were

estimated to be still living in Zaire by the end of 1974, but this was
'necessarily a tentative figure in view of the substantial discrepancies
between available statistics' (UNHCR 1975: 55).

Angolan refugees in Zaire, 1975–1992 (civil war)

Many refugees repatriated around the time that Angola became independent (1974–5), but the initiation of the Angolan civil war in 1975 created
more refugees from Cabinda Province and northern Angola, until there
were an estimated 620,000 in Zaire by 1978. 'These ... were approximations,
as actual statistics were not available and the majority of the refugees were
living independently amongst the local population' (UNHCR 1976: 69).

Only a small minority (eight per cent by mid 1977) of the Angolan
refugees in Zaire were receiving relief (UNHCR 1977: 73). This changed in
late 1977 because of environmental crises (a drought, a cassava blight and
an acute food shortage) that affected both refugees and local hosts. Many
(60,000) new refugees arrived during the rainy season who were 'totally
destitute, under-nourished and in urgent need of medical care', and the
crises 'caused large numbers of refugees who had almost succeeded in integrating on their own' to move into and overload the new organized
settlements (UNHCR 1978: 75).

The number of Angolan refugees in Zaire dropped dramatically (620,000
to 215,000) in 1979. A large number (50,000) of refugees repatriated that
year (UNHCR 1980: 5, 99), but more important was Zairian legislation
that changed the criteria for refugee status to exclude people who had
sought asylum in Zaire before 11 November 1975. Based on UNHCR data,
about 360,000 Angolans remaining in Zaire were declassified as refugees,
and, 'as a result of changes in refugee legislation, the official caseload
[changed to include only] ... 215,000 Angolans' (UNHCR 1979: Adden-
dum I: 5, 1980: 96–7).

The movements of Angolans, either fleeing as refugees or repatriating to
Angola, also rose and fell through the years in response to changes in the
level of warfare. An increase in the intensity of warfare in Angola's Moxico
Province in 1984–5 caused a large influx of Angolans into Zaire's Shaba
Province. At that same time Zairian refugees in Angola were also fleeing
Moxico Province (see Figure 2.1) for other sites in Angola or were repatri-
ating to Zaire.

Small-scale spontaneous (i.e. not organised by the UNHCR or governments) repatriation increased after 1988 as South African and Cuban
troops were pulling out of the war, which seemed to be winding down. An
official large-scale repatriation of Angolans (from Shaba Province) and
Zairians was attempted in 1989, but was cancelled after fewer than 5,000
Angolans had repatriated. This attempt had tragic consequences for many
refugees because, in anticipation of leaving, they had 'abandoned their fields

and sold their possessions. This adversely affected the relative self- sufficiency and integration they had attained and ... their acceptance in the framework and life of the surrounding local communities' (UNHCR 1990: 104).

By 1991, only a small minority of the Angolan refugees continued to require assistance; 'most of them have achieved self-sufficiency, especially those in Bas-Zaire, and an appreciable number is integrated into the working life of the large towns' (UNHCR 1992: 145). With the 1991 signing of the Bicesse Peace Accord that ended the civil war in Angola, 200,000 Angolans in Bas-Zaire and 30,000 in Shaba applied for voluntary (organised) repatriation. However, this organised return was pre-empted by 'social and political events in Zaire' in late 1991 that prompted many Angolans to flee (spontaneously return) to Angola. The 'unstable security situation in Zaire' also caused the evacuation for several months of UNHCR and NGO staff (UNHCR 1992: 145–50).

Continuing spontaneous repatriation caused the number of Angolan refugees in Zaire to drop dramatically to 197,954 during 1992. The remaining Angolans were distributed in Bas-Zaire (where all refugees were Angolans) and Shaba (with 30,000 Angolans) Provinces and in the city of Kinshasa (where most refugees were Angolans). Unfortunately, after the August 1992 national elections in Angola, the peace was shattered with the resumption of the civil war between UNITA and the government. The repatriation of Angolan refugees diminished and stopped in late 1992. Although the refugees in Bas-Zaire and Shaba had become largely self-supporting over the years, they now needed relief again, as they had been mistakenly 'confident of their imminent repatriation ... (and) had destroyed their houses and uprooted their crops ...' in preparation for travel. They were 'completely destitute.' Eight thousand Angolans in Kinshasa also needed assistance (UNHCR 1993a: 185–6).

Angolan refugees in Zambia, 1966–1974 (colonial period)
Once Zambia became independent in 1964, it provided a hospitable base for liberation movements. In 1966 the MPLA and UNITA opened an eastern front in the war against Portugal, and small numbers of Angolan refugees began moving into Zambia, settling near the border in Zambezi District (North-Western Province) and several districts of Western Province (see Figure 2.1) (UNHCR 1966c: 1; 1967a: 79). Eastern Angola (adjacent to Zambia) was sparsely populated, so the numbers of refugees in Zambia never approached the numbers in Zaire, which was adjacent to a more densely populated region of Angola. In Zambia as in Zaire, the basic features of the refugee population, its settlement and the responses of local hosts and government were established during the first few years.

The Zambian government established the policy that refugees were to be moved away from the border into agricultural settlements, and two settlements

(Lwatembo in Zambezi District and Mayukwayukwa in Western Province –
see Figure 2.1) were started. Several problems developed at the settlements,
including the recognition that there was not enough agricultural land. A
study reported that one settlement (Mayukwayukwa) could continue if more
land could be acquired and individual farming established, but also stated
that the poorer soils meant 'refugees would not be able to support themselves from the cultivation of crops' (UNHCR 1969: 97–8; 1970a: 97–9).
Zambia wanted the settlements to depend entirely on mechanized communal farming, but allowed refugees to have small plots for private
cultivation (UNHCR 1968a: 97, 1968c: 18). Refugees complained about
communal farming, and the communal farms were not very productive.
Finally, in 1970, the government changed its policy from communal to
private farming in the settlements (UNHCR 1970a: 98–99, 1971: 88–90),
and production improved.

There were also 'difficulties of a tribal nature' at the site in Zambezi
District. The 'serious tribal problems' (UNHCR 1967b: 94; 1968a: 95)
dealt with the relationship between two Zambian ethnic groups (Luvale and
Lunda peoples) in the district. The ethnicity of the refugees was not noted
in the UN reports, but my 1970–2 research revealed that the majority of the
Angolan refugees in that district were Luvale, and the influx of Luvale had
strengthened that group in their continuing disputes with the other ethnicity.

Because of the problems with the first sites, the government allocated
360 square miles for a new settlement at Meheba in Solwezi District
(North-Western Province – see Figure 2.1) and transferred almost all of the
Angolan refugees from the other settlements to Meheba in 1971. The
Lwatembo settlement was closed, but the Mayukwayukwa settlement
continued with fewer refugees. Each family at Meheba was allocated five
hectares (twelve acres) of land to farm (UNHCR 1971: 88–91, 1972: 69–
72). Not until 1973 was it decided to begin progressively cutting the full
food rations that all of the refugees in the settlements had received since
their first arrival in Zambia.

The Zambian government wanted all Angolan refugees to reside in
government-controlled settlements, but, from the beginning, fewer refugees
than expected were resettled from the border into the organised settlements.
Little was known about those who never resettled; they were assumed to
have repatriated (UNHCR 1967a: 79) or to have 'left to live with the local
population' (UNHCR 1968a: 96). They 'returned home voluntarily or
found a way to fend for themselves elsewhere in Zambia' (UNHCR 1968b:
89; 1969: 98).

Until 1972 the Angolan refugee population in Zambia had grown slowly,
and most of those refugees were estimated to be living in organised settlements. The estimates for self-settled refugees, people living outside the
organised settlements, changed dramatically during 1972–4 (UNHCR 1974:

66), reflecting the government's 'belated recognition of the large existing village refugee population rather than new refugee influxes' (Hansen 1977: 30). The UNHCR noted without comment that '6,000 Angolan refugees living in border areas are also being transferred by the authorities, with UNHCR assistance, to Meheba' (UNHCR 1973: 74). This transfer was really a 'sweep', or concentrated effort by the police and immigration authorities to identify and collect self-settled refugees who did not want to move to the settlements. Both the increase in population estimates and the sweep may also reflect the government's awareness of my research (1970–2) among self-settled Angolan refugees in Zambezi Province. Although I delayed publication of my research until 1979 (Hansen 1979a, 1979b) in order to protect my informants, my findings had been reported in a research seminar at the University of Zambia before I left in mid-1972. My research may have contributed to the government's decision to 'sweep' the border.

The total number of Angolan refugees in Zambia continued to climb during the 1970s and was estimated to be 25,000 by the end of 1974. During 1974, Angolans began anticipating repatriation. In the Meheba settlement, 'only the minimum land area is being cleared for cultivation' (UNHCR 1975: 63).

Angolan refugees in Zambia, 1975–1992 (civil war)

Repatriation stopped when the civil war began; some of those who had repatriated fled again; and the number of Angolan refugees in Zambia remained around 30,000 during the rest of the 1970s. Some Angolans repatriated spontaneously during this time, while new Angolan refugees continued to arrive in Zambia. The major change in the 1982 estimated population of Angolan refugees (almost doubling) was the result of increasing the estimate of the extent of spontaneous settlement. This change was based on UNHCR-sponsored research (Freund and Kalumba 1983, 1986). Revised estimates were that 85 per cent of Zambia's refugees lived spontaneously, 13 per cent in organised settlements, and two per cent in urban areas (UNHCR 1983: 169–70, 1984: 138–9). In the border areas where they had self-settled, 'Angolans share ethnic and other socio-cultural ties with their Zambian hosts' (UNHCR 1987: 88).

By the early 1980s most of the refugees in the Meheba settlement were self-supporting in food production, and food rations were given only to new arrivals (UNHCR 1978: 81–2). UNHCR handed over administration of the settlement (with 10,503 refugees) to the Zambian government in 1982, so that Meheba 'could be integrated into Zambian economic and social structures'. A 'firm Government decision' was reached in the mid-1980s that all newly arriving refugees would be moved to new sites or repatriated (UNHCR 1986: 92), and the Meheba settlement was expanded to accommodate 10,000 to 12,000 new refugees (for a total of more than 20,000).

With the signing of the 1991 Bicesse Accord, the Zambian and Angolan governments and the refugees in organised settlements anticipated that repatriation would occur soon. 'High expectations among refugees regarding repatriation, coupled with the drought ... (affecting all of southern Africa), resulted in decreased prospects for self-sufficiency in food production' (UNHCR 1992: 154–5).

The resumption of warfare in late 1992 stopped repatriation and initiated the flight of more refugees. By the end of 1992, 101,779 Angolan refugees remained in Zambia, with 25,000 living in the two rural settlements (Meheba and Mayukwayukwa). Some of the Angolans who had repatriated had returned to Zambia, and some refugees who had intended to repatriate were now in need of relief again (UNHCR 1993a: 199–203).

TRANSIENT STATUS AND GENERATIONAL REALITY

Citizenship is understood to be a permanent or long-term status. Refugee, to the contrary, is assumed to be a transient status, or temporary condition, and refugees are assumed to be temporary, short-term phenomena. The Portuguese colonial authorities and the Zairian and Zambian governments expected that the flight of Angolan refugees into Zaire and Zambia would be brief and resolved through repatriation. In 1962 the UN noted that the 'Portuguese authorities have given assurances ... [that they are ready to] facilitate the return of refugees to their home and their re-establishment in Angola' (UNHCR 1962: 7), and Zairian authorities hoped the refugees would 'shortly be able to return to their homeland' (UNHCR 1963: 2). The reality is very different. Most African refugee populations have been relatively stable and long-term (Hansen 1992), and the growth of refugee populations is not a simple matter of adding more new arrivals to an existing population.

Demographic, social and political factors combine to explain the generational reality of African refugee populations. Socio-political status is critical in understanding refugee statistics. A major reason why the number of African refugees continues to increase every year is that each new wave of refugees supplements an earlier, relatively stable, existing population. Most Africans who become refugees continue to be considered (and counted) as refugees for many years. To some extent, this stability has been caused by the continuation of wars and disturbances that prevented refugees from repatriating, but another reason for the stability has been that refugees were rarely allowed the opportunity to become naturalised citizens of their host country, even after decades of residing there (Hansen 1993). The number of immigrants in Africa does not increase in the same way as the number of refugees because immigrants are no longer categorised as immigrants after they have resided in their new location for a time.

Even refugees who have completely integrated themselves socio-economically into the host society are rarely allowed to integrate themselves socio-politically by naturalising. When I returned to Zambia in 1989 to re-examine the status of self-settled Angolan refugees, almost all of them were completely integrated (socio-economically) into the local society. That integration forced me to re-examine the basis and perspective for continuing to categorise them as refugees. On reporting these findings and conclusions to the Zambian Commissioner for Refugees, I was reminded that, given Zambian law and policy, all refugees remained 'strangers' (refugees) forever (Hansen 1990: 35–6).

The relative permanency of refugee status is also generational because the status is inherited by the children of refugees, and by their children. Some Angolans became refugees in Zaire over thirty-five years ago, and others in Zambia over thirty years ago. They have been refugees for almost two generations, and have married and had children, some of whom also have married and had children; and all of these people remain refugees.

Refugee populations can grow, therefore, because of natural increase (a surplus of births over deaths). Natural increase can have a dramatic impact on long-term populations, which helps to explain a continual increase in the number of African refugees. Sub-Saharan African populations have been characterised for some time by relatively high annual growth rates. For instance, the average annual population growth rate of the Eastern, Western, and Middle African regions (1990–4) was 3.0 to 3.1 per cent, while the developing countries in southern Africa ranged from lows of 2.6 to 2.7 (Botswana and Namibia) through 3.3 (Malawi and Zambia) to highs of 4.4 to 4.5 per cent (Zimbabwe and Zaire) (UN 1996). Statistically, the annual growth rate times the number of years to double in size equals 70 (the 'rule of 70'). Assuming, for the sake of argument, that the natural rate of growth of the Angolan refugee populations in Zaire and Zambia was 3.3 per cent (Zambia's rate), those populations would double in size in less than twenty-two years without the arrival of any new refugees from Angola.

AGE, SEX AND DEMOGRAPHY

It is important to understand the distribution of people by age and sex, but statistics can be misleading. Reports often emphasise that African refugee populations consist mostly of women and children. This true statement creates the misleading impressions that these refugee populations are dramatically different from the pre-flight populations that generated the refugees and that there is a disproportionate presence of women among African refugees. The questions to ask about refugee populations are the extent to which these populations differ from the populations of origin (and the host populations), and the reasons for the differences. In situations of forced migration, such as occurs with refugees, the migratory population usually demographically resembles the original population because people in all of the age and sex categories ('everyone') flee.

Table 2.2 Age and sex among some rural African populations

Rural population (Census date)	M:F Ratio (All people)	M:F Ratio (Only adults)	Children and women (%)	Children and men (%)
Malawi (1987)	92	86	75	71
Namibia (1991)	92	84	75	71
Zaire (1985)	93	86	74	70
Zimbabwe (1992)	91	84	77	72
Angolan refugees in Zambian Settlement (Meheba)(1996)	99	96	74	73
Internally displaced Angolans (1996)	83	62	87	79

Key: The M:F (or sex) ratio is the number of men per 100 women (a ratio of 100 would be sexual parity). Children in these statistics are people less than fifteen years of age, so adults are fifteen and older.
Sources: Country data are from the 1994 Demographic Yearbook (UN 1996), refugee data from a UNHCR census report (UNHCR 1996a), and internally displaced data from an Angolan National Institute of Statistics report (Government of Angola 1996).

Are African refugee populations disproportionately female in comparison with other African populations? The key for most Third-World populations, including refugees, is that there are many children, not that there are many women. The number of children depends on how children are defined (those under fifteen years of age, or under eighteen) but, in either case, children compose approximately half of African and other Third-World populations that are growing rapidly because of natural increase (UN 1996). If half of a population were children and the adults were divided more or less equally between women and men, about three-quarters of the population would be children and women. Conversely, about three-quarters would be children and men.

Our demographic understanding is improved if we separate the factors of age (children versus adults) and sex (males versus females). The male–female (M: F) ratio (number of males per 100 females) is a demographic measure to check distribution by sex. The sex ratio may be determined for the entire population, or for certain sectors. Since the majority of African refugees are rural people, especially relevant for comparisons is the sex ratio in rural populations, especially the ratio among adults in the rural population. The proportion of women and men among adults is a variable that depends on a number of factors, such as patterns of labour migration, differential mortality (including war-related deaths), recruitment as soldiers, etc. Thus, a disproportionate percentage of women does not mean necessarily that many men are fighting as soldiers or were killed in warfare. Many southern African rural populations show a preponderance of women to men because of male labour migration to urban areas, where there is a corresponding preponderance of men to women (UN 1996).

There are adequate census data (UN 1996) from four southern African countries (Malawi, Namibia, Zaire and Zimbabwe) to examine the relationship of age and sex in their rural populations (see Table 2.2). Children (younger than fifteen) compose 46 to 49 per cent of the rural population of those four countries. There are more females than males (sex ratios of ninety-one to ninety-three males per 100 females) in the rural areas, especially among adults (sex ratios of eighty-four to eighty-six men per 100 women). This sexual imbalance is masked when age and sex are considered together; the presence of many children masks the preponderance of women. Because there are so many children, women and children compose three-quarters (74 to 77 per cent) of these rural populations, but there are almost as many men and children (70 to 72 per cent).

The age–sex distribution of two regional populations of Angolan refugees in Zaire in 1961 was estimated to be approximately half children (45 to 60 per cent), with the percentage of women and children being 75 to 85 per cent (UNHCR 1962: 5). In 1991 the age–sex distribution of the Angolan refugee population in Zaire was 21 per cent adult (eighteen and older) females, 18 per cent adult males, and 61 per cent children (31 per cent girls and 30 per cent boys). Women and children constituted 82 per cent of the refugee population, but men and children constituted 79 per cent (UNHCR 1992).

The most recent surveys of rural Angolan refugees show higher sex ratios (all ages), ninety-seven in Zaire (UNHCR 1996b) and ninety-nine (ninety-six when counting only adults) in the largest rural settlement (Meheba) in Zambia (UNHCR 1996a). These high ratios, especially those for Meheba, are unusual for southern African rural populations and reflect a stable, long-term (non-emergency) situation in which the normal migratory patterns of men are restricted, as movement and occupation in the host country are restricted. In these circumstances the rural refugee populations have higher male–female ratios than the resident rural populations.

By contrast, a large-scale survey of recently displaced (1992–4) Angolans in seven provinces of Angola reveals very low sex ratios (eighty-three for all ages, sixty-two for adults – see Table 2.2). These ratios indicate that this internally displaced population (not refugees) is structurally different from normal southern African populations, and that there is a disproportionate number of women (Government of Angola 1996). Research is needed to learn the reasons (military recruitment, labour migration, differential mortality, etc.) for the marked absence of adult men among these internally displaced Angolans.

BECOMING (AND DEFINING) A REFUGEE

Becoming a refugee is not a simple clear-cut matter. The UN and OAU have different ways of defining the status or identity of refugee. Even when, using either the UN or OAU definitions, observers assume that people are refugees and label, or impose, refugee status on them, that overlooks the socio-political reality that becoming a refugee is a matter of perspective. First of all, host-country authorities must agree to recognise immigrants as being refugees. This is not an automatic process. The host government may also declassify refugees, as occurred in Zaire in 1979. Second, there are the perspectives of the people in flight and the people they encounter and settle among.

Since 1970, I have been studying Angolan refugees who self-settled in Zambian border villages. Refugees and villagers live intermixed in rural settlements, speak the same languages, practise the same, or very similar, customs, and are often related in some way. Zambian policy required all refugees to live in organised settlements, so all of the self-settled refugees were illegally in the villages and sought to conceal their status as Angolans and refugees. I lived in a rural settlement and learned to speak the local Luvale language, but it was difficult to identify who was a refugee. I conducted research on local social and economic systems for a year before I could positively identify the first refugee. After he identified himself to me, I could begin to identify other refugees using the snowball sampling technique.

From the beginning, because of the existence of the war across the border, I accepted the basic premise of the UN and OAU definitions; a refugee was someone who fled across an international border to escape a war. I then devised an empirical definition to differentiate between the refugees and the villagers among whom they lived, defining a refugee as someone who came from Angola since 1965 (just before the war erupted along the border); leaving the country during wartime made the person a refugee.

There were always complications. The Luvale and related peoples had lived on both sides of the border before it became a border. Many people had lived on both sides at different times in their lives and had travelled in both countries to visit family, and to fish and trade. Migration for various reasons was a normal part of their lives, and Angolan labour migration to the mines and farms of South Africa, Zimbabwe and Zambia's Copper Belt had caused a major migratory drift during this century that had populated that part of rural Zambia with people who had originated in Angola (Hansen 1979a).

Nonetheless, my objective definition served my research objectives until 1989, when I returned to compare the long-term consequences for Angolan refugees of being self-settled versus living in an organised settlement. Two dimensions of interest to me were psychological security and dependency, and the extent to which refugees had become integrated into the Zambian society and economy. In addition to a long (two-hour) semi-structured interview and group discussions, I also used a physical instrument, a model ladder, to elicit the attitudes of refugees and villagers in the villages and refugees in the Meheba settlement.

The English concept of 'refugee' does not translate directly into the Luvale language. The closest equivalent was *ungeji*, which means a stranger, or newcomer. Using the ladder, I indicated that an *ungeji* coming to a place was on the first rung and asked each refugee where he or she was now on the ladder.

Objectively, using economic and social indicators, all of the self-settled refugee men and women were integrated into Zambian society. Based on their responses to the ladder, it was obvious that they also felt completely integrated. In addition, the local villagers considered the self-settled refugees to be completely integrated. In fact, it became apparent that neither the self-settled refugees nor the villagers felt comfortable in 1989 with the cultural or linguistic implications (of estrangement, displacement and alienation) that accompany the refugee concept. Essentially, the self-settled refugees and the host villagers denied that the refugees had ever been 'refugees'. They did not deny that people had fled across the border to escape the war, but their perspective was that people who had fled the war to come stay with their kin and co-ethnics were (using the distinction in English) newcomers on their arrival, but not strangers. (I shall continue to refer to these people as self-settled refugees for the remainder of this chapter, but the use of the refugee concept is clearly disputable.)

The implications of this difference in cultural perspective became clearer with the data from refugees in an organised settlement. Although they were economically better off than the self-settled, refugees in the Meheba settlement were not as well integrated. The key was the relationship between refugees in a settlement and villagers living around that settlement, many of whom resented the presence of the refugees. Twenty per cent of the men and women in the organized settlement still saw themselves to be *ungeji* after living in Zambia for almost twenty years, and by their use of *ungeji* they really did mean stranger, or refugee (see Table 2.3). In fact, they even noted that the English term 'refugee' was one of the pejorative insults used against them by local villagers. This was confirmed in discussions with villagers around the Meheba settlement, who revealed that they clearly thought of the Angolan refugees as outsiders, Angolans, and refugees who were temporarily sheltering in Zambia.

From the perspective of the refugees (both the self-settled and those in Meheba) and of the villagers living with the self-settled refugees, moving across an international border had not made anyone a refugee. In their social and cultural terms, those people from Angola had become 'refugees' when they were moved in 1971 from the first settlement in Zambezi Province, surrounded by their co-ethnics, to Meheba in another district that was dominated by another ethnicity (Kaonde). The forced movement within Zambia between ethnic territories had transformed them into refugees, whereas the self-settled 'refugees' (in our terms) living along the

Table 2.3 Refugee self-reported scoring as strangers (*ungeji*)

Self-settled male refugees in villages	nobody
Self-settled women refugees in villages	nobody
Male refugees in organised settlement	20 per cent yes
Women refugees in organised settlement	20 per cent yes

Key: Data from Hansen 1992.

border had never become strangers (in our terms) because they had remained within their own ethnic territory among people who accepted them.

There is another possible explanation that I could not test because I did not interview refugees living in an organised settlement within their own ethnic territory. Almost all of the Angolans living in organised settlements had been picked up by the government, either immediately after arriving at the border or in a police sweep, and taken to a settlement, but over the years some people had voluntarily moved to the settlements to escape the effects of drought or poverty. Living in an organised settlement was also called living with the government (*fulumende*). Some of the self-settled refugees alluded to people 'becoming refugees' when they moved from the villages to 'live with the government', to live in an organised settlement. The same idea and use of the refugee concept was noted among Ugandan refugees in southern Sudan (Harrell-Bond 1986).

NATIONALISM, SETTLEMENT AND REPATRIATION

Examining the demographic structure and cultural perspective of Angolan refugees is not simply of academic interest. Assuming sustainable peace is achieved in Angola, what will be the response of the refugees in Zaire and Zambia? African governments and the UN espouse repatriation as the only appropriate action that refugees could take, and the UNHCR predicts that almost all of the refugees want to, and will, repatriate (UNHCR 1996a, 1996b). I disagree for the following reasons.

If repatriation is to be voluntary, it requires a high degree of nationalism. Nationalism is a variable, not a constant value among all peoples. Repatriation requires a degree of orientation, or attraction, towards the country of origin that does not exist for everyone, and also implies that the refugees (with a transient status and condition) are unsettled. Unless repatriation is enforced, or coerced, I predict (contrary to UNHCR predictions) that many refugees (especially the self-settled) will choose to remain in the host countries where they already have established themselves to varying degrees.

Many of the Angolan refugees in Zaire and Zambia were born in those host countries. They are second (or third) generation refugees who are at home in Zaire or Zambia and have been socialised there. If they have gone to school, they have learned French or English, not Portuguese, and have studied Zairian or Zambian history, not Angolan. Angola has been at war

Table 2.4 Refugee self-reported desire to repatriate to Angola

Self-settled men in villages	nobody said yes	10 per cent unsure
Self-settled women in villages	nobody said yes	31 per cent unsure
Men in organised settlements	58 per cent yes	10 per cent unsure
Women in organised settlements	42 per cent yes	16 per cent unsure

Key: Data express opinions in 1989 (Hansen 1992, 1993). Compare with UNHCR surveys from 1996 showing almost unanimous desire to repatriate by refugees in Zaire and Zambia (UNHCR 1996a, 1996b).

for the entire lifetime of many of these young refugees, and they have never looked there for opportunities or jobs. Many of them have married and settled, built homes, cleared fields, etc. These are immovable assets. Meanwhile, the first generation refugees have aged: a twenty-year-old who fled in 1966 is now over fifty years old. Many of these older people have houses, fields, jobs and families in the host country and are too tired or apprehensive to be enthusiastic about returning to a country they associate with warfare and death, and having to rebuild again.

On the other hand, there may be economic, social and political reasons why people might want to return. Some people are patriotic, while ambitious people may think there is more opportunity in Angola. Some of the Luvale in 1989 pointed out the importance for them of *usolo*, or the hunger for fish, as a motive for returning to Angola. With the decades of war, they said, the streams in Angola were full of fish to be caught, and the untilled woodlands were ready to be cleared of trees again and planted.

The attraction to repatriation and the decision to repatriate are inversely related to the degree of integration in the host country and to the degree of self-control that the refugees exercise. In my 1989 Zambian study, none of the self-settled refugees, all of whom were well integrated, wanted to repatriate. Approximately half of the refugees in the Meheba settlement, where people felt more like strangers, 'wanted' to repatriate (see Table 2.4). The 'desire' to repatriate among the refugees in the Meheba settlement expressed more than their own motivation. Many of them expressed directly (or alluded to) their belief that they did not have any real freedom of decision: the 'government' would decide for them; and they would do whatever the government wanted.

In contrast to my findings, the 1996 surveys conducted for UNHCR in Zaire and Zambia found that almost all refugees wanted to repatriate (UNHCR 1996a, 1996b). How can this contrast be explained? First of all, the 1996 Zambian survey only interviewed refugees in the organised settlements; self-settled refugees were not interviewed. My incomplete copy of the 1996 Zairian survey does not explain its methodology, so I cannot comment on the sampling. Second, the UNHCR and the governments (of Angola, Zaire and Zambia) have conducted a long educational campaign (including visits to refugee settlements by representatives of the Angolan government) to convince refugees of the importance of their returning to Angola. This campaign clearly expressed the wishes of the governments and may have changed people's minds, or clarified what they were supposed to do. Third, the war was ongoing when my 1989 survey was conducted, while the 1996 surveys were conducted more than a year after the cease-fire. Because of peace and other events (in Angola and the host countries) in the intervening years, refugees may have changed their minds about the advantages of returning.

I still predict that the majority of self-settled refugees in Zambia (and probably in Zaire) will remain in those host countries unless they are coerced to return to Angola. Almost all (or all) of the refugees in organised settlements will return to Angola (in organised convoys), but some may again return to Zaire and Zambia if economic conditions in Angola do not improve. The borders between Angola and its two neighbours are porous, and back-and-forth movements (voluntary migration) will continue as people on both sides (refugees and residents) attempt to improve their personal situations.

Even for the refugees who wish to return, completely voluntary repatriation may take years. Over the decades, many refugees repatriated when it looked as if the war was over, only to be killed or forced to flee again when warfare resumed. Experience has made people cautious about rushing back to Angola before they are convinced that the war will not resume. Fighting has flared up intermittently since the cease-fire in November 1994, and only a small minority of the refugees have repatriated on their own.

SUMMARY AND CONCLUSIONS

This chapter began by summarising the movement and settlement of Angolan refugees in Zaire and Zambia from the beginning of the war for national liberation (1961) through the brief peace (1991–2) after the Bicesse Peace Accord. Reviewing the year-to-year statistics provided by the UNHCR permits the reader to appreciate the quality and imprecision of refugee-population data, and following the movements of refugees from year to year provides a sense of the stability and fluidity of refugee populations.

Refugee-population estimates are notoriously imprecise, but there are patterns to the imprecision of refugee (and other crisis-related) population statistics. The magnitude of these estimates expresses qualitative, symbolic and emotional statements.

The composition of African refugee populations was analysed, as was the discrepancy between the idea that refugees are temporary phenomena and the reality that refugee populations are stable through generations. The stability and growth of these populations are influenced by natural increase and political decisions that deny the opportunity to naturalise. The relative importance of age over sex was also examined, as was the variation in male–female ratios among different populations.

Refugee status is a complex concept. At one level there is variation between the UN and OAU definitions, and at another level there is significant decision-making by the host government. This became dramatically clear in 1979 when Zaire declassified almost two-thirds of its Angolan refugees.

Identifying refugees can be difficult, and operational definitions for measurement purposes can be complicated by African social realities, such as high levels of normal and antecedent migration. The 'refugee' term also emerges from a particular western culture and language and does not necessarily have an exact equivalent in other languages and cultures.

Objective indicators are helpful, but there are levels of meaning and attitudes that must be approached or measured in other ways. While the refugee term is defined at one level by the necessity for international movement, the emotional or psychological feelings that are associated with being a refugee may be triggered by other movement, and not necessarily by international movement. In the case of Luvale-speaking Angolans in Zambia, movement to an organised settlement, or to one in another district that was dominated by a different ethnicity, may have triggered a level of alienation that was not initiated by international movement.

This discussion is of both theoretical and practical interest. Ongoing civil war and flight in countries such as Angola and the Democratic Republic of Congo mean that host governments in southern Africa are still sheltering many refugees. Ideas about the creation of refugee status and the composition of refugee populations help predict the post-war movement and motivation of refugees who are usually expected to repatriate.

NOTE

1. In this chapter, 'Zaire' is used rather than 'Democratic Republic of Congo' as the country was known as 'Zaire' for the period dealt with in this chapter, i.e. 1961–1992.

SOUTHERN MOZAMBIQUE: MIGRANT LABOUR AND POST-INDEPENDENCE CHALLENGES

It is well known that migrant labour to South Africa has been an important factor of integration in the southern African economy for the last 150 years. In some of South Africa's neighbouring countries such as Mozambique, migrancy is amongst the most important foreign sources of income. In Mozambique the dependence on wage labour income is dramatically noticeable in the rural economy of the three southern provinces, namely Maputo, Gaza and Inhambane (see Figures 3.1; 3.2).

In recent years there has been considerable debate about the implications of migrant labour for both the sending countries as well as for South Africa. Concern within South Africa has focused on the continuation of the system or on introducing changes into it. Government departments and research institutions have looked very carefully at the influx of migrant workers into the newly democratic South Africa.[1] This relates to the expectation of positive social and economic transformation under the Reconstruction and Development Programme (RDP), recently restructured into the Growth, Employment and Redistribution Programme (GEAR), in areas such as housing, employment, better working conditions, health-care facilities, and education. Ongoing immigration is seen to reflect increasing numbers of people competing for these resources.

Under apartheid, migrant labour from the neighbouring countries to the mines and plantations in South Africa had both political and economic implications. I am not going to deal with this aspect, or with the history of migrant labour to South Africa, as they have been extensively researched and a vast literature is available on these issues. Current debates have tended to underemphasise or overlook crucially important matters, which lent a complex economic and social dimension to migrancy during the colonial and post-colonial period (1928–78). These matters include contracts and compulsory repatriation, the deferred pay system, compensation and indemnity procedures. For Mozambique, all these procedures were a result of complicated negotiations between Portugal and South Africa in the

1920s. To some extent they represented a victory for Portuguese rural commercial interests, and for African families. It is not my intention to analyse those negotiations, but I would argue that compulsory repatriation after completion of a twelve- or eighteen-month contract, and deferred pay, were but two sides of the same coin. They were important strategies, according to the Portuguese negotiators, to prevent permanent immigration and to help people to save money. But they also fuelled rural commerce, and gave rural families a more substantial interest in migrancy as a system.

In the 1920s it was South African commercial interests which resisted deferred pay, because it meant money leaving South Africa in order to develop Portuguese trade. Portugal insisted on it, saying that she wanted to minimise the suffering of the families of the so-called *manparra magaiças*.[2] Assuming that almost every migrant worker had on average between five and ten dependents left in Mozambique, it is clear that the outcome of such negotiations would have very serious social and economic implications.

In this chapter my main objective is to describe and discuss the social and economic changes related to migrancy in Mozambique over the last twenty years. There have been four major factors making for change:

- the rise in wages in the mining industry;
- the independence of Mozambique and Frelimo's socialist project;
- prolonged warfare and natural calamities;
- the democratic changes in both Mozambique and South Africa.

THE RISE IN WAGES IN THE MINING INDUSTRY

In the mid-1970s migrants saw their wages rising and as a consequence developed more ambitious goals. These changes in wages in South Africa helped to sharpen peasant differentiation in southern Mozambique. The reduction in the numbers of foreign workers in the mining industry meant that many workers lost their jobs, or became semi-employed in Mozambique. However, those who succeeded in getting job contracts were now more easily able to accumulate and invest their money in ploughs, oxen, cars and lorries, and improved brick/block houses than before. Interviews suggest that the degree of social and economic differentiation in the area has increased sharply in the last twenty years.

> Before the 1970s people working in the mines were not socially important in the community. In that period I took contracts but I had to hide the fact that I was working in South Africa from my family and friends. However after 1974 people working in South Africa became respected.[3]

Interviews and my own experience indicate that it was in the 1970s that the designation *magaiças* for the returning migrant workers was replaced by *madjonidjoni*.[4] The difference between these labels is that the latter group had comparatively more money and as a result could afford to buy a car, to rent a flat and live in town, or to build a modern house, and to compete

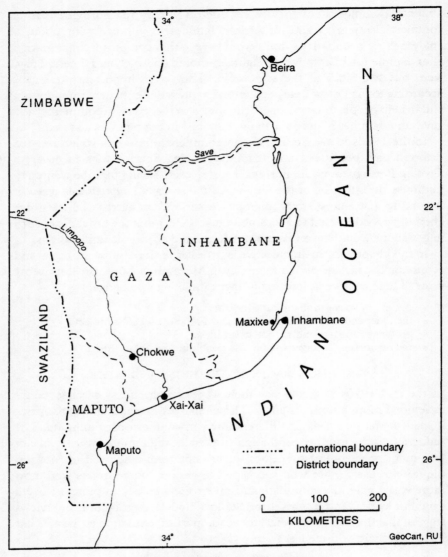

Figure 3.1 Southern Mozambique

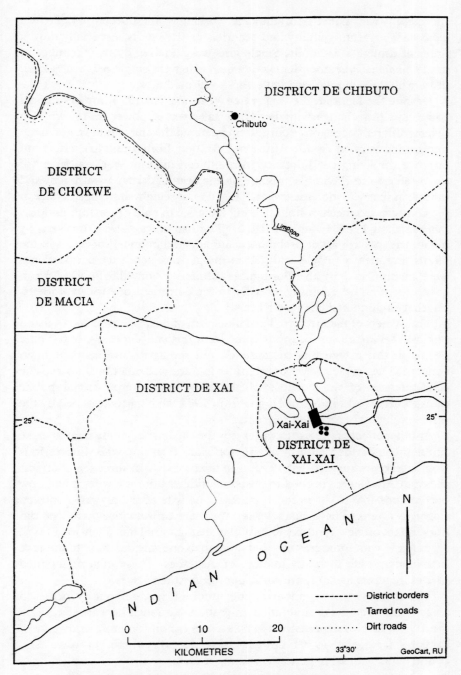

Figure 3.2 Mozambique: The lower Limpopo valley *circa* 1990

successfully with skilled Mozambicans working within the country. To be a *madjonidjoni* meant stability and security for the family, especially during times of droughts or floods. Single girls were advised by their families to marry *madjonidjoni* rather than young men who were employed locally, even those who were in relatively skilled and well-paid jobs.

Despite the fact that the wage rates went up from 1973, my informants connected this change with Frelimo's takeover of power in 1974/5. On several different occasions informants explained the changes in wages in the mining industry in South Africa as resulting from Frelimo's efforts to improve the living conditions of Mozambican migrant workers. Many of them referred to Frelimo's pressure on the South African government and mining industry to increase wages. They do not seem to have been aware of the complicated mechanisms affecting the price of gold or the international market (First 1983; Houghton 1976). The rise in wages was thus seen by my informants as part of Frelimo's economic and political successes in the 1970s. Frequently people said that in the pre-independence period wages were manipulated by the Portuguese administration, the South African government and the mining industry to the detriment of African workers, but that Frelimo had changed all that.[5]

The owners of the means of local transport, of restaurants in Xai-Xai and of kiosks selling all sort of goods come from this *madjonidjoni* group. Some people in this category of migrants do not see agriculture as their main concern. They exploit new opportunities in trade and other businesses. The consequences of the collapse of the local and interprovincial public transport networks in Mozambique from 1974 were partly lessened by the private vehicles of returned migrants.[6]

Another effect of the rise in wages was the capacity of young men to make simultaneous bridewealth payments for more than one wife. Impressions from interviews suggest that whereas in the past, two or three job contracts in South Africa were needed to raise the bridewealth for a wife, it had now become possible to do so for more than one wife after only one contract. Polygyny seems to have characterised the more conservative men, who did not embark on new ventures to improve their material life. They might well argue – and with some reason – that more than one wife did more to improve their material life than any number of machines. These men maintained that more wives meant more womanpower for themselves.

The changed socio-economic opportunities brought about by increased wages reinforced the desirability of migration. Although he was referring to the 1990s, L. N.'s experience can be seen as epitomising migrant workers' thinking from the 1970s onwards. People everywhere, in town and countryside, wanted to go to the mines, he said:

> I do not think that I can work here [Mozambique] any more. I also would like my children to go to school and later work in South Africa. When you are educated

you get a very good job in South Africa. When I work [he has no academic qualifications] I get R1,500 per month and when I have the opportunity of working overtime, I can earn R2,000 per month. This money has been sufficient to feed my family and to buy some commodities which are used in paying people who help on the farm.[7]

Despite a history of nationalist critiques of migrant labour to South Africa, and studies of its possible substitution, political and economic conditions in the mid–1970s did not favour any policy of terminating migrant labour (Frelimo 1983a: 10; Mondlane 1983: 92–3; *Noticias* 9 June 1975). After 25 June 1975 the government of independent Mozambique, like its Portuguese predecessor, was not in a position to offer alternative employment to migrant workers. On the contrary, Mozambique needed to increase the number of migrants (Government of Mozambique 1989: 19–20; 1990: 16–19). In 1979 Mozambique initiated a large programme of sending workers to the former German Democratic Republic for four-year contracts. Local agriculture and industry were still unable to absorb the labour force. The destruction of industrial and agricultural equipment by Portuguese settlers before they left the country in 1974 and 1975 worsened the already limited job market in Mozambique.

In 1974 and 1975, migrant labour from Mozambique to South Africa continued to be crucially important to the mining industry, and an important source of income in the post-colonial period for thousands of families in southern Mozambique as well as for the independent state. The pre-independence political discourse, condemning not only the nature of migration under colonialism, but the migrant labour system as a whole, had now to be adjusted to the economic reality of Mozambique. The new authorities had to be wary of the criticism that had been directed against Portuguese colonists: that they had been criminally selling Mozambicans to the mines, where they had contracted incurable diseases, and that migrant labour had brought other horrifying consequences to the rural communities of southern Mozambique.[8] Frelimo's political fight against apartheid now had to be conducted within the context of her economic dependence.

THE INDEPENDENCE OF MOZAMBIQUE AND FRELIMO'S SOCIALIST PROJECT

When Frelimo came to power in Mozambique, the socialisation of agriculture was among the first of its revolutionary tasks. Frelimo's economic development plan was based on three main pillars: agriculture was seen as the 'base', manufacturing as the 'dynamising factor', and heavy industry as the 'decisive factor'. According to Hanlon (1990: 73):

With respect to agriculture, Frelimo came to independence with reasonably clear ideas about rural development, which is not surprising since it fought the armed struggle in the rural areas. The policy was 'socialization of the countryside', involving state and cooperative farms, with people living in new villages. This is the central issue of economic transformation, as 85% of the population live in rural areas.

The Third Party Congress in February 1977 decided that the state farm sector must be 'dominant and determinant' and that 'technical resources must be concentrated on state production units'. Co-operatives were to be 'actively supported'. Family farming was ignored.

The political economy of the new government was basically designed to give priority to the socialisation of the countryside. Learning from the agrarian policies of socialist Eastern Europe and to some extent from its own experience in the liberated areas, Frelimo believed that the best way to fight misery and poverty was to set up big state farms, communal villages and co-operatives.[9] The customary system of land tenure, virtually ignored or disregarded by the Portuguese, was not revived. Peasants who hoped to recover the lands forcefully usurped by the Portuguese were disappointed, as cooperatives and state farms replaced the Portuguese farms (Hermele 1988: 44–6).

In 1992 I interviewed a former *regulo*,[10] who told me that the major mistake of the Frelimo government had been to try to supplant the small producers by big state farms. He added that Frelimo had believed that all people could be fed on the basis of wage-labour on the state farms. The government had not provided room for manoeuvre for the poorest peasants, as the Portuguese to some extent had.[11]

In February 1977 devastating floods in the Limpopo river valley resulted in the loss of large quantities of food crops. Irrigation works, granaries, housing, road infrastructure and transport equipment were destroyed. For example, on a single day, 14 February, in Chókwe district the floods left some 740 people homeless, more than 200 houses were destroyed, the Limpopo railway line was severed, cattle disappeared, state, collective and family farms were seriously devastated, and rice-peeling factories were inundated (*Notícias* 14 February 1977). On 19 February it was announced that 10,000 people had been affected by the floods. In Xai-Xai alone there were 3,323 displaced people and in Chókwe 4,000 (*Notícias* 19 February 1977).

In Inhamissa, as in other parts of the Limpopo valley, these floods accelerated the implementation of communal villages and cooperatives (Frelimo 1983b: 20). Relief operations including food and medicine distribution were carried out in combination with the setting up of communal villages. The press frequently quoted Frelimo officials as saying that the communal villages operation was welcomed by the local affected people (*Notícias* 20 February 1977, 23 February 1977). A provincial Brigade of Communal Village Building was formed to accelerate the process. (*Notícias* 21 February 1977).

Hundreds of families from the valley were forced to seek protection in the highlands. This was not their first such experience. During floods temporary migration to the highlands had been a common practice for generations. But the floods of 1977 brought new challenges to the population of Inhamissa. For the first time they had to leave forever (Hermele 1988: 47). The 1977 catastrophe led Frelimo to form a special commission to resettle the affected people. Among the decisions taken by the commission were the following: the population should be resettled on high lands in communal villages; if the population refused to comply, 'administrative measures' could be taken; and state farms and cooperatives should have priority access to the Colonato lands (irrigated areas).

The Limpopo floods of 1977 also had important effects on migrant labour. Many informants said they had been forced to break the conditions of their re-employment guarantee certificates.[12] The fact that the Frelimo government was engaged in transferring people from the valley to the highlands and was setting up houses in the communal villages worsened the situation by making it necessary for them to spend a longer period at home. Male labour was needed to build houses and they had to help their families settle in a new and strange social and physical environment. This is why many of my informants referred to 1977 as the last year of their job contracts in South Africa. They pointed to the establishment of the communal villages and the floods as the main reasons why they failed to renew their jobs contracts in South Africa.[13] Yet this was the opposite of what one might expect. In the past natural disasters had led to increased labour migration. Of course, it was not completely correct to associate the floods with the end of the contracts. This may well have happened anyway, given the policies of the Chamber of Mines, which resulted in a decline in recruitment and which my informants would have not known about. It is not unusual for informants to attribute a causal relationship to the most dramatic preceding event.

With reference to the periodic floods of the Limpopo river, people of the valley had already developed their own survival strategy. During floods people took refuge in the areas of the valley which were not normally affected, and in big trees (Serrano 1894: 432). Informants told me that in their own experience it was possible to keep clothes, food, firewood, pots, other items and even domestic animals in trees and to maintain a family during periods of flooding. Men swam periodically to the highlands to maintain stocks of food and firewood. Only those who had family in the highlands used to move with their belongings until the end of the calamity. This highlights the importance of marriages between families from different ecological zones.[14] Pilots of helicopters in rescue operations found people in trees who did not want to be evacuated. They wanted to continue in the trees with their belongings until the floods came to an end, and serious efforts had to be made to convince them to get into the helicopters (*Notícias* 16 February 1977).

Circumstances thus accelerated the Frelimo policy of organising people into communal villages in Inhamissa. People who were temporarily displaced were encouraged not to go back to their land, and new settlement schemes were designed involving people from the valley and the highlands.[15] The press frequently stated that peasants were unanimous in not wanting to return to their home villages.[16] A peasant testifying to the press manifested his gratitude to Frelimo by saying that without it, 'We were condemned to putrefy in the river'.[17] By 25 February 1977 more than 10,000 people were reported as living in safe areas where they had begun to build communal villages. In less than a week five brigades from the provincial Frelimo headquarters in Xai-Xai were working with the affected people to 'dynamise' the communal villages movement. The government distributed food and implements such as axes and hoes, and sent tractors to help peasants engaged in building communal villages (*Notícias* 25 February 1977). However, it is clear from interview material reported above that the process of villagisation based on flood rescue was not universally supported, and encountered resistance.

Even in 1976 Frelimo had attempted to form communal villages among the people living in the Limpopo valley. In that year, however, Limpopo river floods had barely affected peasants' crops, housing and cattle. That flooding was not sufficient to persuade people to move from the valley to the highlands. Frelimo and government officials failed to mobilise the peasants behind the communal villages project. Only a handful of peasants were persuaded to set up the communal village 3 de Fevereiro.[18] In 1977, 3 de Fevereiro was taken by party and government officials as a model because it was not affected by the floods (*Notícias* 27 February 1977). The devastating effects of the floods of that year made the task of the party and government communal villages brigades easier. (*Notícias* 27 February 1977). They acted as a catalyst for 'socialist transformation'.

In the mid-Limpopo area, the focus on state farms in the government's rural strategy emphasised rapid mechanisation and the expansion of the area under cultivation. Massive purchases of 1,200 tractors and more than 500 combines were made in 1977. Overall, before 1983, 90 per cent of centrally planned agricultural investment went to the state sector. Agronomists from socialist countries were brought in to assist in coordinating state farm production (Kyle 1991: 638).

The ten-year plan approved in 1981 saw family farming only as something to be eliminated by the end of the decade. Cooperatives had an important social and political role, but priority was to go to the 'accelerated development of the state sector'. This style of development promoted conflicts between family and state farms. Thus the struggle for land continued to be a central issue for peasants under the Frelimo government.

By 1983 the government had recognised the failure of its large-scale, centrally planned, capital-intensive and import-dependent development projects. Emphasis was now placed on more decentralised capitalist-oriented, small-scale projects. It dismantled most state farms, redistributing the land to peasants and private farmers (Bowen 1992: 256). The Eastern European model, centred on large state farms and centralised allocation and pricing, could not succeed under the extremely unfavourable political, economic and natural circumstances of Mozambique (Kyle 1991: 643).

My informants believed that it was from the 1980s that government attempts at encouraging and facilitating the general use of new and advanced agricultural implements such as tractors and ploughs were made. In a collective interview I was told that until 1983 there was only one African-owned tractor in the locality of Inhamissa. That tractor had been provided on a credit basis during the colonial period. No migrant worker was referred to as having brought such machinery from South Africa or as having tried to buy it during that period.[19]

Aiming to ease the system of credit and to benefit as many peasants as possible, the government encouraged the emergence of agricultural associations. Two or three peasants could join together and apply for credit to buy a tractor, a plough or a span of oxen. My informants asserted that these arrangements were frequently fraudulent. Peasants without any experience of banking were invited by the more informed to join these associations. They were simply used to gain access to additional funds, and did not feel themselves owners of the implements or as having obligations to the bank. They had simply been deceived and used by the more informed, who took advantage of their ignorance and connected their names to businesses with which they had no concern.

Another problem was faced by people who succeeded in acquiring ploughs and spans of oxen, but lacked any previous experience or training in the care of animals. Informants said that there were situations in which animals died because they were not properly pastured, fed or protected. There were also extreme situations in which peasants killed the animals for meat. This latter situation was frequently cited as resulting from cultural pressure, as oxen were often killed to provide meat required by the ancestors in ceremonies. One of my informants referred to a long list of people who had loans to buy cattle and who did not honour their obligations to the bank.[20]

From the mid-1980s, different transformations in the country and in the world, such as Perestroika and the collapse of Eastern European socialist regimes, put further pressure on Frelimo to introduce political reforms. In 1989 it was forced by circumstances to drop 'Marxism–Leninism' and change the party from a 'worker–peasant alliance', to a party for all Mozambicans, and subsequently it accepted the introduction of a multi-party system and initiated dialogue with Renamo.

Natural disasters (droughts, salinity and floods), combined with inexperienced management, lack of skilled and technically qualified Mozambicans to operate and assist the sophisticated agricultural equipment before 1983, and the war of destabilisation waged by Renamo backed by South Africa, all conspired against socialist transformation.

PROLONGED WARFARE AND NATURAL CALAMITIES

From 1981 catastrophic drought and war began to ravage the area.[21] Tens of thousands of cattle died due to lack of water and pasture. Peasants from affected zones began to look for security in the surrounding areas of Xai-Xai (Frelimo 1983b: 22). Inhamissa and Chókwe received thousands of displaced people. Pastures were transformed into agricultural areas and some farms disappeared simply to provide space for shelters. The land had to be redivided. Almost all my informants in Inhamissa and Chókwe confirmed this. I was shown places which had previously been farms, but which had subsequently been transformed into residential areas.

Cultivation and livestock farming, which constituted the main sources of peasants' subsistence, were seriously affected. People were forced to build new houses in Inhamissa near the city of Xai-Xai. In Inhamissa wood, cane and grass, which were basic hut-building materials, were not available in sufficient quantity. Huts, which were normally made of local and freely available construction material, had now to be built out of expensive materials such as cement and zinc.

The huge difference between wages offered in Mozambique and South Africa enabled those who were fortunate enough to get job contracts to live quite comfortably in Inhamissa. In addition to clothes, blankets, saws, hammers, chains and the other basic items for rural life, which constituted the traditional merchandise brought home by migrants, they also brought back hi-fis, TVs, and video-cassettes. In Inhamissa there is now electric current.

Most returning migrants did not devote their incomes to agriculture, becoming involved in providing transportation. Owing to their ability to purchase pickup trucks and small lorries at relatively low prices, migrant workers came to have a virtual monopoly of the transport links between South Africa and Mozambique and, within Mozambique, between towns and the countryside. The heavy dependence of rural areas on the commercial network established in the main towns made transport an attractive sector of accumulation. The main movement from the countryside to the towns was of people; from the towns to the countryside it included the transportation of goods, with the circulation of goods in the countryside having been secured by incomes from migrancy.

Under these circumstances, families with members working in South Africa had considerable advantages. Migrants turned their attention to the minimisation of the problems created by the war. They imported galvanised metal sheeting, cement and even maize, while cultivating peanuts became a major concern. In Inhamissa there was not enough land to reproduce the style of life they had enjoyed in their home villages. Some of the displaced people were now fully dependent on their income from migrancy. This was in contrast to what had happened in the colonial period when people had to depend on the income from migrancy to buy food in the local shops only when drought and floods had completely destroyed their crops. Now there were fewer inputs from agriculture to offset the spending of the money earned from migrancy.

In the past people in their rural environment had not viewed housing, food, firewood and water as objects of purchase and sale; they now became commodities. War and natural calamities conspired against the rural basis of migrancy. Income from family agriculture was no longer able to offset a low wage on the mines. The Chamber of Mines' policies of internalisation, stabilisation and mechanisation had worsened the life of thousands of families in southern Mozambique. The reduction in recruitment and the difficulty in obtaining access to land created a new type of unemployed person in the overcrowded Inhamissa district. Men in Inhamissa and Xai-Xai who might have become full-time peasants now became involved in the informal sector or in other survival strategies such as begging or thieving.

The degree of poverty has grown dramatically in the last sixteen years, threatening to reach levels of starvation. Everybody wants to go to South Africa. For more than one hundred years migrancy has been an economic escape route for non-literate peasants. But in the current period it is increasingly attracting young people from the cities with technical skills and formal education, who see greater opportunities in the relatively much more advanced South African economy.

GOING HOME AFTER THE WAR

There are peasants who decided to return to their home villages to restart their peasant life after the Rome Peace Accord in October 1992. Their euphoria at the prospect of returning to the stability of fifteen years ago, was however confronted by a very changed rural environment. Places where they had once planted maize and cassava were now inaccessible bush. Wild animals which had disappeared a long time ago had had enough time to re-establish themselves. The environment was strange to many peasants. The humanised landscape, previously characterised by farms and pastures, had in many cases given way to forests inhabited by wild animals. In addition to this there are landmines planted everywhere which have not yet been removed. Going back to their home villages is seen as once again coming into an area as pioneers.[22]

Those who are involved in the informal street markets, so-called *dumba nengues*,[23] will find it extremely hard to return to dependence on the irregular rainfall. The selling of cigarettes, bread, and sweets has, to some extent, ensured a regular income to buy sugar, maize, firewood, water and paraffin to maintain a family. In the towns it was less difficult to have three meals a day. In the countryside alternatives were dramatically almost non-existent. The habits developed over fifteen years or more in towns make people see rural life as extremely harsh and difficult. There are also young people whose parents went to live in Inhamissa when they were babies or young children. They have had no opportunity to learn basic strategies for living in the countryside. This suggests that it will be amongst older migrants and those from the areas less affected by warfare that rural economic reconstruction will first take place.

For those who have succeeded in securing regular sources of income in the urban areas, it is hard to think of returning to rural struggles. To forsake daily bread, TV and other city attractions and to go back to growing cassava and maize, to hunting for meat and to building huts, is not a decision to be taken lightly.

People face another serious problem: even those refugees who want to go back to their home villages, now have strong socio-economic ties with Inhamissa and Xai-Xai which they do not wish to break. These families attempt to maintain a home both in their native home villages, as well as in the area where they were refugees; as a song collected in Chimbimbanine in 1994 suggests:

> Goodbye my neighbour
> You will stay to look after my chickens
> You stay to look after my house
> You stay to look after my children
>
> Goodbye my neighbour
> The war is over
> My children are in the secondary school
> The trees I am leaving here in town are seeds
> The real trees are in my home village.[24]

One of the most interesting social realities portrayed by the song has to do with the education of the children. It was generally difficult for children in the countryside to gain access to secondary education. The rural school network was extremely limited and did not go further than primary school. The movement of entire families to Inhamissa gave some families the opportunity to send their children to secondary school.[25] This was partly facilitated by the government's efforts to integrate displaced children into the local primary schools. Children who succeeded in passing at the primary level in town took advantage of the proximity of secondary schools to pursue their education further.

The song indicates parents' concern to educate their children. It tells the story of families who decided to leave Chibuto to reconstruct their lives in their home villages. But as their children were in secondary school, they decided to maintain their houses and other property in town to provide support for their children. The song says that the fruit trees they planted in Chibuto may be considered as simply seeds, and maintains that the real trees are those left behind in their home villages. They ask the native people of Chibuto, who were their neighbours by chance, to help in providing assistance to their children and to protect their property. This song helps us understand the different ways in which the war pushed people to semi-urbanisation, and also to creating new networks of support and even new communities in town.

In a recent interview I was told that people who were leaving for their home village were selling the land they had initially received free of charge. There is no space for new residential sites for young new families in Inhamissa. This is affecting the junior members of the families who, as already explained, were to be allocated land. There are no legal provisions against such selling of land.[26]

CONCLUSION

The change in migrant labour policies had devastating effects on the economy of the majority of peasants, due mainly to its coincidence with other unfavourable internal natural and political factors. Wages from the mines increased stratification and shaped new survival strategies, which paradoxically did not emphasise agriculture in the 1970s and 1980s. Perhaps it was because of this diminished importance of agricultural investment that my informants did not talk about buying implements. Connections between migrancy and agrarian innovation or expansion were extremely tenuous.

In the 1990s important internal and regional political transformations took place which will again further influence migrancy. In Mozambique the war is over. Legal apartheid no longer exists in South Africa. On the one hand these changes mean that Mozambique's countryside is now accessible to peasants who for a long period took refuge in the main cities and district capitals. Peasants are going to restart agricultural production. Those who left their home villages as communal villages, state farms, and cooperatives are returning to live and work in the new circumstances of the market economy. They face all sorts of land disputes arising out of conflicts among themselves and with newcomers, in the context of a resuscitated capitalist agriculture. In addition, they need support in the form of seeds, implements and food before the first harvests. The question now is whether migrant workers will use their incomes to take advantage of the opportunities offered by the new economic policy. Are they in a position to compete with the emerging national bourgeoisie and with foreign capital? To what extent will the maintenance of both their rural and urban bases contribute to the transformation of peasant–migrant worker attitudes towards agriculture?

On the other hand, it is important to understand how South Africa will restructure migrant labour from neighbouring countries without destabilising their economies[27]. Part of the ANC-led government's agenda is to reduce the high rate of unemployment among its own black population. Will this aggravate the economic difficulties of the labour-sending countries? It is undoubtedly true that under present economic circumstances any rupture of this source of income will worsen the already poor standard of living of many families in southern Mozambique.

The proximity of Inhamissa to Xai-Xai and the decision taken by the Frelimo government to transfer people from the Limpopo valley to the highlands destroyed the peasants' economic base. Nowadays the highlands of Inhamissa are no longer an agricultural area for drought-resistant crops. Ecological and political factors have transformed this part of Inhamissa into an overcrowded semi-urban residential area. There is no way to practise viable agriculture there. The combination of the Limpopo river floods of 1977 with Frelimo's project of building communal villages has transformed Inhamissa from a productive to a purely residential area. In addition to these factors there was the warfare which forced people from neighbouring districts to come into the area, fleeing Renamo attacks.

The city of Xai-Xai did not have the industry, commerce and public services to absorb the growing population of Inhamissa and other surrounding areas. Local people lost their farms, fruit trees and pastures.[28] There is no real prospect that these people will return to their native areas, leaving behind them the new and modern houses they built at Inhamissa.[29]

Given the present technical facilities and skills, Inhamissa has very little likelihood of recovering from cyclical crises in the near future. When there is no rain it is impossible to grow crops in the lowlands because the soil becomes extremely dry. But when it rains there is flooding because the irrigation channels do not drain the water to the Limpopo River properly. At the moment the government Department of Agriculture has neither the financial nor the technical capacity to assist in cleaning the channels.[30] The result is that almost any rainfall has meant flooding and any lack of rainfall has meant severe drought.

Frelimo's project of socialist transformation and the development of agriculture in southern Mozambique did not undermine the migration of male labour to South Africa. On the contrary, the economic and political factors which contributed to the failure of the communal villages, state farms and agricultural cooperatives to attract and stabilise male labour, have intensified continued migrancy to South Africa.

NOTES

1. See the papers presented at the international conference on 'Transforming mine migrancy in the 1990s', University of Cape Town, Cape Town, 27–29 June 1994, and at the workshop convened by the Centre for Policy Studies on 'Southern African migration: domestic and regional policy implications', Johannesburg, 10 April 1995. See also Reitzes (1995).

2. *Manparra magaiça or màmbárha gàyisá*: *manparra* is from 'baar' in Afrikaans, which means a raw, unskilled person, a greenhorn, and *gaiça*, which in Shangaan means a worker returning home from town or the mines. This expression was the classification commonly given to migrant labourers who used to spend all their salaries in South Africa, neglecting their families.

3. Interview with N. D. and verified by J. B., Inhamissa, 27/10/1993. They provided me with this information during a collective interview, during which nobody contradicted them.

4. *Madjonidjoni* is from *djoni* which derives from Johannesburg. In Shangaan, like *magaiça*, *madjonidjoni* means people coming from Johannesburg or simply wealthy people.

5. In a sense there is some truth in the notion: fears that the mines would lose their 'foreign' labour played a major role in the changes – and Frelimo's victory was a potent spur in this respect.

6. After the independence of Mozambique many Portuguese shopkeepers left the country. They had played an important role in the rural transport system.

7. Interview with L. N., Inhamissa, 31 January 1992. The amounts referred to are twenty times the average monthly salary of an unskilled worker in Mozambique.

8. See the daily newspaper of Maputo, *Notícias*, and the weekly magazine *Tempo* of June 1975. Samora Machel's speeches during his triumphal tour in June 1975 were extremely critical of migrant labour. He attacked and condemned the poor conditions under which migrant workers were recruited, employed and paid in South Africa. This triumphal trip was part of the series of pre-independence visits that the President of Frelimo made to the main cities of the country from Rovuma river to Maputo. He arrived in Maputo to proclaim the independence of Mozambique on 25 June 1975.

9. Liberated zones were the areas from which the colonial administration had been expelled during the war for independence (1964–74). The northern provinces of Cabo Delgado and Niassa had areas fully controlled by Frelimo before independence.

10. *A regulo* was an African traditional leader under direct control of the colonial administration.

11. Interview with E. C., Chókwe, July 1992.

12. For details on re-employment guarantee certificates, see First (1983: 59–61); see also Chamber of Mines of South Africa Archives (CMSAA)/0457(000431), Circular nr.208/77, 13 October 1977, Strictly confidential , 'Allocation of Mozambicans: holders of Valid Re-Employment Guarantees'; CMSAA/0457 (000419–31), Correspondence between the East Rand Proprietary Mines, Limited and the General Manager of The Employment Bureau of Africa (TEBA), 1976–7.

13. For more details on the social and economic effects of the floods see *Notícias* for February 1977 and following months.

14. Collective interview, Inhamissa, 26 October 1993.

15. *Notícias* 16 February 1977: People evacuated from the valley were mobilised not to return to their home villages after the floods to prevent future crises. Frelimo

and state officials explained to the people the need to build their new houses in the highlands where they also could establish their farms without any threat of danger; *Notícias* 18 February 1977: Five brigades were set up to conduct the process of building communal villages.

16. Maputo, *Notícias* 24 January1977. However, during interviews, particularly after the 1992 peace accord, peasants recalled the violence perpetrated by government officials to pressure them to leave the inundated areas and build communal villages.

17. Filipe Sigaúque, interviewed by *Notícias* 27 February 1977.

18. 3 February was proclaimed Heroes Day in Mozambique. The first president of Frelimo, Dr Eduardo Chivambo Mondlane, was killed by a parcel bomb in Dar es Salaam on 3 February 1969.

19. Collective interview and interview with B. C., Inhamissa, 26 October 1993.

20. Interview with B. C., Inhamissa, 26 October 1993.

21. On 4 October 1992 Frelimo and Renamo signed a peace agreement in Rome, Italy.

22. This is what people who had visited their rural home villages told me and it is also to some extent what I felt myself when I revisited Mahuntsane, my home village.

23. 'Trust your legs' – meaning 'run from the police' – from the period when officials attempted to suppress such informal trade.

24. Song recorded in Chimbimbanine, district of Chibuto, Gaza Province, February 1994.

25. In Inhamissa, besides primary schools, there is the Gaza provincial Pre-University School and the primary school training centre.

26. Interview with B. C., Inhamissa, 29 November 1994.

27. The South African government's Green Paper on International Migration (Government of South Africa 1997) seeks to facilitate the movement of people between SADC-countries and South Africa (the editors).

28. Interview with A. C., Inhamissa, 6 September 1994.

29. Almost all informants who are not originally from Inhamissa expressed the same feeling.

30. Collective interview with technicians of the Department of Irrigation, System of the Lower Limpopo, Xai-Xai, 2 September 1994.

STRUCTURING THE DEMISE OF A REFUGEE IDENTITY: THE UNHCR'S VOLUNTARY REPATRIATION PROGRAMME FOR MOZAMBICAN REFUGEES IN SOUTH AFRICA[1]

INTRODUCTION: RECONSIDERING THE POLITICS OF 'REPATRIATION'[2]

In April 1994 the United Nations High Commissioner for Refugees (UNHCR) formally implemented a programme to facilitate the 'voluntary' repatriation of an estimated 250,000 Mozambican 'refugees' from South Africa. By March 1995, when this phase of the programme was terminated, a total of only 31,985 persons had returned to Mozambique (UNHCR, Johannesburg, Personal Communication, August 1995). Through tracing the planning, implementation and initial impact of this 'Voluntary Repatriation Programme' (hereafter VRP), I examine some of the implications of this limited response for the majority of Mozambicans who remained in South Africa with fewer resources and no longer formally recognised as 'refugees'. My assessment of the VRP, therefore, examines its relevance for social identities within the emerging state discourses of post-apartheid South Africa and postwar Mozambique.

By focusing on the relationship between local-level social processes and their broader implications, this chapter challenges established ways of understanding the UNHCR and its practice of promoting 'repatriation' as the most desirable 'durable solution' to any refugee crisis (Cunliffe 1995: 286; Harrell-Bond 1989: 41). As the 'principal international actor for the assistance and protection of refugees' (Cunliffe 1995: 278), the activities of the UNHCR are determined largely by international conventions that define its mandate, such as the 1951 'Convention Relating to the Status of Refugees', or regional initiatives that have shaped it, such as the Organisation of African Unity (OAU) 'Convention Governing the Specific Aspects of Refugee Problems in Africa' (UNHCR 1994: 4–5). Recent evaluations of UNHCR operations have led to accusations that the primary role of the organisation is to enforce the will of the powerful states that constitute the principal source of funding for the organisation (Cunliffe 1995: 288–9; Hancock 1989; Harrell-Bond 1986: 188; 1989: 46).

Consequently, this ambiguous position of the UNHCR in the global

context of assistance to 'refugees' has led to analyses of 'repatriation' from
two broad perspectives (Allen and Morsink 1994: 2). Less critical
approaches tend to provide descriptions of specific programmes as socially
reconstitutive, measuring their 'success' in terms of the numbers of refugees
who 'benefited' from the operations (e.g. Compher and Morgan 1991;
Wood 1989). This approach is characteristic of much of the literature
produced by the UNHCR (UNHCR 1995) and other official organisations
that promote assistance to refugees, such as the US Committee for Refugees
(e.g. Drumtra 1993). A second approach is more critical and suspicious of
the explicit intentions of 'repatriation' programmes. From this perspective,
such planned population movements across national borders are examined
as a function of specific political interests that they are held to serve (e.g.
Crisp 1984; 1986: 180; Harrell-Bond 1986: 188–9; 1989: 44–6). This
approach makes the important point of noting that interests which motivate
'repatriation' programmes, are sometimes contrary to the interests of the
refugees themselves.

Both descriptive and more critical approaches assume that a common
understanding of 'repatriation' is shared between refugees and the diversity
of social actors who pay attention to them. This assumption leads assessments of 'repatriation' to maintain a largely macro-level focus which
concentrates on the 'big picture' and glosses over local variations and
peculiarities. A recent collection edited by Allen and Morsink (1994) takes
an important step towards confronting this void in studies of 'repatriation'.
Although the title – *When Refugees go Home* – persists with the suggestion
that repatriation is an inevitable outcome of refugee crises, many of its
contributions highlight the importance of understanding the particular
dynamics of specific incidents of 'repatriation'. By focusing on the social
agency of refugees (Ranger 1994: 283; Wilson and Nunes 1994; Wilson
1994) and the social consequences of experiences as a 'refugee' (Makanya
1994), these writers show how 'refugee' understandings of their predicament and their perceptions of a changed environment influence their
decisions and strategies relating to their possible return.

Unlike the descriptive/critical approaches to 'repatriation' mentioned
above, approaches which emphasise the social agency and experiences of
'refugees' accommodate the potential for countries, homes and other
socially defined places to be creatively imagined in diverse ways. Mapped
representations, claims to autochthony and senses of 'rootedness' and
'up-rootedness' constitute only a few possible configurations of a perceived
relationship between people and places (cf. Anderson 1983; Malkki 1992;
Thornton 1994).

Diverse cultural experiences of place may prompt a myriad of social
responses to organised interventions such as 'repatriation'. Such interventions impact on these responses by either promoting or limiting the

strategies being pursued by 'refugees' – often in ways that are not anticipated by planners (Wilson and Nunes 1994: 167). Far from simply being seen as victims or beneficiaries of programmes, 'refugees' are increasingly being recognised as able to impact powerfully on 'aid' (Colson 1991: 25–7; Harrell-Bond 1985: 3; Wilson 1994: 237).

An emphasis on 'refugees' as active and creative social agents in spite of the 'aid' that they receive does not necessarily help to reach a better understanding of the local-level dynamics that characterise particular 'repatriation' programmes. In order adequately to accommodate the activities of all the social actors involved, I have drawn from some recent theoretical insights to emerge from studies of 'development' (e.g. Escobar 1988; Ferguson 1990; Sachs 1992). These studies emphasise the power of knowledge or ways of understanding as fundamental to understanding the global phenomenon of 'development' intervention. Specifically, they focus on how the subjects of the international development industry are constructed or 'invented' (cf. Escobar 1988) and how these images are in turn shaped by local practices and strategies. By examining 'development' primarily in terms of the social production of knowledge and recognising this knowledge as socially powerful in its own right, these studies are able to transcend the apparent disjuncture between macro and micro levels of understanding, permitting the interpretation of local-level social activity in a global context.

This following section examines some of the major factors that influenced the UNHCR's understanding of the predicament of Mozambicans in South Africa. The chapter then proceeds to trace the development of the VRP in terms of this understanding, as well as how 'refugee' responses impacted on the programme. I conclude by considering the consequences of the VRP beyond questions of 'success' or 'failure' and I examine some of the less obvious implications of implementing a 'voluntary repatriation programme'.

PRECURSORS TO REPATRIATION: PEACE IN MOZAMBIQUE AND THE BUREAU FOR REFUGEES' SURVEY

For the 'international community', the signing of the historic Peace Accord between Frelimo and Renamo in October 1992 was held to set Mozambique on the road to a lasting peace. The devastation of decades of anti-colonial struggle, externally inspired destabilisation and extremely violent conflict had however left its toll on Mozambique. An estimated 1.7 million Mozambicans who had been 'externally displaced' prompted the 'largest repatriation of refugees in the history of Africa' (Drumtra 1993: 1). This involved the development of numerous UNHCR sponsored and coordinated 'repatriation' programmes, set up in Tanzania, Malawi, Zambia, Zimbabwe, Swaziland and South Africa.

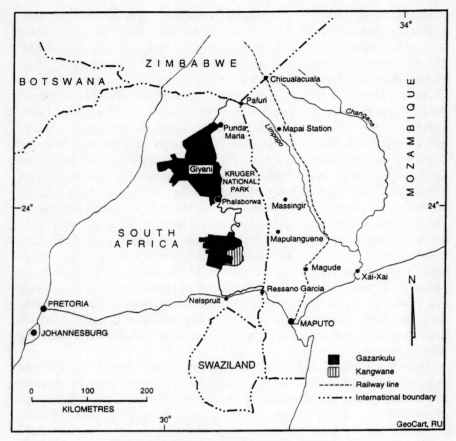

Figure 4.1 Movement of Mozambican refugees

From the perspective of the UNHCR, the dynamics around the presence of Mozambican 'refugees' in South Africa were highly peculiar. Throughout the war, the white minority 'central government' refused to grant 'refugee' status to Mozambicans who had fled to South Africa, regarding them as 'illegal immigrants' or 'aliens' who were subject to deportation if arrested. However, thousands were able to settle in relative safety within the 'home-land' territories of Gazankulu and Kangwane, which comprised pockets of land situated relatively close to the Mozambican border (see Figure 4.1).

In Gazankulu, the Mozambicans who arrived from the early 1980s onwards were permitted to settle in designated areas by chiefs and other local authorities. This prompted the development of distinctly Mozambican settlements, ranging in size and often situated on the periphery of 'closer-settlement' villages.[3] The Mozambican settlements were discernable through high levels of poverty, relative to the majority of South Africans living in the villages. The poverty, suffering and terror associated with these settlements attracted the attention of numerous church groups and non-government organisations (NGOs) which provided humanitarian assistance to what came to be regarded as 'refugee camps'. These organisations were mainly South African based and included Operation Hunger, the Catholic Church and the South African Council of Churches (SACC). The Paris based emergency aid organisation, Medecins Sans Frontières (MSF) was also active amongst the Mozambican 'refugees' in some areas.

The UNHCR was noticeably absent from this 'refugee crisis'. It was almost a year after the signing of the Peace Accord, when South Africa was firmly on the path to a non-racial democracy, before the UNHCR received a 'mandate' from the South African government to consider Mozambicans in South Africa as 'refugees'.

The sense of an impending large-scale 'repatriation programme' represented by the arrival of the UNHCR drew attention to problems associated with the ambiguous status of the Mozambicans in South Africa. The absence of a coordination body prior to the involvement of the UNHCR resulted in 'relief' being implemented on an *ad hoc* basis, and basic information on the 'refugees' was mostly lacking for all but the larger 'refugee centres'. Following a meeting in February 1993 with their counterparts in Mozambique, the Bureau for Refugees (established by the Southern African Catholic Bishops' Conference) responded to this void by conducting a basic demographic survey of Mozambican 'refugees' in South Africa. The survey focused on the size and composition of 'refugee' households, dates of arrival, reasons for crossing over into South Africa and, most importantly, intention to return.

In the Giyani district of Gazankulu, data for this survey was collected by the Giyani Catholic Refugee Relief Group (GCRRG) – the most active Catholic sponsored group in the area. The fourteen settlements that they focused on were identified by using MSF's food distribution figures. The required data was collected through the assistance of the *vandunha* (sing. *ndunha*) of the various settlements. (In the context of the 'refugee' settlements, these were mostly Mozambican men who were appointed by South African chiefs.) In most cases, when the research team arrived, those present in the settlements were summoned to a meeting by the *ndunha*, where 'heads of households', or another representative in their absence, lined up in front of the researchers to answer the short questions that were put to them. The team dealt with each household representative quickly, recording their abrupt answers in the small spaces permitted by the form, before moving on to the next in line.

This survey was the first organised attempt to consolidate basic socio-economic and demographic information on the Mozambican 'refugees' in South Africa. A focus on 'intention to return' highlighted an urgent need for organised intervention to promote a 'repatriation' process. This was emphasised when the results of the survey were published in October 1993 and the coordinator of the survey and Director of the Bureau for Refugees, Father J. P. Le Scour, argued that:

> The result of this survey should motivate people and stimulate action and interest. It is important that the governments concerned, NGOs and UNHCR, churches and all groups working with refugees, have access to and use reliable demographic and socio-economic data in order to organise efficient help and programmes of repatriation. (Le Scour 1993: x)

For the UNHCR, which covered most of the costs of producing the report, the survey provided confirmation of a previously guessed figure of 250,000 Mozambican 'refugees' resident in South Africa. This was rather odd since the sample size of 6,348 households represented only about 27,804 individuals.[4] Through the recognition that the survey did not extend to all recognised settlements, the previously entrenched guess of a total 'refugee' population of 250,000 remained intact (Le Scour 1993: viii).

Stated in the report as 'one of the most significant findings', 83.7 per cent of the refugee 'households' interviewed indicated that 'they wanted to return to Mozambique' (Bureau for Refugees 1993: 46). This conclusion was reached from a single and direct question posed to the 'refugee' household representatives during the survey – 'Does this household intend to return to Mozambique? – Yes or No' (Bureau for Refugees 1993: 68). The report gave no indication of when or how long this process would take.

The Bureau for Refugees' survey was conducted in identified settlements within Gazankulu, Kangwane and Winterveld – where the organisation was most active (see Figure 4.1). It is important to note that this survey effectively mapped the settlement patterns of those 'refugees' who fell under the 'aid umbrella' (Harrell-Bond 1986) of the Catholic Church and other organisations such as MSF and SACC. The thousands of Mozambicans who were surreptitiously settled in and around urban townships such as Alexandra (Lucas 1995) and Soweto (Dolan 1995) were not included in this survey. Mozambicans from these areas were subsequently not considered in the planning or implementation of the VRP, even though the UNHCR was clearly aware of their presence in these areas (UNHCR 1993b: 4). Dolan (1995: 54) has recently highlighted the apparently arbitrary distinction between Mozambicans in rural areas being regarded as 'refugees' whilst those in urban areas are defined as 'illegal aliens'. Winterveld, the sprawling squatter settlement north of Pretoria, appears to be exceptional in that Mozambicans were regarded *prima facie* as 'refugees' by the UNHCR. This was probably due to the prominence of a group of Catholic 'Sisters of Mercy' who were active in the area .

The VRP that developed after the publication of the survey focused specifically on Mozambicans who were receiving 'relief' from humanitarian organisations. These Mozambicans were rendered highly visible to the UNHCR by organisations who justified their activities through highlighting the terror and injustice experienced by the 'refugees' in Mozambique, as well as in apartheid South Africa.

The UNHCR's perception of the Mozambican 'refugee crisis' in South Africa was clearly influenced by the 'relief' activities of the humanitarian organisations that were established in certain areas. The aims, structure and size of the survey conducted by the Bureau for Refugees comprised a particularly influential representation of Mozambican 'refugees' to the UNHCR, providing a solid geographical and conceptual framework for the development of the VRP.

'EXACTITUDE ON THE MATTER': PLANNING FOR THE VRP AND THE SIGNIFICANCE OF LOCAL-LEVEL INTERACTION

The UNHCR entered the social field of 'Mozambican refugees' primarily by asserting their international competence in defining refugees. This was through various 'missions' undertaken by persons with specialised 'expertise' and experience – mainly in international law. In August 1993, a Senior Protection Officer and a Senior Liaison Officer from the UNHCR's main office in Johannesburg conducted what appeared to be their second 'mission' since May 1993. Their intention as stated in their report was to:

- Determine the extend [*sic*] to which Mozambicans reported to be residing in South Africa may be regarded as being of concern to UNHCR;
- Establish the protection concerns and needs;
- Determine the willingness of persons of concern or potential concern to voluntarily repatriate to Mozambique. (UNHCR 1993b: 1)

Interviews and discussion with a few 'refugees' and NGO workers led the 'mission' to conclude that: '[a] significant interest in voluntary repatriation was evident in all the areas visited' (2).

The reasons for this 'readiness' were ascribed to deterioration in the quality of life in South Africa, set against the potential that peace in Mozambique represented:

> The persons involved would like to cease working in the employ of others on condition of being able to return home even now in order to cultivate Mozambican land, in total peace, if total peace can be guaranteed. (UNHCR 1993b: 8)

The above statement gives the impression of a widespread reluctance on the part of the Mozambicans to remain in South Africa and a strong general desire to 'return home'. This understanding created the conditions for the UNHCR to assert their own expertise and thereby define the limits and conditions of their involvement:

> [a] major task that will precede UNHCR involvement with the Mozambicans will be the determination of persons of concern ... verifying existing information on numbers and whether the Mozambicans so identified, prima facie, fall within the wide OAU 'refugee' definition. (UNHCR 1993b: 3)

More specifically on the question of numbers, they argued that:

> [u]ntil UNHCR's own determination of the number of authentic refugees in South Africa sees the light of day ... a cloud will continue to hang over any attempts to obtain exactitude in the matter. (UNHCR 1993b: 5)

This independent assessment was deemed necessary because:

> the UNHCR exercise will definitely separate the genuine refugees from pretenders or economic refugees, a distinction which the NGOs hardly make due to their emotionalism ... (UNHCR 1993b: 5)

These statements show how UNHCR 'missions' generated new forms of 'expert' knowledge of the 'refugees' through impressions created within 'mission' reports. This knowledge was based on a claimed technical or legal expertise on the part of UNHCR staff. It is difficult to understand exactly what the authors of this report meant by 'emotionalism', but one can plausibly interpret it as a fixation on the terror, poverty and exploitation that characterised the predicament of the Mozambicans in South Africa. This 'mission' thus strongly asserted the UNHCR's authoritative assessment.

Shortly after the UNHCR received a full mandate to implement a repatriation programme some of their recommendations were put into practice.[5] A 'Status Determination Survey' was undertaken in November 1993. In the Giyani area, a two-person delegation representing the UNHCR, both of whom were trained in law, arrived with the intention of conducting an 'individual assessment'. Because of constraints on their time they focused on selected individuals from the recognised settlements. 'Refugees' who were interviewed were asked to provide information on dates of entry into South Africa, areas of origin, reasons for relocating to South Africa and whether or not they had any documents in their possession. The following extract from an interview conducted in Hluphekani settlement provides some insight into the interactive dynamics that justified and shaped the VRP:[6]

I: Do you have relatives in South Africa?

R: Many many relatives in South Africa. Some were born here. I have a brother, Johan, who works at Giyani Technical (college). I have a wife and two children, but I took them home ['*kaya*' – Mozambique] in July. My brother was born in South Africa and has stayed here all his life. His father is the brother of my father. His father married a South African woman from Phalaborwa. I took two wives and four children with me to Mozambique in July and then I came back. I have not been back since.

I: Our purpose here is not to return you, but to know if you want to go back or not.

R: I would just like to come to South Africa to work. My problem is that I don't have a passport. I don't like to come here by walking across the game reserve.

I: Why did you take your family back?

R: My father is alone since my mother is already dead. I took my family back so that they could look after my father. I would like to ask a question. I would like to know how I can get a passport. I would like to bring my father here since my father cannot walk here.

I: UN policy all over southern Africa is to help people to go back to Mozambique, not to help people to come to South Africa.

R: [R repeated his wish to get a passport.][7]

This extract shows that the Mozambican respondent in this interview did more than simply answer the questions that were put before him, in order to express the importance of maintaining links to South Africa. For the interviewer, the 'status' of the respondent could only be determined with reference to answers to the questions and she had neither the time nor reason to record the full responses in her notebook. The narrow legal framework imposed by the UNHCR to conduct the task effectively silenced the narratives of the Mozambicans.

The interviewer needed to confirm a disruption of the relationship between Mozambicans and Mozambique to justify the expensive infrastructure that characterised the VRP that was to develop. Everything else was simply history.

THE DEVELOPMENT OF THE VRP AND THE TRANSFORMATION OF AID

To implement the VRP, the main 'Branch Office' of the UNHCR in Johannesburg established a 'Sub Office' in Nelspruit, as well as three 'Field Offices' in Giyani, Phalaborwa and Winterveld respectively (see Figure 4.1). These offices were placed near to six 'staging areas' – sites near densely populated 'refugee' settlements from which 'repatriation' movements could be effectively launched, by transporting people back to Mozambique on specially adapted trucks.

Following a standard UNHCR practice of implementing programmes through partner organisations, contracts were drawn up with MSF, the

International Organisation for Migration (IOM) and the Masungulo Relief and Development Organisation (locally referred to as 'Masungulo'). Of the three organisations, MSF had been the most prominent international NGO amongst Mozambican 'refugees' in South Africa and was responsible for constructing, staffing and managing the 'staging areas'. These comprised fenced off 'camps' and constituted centralised points where the trucks transporting the 'refugees' back to Mozambique would leave from. They conformed to a fairly standard design which included an office, a small clinic, a number of thatched shelters for the 'refugees' to sleep in, as well as ablution facilities. IOM was frequently contracted by the UNHCR to undertake 'repatriation'. Masungulo was a small South African based NGO which also operated in Mozambique. When the Bureau for Refugees was faced with abrupt closure just before the implementation of the VRP, Masungulo incorporated some of the Catholic Church sponsored 'refugee' relief groups into the organisation, thereby significantly expanding its capacity to be involved with the Mozambicans. Masungulo was contracted to register the Mozambicans – in the staging areas as well as in the 'camps' – and to provide the Mozambicans with information on the situation in the various parts of Mozambique that they were returning to so that they could make a more informed decision over whether to 'volunteer' for 'repatriation' or not.

In order to secure their respective contracts as 'implementing partners' to the UNHCR, Masungulo and MSF had to demonstrate their ability to realise the aims of the VRP, and this diverted attention and resources away from the 'relief' that both organisations had been involved in. An example of this was the decline of two aid programmes supported by MSF which were the most reliable source of food aid in the Giyani area. At the end of 1993, on the eve of the VRP, the organisation stopped all food-distribution programmes. In addition, they also withdrew their involvement in a clinic that they had established in a large 'camp' less than a year before. From the beginning of 1994, MSF's interest in the Mozambican 'refugees' in South Africa was limited to the VRP.

In the context of an apparent lasting peace in Mozambique, it became increasingly difficult for organisations like MSF to continue justifying programmes of 'refugee relief', and the VRP provided the potential for these organisations to continue with their involvement. A perceived *need* to assist the Mozambican 'refugees' in South Africa was largely transformed from a response to the violence, terror and destruction of the war in Mozambique, to the promotion of a return 'home' and the resumption of 'normality'.

On at least one occasion, the UNHCR actively undermined a project deemed to threaten the success of the VRP. In response to the abrupt cessation of organised food aid to 'refugees', Catholic Church 'refugee' relief groups collectively applied for substantial support from the South African Government sponsored National Nutrition and Social Development

Programme (NNSDP). Initially, a grant of approximately R11 million was approved. This amount was reduced to about R4 million after the UNHCR intervened at a fairly high level and successfully claimed that an extensive food-distribution programme would give the Mozambicans an incentive to remain in South Africa and undermine the aims of the VRP.

The 'relief' efforts of organisations that were not formally part of the VRP, such as the Catholic Church and SACC, were also directly affected by a flow of human resource potential toward the VRP. In Giyani alone, twelve people who had experience 'working with the refugees' prior to the VRP were employed to work on the VRP as 'local staff', either by the UNHCR directly or by one of the three implementing partners. Decisions to work within the VRP were often made with reference to the relative stability (albeit temporary) of employment and in some cases, higher incomes offered.

The assimilation of people with local experience into the VRP was integral to transforming the VRP into the principal form of aid offered to 'refugees'. Firstly, through their pre-'repatriation' work, many had established effective social networks within the 'refugee settlements', which were later drawn upon to facilitate the VRP. This process also weakened 'aid projects' that were not part of the VRP. The Hluphekani Information Centre stood as a monument to this. During the opening ceremony in October 1993, the new Director declared that the Centre would operate every day, making current information on Mozambique directly accessible to those who were interested. However, in April 1994 he was employed as a Mine Awareness Instructor by MSF. After this, he was in the field for most of the week and hardly ever present at the Centre.

Within the wider context of humanitarian assistance to Mozambican 'refugees' in South Africa, the development of the VRP fundamentally transformed the nature of aid to 'refugees', largely through introducing a sense of an international moral obligation to provide them with assistance to return to Mozambique. The realisation of this obligation involved a systematic dissolution of humanitarian concern over the terror and suffering that brought the Mozambicans to South Africa – the 'emotionalism of the NGOs'. This was reflected in the dramatic changes in aid practice that followed the arrival of the UNHCR. Such a successful shift in focus from 'relief' to 'repatriation' was also dependent on the participation of the 'refugees' themselves.

CONCLUSION: CONSEQUENCES OF THE 'VOLUNTARY REPATRIATION PROGRAMME'

The official termination of the VRP at the end of March 1995 was not marked by the dramatic transformation in Mozambican patterns of settlement in South Africa that the UNHCR had initially anticipated. The vast majority of Mozambican 'refugees' were not 'officially repatriated' through the VRP and continued to reside in 'camps' in South Africa. Of those who were 'repatriated', many subsequently returned to the 'camps', which either allowed for better living conditions than in Mozambique, or offered a greater potential for improvement and development of the homestead. In addition, significant numbers of Mozambicans continued to cross back and forth across the border unofficially, mostly by walking across the Kruger National Park. This outcome has led Dolan (1995: 53) to consider the VRP, along with the South African government's long-term policy of forced deportation, as '... failures, in terms of the objectives they set themselves'. An assessment in these terms, which is limited to a consideration of the stated intentions of the programme, does not necessarily reflect the perspectives of persons involved with, or affected by, the programme. In addition, this assessment fails to recognise the potential for the social implications of the VRP to extend beyond the actual resettlement of people across the national boundary.

The VRP was not a failure in its own terms – in spite of the low number of people who were 'repatriated' through it. For the UNHCR staff who planned and implemented the programme, it successfully provided those Mozambicans who were recognised as 'refugees' with *every opportunity* to return to Mozambique. The commitment of UNHCR staff was not simply to move Mozambicans from South Africa to Mozambique, but to facilitate and promote their *voluntary* return. Through meticulously addressing 'problems' that they identified as confounding these aims and preventing or discouraging 'refugees' from 'volunteering' to return to Mozambique, the UNHCR successfully created an environment in which all 'refugees' were potentially assisted to return to Mozambique with their families and belongings. In this sense, the VRP impacted on all 'refugees' by providing them with a reasonable opportunity to return to Mozambique, for the duration of the programme. The fact that the majority of 'refugees' did not respond to this directly, did not imply failure on the part of the UNHCR (cf. Harrell-Bond 1989: 52).

Active 'refugee' responses to the VRP did not necessarily indicate the establishment or re-establishment of a relationship to Mozambique as a *patria*. The discussion above has shown how the programme was socially incorporated by the Mozambicans through strategies that they pursued in terms of rather distinctive cultural notions of home, family, personhood and mobility. Some of these strategies – which were not formally recognised within the UNHCR's discourse on 'repatriation' – were however interpreted by the UNHCR as supporting the aims and ideals of the VRP. In other cases, such as the high numbers of single males that volunteered for 'repatriation', 'refugee' responses were interpreted as abusing the hospitality of the UNHCR and the 'international community' that it represented. In either situation however, the Mozambicans were able to invoke the programme to enhance their own strategies and pursue processes of social reconstruction in terms which made sense to them – even when, ironically, these strategies were regarded by the UNHCR as contrary to the aims of the VRP. It is not surprising that there was widespread support from the 'refugees' for the programme, as well as some critical regard for its relatively short duration.[8]

In relation to a broader context of 'repatriation', this VRP was not characterised by a particularly low number of 'returnees'. Cuny and Stein (cited in Wilson and Nunes 1994: 172) report that since 1975, less than 10 per cent of 'refugees' who 'repatriated' did so with official assistance. Compared to other programmes, this VRP appears to have directly affected a considerably higher percentage of 'refugees' than most programmes. Wilson and Nunes (1994: 173) argue that the limited impact of organised attempts to 'repatriate' people results from the fact that they are seldom sophisticated enough to accommodate the complexities of human agency or flexible enough to respond to the rapidly changing needs and aspirations of the people affected.[9] Whilst this explains the limited impact of planned efforts to promote 'repatriation', it also raises the question as to as to why such programmes continue to be planned and implemented with such regularity.

Taking the 'organised repatriation' of Mozambican 'refugees' from South Africa as a case study, this chapter has shown that the VRP was not simply about 'repatriating' people who had been 'displaced'. One important unplanned and unacknowledged feature of the programme was, as I have highlighted, the structured decline in 'relief' assistance. This claim is supported strongly by the observation that the VRP effectively focused solely on those Mozambicans who had been recognised as 'refugees', through the 'relief' assistance that they were receiving from humanitarian organisations. From the perspective of the local level, the structured decline in 'relief' efforts halted many of the social processes that defined or emphasised Mozambicans as 'refugees'. This effect was not an explicit intention of the VRP but was largely achieved through emphasising assistance for the 'refugees' to return to Mozambique as a priority for both resources and effort.

The demise of various forms of 'relief' assistance that Mozambican 'refugees' had received from the late 1980s onwards was important, not only because of the reduction in physical resources made available to the 'refugees', but also for what these resources represented through the context of their provision. Responses to a perceived need for 'relief' to the Mozambicans in identified settlements emphasised their presence in South Africa as involuntary and resulting from experiences of terror and acute social destruction. It also suggested an inability on the part of the Mozambicans to survive in this foreign landscape, hence the need for 'relief'.

Regardless of the numbers of Mozambicans who were 'officially repatriated' from South Africa, the VRP ultimately constituted a highly visible mechanism for facilitating the re-organisation of 'official' social identities of those Mozambicans who remained in South Africa after the conclusion of the VRP. A cessation or reduction in programmes of 'relief' contributed significantly towards potential processes of re-identifying vulnerable and disorientated 'refugees' into categories of manipulative deviance, such as 'alien' or 'illegal immigrant'.

A year after the conclusion of the VRP, in early 1996, large numbers of Mozambicans continued to reside in settlements in the former 'homelands' of Gazankulu and Kangwane. Through the intensive 'information campaign' that accompanied the VRP, many were probably also aware that, following the conclusion of the VRP, the South African government could invoke a 'cessation clause' which would entitle it to forcibly deport Mozambicans living in the 'camps'.[10] Although this had not taken place, it remained an option for the South African government to pursue – this time with the blessing of the 'international community'.

NOTES

1. This chapter is taken from my MA thesis, Rodgers 1996.
2. I use single quotation marks extensively throughout the chapter to emphasise that the concepts and categories that I invoke are located within the UNHCR's discursive practices, constituting part of their language of operation, and not necessarily reflective of my own framework of analysis.
3. These villages developed largely from government initiatives to move people from scattered settlements into more concentrated villages. See de Wet (1995: Chapter 3) for a discussion of this practice in the national context of South Africa and Harries (1987: 106–7) for the case of the (old) Northern Transvaal.
4. This figure is calculated from the finding that there was an average of 4.38 people per household (Bureau for Refugees 1993: 12).
5. This was achieved through two major agreements. The first was a 'Basic Agreement' between the UNHCR and the South African Government defining the conditions under which the UNHCR would be able to operate in South Africa. The second, signed on 15 October 1993, was a 'Tripartite Agreement' between the governments of Mozambique and South Africa and the UNHCR, expounding the conditions under which the UNHCR could assist Mozambican refugees to 'repatriate' voluntarily from South Africa.
6. I=Interviewer; R=Respondent.
7. This extract is reconstructed from an interview in which all responses were translated from Tsonga.
8. During the planning phase of the VRP, UNHCR staff presented the programme to 'refugees' as lasting between two and three years.
9. In her classic study of the social impact of resettlement, Colson (1971: 43) supports this conclusion, suggesting that this is a broad feature of organised programmes of resettlement and not peculiar to 'repatriation'.
10. The 'cessation' clause has subsequently been invoked. This has the implication that Mozambicans who came to South Africa as refugees and who are still in South Africa no longer automatically have refugee status, but have to demonstrate that they are entitled to refugee status (the editors).

5 Malefane Maema, Tsebang Putsoane, Per Bertilsson,
Keketso Sefeane, Mampho Molaoa and Thando Gwintsa

MAKING RESETTLEMENT A COMMUNITY DEVELOPMENT PROJECT: A CASE STUDY OF KATSE DAM RESETTLEMENT IN LESOTHO

Resettlement projects, whether spontaneous or assisted, are always fraught with social, economic and environmental problems (Cernea 1991; Kinsey and Binswanger 1993; Guggenheim 1994; McDowell 1996). These include homelessness, landlessness, unemployment, food insecurity, disease and marginalisation. Those who are displaced often have to suffer most of the disbenefits while others reap what benefits may ensue (Cernea 1994, 1996c).

Much of the recent focus on resettlement has concerned innovative development policies (World Bank 1994b). While some success has been achieved in this area (Cernea 1996c), there remains the challenge of implementing these policies to maximise the benefit for those to be resettled.

This chapter describes an attempt to implement a resettlement project associated with Katse dam in Lesotho as a community development project where those involved seek to maximise short- and long-term benefits. We begin by describing the project in its regional and national context and then examine its impact on those involved.

PROJECT DESCRIPTION

Lesotho emerged from autocratic and military rule following democratic elections in March 1993. A new local government structure has yet to be put in place, and meanwhile local administration is undertaken at District, Ward, Principal Chief and Village Development Council levels.

The Lesotho Highlands Water Project (LHWP) is a large hydropower-generation scheme undertaken jointly by the Kingdom of Lesotho and the Republic of South Africa. It will be implemented in a number of phases. This initially involves the construction of Katse dam (180m high), a tail-pond (Muela dam, 55m high), with a tunnel between these (45km long), and another (40 km) tunnel between Muela and the outfall on the As River, a tributary of the Vaal River. Subsequently, this will involve constructing a series of further dams: Mohale, Mashai, Tsoelike and Ntoahae. These latter phases will depend on feasibility studies that currently indicate that only the

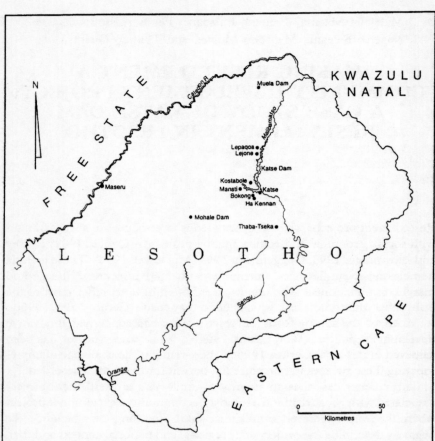

Figure 5.1 Location of Lesotho Highlands Water Project

first four constructions are likely to be implemented. The aim of the project is to augment the supply of water to Gauteng Province in South Africa, a major industrial and residential complex, and to supply Lesotho with enough electricity in the medium term to replace imported electricity from Eskom, the power generation company in South Africa.

The LHWP is a major undertaking relative to the small economy of Lesotho. It is expected to contribute at least 8 per cent to the country's GDP through a combination of revenues from sale of water, import taxes on labour, materials and capital equipment and employment generation. Mining remittances from South Africa currently contribute a large share of the GDP of Lesotho. The prevalence of poverty in Lesotho is high [Sechaba Consultants 1991; World Bank 1995a] with a lack of natural resources, but mainly lack of vision and implementable strategies to take the country out of the poverty trap.

The project area itself is characterised by harsh weather with a relatively high precipitation of about 800–1,000mm per year. Snow falls during the winter months of May to July. Temperatures range from minus ten to plus thirty degrees Celsius. The highest mountain range in the area is slightly over 3,000 metres above sea level. Soils are shallow and poor, of dolerite parent formations and highly erodible. Agricultural land is limited to small areas in river valleys, although people cultivate the mountain slopes. There are few natural resources, including limited vegetation cover. The high population densities of livestock (sheep and cattle) have led to overgrazing and a further deterioration of the grazing land. Water resources are considered abundant and the rivers are perennial except during severe droughts. The area is well known for alluvial diamonds, but their exploitation is limited.

In 1992, the Environment Division of the Lesotho Highlands Development Authority (LHDA) started to prepare budgets for the relocation of twenty-five households under the Compensation Plan, but this was not fully integrated into the main dam and tunnel construction programme. The LHDA defined the scope of the project, but tenders were rejected in late 1994 because of the high cost and lack of community participation. This led to a cheaper community-based construction option for the replacement houses.

The Land Act of 1979 recognised the need for compensation at 'replacement value', but this 'value' did not always allow for long-term sustainability of affected households. The Lesotho Highlands Water Project Order No. 22 of 1986 and the Treaty on the Project provided better legal mechanisms for compensation and resettlement in line with international best practice. The LHWP Compensation Policy and Regulations of 1990 provide for compensation and resettlement, and require that where relocation cannot be avoided, it should take place within the same area and provide compensation or alternative property at replacement value combined with economic rehabilitation, recognition of usufructuary and common property rights to land, environmental conservation and attention to host populations. This gave effect to the creation of new institutions. The Lesotho Highlands Development Authority was established and the Environment Division was created to take responsibility for the social and environmental aspects of the LHWP.

The Katse Shoreline Resettlement Project (KSRP) involves the removal of households which will be directly affected by the flooding of the Katse reservoir area. The total number of households to be resettled is seventy-one, of which twenty-five are involuntary and forty-six 'voluntary'. The project is divided into two phases, I and II. Phase I requires the involuntary resettlement of twenty-five households that are less than 100m above the full supply level of the reservoir. Phase II entails the 'voluntary' resettlement of forty-six households above this level, and these can move of their own choice after taking advice.

At the end of October 1995, the World Bank supervision mission visiting the project concluded that satisfactory progress had been made in the initial stages of the Phase I project, and that impounding the dam could take place.

First, a full inventory of each household's resources was undertaken, updating the 1988 census and noting the socio-economic characteristics of all households, a skills profile, number and type of house structures, household resources, the preferred relocation area, and also communal resources, structures and properties (e.g. schools, churches, roads, water supply, grazing land and tree clusters).

Phase I consists of the relocation of people from three villages with twenty-five households and forty-nine housing units, and these were to be replaced by thirty-four housing units in ten existing villages. Phase II involves forty-six households in six villages, with 113 housing units, one business unit, four school units, and the loss of several river crossings to Katse, Thaba-Tseka and other nearby towns (see Figure 5.1).

Each household was requested to select a suitable relocation area and replacement site within the existing chief's jurisdiction. The LHDA officials provided advice on suitability of land and planned and formally registered the sites. In Lepaqoa, the topography allowed for each household to have a garden, and there was additional land for a community garden. The relocation site at Lepaqoa (see Figure 5.1) was the only 'new' settlement and it was selected with the planned regional infrastructure, feeder roads and schools, in mind.

Phase I was split into two contracts for implementation under the supervision of the LHDA Environment Division. A Project Steering Committee consisting of members of the Joint Permanent Technical Commission and the LHDA Executive oversaw the project, while a Project

Management Team was involved in the day-to-day running of the project. The community and individual households were authorised to mine stones from local quarries, to transport fencing material and to build cattle byres. Tools and training for fencing were provided free of charge. Materials were procured by the LHDA and construction of byres and stables was done by the villagers for a wage. All sites are ready to be fenced.

Initially, there was little integration of the infrastructure projects to be undertaken under the Rural Development Programme and delays created problems of access necessary to enable cheaper construction of houses, and to facilitate social and economic activities in the affected communities.

The LHDA Field Operations Team has therefore provided extension and support services to the affected communities. Participatory planning sessions, community organisation and capacity building are conducted. Compensation for lost cropland exceeding 1,000 sq.m will be paid over a fifteen-year period, and for lost grazing land over a period of five years. Community resources, such as tree clusters, thatch and grazing land, are allocated according to the wishes of the community. Reburial from displaced graves will be a relatively large undertaking.

PARTICIPATORY PLANNING

The approach of the LHDA recognises the stages of the resettlement process, but fails to give sufficient emphasis during planning to the last 'Handover' stage or to provision of infrastructure before relocation. This limitation is apt to lead to the phenomenon of 'agency paternalism' and problems with social services which have been observed in other land-settlement projects in Zimbabwe, Guatemala and Malaysia (Kinsey and Binswanger 1993). Models which recognise the importance of handing over to communities at the earliest stage of planning include that proposed for the LHDA in the form of a Highlands Trust (Reynolds 1995) or a progressive handover, as in the case of Indonesia and Kenya (Kinsey and Binswanger 1993).

The notion of community participation in a mandatory settlement project is problematic, not least because, in this case, the process was largely driven by the construction programme. A participatory planning process was initiated by the LHDA in order to optimise the resettlement process in terms of selection of relocation sites and house structures, and the involvement of both relocatees and host populations. Villages involved in resettlement identified and prioritised their social and development needs through Participatory Rural Appraisal workshops. However, the creative potential of such participation was restricted by the menu of options already identified in the Rural Development Projects (RDP). The alternative proposed Highlands Trust model is likely to enhance participation by enabling communities to access information on the available budget, and then to plan to meet their needs around that budget (Gillis *et al* 1992; Spalding 1990; Todaro 1981).

Unsatisfactory performance with regard to the implementation of resettlement has been associated, *inter alia*, with the interpretation of the compensation policy. The lack of a comprehensive national policy framework for resettlement allows room for unproductive debates on policy. For example, there was much debate in the Katse case on the criteria for defining involuntary and voluntary resettlement. If the housing replacement project had initially been perceived as a resettlement project, it could have been done earlier and in a more integrated fashion. In the case of resettlement at Lepaqoa, the community decided to move as a single social unit. In one case, the resettler chose to distance his household from neighbours with whom he had had problems. It is clear that community cohesion influences the chances for successful resettlement (Downing 1996). A spatial analysis of the distance of relocatees from their original homes indicated that the majority of households (87 per cent) were relocated within 5km of their original homes. Each household had a choice of house structures that were either replicas, standard designs or an amalgamation of house units. Building materials were either locally made concrete blocks or local stone. Roofing options included thatch or corrugated iron sheets.

Although the programme of housing construction had no monetary float, all houses were completed on schedule and within budgeted cost. The houses were of a higher standard than the traditional huts being replaced, but of similar floor area. During the construction period, at least twenty-one labourers were members of the affected households or their relatives. The majority of labourers were women (130 women were employed per day) who carried water and sand from the river. All the catering was done by women from the villages after having been given a brief course on catering and nutrition. Additional income was derived from the hire of donkeys and ox carts for transporting construction materials. Wages were earned from the construction of houses, byres and toilets, and the rehabilitation of springs.

A report of a visit to the project area concluded that there was 'total satisfaction with the quality of the houses built' (World Bank 1995b). Modification of technical specifications and the adoption of a community participatory approach could well enhance the quality of a project and lead to substantial cost savings. The challenge is to make house construction an 'owner-build' approach, where the owner is provided with funds and/or materials to organise his/her own construction team. An incentive mechanism to actually use the funds to build a house and to complete it on time would be an important part of the package.

A public-health baseline survey has been undertaken in order to establish the health of the resettlers, monitored through key indicators. At present, support services provided to the communities include free medical services to resettlers, public-health outreach, and agricultural-extension services.

Substantial injections of financial support, even on a short-term basis, have been shown to be important in the support of land settlements. To this end, public works programmes are recommended to support long-term resettlement (Gillis *et al* 1992; Narayana *et al* 1988). Such programmes should be labour-intensive, use local materials and be community based for them to have an impact on poverty reduction. Compensation cash payments should also be treated as seed capital in the development of income-generation opportunities for the relocatees.

Household income generation plans are being prepared, based on the choice of type of economic enterprise by the household members, and with advice from the Rural Training and Development Centre (RTDC) on whether an enterprise will be viable when construction work stops. The RTDC will assist the households to obtain the necessary training, experience and credit facilities. Whereas access to credit will be market driven, the RTDC will provide a grant component to the affected household and link up the household with the RDP project relevant to their needs.

The focus of the economic-support programme was on those households affected by the LHWP. Consultations are at present under way to integrate the RDP with the national programme for community development which is funded by capital inflows from the LHWP royalty government fund. The latter programme is driven by Members of Parliament and their respective constituencies. Although this programme is 'people driven' to the extent that it focuses on a constituency's basic needs, the investment programmes do not necessarily emanate from a regional or national strategic vision. Experience from Japan and the mid-west in the USA suggests that rural community revitalisation or renewal can be promoted through strategic investments at community level (Fujimoto 1992; Wells 1991). Potential strategic investments in the project area appear to be in the eco-tourism, entertainment, mining, wool and mohair processing and health spa sectors. The issue for resettlement is, therefore: to what extent can resettlement be designed so as to have a strategic development focus or to create new opportunities for resettlers?

CONCLUSION

The progress which is being made in converting resettlement into a community development project at Katse would seem to be the result of the various interrelated ways in which the LHDA has invested in the relocatees and the wider community affected by the dam and the resultant resettlement. The project has given affected people the right to make their own choices in a number of important areas, making use of local people and resources. Households have been allowed to choose suitable relocation areas and replacement sites. They have had a choice of housing structures, and an input into housing design, with cooking areas (an important locus of social interaction) not being incorporated into the houses as a standard measure, as many families preferred to build their own. Participatory planning workshops were introduced to facilitate choice at a group, as well as at an individual, level, with villages involved in resettlement prioritising their social and development needs – although having to do so within the set of alternatives offered by the planners.

Employing those affected during implementation is a two-edged sword, as they may become too dependent on the wages they receive. However, LHDA is attempting to look beyond the implementation stage, with a view to helping household members with the necessary training, experience and credit facilities for the various local enterprises they need to pursue.

It remains to be seen what has been learned during the construction exercise, and how this may be turned to good effect as people move from the protective umbrella of the LHDA. It is still early days, but a sensible start has been made to the long and ongoing process of community development in an impoverished enclave of southern Africa.

The Katse project involves the movement of up to seventy-one households only, and thus is not a typical case when compared to projects involving tens of thousands of people. The small number of relocatees has probably allowed for much more choice and participation than in more usual cases of resettlement. The three main areas in which the community development initiative at Katse has developed would nevertheless seem to have a wider application.

Firstly, it is desirable to set up mechanisms that will enable community-based involvement and planning in the project cycle in as many stages as possible. Increased participation results in greater choice for those whose options are normally limited by resettlement. This not only accords a resettlement project greater legitimacy, but also ensures that it is based on accurate information, which is being obtained in negotiation with the project-affected people, who will surely see proper planning as in their long-term interest. This participation could also be extended into the ongoing monitoring of the project over time, with those affected gathering the information.

Secondly, relocatees often struggle to get back on their own feet, and if projects are not to fail, it must be accepted that relocatees need support for a number of years after being moved. Schemes such as that involving affected people in house construction and the provision of community services at Katse, are in the nature of public-works programmes, which require injections of capital. These are investments which will bear fruit as they enable communities more rapidly to pull out of the position where they are simply a drain on state resources.

Thirdly, if resettled communities are finally to cease being a nett source of demands, they need to be helped to become independent. There is a need for plans to include preparations for getting local income-generating programmes off the ground. This requires making provision for market information, advice, training and credit facilities.

One way of promoting such entrepreneurial independence is through the formation of community trusts, whereby a portion of money is put into a trust fund, over which members of the resettled community exercise control. This enables them to plan to meet their needs around that sum of money, and to borrow from it to kick-start household entrepreneurial projects. Such an approach acknowledges the importance of people moving away from the dependency that often characterises poorly planned resettlement. It provides an organisational and financial mechanism that, if it has been developed effectively through genuine participation from the initial stages of the project, allows the implementing agency to hand over the running of their own affairs to relocatees as early as possible.

MICRO AND MACRO FACTORS IN RURAL SETTLEMENT: A CASE STUDY OF CHIWETA IN NORTHERN MALAWI[1]

This case study examines rural development in the context of the development of a settlement which has been facilitated by a combination of micro-level spatial/geographical and macro-level economic and political factors. It shows how the presence of a lake and its two tributaries has created an agriculturally rich area and a delta for human settlement. The growth of this settlement has been enhanced by political instability in Mozambique, which led to a transport crisis in Malawi. This country's traditional route (the Nacala Railway line through Beira) to the sea was disrupted by the war, and the need for alternative routes thus led to the upgrading and increased use of the Northern Corridor route, which passes through the northern region of Malawi to the port of Mbeya, in Tanzania. The increased use of the route, combined with favourable environmental conditions, has facilitated the growth of the settlement of Chiweta (see Figure 6.1). Unlike the growth pole approach which Malawi adopted as a means of filtering growth downwards and curbing urban migration, the growth of Chiweta has occurred due to local people taking advantage of micro- and macro-level factors. It is argued therefore that, as people take advantage of favourable conditions, more endogenous settlements will emerge and it is through this process that rural and national development will occur.

It is generally agreed that rural development is an integral part of the process of overall national development. Attempts by governments to facilitate this process result in a tension between centralisation and the need for decentralisation. Thus, there is a need to strike a balance between the desire to implement central policies and to generate local development initiatives, while at the same time resolving the often conflicting claims of centralisation and decentralisation of political and administrative power (Rakodi 1990a: 148). A number of countries have adopted policies that emphasize rural decentralisation while the political and financial implications of such programmes have meant a continuation of centralisation.

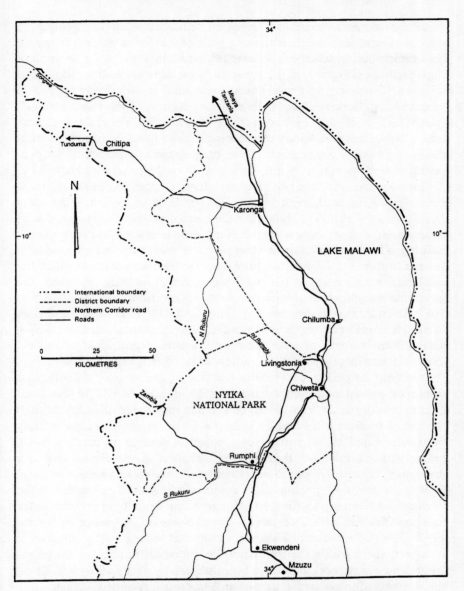

Figure 6.1 The Northern Region showing the location of Chiweta

Thus the centralisation–decentralisation tension is seen in attempts by various governments at implementing policies that focus on such issues as: land redistribution schemes (Nicaragua); rationalisation of the location of rural facilities (Bhutan); development of agro-industries and villagisation schemes (Tanzania); and rural housing and rural growth centre upgrading programmes (Burkina Faso, Côte d'Ivoire, Kenya, Malawi and Senegal) (HABITAT 1987: 70). However, the success of any of the above programmes is dependent on whether the 'ideological and financial commitment of the government is guaranteed ... and the popular acceptance of the programme by the peasantry is unquestioned' (Akwabi-Amayew 1990: 332).

Rural settlements have not received adequate attention in the development agenda, particularly in Malawi. For example, in its first *Statement of Development Policies: 1971–1980* (Government of Malawi 1971), the Malawi government looks at the question of rural settlements within the context of housing. The view is put forward that people in rural areas have the capacity (labour and raw materials) to provide their own housing, and that the challenge therefore lies in the provision of urban housing, on which the government should concentrate its activities (Government of Malawi 1971: 107). A similar view is expressed by HABITAT (1991: 1), with the neglect of rural housing being explained on the grounds that rural inhabitants have always been able to provide their own shelter, using locally available materials, and largely within the context of subsistence economies.

It is thus the policy makers who feel that in the context of inadequate resources, subsistence alternatives should be utilised. As will be illustrated later in the case study, rural housing is in fact mostly provided for through the use of traditional materials. Malawi's shelter strategy has accordingly been formulated in the context of a policy of containing urban growth, redistributing population through the relocation of the capital city to a previously underdeveloped area (Lilongwe), the establishment of rural growth centres, the opening up of commercial agricultural estates in the Central and Northern regions, and stringent land use zoning ordinances for the cities (Kalipeni 1993: 2). It was the second *Statement of Development Policies: 1987–1996* (Government of Malawi 1987) that looked at the question of rural settlement within the context of the spatial distribution of the population, and as a process that could be influenced by policy initiatives. Thus, the strategy adopted in this particular *Statement* was aimed at promoting development of a decentralised hierarchical settlement pattern, and at strengthening functional linkages between settlements in order to improve employment opportunities and rural living conditions, while at the same time creating and maintaining a pleasant and efficient urban environment and economy. Thus, by 1987, ten rural service centres had been established with the aim of building up a network of rural market centres and generally improving economic and social conditions in those areas (Government of

Malawi 1987: 172–3). Influenced by the two Statement of Development Policies, we here approach the question of settlement in terms of housing as well as of the spatial distribution of the population. Housing is presented as an indicator of both settlement emergence and growth.

The need for government to provide housing for its employees and the inability of the private sector to cope with the housing requirements of a rapidly growing urban population has resulted in government involvement in urban housing provision. The Malawi Housing Corporation (MHC) was accordingly established in 1964 as the government's implementing agency. By 1980, the MHC had delivered 9,690 permanent houses and had established 25,636 serviced plots for rental in traditional housing areas. Similarly, the Capital City Development Corporation (CCDC), which was established to develop the new capital city, had by 1983 built 870 permanent houses and developed 10,000 serviced plots in Lilongwe. In addition, the government had 18,609 permanent houses of varying sizes being used by its employees (Government of Malawi 1987: 121). Most of the construction was done between 1964 and 1979. By 1980, demand exceeded supply and as a result, squatter settlements had emerged in the urban areas of Blantyre, Lilongwe and Mzuzu with 100,000, 19,000, and 10,000 squatter structures respectively (121).

Within the urban areas, Malawi's shelter strategies include the provision of sites and services in traditional housing areas, provision of intermediate housing areas with core units or complete units for sale, and a loan scheme for building materials and the upgrading of squatter settlements and urban villages. For other areas, there are the rural housing and the secondary cities programmes (HABITAT 1990: 91). Under the site and service scheme, basic amenities such as roads, water and pit latrines are provided and tenants are left to build their own houses, using either traditional materials (earthen walls and grass roofs) or modern materials (brick walls and iron sheet roofs), or a combination of both, depending on their financial circumstances. These strategies are viewed as the best way of combating the growth of squatter areas, although demand is higher than supply. Thus, despite these strategies and the strict ordinances, 'illegal settlements' continue, often because the alternatives given to people are limited. As will be shown below, low-income urban populations do take the initiative and provide themselves with shelter, water and sanitation, even if they are minimal and sub-standard. It seems therefore, that facilitating local initiative is the best means to achieve access to shelter and services, even in urban areas.

Although it is clear that Malawi's shelter strategies are mainly urban oriented, only 10 per cent of Malawi's population resides in urban areas, with the rest residing in rural areas where 'over 50 per cent of the houses are sub-standard and urgently require replacement' (HABITAT 1990: 91). The rural housing programme that the government established in 1981 in

Table 6.1 Access to toilet facilities in Malawi by percentage of households

Type of access	Rural (%)	Urban (%)
Pit toilets	60.8	72
Flush toilets	1.4	23
No toilets	35.8	5.1

Source: Government of Malawi 1991: 80.

all the districts of the country has had limited impact. It was established to provide loans, house designs and training skills for rural households to build or improve their housing. The target was to reach at least 750 families (*ibid.*) each year, which is a very small figure when one allows for population growth. Thus, the 1977 Population Census showed that the population had increased from 4,039,583 in 1966 to 5,561,821 in 1977, representing a 37.68 per cent increase (Government of Malawi 1978: 1). The 1987 Population and Housing Census further illuminates the situation by showing that there were 2,249,771 dwelling units in rural areas, whilst the figure for urban areas was 224,831 (Government of Malawi 1991: 76).

The government's shelter policy is not conducive to rural settlement development because of its failure to provide improved rural housing as well as the necessary amenities. Thus the 1987 census looked at sources of drinking water and toilet facilities as indicators of the standard of housing. It showed that the well is the most important source of drinking water, catering to 1,060,691 rural dwelling units, while in urban areas, the communal standpipe is the most important source, catering to 101,373 dwelling units. The rest of the rural households get their drinking water from taps inside the housing units (8,217), taps outside the units (24,305), communal standpipes (346,614), boreholes (320,315), springs (19,054), streams/rivers (430,653) and lakes/dams (39,922) respectively. The same sources are utilised by urban households with varying levels of intensity (Government of Malawi 1991: 76). Access to toilet facilities is shown in Table 6.1 above.

It is thus clear that even in urban areas where the government has a comprehensive settlement plan, it is failing to provide basic amenities.

As an important element in the development process, rural settlements are an adaptation to natural and socio-economic conditions (Sanders 1977: 23) and are therefore a key aspect of the spatial dimension and physical expression of economic and social activity. The viability of settlements (the ability to emerge and to sustain themselves) is an indicator of a society's ability to satisfy the basic needs of its members within a local geographical area. Settlements should thus be seen as a prerequisite for social and economic development in that no social progress can occur without efficient settlement systems and networks (HABITAT undated: 3). Yet small settlements continue to be inadequately focused in terms of creating factors conducive to their sustainability, due to the persistence of the 'masterplan' mentality in Third-World bureaucracies, where the emphasis is often on physical planning to the neglect of economic and social relations (Simon 1992b: 33). This often results in the replacement of local authority management by national control for national objectives, thus failing to incorporate the poor into decision-making, planning and administrative processes (Drakakis-Smith 1988: 154). Planning should involve methods of ensuring locally appropriate development through maximum mobilisation of endogenous material, human and institutional resources (Simon 1992b: 39). This is an important aspect of the development process since even small settlements in rural areas are affected by factors beyond their geographical boundaries at the regional, national and global levels. Thus, the impact of global restructuring, with its implied social and economic differentiation, has affected the pricing of rural agricultural commodities, the withdrawal of subsidies, accessibility to credit and establishment of small-scale businesses (Simon 1992b: 30).

Whilst acknowledging the role of planning in settlement and economic growth, it is important to view growth as a locally induced process that cannot be imposed from above. If local conditions are appropriate, growth may occur despite overall structures and central planning. Aerøe (1992), in an empirical study, shows how Makambako, a small town in Tanzania, illustrates development from below, with locally based industrialisation which was influenced by favourable overall structural conditions without assistance from government or donor agencies. A business town located in the Iringa region in the Southern Highlands of Tanzania, Makambako has taken advantage of its strategic position, as well as of changes in the country's economic structure, in order to develop. Thus, the introduction of hybrid maize in the mid-1970s, the development of rail and road infrastructure that made it an important junction for trade and services, and trade liberalisation introduced in Tanzania in 1986 which directed investments into private business (Aerøe 1992: 61), have resulted in the social and economic growth of the area.

Chiweta, a rural settlement in Rumphi district of the Northern region in Malawi[2], shows how the interaction of micro-level environmental factors and macro-level political and economic factors can work towards a rural settlement's establishment and its growth. The settlement is sandwiched between two adjacent rivers, both of which flow into Lake Malawi, which lies along the eastern side of the settlement. The development of a road network through the area provided an important alternative route for transporting Malawi's goods to and from the sea ports during the political crisis in Mozambique, especially from the late 1980s onwards (see Figure 6.1). This, coupled with a generally literate population in the area, has resulted in a locally induced settlement development. However, unlike Makambako – which has the advantage of a broader economic base, where private entrepreneurs have diversified, thereby getting rapid, short-term returns from services (bars, guest houses, minibuses, etc), medium-term returns from production (furniture production, metal works, etc.), and trade (at the market or via shops), and long-term returns from investments in real estate and children's education (Aerøe 1992: 64) – Chiweta's economy is at present based on non-renewable natural resource exploitation and the utilisation of the Northern Corridor road.

Rumphi district is mostly hilly, and on its eastern side the altitude drops dramatically, forming a valley along the shore of Lake Malawi. The uniqueness of Chiweta lies in the fact that it lies on the delta area of two rivers (South Rukuru and North Rumphi). It thus has conditions conducive to agricultural production, which has been a positive factor in settlement development. Unlike the hilly areas which are sparsely populated, with limited agricultural production, the delta region is densely populated. The 1987 Population and Housing Census showed the Chikulamayembe Tribal Authority (under which Chiweta falls), as being the most densely populated TA in Rumphi district (36,954 people out of a total district population of 94,902) with a growth rate of 5.5 per cent, while that for the district is 4.2 per cent. Population projections indicated that by mid-1995, Chikulamayembe would have about 46,800 people (Government of Malawi 1995: 1, 3). Malawi generally has a high rate of population growth, with a total fertility rate of 6.9 and 5.5 for rural and urban areas respectively. This is due to low levels of education among women, early onset of childbearing, an almost universal pattern of marriage for women, limited access to modern family-planning methods and a high infant-mortality rate (Government of Malawi 1994: 4). The favourable conditions at Chiweta that are conducive to population concentration, are thus compounded by general population growth trends in Malawi.

Seventy-five per cent of the land in the Chiweta delta is used for agricultural production, with the remaining land being used for housing, roads, school, health and other social facilities. Cassava is the staple food and bananas are a cash crop. Other crops grown are rice, potatoes and, to a limited extent, groundnuts and maize. Despite its close proximity to abundant water, there is no irrigation and agricultural production is rain-fed. This accounts for famine in recent years that has affected not only Chiweta, but also Malawi and the southern Africa region. The issue however is that this particular area, because of its location, should not be subject to weather changes to the same extent as other areas. Famine conditions in Chiweta are a reflection of the general lack of optimal utilisation of agricultural potential in the area, which has in turn negatively affected its pace of development. The lake is only utilised for fishing; thus there is a thriving fishing industry where both women and men are involved (the former in trading and the latter in both the actual fishing and trading). However, with the dwindling fish stocks in the Lake, the sustainability of this resource as a basis of development is threatened.

Rumphi district is managed by a District Commissioner who is a government representative and is assisted by a District Executive Committee (DEC) of which he is chairperson, which is composed of representatives of all government departments available in the district. The committee's (and therefore the government's) impact on Chiweta is felt through the presence of technical staff: nurses, clinical officers and health assistants, primary school teachers (the settlement has two health centres and two primary schools), agricultural field staff and a community-development assistant. Government has taken a top-down approach, and the DEC is responsible for the coordination of government activities at the local level. Its role has mostly been that of support for the Livingstonia Mission, which has traditionally provided health care and education to the area. In addition, there is a post office and a police unit which also acts as a security check point.

The District Development Committee (DDC) is composed of Members of Parliament, ward councillors and a chief from each Traditional Authority. The District Commissioner acts as a convenor of the meetings as well as a liaison between the DDC and the DEC. The DDC is responsible for initiating local development projects but due to inadequate resources, such activities are carried out by the Livingstonia Mission and the Malawi Red Cross Society, and are limited to health and education. People's involvement and representation in government is through the Member of Parliament whom they elected in the democratic general elections of 1994. He has been instrumental in the formation of the Rumphi East Development Foundation, whose aim is the long-term development of the area. However, the Member of Parliament lives in town, and thus may not have sufficient information regarding local people's concerns and priorities. This may lead him to support inappropriate policies in Parliament. A cassava and maize grinding mill that was abandoned in the early 1970s when it broke down after the benefactor, a missionary, had to leave the country, has since been revived and is serving the entire settlement area. In the hilly country twenty kilometres from Chiweta, a coal mine (Mchenga coal mine) was opened up as an alternative to importing coal for Malawi's industrial use. The demand for labour on the coal mine has provided employment opportunities at the local level. At peak, the labour force was at 800, but had by June 1995 been reduced to 160 for reasons of economy and efficiency. The cash obtained from the mine is generally spent at Chiweta, which provides entertainment during weekends and is a source of material goods, thereby stimulating petty trade.

The quality of human resources is very important in the development of an area. In most developing countries, education is generally viewed as the only viable means of improving one's socio-economic status. Thus, being located in a relatively undeveloped region, and taking advantage of the Livingstonia Mission, which has for a long time provided education, people in Rumphi have acquired high standards of literacy and education. At the national level, 42 per cent of the population aged five years or over is able to read and write either Chichewa or English, or both languages. Of all the twenty-four districts of the country, Rumphi (the district where Chiweta is located), has the lowest proportion of the population aged five years and over with no education (23 per cent for both sexes, 19 and 26 per cent for males and females respectively) (Government of Malawi 1991: 10–11). Chiweta itself has a literacy rate of 61.7 per cent for both sexes and 55.4 per cent for women. Furthermore, 25.1 per cent of women have not been to school while 70.3 per cent and 4.7 per cent of women have had primary and secondary school education respectively.

Education and literacy have had long-term investment implications for the development of the area since education puts a young family member on a track which might lead to a future position as a patron with control over resources (Aerøe 1992: 64). This phenomenon is evidenced in the building of motels and guest houses along the lakeshore by people who are educated and working outside the area but who are sending remittances home. Similarly, the quality of housing is relatively high compared to most rural areas. It is common to find houses whose walls are made of burnt bricks with corrugated iron sheet roofs. This type of housing is an indicator of settlement development. In the area, it is also seen as a sign of achievement to have sent a child to school who is now in gainful employment (usually as a migrant in urban areas within the country for the more educated or in the neighbouring countries for the less educated) and is sending remittances home, from which such investments as home building are made. While an argument may be advanced in terms of the loss incurred by sending away the able bodied and most educated, and therefore most capable to initiate develop-ment at the local level, migration has had a positive development impact on Chiweta. It is however important to acknowledge the fact that migration has had negative impacts on other areas, and may be indicative of problems in the sending area, such as population pressure and the failure to provide local employment opportunities. Nevertheless, all indications point to the fact that migration has indeed had a positive impact on the Chiweta area.

The question of macro-level political and economic effects on a small settlement is best illustrated by the way in which the transport sector crisis in Malawi has contributed to the growth of Chiweta. The historical pattern of transport development in southern Africa has been such that it was intended to serve economic enclaves which are heavily dependent on the exporting of primary agricultural commodities and the importing of manufactured goods for their economic well-being (UNCTAD /UNDP 1990: 9). Malawi is a landlocked country and as such its situation is complicated by additional constraints posed by long distances to the maritime ports, high transport payments (mainly in foreign currencies) and lack of sovereign access to the sea.[3] Up until the early 1980s, the route to the ports of Beira and Nacala in Mozambique was the most important, and in 1981, 531,800 metric tonnes of merchandise goods valued at MK257.5 million[4] were exported and 293,000 metric tonnes of goods valued at MK322.0 million were imported, mostly through this route (UNCTAD 1983: i). Some 60 to 65 per cent of Malawi's imports and exports were thus being carried through this route (Government of Malawi 1984: 1).

By mid-1982, Malawi was experiencing a transportation crisis, mainly due to the virtual closure of Beira and Nacala as a result of insurgent activity in Mozambique. This affected everyone in Malawi since the economy is critically dependent on imports and exports (Government of Malawi 1984: 1). The urgent need to consider alternative routes to the sea resulted in the strengthening of the Northern Corridor to Tanzania, which is the third option to the ocean (see note 3 and Figure 6.1). By 1992, full-scale operations had begun on this route, using a combination of rail, road and water transportation systems. By the end of that year, the route had handled 17.1 per cent and 16.8 per cent of Malawi's imports and exports respectively (UNCTAD/UNDP 1993: 18).

The opening of the Northern Corridor has not only benefited the country generally, but has also helped Chiweta, which lies along the Northern Corridor to the port of Mbeya in Tanzania. The road has provided accessibility to the lake, thereby facilitating its utilisation. Thus, fish traders are able to transport fish to the interior markets where they charge higher prices, thereby getting higher returns. This is in line with what Irwin Sanders (1977) showed to be a feature of rural settlements where periodic markets are held at set times in a central place for selling agricultural produce and merchandise. He further showed that roads increased economic activities and accessibility, as is also being experienced at Chiweta. The difference, however, is that the market at Chiweta is held every day and has developed more to cater for the needs of travellers. It is thus located along the main road at the Police unit which acts as a check point for travellers. One finds small-scale petty traders, with women selling agricultural produce, mostly bananas and other cooked foods, whilst the men are selling manufactured goods like cold drinks. The three stalls found at the market are owned by men. There is an increased amount of cash flowing amongst the settlers, which creates demand for more goods and thus for a good business environment.

Three kilometres from this centre of activity, one finds a number of modest motels and lodges. Thus, a travelling performing arts group has a lodge to facilitate its travel further up north, and there are about four motels owned by locally born individuals, some of whom are working in town but have invested at home. Not having access to electricity, the motels use power generated by diesel engines. Even though tourism in the area is not yet fully developed, it is an alternative that has a lot of potential, especially now that tourism is gearing itself towards lesser-known places. Apart from opening up the area, it will provide gainful employment for the local residents. It is clear that the population, which is growing fast, will not continue to depend solely on rain-fed agricultural production and dwindling fish stocks from the lake.

Just like Makambako, which has become a centre for all kinds of illegal trade and smuggling (Aerøe 1992: 61), Chiweta is also experiencing similar problems. Thus, police at the check-point report often finding people with illegal drugs and some entrepreneurs who have bypassed customs officials at the border with petty goods for sale. The local community has to deal with sexually transmitted diseases, particularly HIV/AIDS, and, as has been shown with experience from the Mchenga Coal Mine, unplanned pregnancies and young mothers who drop out of school have become very pertinent issues. There is also the question of pollution, since most of the vehicles are ferrying petrol which may leak if there is an accident, thereby affecting water quality in the lake. The road lies along the lake, and at some points, is less than 500 metres away from the lake.

Notwithstanding the above challenges, Chiweta has, because of the fishing industry, the Northern Corridor, a high education rate and good agricultural land in the delta, transcended the constraints of an urban-orientated government settlement policy, to emerge as a thriving settlement with potential. However, there are threats to the sustainability of the settlement, given that: fish is a depletable resource; the Northern Corridor may lose its strategic importance now that Mozambique has stabilised; education alone will not guarantee employment; there is insufficient land for agricultural expansion to cater for the high population growth rate. These threats pose questions regarding the long-term future for Chiweta. It is felt that this will depend on options taken at the micro- and macro-level and the way in which they interact with environmental conditions. Sustainability may be attained through the option of creating a conducive environment (by both central and local government), through the provision of technology that will facilitate irrigation agriculture and, if possible, electricity to be used for local development. The local people do not have the financial capacity to acquire such technology, but could easily manage it given their literacy levels. On the other hand, this could make for the kind of centralisation–decentralisation tension referred to earlier in the case study, and could affect the viability of development as a locally induced process. Perhaps empowering local people through involvement in planning the course of the development of their settlement, especially if central government or foreign finance is used, is the path to take. This will act as a safeguard to ensure that the local people do not eventually become only secondary beneficiaries of their own development efforts.

NOTES

1. The author is indebted to Norconsult of Norway and to Escom of Malawi for including her in a reconnaissance pre-feasibility visit to Chiweta in June 1995 to determine social and environmental impacts of a proposed hydro-electricity scheme in the Chiweta area. Views expressed in the case study are entirely those of the author.
2. The country is divided into three administrative regions: Northern, Central and Southern. There are twenty four districts: five in the North, nine in the Centre and ten in the South. In each district there are Traditional Authorities (TAs), and the smallest administrative unit is the village. There are forty-three TAs in the North, seventy-nine in the Centre and eighty-three in the South (Government of Malawi 1994: 1).
3. The three main transit routes are from Malawi to: (i) Mozambique, either by rail to Beira or Nacala, or by road/rail to Beira via Harare; (ii)South Africa, either by road/rail to Durban via Johannesburg, or by road/rail to Durban via Lusaka; (iii)Tanzania, either by road/rail via Dar es Salaam to Mbeya, or by rail/lake/road/rail to Mbeya via Dar es Salaam (UNCTAD/UNDP 1990: 9).
4. On 28 December 1981, one United States Dollar was equivalent to Malawi Kwacha (MK) .9079 (Reserve Bank of Malawi 1981).

THE ECONOMIC ROLE OF GARDENS IN PERI-URBAN AND URBAN SETTLEMENTS OF LESOTHO

In the past ten years many African countries have experienced a rapid growth in rural and urban populations although Africa remains the world's least urbanised continent, with only 35 per cent living in urban areas as compared with a global average of 45 per cent. During the last thirty years, the urban population in Africa increased at an annual rate of 4.8 per cent due to rural–urban migration and lower mortality rates, and correspondingly during the ten-year period from 1976, this growth rate in Lesotho has averaged 4.9 per cent (Government of Lesotho 1992; United Nations Economic Commission for Africa 1996). Rising populations in rural areas have resulted in land shortages, forcing people to move into the urban areas. Some assume that life in the peri-urban and urban areas has advantages, but once they move into these areas, they find that their expectations are not met and that life is really very difficult.

The lack of employment opportunities in the public and private sectors lead people to work in the informal sector and urban agriculture. Gardens are not a recent phenomenon in Lesotho and can be traced back to the nineteenth century. However, there has been an increasing number of gardens in Maseru, the capital city, and in other peri-urban and urban areas.

SETTLEMENT PATTERNS IN LESOTHO

From the days of Moshoeshoe I to the present, the settlement pattern of Lesotho has changed from a traditional structure, characterised by concentrated village settlements, to a more complex pattern in recent years. Cultivation and grazing areas were usually located at a distance from the village. Expansion has proceeded in stages. In the first stage, the mountain lands were used mainly for grazing livestock with a few isolated herdsmen's huts. The rest of the population was scattered in lowland villages. In the second stage, the huts gave way to small settlements, which eventually became villages. The best grazing land in the villages was put under the plough. Instead of land supporting a small group of people, it was forced to support a growing number of agriculturists, leading to soil erosion and reduced soil fertility. Often close to the huts, a garden was cultivated with a limited variety of vegetables for consumption. In the third stage, mission stations, which became important centres for education, health care and other social services, were introduced by the colonial administration, often some distance from villages. The growth of these centres, which eventually became district centres was, *inter alia*, the result of the relocation of migrant families, who wanted to be closer to the border posts to see their migrant members more regularly. Home gardens existed but production was solely for household consumption. However, after independence some planning control was achieved in Maseru, with the establishment of Mohalalitoe Estate within the older urban area, and later at Khubetsoana and Ha Mabote in the peri-urban area (Ambrose 1995).

In the 1970s and 1980s, encroaching settlements and cultivation in urban areas became more predominant as the national population continued to increase at an average annual rate of 2.0 to 2.5 per cent. The land was subdivided further and several new settlements were established. The increasing population pressure in Maseru and other district centres was the result of several factors, such as decreasing access to land in rural areas, increasing desire for a cash income, better job opportunities and improved health and education facilities which attracted people to towns. However, only 9 per cent of the land in Lesotho is arable and with the increasing population pressure, the available agricultural land decreases as it is taken up for settlements, as well as industrial developments.

Although production of cereals and field crops has declined, the cultivation of vegetables on plots in the peri-urban and urban areas is a common occurrence. Aerial photographs of the Maseru area were contrasted by Mapetla *et al.* (1994) for 1960 and 1980 and indicated that in 1960, the area had a large number of fields used for cultivating crops. By 1980, the fields had been replaced by residential sites, on which trees were planted and vegetables cultivated. Over a period of twenty years, the bio-mass had increased and this was a positive trend. However, other problems of urbanisation have become visible, such as overcrowding, poor main-tenance of infrastructure and rising poverty (United Nations Economic Commission for Africa 1996).

A study undertaken in 1986 revealed that over 80 per cent of the plots in Maseru contained vegetable gardens, and about 50 per cent were used for rearing livestock, such as dairy cows, sheep, pigs and poultry (Government of Lesotho 1987). With decreasing access to land for cultivation in the rural areas, the urban household with a small plot is better off (Sechaba Con-sultants 1995). Households engage in other activities such as beer brewing, hawking prepared foods and fruits (not from their own gardens) and sewing. Phororo (1996) noted that very few (5 per cent) of the households who cultivated home gardens generated cash income solely from the sale of vegetables. The majority (66 per cent) generated income from gardens in addition to other sources such as wages, miners' remittances and the sale of beer; and 21 per cent did not generate any income from gardens, since production was only for home consumption.

VEGETABLE PRODUCTION FROM HOME GARDENS

A variety of vegetables are cultivated in the peri-urban and urban gardens, which range in size from 60m^2 to 130m^2. A 1992 study conducted by the Ministry of Agriculture indicated that 5,140 hectares of land were planted with vegetables in the summer season of 1991–2 in rural home gardens, 121 hectares in urban areas and 2,639 hectares on institutional farms. The yield was 21,800 tons of garden vegetables, of which only 2,600 tons were sold, indicating that the majority was produced for home consumption. Nine different types of vegetables (pumpkin, spinach, potatoes, cabbage, carrots, green beans, lettuce, beetroot and onions) were cultivated in the summer, whereas there were only five different types in winter (Phororo 1996).

The Maseru Development Plan indicated that low- and medium-income households had gardens to supplement household food supply and to save money, whereas high-income households had gardens because they enjoyed gardening as a hobby (Government of Lesotho 1987). Phororo (1996) found that 32 per cent of households interviewed engaged in gardening solely for home consumption. Another 61 per cent who produced a surplus, sold this to neighbours rather than organisations or vendors because the quantities were small and irregular.

Home-gardens in peri-urban and urban areas tend to thrive because households are close to inputs such as seeds and water. The gardens are generally well managed and other positive features include fencing and vegetation cover throughout the year, promoting water and soil retention. Households also undertake practices which ensure a high quality crop, such as terracing, manuring, intercropping and raised beds (Phororo 1996).

Home-garden production is not restricted to women. Tasks are divided along gender lines; if a man is present then preparing the soil and planting will be left to him whilst weeding and harvesting is done by women. However, a majority of the men are employed in South Africa, leaving women to fend for the children, who have a role to play in attending to the watering. One reason for both men and womens' involvement in home gardens could be the result of a decreasing number of fields that are available to households. Considering how expensive food is, accounting for about 50 per cent of household expenses (Government of Lesotho 1987), access to a garden saves money. Not only do individual households benefit in savings and nutrition from vegetable gardens, but so does the national economy, which imports 75 per cent of its vegetables from South Africa.

However, a serious constraint to increased home-garden production is the competing uses for land. Unbuilt areas that could be used for gardening need the approval of the landlord. Low-income households live in *malaene* (long buildings with a series of single rooms with doors to the outside), and with no access to a garden they have to cultivate vegetables in plastic bags, cut tyres and half-filled sacks in order to save money, or as a result of theft, they may be reluctant to cultivate.

LAND USE AND TENURE

There is competition for land for agricultural, residential and industrial purposes. Under the customary land-tenure system, no Mosotho could have freehold ownership of land; and it was only when a man got married that he would be allocated land. Land for residential purposes was also allocated and on the arable land, people had exclusive rights to the crops produced. After the crops were harvested, the land reverted to communal grazing. However, this traditional land-tenure system has limitations that cannot be resolved by land planners. Mosaase (1983: 4) suggests that:

> More important, the allocating of land for urban development without the necessary services encouraged chiefs to allocate sites in the peri-urban areas, making no allowance for proper planning in the future. Now the landscape around urban centres is an uncontrolled urban sprawl and there is ribbon development along the main roads.

This, among other factors, resulted in the gazetting of the Land Act of 1979, which delegated allocatory powers to land committees in urban and rural areas, and not to chiefs, as previously had been the case. Some of the benefits that came with this Act included security of tenure, land acquisition for public purposes and a mandate for the government to declare Selected Development Areas (SDA) for the development or reconstruction of new residential, commercial and industrial sites.

Chiefs felt that the Act eroded their powers to allocate land and were reluctant to abide by it, resulting in a sprawling mass of unplanned, un-serviced and peripheral settlements. With a poor infrastructure, upgrading such settlements is expensive and may encroach onto residential plots, where owners resist having their gardens reduced below 1000m^2 (Government of Lesotho, undated). However, with a general shortage of land for commercial expansion in the Central Business District (CBD), it seems inevitable that the residential plots in the peri-urban and urban areas will only become smaller, and that vegetable production will occur on a reduced scale.

To shift from production for home consumption to a more commercial production for sale would require several factors such as procuring a regular supply of improved quality vegetables, a market and improved terms of payment.

Problems such as an excess supply of vegetables during the summer, and the practice of customer credit, will continue to affect households who sell vegetables. Excess supply is the result of many households cultivating vegetables which are harvested at the same time, so other markets have to be found for the sale of the vegetables before large quantities perish. Default on credit leads to loss of household income (Phororo 1996).

CONCLUSION

This study has outlined the expansion of settlements from the traditional setting to the development of peri-urban and urban areas. As more people have migrated into towns, they have become disillusioned with the prospect of finding employment and therefore have become involved in other activities, such as cultivating vegetables, brewing beer, hawking fruits and selling prepared foods. The settlement pattern of Lesotho has been conducive to transferring the culture of having a vegetable garden from the rural areas to the peri-urban and urban areas to meet the consumption needs of the household. The cultivation of a garden is on a part-time basis and often involves the assistance of most family members, playing an important economic role for households. This is not necessarily because large amounts of income are generated from cultivation, but because cash income is saved that otherwise would be spent on food, providing a good return on investment, mainly because the input costs are very low and returns are high. Where surpluses are available, they supplement earnings generated from other activities.

The likely trend in the future is that gardens in peri-urban and urban areas of Maseru and other district centres will continue to be cultivated on even smaller plot sizes, due to the competing uses for land. In addition, it could become as it is in other African cities, that gardens will not just exist on plots but will be on public land, such as parks, roadsides and steep slopes, and even in containers such as half filled sacks, plastic bags and garden pots.

ON MIGRATION AND THE COUNTRY OF THE MIND: CONCEPTUALISING URBAN–RURAL SPACE IN KWAZULU-NATAL, SOUTH AFRICA

> What is now clear is that from both a welfare and a developmental point of view, South Africa's full settlement system – including the rural areas – needs to be understood in terms of a delicate balance... Metropolitan destinations are not necessarily the automatic choice for all migrants. (McCarthy, Bernstein and Simkins 1995)

This chapter has taken shape at the intersection of several lines of research inquiry relating to the urban–rural interface in KwaZulu-Natal after the end of apartheid. In this very violent province, space is a resource being contested with edged weapons, and providing for rural and urban development is an increasingly grave priority as the national and provincial governments struggle for political control. At a level of abstraction, in many ways the political struggle in KwaZulu-Natal represents the struggle of the ideation of urbanism against the ideation of ruralism. It is based on a competing economics, and rooted in population flows and resource flows.

Some of the questions which have developed around population flows relate to changes which have been observed worldwide, and to what is being widely seen as a coming victory of gravity flows over circular migration (van Hear 1994; cf. Mabin 1989), leading to a more settled and permanent urban and urban-fringe population throughout most of the developing world. Other questions approach demographic shifts at a level where economics meets ideas and ways of thinking. Some of the points at issue involve the settlement process and its requirements: how do people take root, and what do they need to put their roots down? What do people have to have to survive in new environments?

These questions emerge against a background of rural marginalisation. Much of the theory of rural–urban relations has concerned whether or not cities are parasitic on the countryside (Lipton 1977; Rondinelli *et al* 1989; Simon 1989c). For South Africa's black rural areas, the situation has gone far past that: the rural communities, mostly excluded from production but once the main suppliers of labour to the urban economy, are again being excluded and marginalised as unemployment has risen and the settled township populations have taken up most of the jobs available. These shifts leave the major rural–urban exchanges taking place between the white large-scale commercial-farming sector and the cities, with the black countryside no longer seen as having resources worth exploiting, and more and more left to support itself as best it can (cf. Cross, Mlamabo, Mngadi, Pretorius, Mbhele and Bekker 1996; May and Trompeter 1992; Yawitch 1981). In this kind of situation, the kind of economic and demographic response which has come from the black rural sector needs to be looked at.

One way to approach the problem is in terms of the resources that households rely on for their livelihoods. As Unwin (1989) notes, this kind of approach has been widely used to understand the various forms of urban–rural interaction (for some classic anthropological versions, cf. Sahlins 1972; more recently, Cernea 1995c). Drawing on Stohr and Taylor's (1981) analysis of development from below, Unwin focuses on resource flows between the urban and rural sectors as the main source of rural disadvantage. His list starts with economic flows, including labour, food, money, commodities, energy and credit, but also includes social, political and ideological flows as essential aspects of urban–rural relations. Unwin's concern for flows of ideas and of people connects effectively with van Hear's (1994) discussion of the concerns of host populations worldwide for how to accommodate in-migrating outsiders, which informs the treatment below of the ideation of migration and settlement in peri-urban KwaZulu-Natal.

Since the rejection of apartheid spatial planning and the explosion of informal settlement in the 1990s, South Africa has seen a general turn to spatial development models based on corridor development and on the compact city, in an effort to hold the cities self-contained, prevent urban sprawl and encourage efficient transport (cf. Urban Foundation 1990). Some questions have begun to come up about where and how the rural–urban interface is located – that is, where the rural–urban boundary would lie if such a separation could be identified, and what it would mean. Dewar (1994c) has suggested that strenuous efforts be made to peg down the urban edge so as to leave space for small-farmer agriculture in the peri-urban zone, an approach also endorsed by McCarthy (1994) at the time with reference to tourism development.

However, in the recent Centre for Development and Enterprise review of the earlier Urban Foundation policy recommendations on corridors and compact cities, McCarthy et al. (1995) now remark cautiously that planning policy can do little about controlling flows and shifts generated in the macro-economy, so that the role of spatial planning will be limited. They also ask how to categorise dense rural settlements in relation to what is urban and what is rural.

The analysis presented here looks at how ideas and institutions that manage the settlement process in KwaZulu-Natal relate to flows of resources and people, and how they constrain the settlement process under conditions of rapid change. Results from some recent studies dealing with migration and settlement in KwaZulu-Natal so far suggest that institutions at the micro-local level are closely tied up with the direction and accommodation of population flows, and play a central role in shifting urban–rural flows of resources. These institutions, and particularly the tenure system, in turn respond strongly to ideas held by people on the ground of how space and resources should properly be distributed. To a considerable extent, the urban–rural linkage can be looked at as a country of the mind, more than as map space or economic space alone.

The sections that follow look first at regional population flows related to urban–rural migration, and then focus more closely on urban–rural inter-action in the mobilised peri-urban periphery, especially around the economy of natural resources. The last section returns to the question of urban and rural identity, and sums up by trying to problematise some of the processes involved.

REGIONAL OVERVIEW

KwaZulu-Natal is located on the southeast coast of Africa, and the regional metropole is the port city of Durban, South Africa's main gate for sea trade (see Figure 8.1). The province's primary economic sectors are agriculture and a declining mining industry in its northern coalfields. Secondary sectors are manufacturing, electricity and construction.

Economic activity is concentrated heavily in the short interior corridor between Durban and the inland colonial capital of Pietermaritzburg, and in a narrow strip up and down the coast. The interior of the province is spati-ally divided between the white large-scale commercial farming sector and the impoverished and marginalised economy of the former black reserves in the old KwaZulu homeland.

The regional transport network is dominated by the metropole. Land use for the province as a whole comes close to a classic von Thunen pattern, with concentric zones of decreasing land use intensity stretching outward from Durban. Most road and nearly all rail lines stop short of the borders of the former reserves.

The interior white farming areas, historically committed to uncompeti-tive maize production, have been stagnant overall. Many are declining, and shedding jobs. The most productive agricultural areas are sugar land located in the belt just inland of the coastal strip, though timber production is expanding into many former sugar areas (Makhanya 1996). The limited industrial base of the interior is generally old and has been assessed as unlikely to expand other than in a few advantaged locations. Over the drought years of the 1980s and early '90s, agricultural activity seems to have shifted towards the better watered south of the province, further weakening

Figure 8.1 KwaZulu-Natal

the position of the dry north. Overall, the provincial interior is losing ground economically against the coastal strip.

Against a background of national planning which is emphasising local economic development in the rural sector, provincial planning seems to be focusing on redeveloping KwaZulu-Natal's interior around tourism (McCarthy 1994). At the same time, a local boom in infrastructure and service delivery on behalf of the dense black population of the areas around Durban seems to be encouraging industry to extend into the designated tourist areas (cf. Cross, Mzimela and Clark 1996). This industrial spreading may endanger the tourism strategy. For the overcrowded black communities in the area – which are facing pollution, drying up of surface water and the collapse of their natural resource base – services are a much higher priority than tourist facilities. However, as will be argued later in the chapter, the economic implications may be double-edged.

The African rural areas

For the areas of black settlement, the time of the drought has been a period of economic decline, with net out-migration. Urban unemployment has soared since the early 1980s, and jobs for unskilled labourers have dried up countrywide. This tightening and shifting of the urban job market towards skilled and white collar jobs has acted to undermine the migrant labour system, which, notwithstanding its historical inequity, provided a broad base of cash inflow to isolated rural families (May 1989; Nattrass et al. 1986). Many families are now without wage income, or are surviving on state transfer payments and their own local efforts (cf. Ardington and Lund 1995).

Growth in the metropolitan economy in KwaZulu-Natal has been too slow to absorb increases in the number of work seekers in the vast interior poverty reservoirs of former KwaZulu (Roux 1991). By the 1990s, unemployment rates exceeded 50 per cent in many black rural districts (Development Bank of Southern Africa 1991), and the situation has become significantly worse since the 1990 census. The relatively well-educated township populations with greater access to job information now have the advantage for available urban jobs, and even given economic expansion it looks unlikely that KwaZulu-Natal's rural unemployment crisis will be fully resolved in the foreseeable future.

As migrant labour declines, patterns of employment are becoming localised around a commutation model (May and Trompeter 1992), focusing on work in secondary and tertiary centres. Although commutation workers appear to bring home a considerably higher share of their wages than would come from migrant remittances, wages in the interior towns are considerably lower than in the metropole and its close satellite centres. These interior industrial areas have few location advantages, and are likely to decline as the South African economy opens to globalisation. The unfavourable prospects for existing rural industries leave up to half or more of the black workforce competing desperately for work opportunities that are disappearing.

The alternative source of local employment is farm work. This sector is subject to labour shedding, poor conditions of employment, very low wages and, in extreme cases, violence between employers and workers (Alcock 1994; Claassens 1989; Kockott 1993).

In response, families in the former homelands seem to be moving further into the cash economy in an effort to secure their income base, chasing declining cash income (Cross *et al.* 1995). Informal small business activity is expanding as a share of household income, as families without adequate access to employment try to access wages indirectly. At the same time, food production activity seems to be falling, and heavy pressure is coming onto the natural resource base.

There are signs of a deepening rural crisis as households trying to move further into the cash economy are being driven by unemployment out of the urban areas and back into the traditional rural economy, which is not able to sustain the numbers. It appears that a crunch point is being reached in the rural communities, when families trying to retreat into the older subsistence economy exhaust their rural options and are then squeezed back again towards the urban economy, where they had earlier lost their foothold. Rates of demographic mobility seem to be rising, with destabilising effects on rural society (Cross *et al.* 1996).

The collapse of economic options is complicated by prevailing high risks of violence. Shaken by increasing residential mobility and by the political war between the ANC and the IFP, rural institutional structures have lost control over social conflicts. Land-related violence is serious in many areas, and stock theft is undercutting the stock raising option for both black and white households (cf. Cross, Luckin and Mzimela 1996). Households are finding that how they position themselves in relation to the urban sector is increasingly critical to their livelihoods.

Regional migration processes

Against this background, large-scale transfers of population have been taking place. The main flows are the long-standing migration stream from the interior districts in former KwaZulu towards the coastal metropolitan complex, and what seems to be a more recent movement from the rural areas generally towards local second- and third-order centres. These flows appear to have been boosted by the expansion of the long-distance taxi industry, which has significantly reduced the isolation of the rural districts by expanding shopping and commuting flows to towns and cities. In addition to the large migration stream from the interior, large numbers of rural to urban migrants seem to be moving along the coastal highways from the relatively mobilised and better-off parts of former KwaZulu located on the north and south coasts.

Several localised eddies in the regional flow can also be identified. Migration into the metropolitan peri-urban zone has drawn migrant families from the central third of the province (Cross, Clark and Bekker 1994). Pietermaritzburg, as a regional centre for the Midlands farming region, appears to operate as a separate focus of urban migration, and may be drawing a much larger proportion of its peri-urban and shack populations from the surrounding farm areas.

As of the early 1990s, the migrating population appeared to show the usual demographic signatures of rural to urban migrant populations worldwide (cf. Lipton 1995). Individual migrants tend to be young unmarried work seekers at an early phase of their working lives, and an increasing number are women. Many of these individuals form new households while working or living in the urban area. Migrating families show up as the middle poor. They are often young families headed by men with some education. They look upwardly mobile, and seem to be the most employable rural households.

Both movement towards work in terms of the general Harris–Todaro model (Harris and Todaro 1970) and movement towards public goods and amenities in line with Tiebout's theory (Tiebout 1956) appear to be taking place. The most important categories of migrants intending permanent moves within KwaZulu-Natal appear to be work seekers and industrial and commercial workers, women and children moving for family reunification, retirees returning to rural areas with their families, people displaced by job loss and refugees from violence (cf. Champion 1995). With labour migration declining, fewer individuals now seem to be moving back and forth to work, and more families seem to be moving permanently from place to place.

It appears that an urban floating population includes the bulk of the single people in the migration stream, as well as some couples with children. The urban shack areas seem to take in younger couples, and the peri-urban tribal communities accept somewhat older married couples with more and older children. The general migration stream is broken up and directed to destination areas by the intentions of the migrating households, and by *de facto* immigration policy in the receiving areas.

Migration into the Urban Shack Settlements
The main destination of the major rural to urban flow has been the shack areas located around the perimeter of the formerly white metropolitan core, but very large flows went into the peri-urban periphery as well. Very little new urban housing has been built by government in the townships over the last ten to twenty years, and urban accommodation for rural migrants has

been mainly in the vast high-density informal areas located on private, municipal and state land on the edges of the core city. Most of these shack areas fall inside the new metropolitan boundary, and count as part of the city. They are broadly distinct in location, housing type, institutions and economic characteristics from the peri-urban areas of dense but dispersed settlement located further out, and mainly on tribal land.

Significant informal settlement by in-migrating black households began in the shack areas at least by the 1920s and 1930s, and perhaps at around the same time in the inner tribal areas as well (Davies 1991; see also Mabin 1991, 1992). It appears that the urban shacks received their first major flood of population from the 1960s and '70s, at about the same time as the peri-urban periphery was developing. Further in-migration from rural areas was believed to be very rapid, and it was estimated that a massive shack population built up in the informal settlements up to and immediately following the lifting of influx control in 1986. The Urban Foundation (1990) estimated that there were 1.7 million informally housed people in Greater Durban by 1990.

Most of these urban shack areas were under rent tenancy, with landlords accommodating tenants on informal tenancy-at-will agreements, and acting as *de facto* local leaders. In most areas, institutionalisation was weak, and leadership processes were not able to deal with the urgent physical and developmental problems of high-density informal settlement. Conflicts between landlords and tenants were commonplace (Cross, Bekker, Clark and Richards 1992; Cross and Preston-Whyte 1989). Some of these struggles concerned landlords' positions of leadership or control relative to their tenants, and whether tenants could enforce reciprocal, rural-type land relations on landlords, or whether urban land relations in the rental framework were instead mainly impersonal.

Settlement was tightly compressed at the household level due to the shortage of land, and most households were reported to have at least one or two lodgers staying with them in addition to the family itself. Household sizes were reported at an average of seven to nine people in different surveys, and many seem to have been larger.

In the late 1980s, as the transition to majority government approached, the grip of the state over urban black settlement relaxed as the apartheid government turned to accommodation with the black liberation movements. The ANC-supporting youth movements organised openly in the shack settlements, and were able to promote a mass movement against the paying of rent to urban landlords. With rent payment stopped, informal residents found themselves the *de facto* owners of their sites. As the crowded shack populations realised that the state was no longer policing their boundaries strictly, an explosion of informal settlement within and around the white core city followed. Micro-settlements appeared on vacant ground throughout the city and suburbs as new families split from parent households and took up land. Household size crashed to three to five people, and the institution of lodging declined to near invisibility in what we have described as a large-scale process of decompression (Cross, Bekker, Clark and Wilson 1992; Cross, Clark and Bekker 1994).

Precise research by Durban's Urban Strategies Department (1995), with air photography and ground surveys, has shown that the expected massive increase in the shack population due to rural to urban migration in the late 1980s and early 1990s did not take place. The shack population, previously believed to be much larger than the population of the townships, appears in the Urban Strategies study at something over half a million, about a quarter of the total metropolitan population, and close to the same size as the formal township population. Earlier estimates of in-migration rates to the Durban city core suggest that steady rural to urban migration may have reached a low peak just before the lifting of influx control in 1986, and again in the mid-'90s (Cross, Clark and Bekker 1994). It now appears that the total population of the shack communities has not expanded sharply since the political transition. Instead, the physical expansion of the shack areas to take control of large sectors of urban space seems to have been due mainly to households already in place decompressing to shed new households, and to the sudden opening of land access to the floating population of former lodgers. Reasons why people do or do not move to the city from the impoverished outlying districts lie at the heart of the urban–rural relation. It seems clear that in KwaZulu-Natal less rural to urban migration has taken place since the end of influx control than had been widely expected.

In addition to the widespread rural dislike and distrust of social conditions in the urban areas, there are a number of possible reasons for the apparent reluctance of the impoverished rural black population to take advantage of the dropping of influx control. These include dislike of urban economic insecurity; news of rising urban unemployment; the accompanying trend to localisation of the rural economy; the vital importance of local social networks as support structures; violence and the war for the shacks; and the frequent need for rural migrants to join the floating township population and spend time building up urban knowledge or contacts to be able to find a site in an informal settlement.

Lipton (1995) has remarked that migration flows respond quickly to urban unemployment, and a large number of disappointed rural work seekers were reported to be back in their home communities at the height of the drought in the early 1990s: most rural families are reported to have remained stubbornly at home during the drought, instead of moving to town. More generally, livelihoods in the inner urban fringe are heavily dependent on wage income, and relatively brittle in relation to job losses (Cross, Mlambo, Mngadi, Pretorius, Mbhele and Bekker 1996). Violence in the early 1990s also seems to have driven even urban-born people to leave the townships and migrate outward into outlying rural areas not yet affected, creating a small migration counterflow to the main rural to urban drift (Cross and Evans 1992).

In addition, locating an urban shack site is more complicated than is usually thought. Less than a third of the rural individuals or families who have migrated into the Greater Durban region seem to have had the existing network connections needed to move directly from a rural community to an urban or peri-urban destination. For the majority, urban migration is a gradual process of moving on by capitalising on opportunities. Many begin their search for an acceptable urban site by joining the floating population, staying with relatives or contacts in the established townships to start learning about potential options. Finding a site is often a result of chance encounters which bring rural people looking for sites into contact with areas which are within their range of specifications. Recently, households have been moving towards areas receiving infrastructural services.

In this light, informal settlements are not a staging area for people moving into the city. Instead, the city, through the townships, has served as a staging area for introducing rural migrants into the informal settlements. Like the peri-urban zone, the urban shack areas themselves represent an affordable alternative for rural-born families with very limited resources trying to position themselves in the urban context.

Under present conditions, the urban context seems to have become less rewarding for rural-born families. The present rate of flow into shack communities seems to be declining, though it may rise again (McCarthy *et al* 1995). Getting entry into a shack community is fast and easy when the area is new and still recruiting membership, but needs increasingly better contacts and sponsorship as the area fills up, and may need money as well: rent tenancy may be re-appearing, and many local committees are being accused of selling land to new people. Much of the new shack population seems to be sourced from among young township families and shack-community families who have resources, but cannot get formal housing in a township or development area. That is, following the usual trend for gravity-flow migration, the urban population is being replaced increasingly from inside the urban area itself.

Migration into the Peri-Urban Zone
The other major element of inward population flow in KwaZulu-Natal has been migration into the peri-urban zone. Fairly separate from the migration stream reaching the urban core and shifting around within it, a major part of the rural to urban demographic flow has been directed into the former KwaZulu tribal districts in the peri-urban settlement belt surrounding Durban. In spite of its close links with the urban core and its high level of

economic mobilisation, the peri-urban zone is still rural in important ways.

Beginning in the 1960s, rural people wanting access to the job market of the metropole have moved into the nearest spaces allocated by the state to black people, and run under familiar forms of land-based administration. Living in the peri-urban zone at the time allowed workers to commute to jobs without falling foul of the pass laws, while accommodating their families in a relatively secure environment.

The population shift involved was massive, though less noticed than the arrival of black people in the prohibited white urban spaces. Starting from the mid-'80s, estimates began to appear, suggesting that anything up to half the total population of KwaZulu may have moved into the peri-urban settlements around Durban, piling up against the influx-control fence line protecting the white core city (cf. Simkins 1984; also Giliomee and Schlemmer 1985). Present estimates are not very reliable.

This movement of population took place at a time when progressive policy thinking was bewildered at the stubbornness of rural people in their failure to abandon their rural communities and move en masse to town. It was widely assumed that all the families that had moved into the peri-urban context would immediately move into the city if they had not been prevented by apartheid law and policy (cf. Giliomee and Schlemmer 1985). More recent research suggests that this may not have been true in all cases.

LOCAL DYNAMICS

If we move the camera in closer to look at dynamics in the interchange zone on the edge of the city, a more textured picture starts to emerge. The sections that follow try to approach the question of migration and settlement by focusing on the urban–rural question in relation to local and urban resource flows, as they seem to affect levels and incidence of immigration.

Increasingly, research in several fields is identifying peri-urban zones, which are treated here as the innermost edge of rural society and economy, as important and distinctive in relation to factors that divide what is urban from what is rural. They represent a kind of inter-tidal zone. Peri-urban areas in Africa exist because of proximity to cities: they usually carry dense semi-rural settlement in close contact with urban work and amenities. With mixed characteristics and resources, peri-urban settlements are usually highly dynamic. Unlike the metropolitan shack settlements, the peri-urban tribal communities in KwaZulu-Natal have not had any recent opportunity to expand onto new land, and areas with location advantage are often very crowded.

KwaZulu-Natal's main peri-urban zone starts at the coast below the port-city metropole, and extends inland and north in a strip of varying width. It lies mostly west of the city and perhaps twenty to fifty kilometres away. Other smaller peri-urban zones have formed around secondary centres elsewhere in KwaZulu-Natal. Compared to those in rural districts, the metropolitan peri-urban region represents the socially and economically mobilised urban periphery. At the same time, it maintains largely rural-type local structures and institutions, centred on Tribal Authorities, and its people uphold rural values and expectations to a much greater extent than in the urban shacks.

After months of angry negotiation, nearly all the peri-urban districts have been formally excluded from the Durban Metro local-government structures, which have strong ANC constituencies, and put under the direct administration of the IFP-led provincial government. In this administrative sense, these areas of mixed political sympathies have now been moved outside the city boundaries and into IFP territory.

The peri-urban periphery of Durban is characterised by relatively high incomes and high education levels, tightly packed residential density, good urban transport, an informal land market and a reasonably good standard of housing, with only a minority in shacks. Making use of Unwin's (1989) list of urban–rural flows and interactions, KwaZulu-Natal's mobilised periphery provides an analytic opportunity to unpack some of the impacts of urban and local flows in cash, services, power and authority, ideas, energy and raw materials. These resources relate to human migration flows and institutional responses on the ground that feed back to affect interaction with the city. The object of the exercise is to re-examine how what is rural and what is urban are related on the ground, and what distinguishes one from the other.

It has been widely assumed for some time that most or all disadvantaged rural communities in South Africa are 'functionally urbanised' (Graaff 1987; and compare McCarthy et al 1995) – that they depend fully on the urban sphere for their livelihoods, and that their only important rural characteristic is their location on the ground. This may not be entirely the case: rural resource flows seem not to be the same as those used by urban people, though they overlap very substantially. Using data collected by several studies in KwaZulu-Natal, this section takes human demographic flows as a starting point. The analysis presented here suggests that this focus on rural resource flows indicates a fundamental shift in the frontier of the urban in relation to the rural in KwaZulu-Natal.

Demographic flows in the mobilised periphery

Population buildup in the metropolitan peri-urban zone seems to have started to gather force in the 1950s and 60s, as Durban began to emerge as a centre of employment in competition with long-cycle migrancy to the mines of the former Transvaal. Settlement pattern has shifted fundamentally in response to urban access. The main reason has been differentials in access to urban transport, resulting in strong micro-scale migration flows.

In the rugged and broken topography of the north end of the peri-urban zone beyond Pinetown, near-urban residential densities have developed in some of the localities with location advantage. Occupation gradients fall away to the density levels of remote rural districts in the inaccessible areas that represent backwaters in the regional transport flow pattern. Changes in density result partly from the attraction of the advantaged areas to people immigrating from outlying rural districts, but also show the powerful pull of the advantaged localities for local-born families in the inaccessible areas. The result has been compression of settlement in the areas with transport advantages, and decompression in the spatially disadvantaged areas which were less thickly occupied even in the 1960s.

Spatial differentiation accelerated as the relation of work opportunities to the peri-urban settlements changed. Shifts in where people preferred to settle over the period of the 1960s to the 1990s reflected both the localisation of the space economy of employment and the rapid rise in violence. These shifts largely reflect the changing focus of urban–rural resource flows and other flows. As the business cycle rose and fell, Durban's commercial and industrial economy was expanding outward toward the former farming areas and outer suburbs beyond the urban edge, where peri-urban settlement was building up.

Land to live on, secure from government dispossession, remained a central goal for settlement up to the 1994 national elections, but other priorities changed over time. By the mid-'60s peri-urban settlement preferences were dominated by access to jobs, via access to urban transport services: obtaining better access to transport minimised the cost in time and money of reaching urban work, and people moved in large numbers to get it. Transport remained the central priority for twenty years, with major effects on settlement.

By the 1970s long-cycle labour migration from the northern peri-urban zone to the Gauteng mines had given way to monthly commuting to jobs in the Durban regional metropole. Ten years later the expansion of employment in the satellite centre of Pinetown was encouraging weekly or daily commuting. By the 1990s, expanding commercial enterprises in the mainly white suburban communities just beyond the boundaries of the former reserves provided a new source of daily commutation work.

At the same time, national unemployment reached an historic high, and large numbers of peri-urban workers no longer had jobs as the economic cycle bottomed. Although overall mobility in the metro peri-urban region is high, there has been no clear sign that either immigrants or locally born people have responded on a large scale by leaving the peri-urban zone and moving closer to the urban core as unemployment has risen. As of the early 1990s, flows into town from the peri-urban area were moderate (Cross, Clark and Bekker 1994), and seemed to have been more than replaced by natural increase and the arrival of new people from other places.

By the late 1980s, the approach of the advancing urban economy was bringing a rapid expansion of local commerce and the beginnings of industry to that area outside Durban which had been a district of white farms with some suburban land use, mixed with black settlement under Tribal Authorities. Local job opportunities expanded as urban-core work opportunities shrank due to rising unemployment. The spread of violence outward from the city replaced transport as the urgent priority for voluntary moves, and levels of residential mobility were driven upward by an explosion of new refugees and of families desperately searching for peaceful areas. But as violence continued to flare throughout the peri-urban periphery, settlement priorities adjusted.

The 1990s were dominated by the collapse of the natural resource base of most of the metro peri-urban zone. Access to urban services aimed at basic needs – centred on water and electricity – emerged as the urgent settlement priority in the mobilised metropolitan periphery as well as in the urban shack areas. This national trend has compounded the attraction of the most densely occupied settlement nodes in the metro peri-urban zone, which have first priority for service delivery in the local context. Overall, rising levels of mobility, boosted sharply by the spread of violence, have deeply affected the way the host communities in the peri-urban zone have perceived and dealt with people moving in.

Tenure and settlement as local immigration policy

In the peri-urban areas, long-established communities with rural institutions have been faced with very large inflows of outsiders. The dividing line between members and outsiders is much sharper than in the urban shack settlements, which are almost by definition communities of strangers, with few if any local-born residents (Cross, Bekker, Clark and Richards 1993; Cross, Clark and Bekker 1994). The kind of concerns they face are common to how tenure systems on the ground respond to immigration in the rural areas and shack areas of KwaZulu-Natal, and in many areas throughout South Africa.

Concerns related to immigration and settlement which preoccupy communities in rural, urban and peri-urban areas make a striking echo of the list of concerns involved in van Hear's recent (1994) discussion of the globalisation of migration flows at an international level. Surveying how nations react to immigrants from developing countries, van Hear notes concerns in the host population over maintaining core values and identities, and over the basis on which immigrants can be taken into the existing population and can join the political community.

He defines one class of national immigration regimes as falling into an 'exclusionary' model, where group membership is defined on the basis of common descent alone, and where outsiders cannot become members no matter how long they stay. This model is contrasted to the 'assimilation' model, where outsiders can become members of civil society, but only at the price of giving up separate identity, and to the 'multicultural' model, where new immigrants are expected to share cultural values and a sense of identity, but can maintain some cultural diversity. These same issues preoccupy rural and urban black communities in South Africa when they deal with immigration. While the former government virulently enforced the exclusionary approach under apartheid, black communities may tend to the opposite view. Instead of excluding immigrants and holding them separate, *de facto* immigration policies and the deeply held social values behind them tend to insist on the assimilation model – that any new entrants joining the community give up other allegiances and identify themselves with their new group fully (cf. Cross 1991, 1992; Vilakazi 1962). This principle has probably become more central as political contention has spread, making unified communities a condition of avoiding war conditions and the collapse of the social order.

With the increasing complexity of rural society and politics in KwaZulu-Natal, the difficulty is likely to be in moving to van Hear's third model, which accepts diversity and dual allegiances, and may be an important factor in development and local-government issues. Any such change will probably have to come through changes in the tenure system, and the local institutions which give force to community thinking on immigration.

At local and regional levels, *de facto* tenure systems vary significantly in how rapidly they accept immigration (Cross 1991, 1992) and in how immigrants are received and absorbed. It can be suggested that at the local level, tenure is the main filter which breaks up and directs inter- and intra-regional population flows. Perhaps the most critical space in which population flows are staged and directed – and where tenure is under the greatest pressure – is in the mobilised periphery where the rural directly encounters the urban. However, tenure institutions in the shack areas also filter migration, and come under most pressure where sites are in shortest supply (Cross 1994).

Tenure systems in disadvantaged South African rural communities are usually communal or semi-communal, or, more accurately, social or communitarian systems. Under a moral land ethic, they provide the ideation and the ideology of settlement, as well as the concepts that make up its vocabulary, and include the values that structure expectations and reactions. Like any kind of formal or informal law, tenure systems are built up out of accumulated practice in terms of world view and values. They change gradually but continually in relation to the inputs they receive and the way people try to use them; this makes for new precedents. Because they change in response to pressure, on the ground social tenure systems tend to be structured around principles and priorities rather than rigid rules. The main concerns for tenure at community level in black areas of much if not most of South Africa have been over dealing with in-migration, rather than with allocating and transferring land in the narrow sense, or with providing access to production land.

At the local community level, the concerns which van Hear identifies are routed through the tenure system, which determines how the community accepts or rejects in-migrants, and how they are accepted into the social body after they arrive. These priorities reflect the uniquely non-agrarian character of the rural economy for black people in South Africa.

Under apartheid, almost the entire black population was systematically excluded from access to commercial crop markets, and tightly compressed onto land holdings too small to allow risk-avoiding extensive cultivation strategies (cf. Duggan 1986). Agricultural schemes in some of the old homelands provided land to a very small fraction, at the price of cutting back the land access of the majority (Fischer 1987; van der Waal 1991). Shortage of land forced households to raise their risk factor by intensifying production practice with limited chances of being able to sell, or else to reduce their production commitment or exit the production economy completely. At the same time, land shortage and dispossession under apartheid put a high premium on land to live on.

Responding to these artificial scarcities, black tenure systems in South Africa have been directed away from cultivation land and driven to prioritise residential land, instead of developing the agrarian tenures focused on access to crop land which have emerged in most parts of Africa (cf. Bassett and Crummey 1993; Bruce and Migot-Adholla 1994). Most tenure systems in Africa are social/communal, and based on group membership. But more than in other parts of the continent, the tenure systems of black communities in South Africa are driven by apartheid land scarcities, and revolve around controlling in-migration.

Land tenure as a system of human settlement both immediately restricts how much immigration is accommodated, and over time is modified by the pressure of immigration and land transfer to accommodate arriving population flow. Immigration is accommodated by modifying concepts of land rights and of land entitlements to allow for more people and denser occupation, or excluded by prioritising the rights of the people already belonging to the community.

Immigration
The way tenure systems react to immigration is routed through the principles of settlement. These principles govern access to land and to membership of the community, and are discussed in greater detail elsewhere (Cross 1988a; Cross, Bekker, Clark and Wilson 1992; Cross, Mngadi, Sibanda and Jama 1995). The basis of regulation of immigration is the role

of tenure practice in governing the process of recruiting new families into the community.

Tight, communitarian land-tenure systems which give the community a strong say in who is accepted tend to select narrow categories of approved entrants: weaker, individualised ones take a wider range. Probably all the South African social tenures start with the idea that immigration candidates should be households with married couples. The main value behind the selection process from the community standpoint is that new immigrants should be morally upright, stable citizens who will contribute positively to the mutualist interaction of the locality they join. Communitarian tenures therefore prefer older, married couples with children, and usually block single mothers and young people looking for land (Cross 1994; but see also Letsoalo 1987). The adapted tenures of the urban shacks sometimes take less stable young couples or even single people. Where high density leads to competition for land, stable older male-headed families tend to push aside others. These preferences interact with the preferences of the migrants themselves, and have a strong demographic effect on population structure in areas with high immigration.

From inside the system, the most basic principles are that community citizenship is conferred by the process of obtaining the right to a site to settle on, and that all families have a claim on society for the fundamental land entitlements. This land right starts from a claim to all the resources that the family needs to feed and sustain itself from the natural environment, including a house site and cultivation land, and land for the household to settle married children and continue itself. Along with household land come rights to basic needs resources including grazing, water and wood, which are on commonage. However, under today's squeezed conditions the full package of entitlements is rarely available in practice, and people adjust their expectations to reality.

Given this basis in livelihood support, most of the rest of the system revolves around social concerns, based on mutualism, transparency, organisation and leadership. Land transactions involving residential rights are public business, and landholding families use land transfers to build up residential clusters of allied people who will support each other, and who regard the land-giving family head as their local leader. These clusters develop out of face to face relations and established mutual trust within the locality. In conservative areas, the longest-settled families in a locality generally claim precedence and leadership roles.

The land-based locality grouping is suspicious of outsiders, and new families stay on probation for some time while the community looks them over before they are fully accepted and can claim sovereign rights over their land. Entering families are expected to come in one by one, and communities tend to resist the idea of accepting groups of immigrants for fear of creating fault lines around separate identities and divided loyalty (cf. Cross 1991).

The status of outsiders in need of land is the most difficult issue for tenure systems under pressure to manage. The right to claim land is seen as universal and is supposed to be acknowledged by everyone, and the social land ethic and mutual-support values that underpin communal tenure make it difficult to refuse land requests from people in need. However, families already in occupation can turn down requests from outsiders on the grounds that land is needed for their own descendants. This principle of prior and greater need is what people use to defend land against claims put by others. Older forms of communal tenure also hold back flows of in-migration by requiring contacts and references, with screening procedures for outsiders and up to seven or eight levels of approval before land can be obtained. New forms, including the very fast-acting forms found in the shack areas, require much less vetting but make many more mistakes by admitting untrustworthy candidates, who then have to be either chased away or lived with (Cross, Bekker and Clark 1994).

Together, the basic principles – that land transfers are public and require screening, that land transfers create moral bonds between households, and that everyone has a claim to land but too many new entrants can be refused in the interests of families already in occupation – combine to form the framework of the local community's immigration policy. How these principles are applied, and modified to allow for relative degrees of settlement pressure, creates the difference between the older tenures found in remote rural areas, the intermediate peri-urban types and the new forms adapted to quick transfer found in urban shack settlements.

Change
Change in the immigration process takes place as the system adapts to stress and pressure. As areas with location advantage are bombarded with migrating households looking for sites, the stricter conditions of the classical rural tenure system requiring several levels of approval for every land transfer are stripped away by the pressure of demand. The right of local settlement clusters and kinship alliances to approve new entrants largely evaporates, and either the individual landholder or the individual land administrator – chiefs, indunas, or democratic committees in some areas – find themselves coming close to autonomy. Where tenure individualises, landholders and/or administrators find themselves shallowly responsible to the larger community, instead of obliged to report to specific local interests able to hold them accountable.

Where control over the land and citizenship process individualises, it also speeds up. Volumes of transactions spiral upward, and landholdings shrink as landholders assign pieces to accommodate demand. Densification ensues and, in advantaged areas and those where there is little access to alternative land elsewhere, household compression also follows, enforcing larger household size because of the difficulties for new households to get sites.

For the immigrant households, one result is an increasing trend to impersonal or anomic communities, and a change in the climate of their reception. Rather than the close, face-to-face classical rural community based on alliances and mutualist social relations, where immigrant families are accepted gradually into a network of alliances and mutual-support obligations, dense communities partly import urban conditions into the rural fringe. The time needed for new families to be accepted telescopes from a generation or more to a few weeks or days, but the community that results is one of strangers. New families are not required to maintain deferential behaviour for long periods, but little social support is available unless immigrant families work purposively to build their own networks. In many areas, church congregations fill in as routes to acceptance and support where settlement relations have declined or collapsed (Cross, Evans and Oosthuizen 1993).

Institutions
Where rapid and sustained immigration has continued for years, the growing impersonality of relations has broken down the coherence of local land-based institutions. Local settlement clusters and large-scale kinship alliances have weakened or fallen apart as face-to-face social relations have retreated against the arrival of large numbers of unconnected people, and ward and tribal district structures are weaker and less cohesive than they were. This institutional weakness is both a symptom and a cause of systems that accept quick immigration and rapid densification, and these conditions promote commodification of land.

Without institutional support, relatives and neighbours cannot maintain their primordial right to intervene in proposed land transfers to protect their long-term land interests by holding off outsiders. Administrators and landholders often see their immediate interest in entry fees or money from sales, and gradually become less likely to try to protect local interests by limiting in-migration. Throughout the world, informal land markets are characteristic of peri-urban areas, and in South Africa they usually emerge under these conditions. The rate of immigration rises accordingly.

Loss of integrity in local autochthonous institutions has gone along with political contention to weaken local flows or relations of legitimate authority. In the jostling stranger society found in many areas, ad hoc groups organise readily, but new structures of formal authority able to deal with high-density conditions have not often emerged. Committees and comrade movements or other organisations often seem superficial and transient and have not often been effective in replacing the earlier structures rooted in land relations, which grew leadership structures from the ground up through alliances based on land transfers. The weakness of authority relations exposes the inner rural communities in the peri-urban zone to arbitrary exercise of power from outside political actors in both the urban and rural spheres.

Power

Under these conditions, how communities handle immigration through their tenure institutions depends on how much pressure they face from outsiders needing land, but it also relates to power dynamics connected to class formation. The northern peri-urban communities in KwaZulu-Natal show a range of tenure systems/immigration policies, depending on their local advantage and how much immigration they have drawn over time. Changes in local-level immigration policies also relate to how immigrants are accepted into local communities after they arrive, and what resources they bring with them.

In the most closely settled and socially atomised peri-urban areas with urban transport and ongoing service delivery, elite immigrants from the urban townships have begun to appear for the first time. Like the locally born people coming back from the city, these families tend to have significantly higher incomes than the local average, and have started businesses and played a leading role in mobilising development projects. In some areas families from this new urban immigration stream seem to be in the process of using their urban skills to take over power structures: some local office holders have resisted successfully, and others have allied themselves with the new class, but many have been pushed out of power loops altogether. These developments are creating a new kind of power base, rooted in economic capability rather than in land relations. This trend has marginalised many of the old families which previously controlled land and administrative functions, deriving their position of leadership from seniority and from their land-based alliances. Similar trends seem to be appearing widely, in KwaZulu-Natal and elsewhere (e.g. Werbner 1993).

These elite immigrants have been widely resented in their local communities for elbowing aside older residents with seniority, but are also admired and respected for their developmental activities and leadership skills. In the same areas, immigrants with limited means coming into the community through social grant transfers are likely to remain socially subordinate. Still largely barred from public life by tenure principles, they have few resources compared to the urban elite and are much less likely to get into positions of influence. In the older tenure systems of the marginalised transport backwaters, leadership roles and conspicuous economic activity from new arrivals usually remain blocked. However, the settlement system is self-sorting: very few families with urban skills look for sites in the outlying areas with weak economic activity, few services, high suspicion of strangers and relatively slow entry processes.

For the advantaged areas with dense populations, the weakness of land-based institutions seems to be allowing economic and class factors linked to urban settlement to push out the older land-based seniority system in determining the standing of immigrants under the social assumptions of the local tenure system. Where this happens, the tenure system loses much of its interlocking, social/communitarian character, and is drawn much further into the impersonal cash economy and atomised social relations of the urban areas.

The local economy on the urban edge

A wave of economic change has washed over KwaZulu-Natal's peri-urban zone as the edge of the city has come closer. This wave has had a number of direct and indirect economic effects on settlement processes. Migrant labour has nearly disappeared. High unemployment has meant that a broad-based access to relatively low but reliable cash flows from the urban core has been superseded by a limited and very conditional access to work that more and more often requires significant levels of education and skills qualifications.

The overall outcome has been a sharp rise in both average income and income differentiation within the local communities of the peri-urban zone. Processes of class formation have been helped along by migration processes. In terms of the Tiebout model of consumer mobility (Dowding, John and Briggs 1995; Tiebout 1956), people can be expected to move toward the best level of public goods – and particularly infrastructure and services – that they can afford. The probable outcome would be one of sorting localities into a class-related structure tied to levels and costs of service delivery. Population sorting and migration in the peri-urban zone seem to be following this model: at the same time, there are many families that cannot afford to move and who may find themselves in difficulties. The households of many unemployed people seem to be falling out of the bottom of the local cash economy.

Income levels in the densely populated, mobilised settlement nodes seem to be separating rapidly from the average incomes in the outlying margin-alised areas located in the transport shadow of the rough terrain away from the main access roads. The differences in relative wealth and poverty between the northern peri-urban localities that are drawing immigration and the marginalised transport backwaters are now very large.

The typical peri-urban income distribution in the densifying, developing settlement nodes is now looking very stretched out. The very poor, with recorded cash incomes below R250 per month, represented about one in ten households in several samples surveyed in 1995 (Cross, Luckin and Mzimela 1996). They were outnumbered by the very well-off, with incomes over R3,000 per month. This elite group included a high proportion of internal and external immigrants, and represented as many as one in six households. The outlying transport backwaters are different. They are demographically older and less-educated populations which have been dominated by out-migration of younger households with earning potential, and they show income distributions that are strongly skewed toward the low end, and approximate the classical J-shape of poverty. Elite incomes over R3,000 per month were as rare as one case in fifty.

This kind of economy is thought to be functionally urbanised, meaning that people are wholly dependent on cash income flows from the urban economy for their survival. Planners now seem to believe that the economy of the peri-urban zone is entirely urban (cf. McCarthy, Bernstein and Simkins 1995). It is not clear that resource flows involved in livelihoods are that simple, or that the only significant flows are wages and transfers. It has been argued elsewhere that not enough attention has been paid to the role of local flows from the natural-resource base (Cross, Mzimela and Clark 1996). More broadly, migration into the peri-urban zone can be seen as a rural solution to how to survive in an urban-dominated economy without losing all access to rural-resource flows that are part of land entitlements.

The economy of natural resource use for rural black communities can be separated analytically into the *production economy*, based on assigned land rights and involving cultivated crops and livestock raising, and the *extraction economy*, making direct use of the biotic and abiotic environment, both renewable and non-renewable. These are collected resources, and include water, wood for energy and for building, plants for food and medicine, clay, thatching grass and a range of other materials used for subsistence, crafts, housing and manufactures (Cross, Mzimela, and Clark 1996).

Densification and immigration have also cut back and simplified the peri-urban natural-resources economy. The production economy still provides some economic backstop to most families, even in the nodes of dense settlement, but there seems to have been a broad trend across the rural eastern seaboard of South Africa to downsize home production from field crops to gardens, and from staple maize to specialised vegetable production for household food security (Andrew 1992; Cross *et al* 1995). This trend to reduced scales of home-crop production is advanced in the peri-urban zone. It is underpinned by reliance on the urban sector to deliver relatively cheap and reliable flows of processed staple grains from the large-scale commercial-farm industry, and reflects increasing commitment to the cash economy and integration into the urban distribution network.

For peri-urban producer families, down-scaling of home production at a time of drought has gone along with extreme caution in committing scarce cash and labour resources to intensify production for higher yields from limited garden plots. High risk aversion is compounded by perceptions of relatively insecure tenure for production land in the densifying settlements

(Cross, Mlambo, Mngadi, Pretorius, Mbhele and Bekker 1996); but in spite of perceived risks, some intensification is taking place as vegetable production makes inroads against extensive cultivation of staple maize, and hiring of labour becomes more common. Perhaps one-fifth of peri-urban families rely heavily on their cultivation, especially in the transport backwater areas, and among the destitute who have no access to cash income flows (Cross 1988b; Cross, Mlambo, Mngadi, Pretorius, Mbhele and Bekker 1996; May 1996).

A similar trend over the recent prolonged drought has affected livestock raising. Survey results suggest that livestock numbers have fallen steeply by about two-thirds during the prolonged drought of the 1980s and early 1990s. Only the relatively isolated and impoverished outlying peri-urban communities still maintain significant levels of stock ownership, but in these transport backwater areas stock ownership is still the dominant form of savings. In most areas levels of theft are very high, and even household chicken flocks seem not to be being bred back to their pre-drought levels because of theft risks. For densifying communities, loss of savings in livestock is having the effect of making reliance on urban flows of cash and food more precarious at a time of record unemployment. These shifts in production activity are leaving most of these inner rural areas more dependent on unstable wage flows from the urban sector.

Changes in the extraction economy relate directly to localised human density levels. Specific resource flows in energy and water have been identified as critical bottlenecks by policy bodies and service providers. Families that still use natural resources for basic needs have to travel long distances and commit quantities of labour time to find what they need. Pollution of ground and surface water and exhaustion of firewood resources are widespread, and the peri-urban zone is seeing moves on a large scale to deliver urban-based water and power supply to substitute for declining natural resources in the densely populated areas.

However, the continuing importance of the extraction economy as a whole has not been widely recognised, nor has the total cost to the household of substitution been looked at closely. Recent work (Cross, Mzimela and Clark 1996) suggests that even in the nodes of dense settlement, a significant share of peri-urban communities and households still rely heavily on both urban cash flows and the local resource base in an economic context where both are at risk and neither alone provides all of what they need.

Environmental products still seem to be being used heavily by 20 to 40 per cent of the present peri-urban population, to provide local flows of water, food and fuel supplies, cash income, medicine, and construction materials for housing. Others use natural resources from time to time, to backstop paid services and to hold down the total cost. Workshops and interviews emphasised the continuing importance of natural resources to the poor. Results suggest that the total cash equivalent value in paid services of the local extraction economy – counting water, energy, medicine, building materials and transport to reach work instead of living on home production – could, if subtracted from cash income, cut the family's total cash income by what might be very roughly estimated at one third or more.

Conceptualising immigration and rural–urban resource flows

Discussion so far suggests that flows of urban cash and service delivery and flows of local natural resources are both central to the dynamics of peri-urban settlement, and that both respond quickly in a feedback relation to pressure from immigration brought about mainly by location factors relative to the city. The mediating factor is the tenure system and its underpinning system of social ideation in terms of the social land ethic, which determines what claims group members and outsiders can make on the land system.

Perched on the edge of the rural with maximum access to the urban, peri-urban areas in KwaZulu-Natal have offered an effective combination of access to work opportunities and to land entitlements. Rural people looking for ways to improve access to urban resource flows without giving up rural resources have streamed in.

Under this kind of pressure, the immigration policy implicit in the tenure system has tilted 180 degrees from where it started. Classical settlement process was rooted in a system of ideas based on suspicion of outsiders. It required full assimilation of new entrants to maintain a unified and coherent community at local level, but also required multiple approval of new people and accepted them only gradually and incrementally. Driven by demand for easier access, the settlement process has individualised, and now accepts immigrants rapidly. Under these conditions, most families now receive a minimal land right of a residential site, community membership and the option to collect what natural resources they can, often along with access to piped water, electricity and telecommunications, at a price. For mobile families with assets in education and urban contacts, this settlement package meets their needs and continues to draw new arrivals looking for land and opportunities.

Social thinking around settlement and immigration continues to require full assimilation, to avoid splits in the community that could open the door to violence. Compression of settlement in the densifying nodes receiving service delivery keeps the tenure and immigration system under pressure and makes space a scarce resource. This context favours individualisation. Social tenures still equate land rights with group membership, but also accommodate individualisation through informal land markets. Immigrant families buying land require little formal acceptance, allowing many new people to move directly into social and political life, and to reach positions of leadership and influence based on their economic standing and urban skills.

These changes have taken place at the expense of the old families who formerly controlled the land system and monopolised local authority flows, and also at the expense of institutional coherence in general. Without their land base, the older local-born families have few assets useful in the contemporary economy unless they have invested in education. In many cases they represent the new poor, and have been pushed back into the declining natural-resources economy. The very poor do not have money to cover the expense and transaction costs of moving, and usually do not have the option of migrating to less crowded areas.

The immediate mechanisms underpinning the reorientation of the settlement system in the dense peri-urban areas then involve rapid densification supported by urban resource flows from outside the area, and the weakening of the production and extraction economies. Once the tenure system individualises, land transfer rates begin to cascade as market forces take over, commodifying land and causing effective control to slip from the community.

Loss of effective access to the natural-resource base as a form of collective good helps to promote the sequence of change in perceptions of land which opens the area to the penetration of urban or quasi-urban settlement systems. These systems turn over land rapidly and easily and deliver residential rights only, with fragmentary access to the production and extraction economy. In this sense, they align with the priorities of the urban economy, and with the priorities of immigrant and local elites whose household economies are already inside the urban sphere. At the same time, these urbanist settlement systems act against the interests of the local-born and the poor. These groups still often depend heavily on the balancing role of local resource flows, and on entitlements to production land and collection rights, and may not be in a position to be able to afford to lose these rights.

It can be suggested that the distribution of natural-resource dependence across the immigrant and local peri-urban population is a major factor in locating a rural–urban boundary. On the approximation given above based on the 1996 LAPC study (Cross, Mzimela and Clark 1996), perhaps a quarter to two-fifths of the present peri-urban population would be depending heavily on the natural resource base and on their remaining home production, and might not be able to make the jump to paying for a full package of urban-sourced services. These families can be looked at analytically as remaining on the outside (i.e. on the rural side) of an urban–rural meridian dividing the peri-urban zone.

In contrast, the urban-oriented peri-urban elites with better paid work and several sources of household income can probably be considered functionally urbanised. These families are fully committed to buying service flows from the metropole, have much less stake in the rural natural-resources economy, and appear as part of the urban core economy although they live in a suburban relation to the city.

If the relation of urban and rural is problematised in relation to how the household obtains the resources it needs to live, the defining factor for urban society is probably not reliance on cash earning as the major element of support, as assumed by the construct of 'functional urbanisation'. Rural and peri-urban households have been relying on urban work since the nineteenth century without breaking their links to the land.

Instead, it can be suggested that the urban breakpoint occurs when reliance on the natural resource base stops. At this point the household becomes free-swimming in the urban cash economy, shifting from semi-proletarian status to free labour, with no economic connection to the land. In this light, a fairly sharp boundary between the urban and the rural can in principle be located in relation to dependence on urban resource flows against local resource flows. However, this boundary divides economic rather than physical space.

In this sense, the urban–rural boundary would be class-related, and would divide communities along the line of how individual families at any given time use urban and rural resource flows in making up their liveli-hoods. In crossing this economic boundary, the families of the long-term unemployed, the chronically poor, and those with insecure cash incomes are clearly most at risk. Outcomes will depend on whether employed people bring back enough wage income to allow the poor in their community to build up a living on micro-enterprise and the local labour market. Failing this, rural as well as peri-urban communities may remain for the indefinite future divided into urban and rural sectors, and still at least partly tied to their land – or, functionally ruralised.

CONCLUSIONS: THE URBAN AND THE RURAL IN KWAZULU-NATAL

The processes of transformation in settlement systems and their conse-quences which can be observed in the mobilised peri-urban periphery can also be found in earlier stages or in other versions in rural and peri-urbanised areas across the province. Further from the urban centres, traditional leaders have maintained closer control over settlement, and the artificial crowding produced by dispossession and removals has driven up the demand for land by displaced families. The process of individualising tenure seems in some areas to be taken over by leaders, giving chiefs/*amakhosi* scope to sell land informally to refugees and immigrants rather than to community members (Cross, Mngadi, Sibanda and Jama 1995). High volumes of transfer can result because of underpaid leaders' need for income. In these areas, old elites seem less likely to be displaced by immi-gration-related change processes than in the mobilised periphery where market forces seem to have more scope to bring about change.

In the urban shack areas which are accommodating the mass of rural to urban immigrant families, reports and interviews suggest that people frequently lose jobs or earning opportunities and slide out of the urban economy. It seems that in many cases people in this situation migrate back outwards towards peri-urban or rural areas, trying to cross the rural boundary and regain the lost country of the mind where natural-resource entitlements are readily available at no charge.

This outward stream crosses the track of rural and peri-urban families heading the other way, trying to get as close as possible to job markets. These households seem ready to tolerate greater compression to find urban sites, while trying to drag along any land-entitlement rights they can enforce in a contested environment.

The overall picture of settlement systems in the province (i.e. KwaZulu-Natal) today seems to reflect chronic tension between urban-oriented interest groups trying to get control of space for settlement and for narrowly economic uses, and rural-oriented interests trying to maintain differentiated land entitlements and a more exclusionary settlement system able to protect older land principles. Depending on their economic standing, immigrants and local-born community members can line up on either side of the struggle.

More broadly, the situation around settlement and immigration suggests conceptualising the urban and the rural as two fairly distinct economies actively contesting space, rather than as a one-way process of urban expansion and rural retreat. Historically, rural people have reacted to the urban cash economy not by trying to join it, but by trying to use it (Cross, Mzimela and Clark 1996). People who have moved closer to town have often been pushed into motion by the destruction of the classic rural subsistence economy, by overcrowding and by economic change. But they have not always given up the rural resource economy. Instead, many families have tried to bring it with them as they moved toward jobs: they have gone about this by bringing along rural ideation relating to the land economy, and unpacking it on arriving.

The system of rights and ideas underpinning the rural economy continually tries to penetrate the urban ideation and recapture space as rural-born families migrate into town. The recent decompression of urban shack settlement has opened up opportunities on this line that were not available before the last government lost its grip on urban settlement.

Small shack settlements practising social tenure have seeded themselves all through KwaZulu-Natal's urban core, and urban agriculture is common in Durban, Cape Town and Gauteng, and in many other parts of Africa wherever shacks have established themselves. Small stock are common in urban shack areas. Cattle have appeared in the cities of the Western and Eastern Cape, and are appearing in urban KwaZulu-Natal as well. On another level, urban boycotts of service charges owe some of their force to the rural principle that the family's basic needs should be drawn from the natural-resource base as part of the settlement right, a basic entitlement which is not paid for.

These attempts by the rural poor to plant their land economy in the heart of the urban is the mirror aspect of the outward migration stream of elite township-born families taking control of densifying development nodes in the mobilised periphery. It appears that the conditions around compression of settlement push for individualising the tenure and settlement process, while a period of decompression allows the household to try to re-establish some form of the older rural range of resource entitlements.

Against the background of this contentious terrain, the affordability of urban services flows may form the spike which splits black society in KwaZulu-Natal into rural and urban components in areas where the natural resource base is seriously compromised. Institutions at ground level are weak throughout the province, and re-establishing effective management of production and extraction resources looks likely to be a long uphill struggle. If national government is able to hold to its RDP/GEAR[1] commitment to bring services widely into rural communities, it is possible that new provincial migration flows will develop in relation to services affordability, as well as around initial access. If so, these new migrations will help to re-draw the outlines of rural and urban ideation in the mind and on the ground in a new KwaZulu-Natal.

NOTE

1. The Reconstruction and Development (RDP) Programme has recently been reconstituted as the Growth, Employment and Redistribution (GEAR) Programme.

POLITICS, COMMUNITY DISPLACEMENT AND PLANNING: CATO MANOR – PAST, PRESENT, FUTURE

Cato Manor was once a melting pot of Indian and African cultures, a vibrant makeshift community of 100,000 people who wrote their own rules and survived and thrived for half a century in the shadow of the city that excluded them ... in the darkest days of apartheid it was torn down, to enforce racial segregation and open up a prime piece of real estate for white occupation. This never happened. Fragments of the former communities remained, a new wave of settlers moved in and Cato Manor remained largely undeveloped and under-utilised for 25 years. (Cato Manor Development Association 1994: 1)

In South Africa politics played a key role in settlement evolution and community displacement at the macro-(bantustans) and micro-(group areas) levels. A dominant theme in the history of black communities in South African cities was their struggle to construct and 'defend illegal space'. A central focus of apartheid state policy was to annihilate such communities and to 'quarantine them in localities selected by the state where they could be more effectively regimented and controlled' (Bonner and Lodge 1989: 1).

This chapter examines the changing fortunes of one such urban settlement from the pre-apartheid, apartheid and post-apartheid phases. The focus is on the Cato Manor settlement in Durban. Cato Manor is an evocative name in the province of Natal and has powerful connotations with the history of the dispossessed in South Africa. The process of urban dispossession and contestation in Cato Manor has often been compared with the destruction of Sophiatown in Johannesburg (Lodge 1983) and the razing of District Six in Cape Town (Hart 1988).

Cato Manor has been referred to as a 'complexity in place' – 'one of those places about which, and around which, controversy has always appeared to rage' (Butler-Adam and Venter 1984: 1). Furthermore, the 'complexity of Cato Manor is not static. It reflects the interwoven processes of society as it has operated in the past, and is a complexity sustained and created afresh out of present processes' (67).

This chapter is divided into five sections. The first section traces the historical evolution of settlement in Cato Manor. The impact of the Group

Areas Act on community displacement in Cato Manor is discussed in the second section. The re-zoning of Cato Manor for Indian ownership and occupation is discussed in the third section. In the fourth section the recent land and housing invasions in Cato Manor is discussed. Attempts by planners to develop a non-racial settlement in the area is evaluated in the final section.

The intention of the chapter is to extend our understanding of the relationship between settlements and their wider political and economic contexts. Furthermore it will contribute to our understanding of the interplay between the local micro-level social structure and relationships within a settlement, and its wider macro-level political and economic setting. Finally, it enhances our understanding of the community experience of the dispossessed classes in South Africa. The chapter also highlights some of the problems that are likely to be experienced in the process of urban reconstruction, development and planning.

CATO MANOR: CONTESTED TERRAIN

The history of settlement in Cato Manor is very complex, especially in terms of its race–class configuration, types of legal and illegal tenure, and the extent to which the right to live in the area has been 'fiercely and often violently contested' (Edwards 1994: 415). It is located within 5km from the Central Business District (CBD) and is also very close to the industrial areas of Durban (Figure 9.1). Cato Manor has traditionally been a mixed area, occupied mainly by Indians and Africans and its history is inextricably interwoven with the history of Durban.

The area was originally owned by George Cato, the first mayor of Durban, and comprised of about 4,500 hectares (Edwards 1989: 7). It consisted partly of a marshy, animal-infested jungle, and the land was variable in quality. After completing their period of indenture, many pioneering Indians settled here and built simple houses from their modest earnings and savings, facilitated by pooled incomes from the joint family system. They had purchased or leased their land from wealthy white farmers who had made lucrative profits from transactions with Indians. The conversion of undeveloped Cato Manor into a thriving, productive agricultural area resulted from the 'effort of the Indian through industry, resourcefulness and thrift' (Maryville Indian Ratepayers' Association (MIRA) 1958: 4).

The Indians were mainly fruit farmers and market gardeners who ensured that Durban was adequately supplied with fresh fruit and vegetables at reasonable prices. With the passage of time more Indians were attracted to Cato Manor and the area grew by leaps and bounds. This was not unrelated to the fact that being located outside the jurisdiction of the Durban City Council (DCC), they were able to erect substandard dwellings at low cost. Schools, temples, mosques and halls were built and sustained

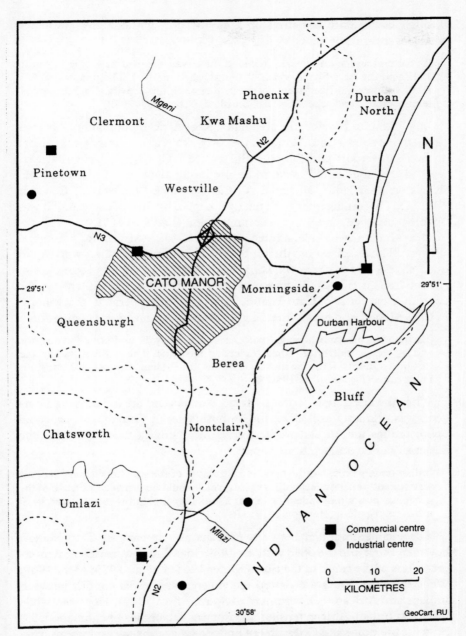

Figure 9.1 Location of Cato Manor in Durban

through community initiatives in Cato Manor, without any assistance whatsoever from the state:

> Its cultural and social centres included the Aryan Benevolent Home begun in 1918 and the Arya Samaj which was established in 1920. The temples at 'first river' and 'second river' were also early foci of Hindu activity. Church groups, temple groups and school boards flourished. (Chetty 1990: 12)

In addition to Indians, the area had a large African population. Africans began to move into Cato Manor in the early 1940s as they were ejected from areas like Overport and Puntans Hill by the DCC. Many Indian farmers realised that they could make more profits by allowing Africans to build shacks on their lands, and many of them became 'shacklords' (Edwards 1983: 4). This arrangement was tacitly accepted by the DCC because it was unable to provide alternative accommodation (Ladlau 1975).

Often Indians would let a huge plot of land to an African for a nominal site rent. The tenant would then sub-lease to hundreds of others who would build shacks and pay rent (*Fighting Talk* 1959). As a result a large class of African 'tenant-landlords' came into being, who had a vested interest in the continued existence of Cato Manor. This group also operated 'shackshops' in Cato Manor, and experienced a great deal of insecurity and competition:

> They lead an insecure, harassed existence squeezed by the authorities on one side and by competition with Indian traders on the other. These illegal traders and 'tenant-landlords' form the social soil for the anti-Indian attitudes that one finds in the area. (*Fighting Talk* 1959: 3)

While the interaction between African workers and the Indian petty bourgeois was primarily exploitive, Indian businesses in Cato Manor provided opportunities for African workers and their families to escape from the austerities of direct local state control:

> Indian traders provided the basic infrastructure of the squatters' slums: the bus services and retail outlets – the services which could be provided because of the particular position of Indian people as a 'buffer group' in the racial hierarchy of urban segregation. (Hemson 1977: 103)

The incipient conflict between Africans and Indians in Cato Manor, however, burst into the open with the 1949 riots. There were different interpretations of the cause of the riots (Kuper 1965; Ladlau 1975; Meer 1969; Webster 1978). The state viewed the violence as a racial conflict between Indians and Africans (Government of South Africa 1949). However, while there was Indian–African tension, the riot was a 'complex phenomenon, fed by white prejudice and Government policy as well as by the aspirations of an embryonic African bourgeoisie' (Ladlau 1975: 19).

The riots were also attributed to the poor socio-economic and housing circumstances of Africans in Cato Manor. Although Cato Manor was incorporated into the Borough of Durban in 1932, no attempt was made to upgrade the area, and it remained a chronically neglected area in terms of services and facilities for some years after consolidation. At the time of incorporation there were about 2,500 Africans living in 500 shacks. Ten years later the population escalated to 17,000, and by 1948 there were about 29,000 Africans living in shacks in Cato Manor (Edwards 1983: 9). In 1950 there were 6,000 shacks in Cato Manor housing 50,000 Africans (Maasdorp and Humphreys 1975: 15). The proximity of Cato Manor to the city centre and surrounding industrial zones contributed to the rapid development of shacks in the area (Maasdorp and Humpreys 1975).

Living conditions in Cato Manor were far from satisfactory. The crime rate in the area was high. The police were particularly concerned about the brewing of illicit liquor and shebeens, important components of the informal economy of Cato Manor. There was overcrowding, inadequate health and sanitation services, and disease was rampant (Edwards 1983). The Durban Housing Survey (1952: 372) stated that Cato Manor was 'the spearhead of an attack on Durban's health', and described the area as follows:

> In general, the area has few water taps. There are a few small and ill-constructed pit latrines, but no system of drainage or rubbish removal. Waste water oozes from the shack surroundings to form stagnant pools. Vermin, flies, cockroaches and other pests flourish in the uncovered food, overflowing pits, neglected refuse dumped a few yards from the shacks and general filth. Unsavoury odours cling to shacks and to whole areas.

The Durban Housing Survey (1952) concluded that trade and industries had developed in the city without any consideration being given to the social and human consequences. The contradictions embodied in Cato Manor, especially with regard to the contribution of its residents to the development of the city, and the responsibility of the DCC, is aptly conveyed by the following *Sunday Tribune* (1957) editorial:

> Cato Manor, with all its burden of pain and misery, its sick and dying children and its insanitary shacks, is Durban's responsibility. A modern city, exemplifying all the highest standards of western civilisation, cannot disassociate itself from its gloomy satellite. Durban also needs Cato Manor, or it needs the 100,000 people who live there, journeying into the city every day to contribute their labour to the general prosperity.

Notwithstanding the poverty and despair, Cato Manor was home to its residents. The Durban Housing Survey (1952: 375) noted that :

> there are many attempts to maintain pride and self-respect, which cannot fail to move deeply, and even hurt, a visitor to these homes. Walls are painted and decorated with pictures cut from newspapers. In more than one case the earth floor is covered with linoleum and the household linen unbelievable in its whiteness. Actually, many interiors of shacks are remarkably clean and tidy, and seem to be out of tune with their environment.

A major advantage of Cato Manor was that Africans were spared the controls which were imposed upon them in the locations. The terrain occupied by Africans in Cato Manor was, however, contested space. Although the area was owned by Indians, Cato Manor 'became ever more central within the state's plans to allocate the spatial and social features of Durban' (Edwards 1989: 192).

RACE ZONING, PROTEST, RESISTANCE AND RELOCATION

In terms of the Asiatic Land Tenure Act (Ghetto Act) of 1946, Cato Manor was zoned for Indian ownership and occupation. By 1950 some City Councillors and the Native Administration Department expressed concern about the future of Africans in Cato Manor. While recognising that the area was primarily owned and occupied by Indians, the Native Administration Committee of the Durban City Council (DCC) suggested that separate zones for Indians and Africans should be set aside in Cato Manor (DCC Minutes 20 November 1950). However, the Committee recognised that 'Cato Manor is ultimately to become an Indian area, and that permanent accommodation will have to be found for the Natives put there under a temporary controlled shack scheme' (Durban Housing Survey 1952: 380).

The DCC subsequently obtained central state consent to expropriate 450 acres of land in Cato Manor, as well as a loan of £153,000 towards the costs to provide temporary accommodation (later known as the Cato Manor Emergency Camp) for Africans. The main purpose of this gesture was to ensure that the shacklands of Cato Manor were cleared. However, the Minister of Native Affairs, Dr Verwoerd, emphasised that the central state would never support permanent African housing in Cato Manor as the area would be zoned white in terms of the Group Areas Act (*Daily News* 1951).

In 1952 the DCC recommended that Cato Manor should be zoned as a white group area. In spite of objections from Indian political and civic organisations, Cato Manor was proclaimed a group area for white owner-ship and occupation in 1958. However, the DCC was forced to reconsider its 1952 recommendation as the financial implications of group area relocations became apparent. In June 1958 it resolved that a 'more realistic approach' be adopted to race zoning in the city, with emphasis on the 'minimum disturbance of the existing population' (DCC Minutes 5 June 1958). As a compromise, the DCC recommended that a portion of Cato Manor which was predominantly Indian owned and occupied should be zoned for this group. This proposal was rejected by the government. By the early 1960s there was evidence of increased central state control over local authorities, and the space for local opposition to central policies was significantly reduced. The weak apartheid state of 1948 was very much in control by the early 1960s (Maharaj 1994).

Removals from Cato Manor commenced in March 1958 and were

almost finished by August 1965. During this period 6,062 shacks were destroyed, and 82,826 Africans were officially relocated in the new townships of Kwa Mashu and Umlazi. It was estimated that 30,000 to 40,000 people disappeared, 'either returning to their rural areas or else taking up illegal residence elsewhere in the city' (Maasdorp and Humphreys 1975: 61).

The removals were resisted by the communities. 'Illegal residents' who were in Durban without permits felt that they were being deprived of their rights to live in the city. Others who were engaged in selling liquor and other illicit activities felt that their livelihoods were being threatened. The main reason for the resistance was that the cost of living would be higher in the townships, especially with regard to rent and transport expenditure (Maasdorp and Humphreys 1975).

In April 1959 residents protested against the razing of shacks at Mnyasana, bringing a temporary halt to the relocation process. In June 1959 spontaneous protest action in the Cato Manor Emergency Camp resulted in the destruction of buildings and facilities and beerhall riots. The rioting and boycott of beerhalls was sustained up to November 1959. While the African National Congress played a role in the protest action, it was mainly 'initiated by the underclass – illicit entrepreneurs and women for whom municipal shack demolition and removals posed an absolute threat to continued city residence' (Edwards 1989: 196). A major problem was the lack of organised protest action and resistance. While shack dwellers affirmed their desire to reside in Cato Manor, 'there was no clear political strategy and a lack of any clear leadership' (Edwards 1989: 207). Removals were resumed in November 1959, under police protection. By the end of 1959 about 10,600 people had been relocated (Maasdorp and Humphreys 1975: 62). The majority of Africans were moved either North to Kwa Mashu, or South to Umlazi (Figure 9.1).

In January 1960 nine policemen who were involved in a liquor raid were killed in Cato Manor. The state of emergency introduced after the Sharpville riots resulted in a reduction in resistance action in Cato Manor as residents were unable to counter the repressive power of the state. There was a further change in attitude in early 1961 when between 400 and 500 families requested to be moved to Kwa Mashu. There were two possible reasons for this change in attitude. The official view was that residents were aware that they were leaving the unhealthy and overcrowded slum areas. However, a more plausible reason was that residents realised that resettlement was inevitable, and to join the queue for new housing as soon as possible was in their interest. Furthermore, allocation to a municipal house would give them rights to live in the urban area and end their feelings of insecurity (Maasdorp and Humphreys 1975: 63).

Indian political organisations were also vociferous in their condemnation of, and opposition to, the Group Areas Act and being uprooted from Cato

Manor. They resolved to mobilise their resources, and to use every available avenue of protest to oppose relocation from Cato Manor, and to defy the unprecedented assault on basic human rights and privileges. In an atmosphere of increasing hostility and intolerance these organisations utilised peaceful measures, which included recourse to law, passive resistance and appeals to India and the United Nations, to expose the injustice and violation of human rights in South Africa. The Maryville Indian Ratepayers' Association (MIRA) made an emotional appeal to the DCC and the government, emphasising the attachment of people to place and community:

> People form deep and lasting attachments to the places in which they live and such attachments are rooted in emotional association with homes, temples, churches, mosques, schools, burial places and with neighbours – years of friendship, the passing on of homes from generation to generation. Such are worthwhile values which cannot be set aside lightly. Is it fair to ask people, now advanced in years, to break up old associations and homes, businesses, etc. and to start afresh? Besides, can monetary compensation, even though seemingly adequate, take the place of homes, businesses, etc.? Enforced removal must necessarily bring *resentment* and resentment can so very easily smoulder into *hate*. (MIRA 1958: 2, original emphasis)

Although Indian political organisations claimed to represent the Indian community, there was very little evidence of mobilisation of the working class. This was because segregation presented an immediate threat to middle-class Indians, and political action and resistance was directed to protecting the interests of this group. For the poor there was the possibility of being housed in municipal housing schemes and a relief from the high levels of exploitation from the Indian landlords (Maharaj 1992).

The main reason for the failure of resistance to the zoning of Cato Manor for Indians was the repressive state apparatus. Many Indian political leaders were arrested and were being tried for high treason. The majority of Indians were low income labourers who were afraid of being arrested, and the consequent loss of jobs, earnings and family support associated with political activism (Maharaj 1995). The majority of Indians from Cato Manor were initially moved to Chatsworth and later to Phoenix (see Figure 9.1). The relocation process was described as follows:

> These mass removals are affected in a manner that reflects an almost uncaring attitude on the part of those who make the decisions to move people hither and thither ... It is almost as if humans are being used as pawns and moved into white and black squares by a manipulator who plans and plots to achieve a desired objective. He annihilates and sacrifices to that all important end. But this is no game that is being played. Human lives are involved and the very core of community life is being seriously affected. Everything that has been built up over many years, and decades, is destroyed ... leaving in its wake resentment, enmity, despair and pain. (*Leader* 1981: 8)

There was a great deal of apprehension about moving to Chatsworth because transport costs would increase by 85 per cent, and rents for substandard dwellings would increase by 78 per cent. Also, recreational, educational and religious amenities in Chatsworth were rudimentary. Furthermore, many Cato Manor residents were home-owners with mortgage bonds which were almost paid off. In Chatsworth they would have to start afresh. As a result of age and economic circumstances, many would not qualify for bonds, and interest rates were higher. Hence, 'many economic house-holders would be forced to become sub-economic householders as a result of higher costs of housing' (Subramony 1993: 80).

There were a number of problems with houses in Chatsworth. Residents had no choice in the selection of individual dwellings, neighbours or neighbourhoods. Generally, the buildings were of a low standard, with many technical and structural defects. Many houses were located in hollows and steep slopes, and there were serious drainage problems. The semi-detached block and mortar cottages were tedious, repulsive and 'did not convey a pride of possession' (Subramony 1993: 82).

By the early 1970s, the process of 'ethnic cleansing' in Cato Manor was complete, and a vibrant community was destroyed. In 1978 Cato Manor was described as follows:

> Today the hillsides of Cato Manor are once again covered by thick tropical bush and grass. A few paved roads, shells of buildings burnt during the 1959 riots and traffic to and from Chesterville are the sole reminders of human settlement. Some Indian families who have thus far survived from the Group Areas axe still live on the periphery. Cato Manor today represents one of the largest undeveloped urban areas in a South African city. (Maasdorp and Humphreys 1975: 63)

RE-ZONING CATO MANOR

In spite of being zoned for whites, Cato Manor remained vacant and undeveloped for almost two decades. There was an abundant supply of land for whites in other parts of the city. Also, parts of Cato Manor geology was Ecca shale, which would lead to a major increase in building costs. The state-appointed South African Indian Council (SAIC), which was established in 1965, made numerous representations to the government for the deproclamation of Cato Manor for Indian occupation. In 1979 the government agreed to deproclaim Cato Manor for Indian ownership and occupation. The main reason for this was to increase the legitimacy of the SAIC in the Indian community (Desai 1986).

While the re-zoning of Cato Manor was welcomed, concern was expressed that only the wealthy would benefit. Very few of the former residents would be able to purchase land in the area if it was sold at market prices. Furthermore, only one third of the original Cato Manor was returned to Indians. Under these circumstances, the re-zoning of Cato Manor was described as 'something of a Pyrrhic victory' (*Sunday Times* 1987).

The Cato Manor Residents' Association (CMRA) was formed in November 1979 in order to represent the interests of past and present residents of the area. More specifically, the objectives of the CMRA were to:

- stop evictions of families living in Cato Manor;
- ensure that housing is provided for all income groups in Cato Manor, and to ensure that preference is given to past and present landowners, tenants and other family members;
- oppose the sale of land by public auction;
- call for the scrapping of the Group Areas Act. (*Daily News* 1979)

Through its campaigns, which included mass mobilisation and petitions, the CMRA succeeded in preventing the DCC from selling land in Cato Manor by public auction. In May 1984 responsibility for the planning and development of Cato Manor was passed on to the House of Delegates (HOD). There were numerous allegations of irregular land sales in Cato Manor. In 1986 the HOD was forced to recognise the CMRA as a representative of the community, and was compelled to work with the Association in the development of public housing in the Wiggins and Bonella areas of Cato Manor (Figure 9.1).

LAND AND HOUSING INVASIONS

Since the late 1980s a new process of informal resettlement began in the area as Africans began to resettle clandestinely in Cato Crest in the wake of violence in the townships and squatter areas on the peripheries of the Durban Functional Region (Makhathini 1992). Africans built their dwellings in bushy areas, and by 1991 their numbers increased to a point where the shack settlements became more obvious and conflict started between squatters, neighbouring white residents and the authorities (Hindson and Byerley 1993). The *Daily News* (1993) maintained that the development of shacklands in Cato Manor in the 1990s was a 'monument to political ineptitude':

Cleared of its African and Indian inhabitants in the name of apartheid in the 1960s – when proper planning, servicing and control were all that was required – it stood for decades as a forlorn wasteland in the heart of an otherwise burgeoning city. Today the squatters and their shacks are flooding back into the vacuum left by the disappearance of apartheid. Once again, proper planning, servicing and control are required. And once again, the authorities are failing to provide it.

All the groups removed from Cato Manor in the 1950s and 1960s have staked moral claims to some form of right in the resettlement and development of the area. Indian families that remained in the area have already been able to realise this claim in the form of new housing constructed for them in Bonella by the HOD. New groups of invaders are also staking claims and are refusing to move. With the advent of a new democratic system in South Africa, Cato Manor has continued to be invaded. It is a large and undeveloped piece of land that is attractive to many low-income residents in the Durban functional region (Hindson and Byerley 1993; Hindson and Makhathini 1994).

On the night of 1 November 1993 houses set aside by the HOD for low-income Indian families in Wiggins were invaded by Chesterville residents. These houses were being sold to Indians, and had been lying vacant for three months. However, most of the dwellings had been allocated to Indian buyers, who were in the process of taking occupation of their houses. The houses were being sold for R35,000. Initially, about four hundred houses were invaded, and in the next few days another four hundred houses were invaded. Initially, the invaders were all from Chesterville. Subsequently, residents from other surrounding Durban townships, for example, Umlazi, Kwa Mashu, and Lamontville also invaded houses in Wiggins (Gigaba and Maharaj 1996).

The Wiggins invasion was linked to the era of political transition when the ruling National Party was at its lowest ebb. The timing of the Wiggins invasion was most appropriate. It was on the eve of elections, and there were three very favourable conditions for the invasion.

- The country was on the threshold of democracy, and the ruling regime did not possess the moral and political authority to address the invasion decisively;
- Since it was on the eve of the election, no party wanted to risk votes by taking sides. All the main political parties failed to respond decisively to the crisis;
- The invaders knew that the moral and political authority of the state was waning, and they took advantage of the situation. (Gigaba and Maharaj 1996)

RECONSTRUCTION, DEVELOPMENT AND PLANNING

It is evident from the preceding sections that Cato Manor has been the subject of social and political contestation since at least the 1940s, and in many respects it has been a political football. There were at least thirty-one organisations, including six political parties, four statutory local authorities, and numerous community and non-government organisations with an interest in the development of Cato Manor.

In 1990 the changing political ambience, as well as concerns about racially exclusive plans for the area, led to intensive negotiations about the future development of Cato Manor among the different interest groups (Cato Manor Development Association 1994). These negotiations led to the establishment of the Cato Manor Development Forum (CMDF). The main purpose of the Forum was to 'guide and advise on the development of the area' (Robinson and Smit 1994: 1). Cato Manor comprised about 2,000 hectares of prime, undeveloped land, of which 850 hectares could be developed. It was possible to provide housing for about 30,000 to 40,000 low-income households or about 200,000 people in the area (Centre for Community and Labour Studies [CCLS] 1992). The community, civic, political and private sector organisations represented on the Forum agreed that Cato Manor should be developed as a non-racial residential area. This was viewed as an example of how Durban could lead the way in physical planning and negotiating the new South Africa on a non-racial basis (*Sunday Tribune* 1992).

In July 1992 the Forum adopted a vision statement in terms of which Cato Manor would provide affordable housing and jobs for low-income people in the inner city. The statement recognised the symbolic importance of Cato Manor and the sensitivity surrounding its development. The development of Cato Manor would contribute towards urban reconstruction and represented a significant deviation from apartheid planning. The emphasis was on holistic planning and development, and the evolution of a sustainable urban environment (Centre for Community and Labour Studies 1992: 4).

In March 1993 the CMDF 'transformed itself into the Cato Manor Development Association (CMDA), a Section 21 Company' which was commissioned with the task of realising the vision charted out by the Forum (Cato Manor Development Association 1994: 1). The CMDA plan for Cato Manor involved the creation of jobs, business opportunities and housing:

> The plan involves developing Cato Manor into a high-density 'city within a city' with residential areas interspersed with commercial, business and light industrial sectors as well as health facilities, schools, recreation centres and parks. It is envisaged that over the next ten years, housing for up to 200 000 people will be built ranging in size and price and available to all people, creating a vibrant cosmopolitan community near to the heart of the city. (*Daily News* 1994b)

In November 1994 Cato Manor was designated as a Special Presidential Project in the Urban Renewal category of the Reconstruction and Development Programme (RDP). This meant it would enjoy priority in terms of RDP funds. Also, Cato Manor would receive preference 'in the budgeting activities of line function departments at all relevant levels of government' (Cato Manor Development Association 1994: 6). According to the CMDA (1995: 3), Cato Manor offered remarkable reconstruction and development prospects, which included the opportunity to restructure the apartheid configuration of Durban by offering low-income housing close to the city centre; allowing low-income families to live close to economic opportunities in the metropolitan region; creating a new sustainable environment; and perhaps most importantly, a chance to promote non-racial housing development which would reflect the reconciliation and non-racialism of the new South Africa (Cato Manor Development Association 1994: 1).

In spite of these opportunities, the CMDA encountered numerous problems as it attempted to implement its plans for reconstruction and development in the area:

- tensions between Indian and African residents as a result of the Wiggins invasions;
- the continued unauthorised invasion of land delayed development initiatives;
- land claims from those who were dispossessed as a result of the Group Areas Act;
- political conflict and rivalry in the region delayed the CMDA's access to RDP funds;
- legal problems relating to the different local authorities who owned different parts of Cato Manor. (Cato Manor Development Association 1994)

These problems have seriously delayed the implementation of development projects in Cato Manor. While the CMDA produced some interesting plans for the development of Cato Manor, there was little tangible progress in implementation. There was also concern that the CMDA development proposals did not 'reflect the concrete realities of settlement and settlement dynamics in the area' (Hindson and Makhathini 1994: 17). It has been suggested that Cato Manor is a 'major political issue, long beyond the capabilities of local planners and groups like the CMDA to control. It will not be easy to solve' (Edwards 1994: 424).

In August 1993, Peter Mansfield, chairperson of the Management Committee of the DCC, warned ominously that unless there was rapid development in Cato Manor 'the dream of a well planned, well located development ... will be replaced by a nightmare of massive unplanned squatting and a lot of conflict' (*Natal Mercury* 1993: 6). In January 1994 a Durban City Councillor, Peter Corbett, cautioned that the future of Cato Manor was precariously poised between orderly development and uncontrolled informal settlements (*Daily News* 1994a). Hence, it would appear the CMDA was walking on a tightrope:

> The scales of success are finely balanced, with risk of failure ever present ... On the one hand, slow progress (or extraneous factors) could result in an invasion of the entire area resulting in a sprawling shackland. On the other hand, the 'easy' route would be to hand over to large scale developers who could construct fairly low density housing rapidly, but most of it would not be affordable by the low income majority of the metropolitan population. Either of these outcomes would, indeed, be a legacy of the past. The reconstruction route is being actively pursued, but at this stage it is too early to reach any conclusion on its success. (Robinson 1994: 14)

At the present conjuncture, it is too early to assess the extent to which the CMDA's projects in the Cato Manor have been successful. Time will tell.

CONCLUSION

Specific localities are often symbolic representations of conflicts in the wider society. Cato Manor similarly reflected at the micro-level the political and economic conflicts which were evident in the broader society. This chapter has examined the development of the Cato Manor settlement against the background of its wider political and economic contexts, and has highlighted the nature of the interaction between local micro-level processes and macro-level political forces, and their influence on the changing fortunes of Cato Manor.

An historical analysis of the development of Cato Manor reveals that settlement in the area has always been turbulent and contested and that it has basically been a political football. In the 1940s there was conflict between Indian landowners and African squatters. The landowners and squatters unsuccessfully opposed the strategies of the local state and central government to relocate them in sterile environments on the urban periphery. By the late 1960s Cato Manor was a vast wasteland.

In 1979 Cato Manor was re-zoned for Indian ownership and occupation in order to give legitimacy to the SAIC. Intervention by the CMRA (Cato Major Residents' Association) ensured that development in Cato Manor would cater for low income families. Squatters began to invade the area since the late 1980s to escape the political strife in the townships in the Durban metropolitan region. The CMDA was established to plan for urban reconstruction and development in the area. Given its strategic location and size, Cato Manor offered a unique opportunity to address the legacy of urban apartheid, and possibly a model for the rest of the country to follow.

Urban reconstruction and development planning in Cato Manor, however, has been impeded by escalating land invasions, political conflict and rivalry, racial tensions and land claims from those who were dispossessed by the Group Areas Act. There have been dire warnings that the future of Cato Manor is perilously poised between orderly and planned development and the rapid expansion of uncontrolled informal settlements. Hence, Cato Manor remains today, as it was in the 1940s, a politically contested terrain.

10   Leslie Bank[1]

'DUNCAN'S INFERNO': FIRE DISASTER, SOCIAL DISLOCATION AND SETTLEMENT PATTERNS IN A SOUTH AFRICAN TOWNSHIP

In the mid-1990s, increasing numbers of residential fires were reported in informal settlements in metropolitan centres throughout South Africa. In the Western Cape, the high-density shack settlement of Maconi Beam was burnt to the ground twice in the first few months of 1996, leaving a dozen shack dwellers dead and thousands more homeless. These disasters were almost immediately followed by another runaway shack fire in the Glendene squatter camp which left over 1,500 people homeless. In Gauteng, several smaller residential fires have been reported in the high-density shack areas such as Phola Park and Alexandra. In July 1996, one of the largest shack fires ever reported in South Africa occurred in Duncan Village, East London. This fire, started by a paraffin flame stove in a densely settled shack area, destroyed over 1,000 homes in a single afternoon (SABC TV News 1996).

The increasing frequency and severity of shack fires in metropolitan areas has raised a number of vexing questions about contemporary urbanisation trends and settlement patterns in South African cities, as well as about fuel-use practices in low-income urban neighbourhoods. Analysts are asking whether the current wave of urban disasters might not better be described as structural disasters, linked to social and economic forces, than as natural disasters. Fires, in particular, have raised public consciousness about the dangers of unplanned informal settlements, the high levels of dependence on paraffin as the primary domestic fuel among the urban poor, and about the types of appliances and fuel-safety standards applied in these areas. What is the responsibility of the state in ensuring that the urban poor have access to safe, affordable shelter and domestic energy sources which will not threaten lives and possessions? How can local-level fuel-use practices be modified to minimise the potential for fire disasters in shack areas? And, most importantly, what are the consequences of repeated residential fires on the social fabric of urban communities?

This chapter is primarily concerned with the last of these questions. It seeks to document the long-term consequences of repeated fire disasters in

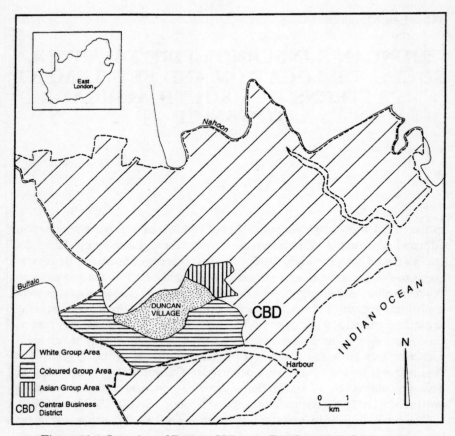

Figure 10.1 Location of Duncan Village in East London's Group Areas

a single urban community. The case selected for investigation is Duncan Village in East London (see Figure 10.1) which has experienced over 400 residential fires since 1986. These fires have collectively destroyed over 4,500 homes. In other words, a fire breaks out, on average, once every ten days and approximately one home has been destroyed every day for the past ten years. These staggering statistics point to the gravity of fire as a social problem in this township. In this chapter, we explore the phenomenon of fire disasters in Duncan Village and relate them to local living conditions, fuel-use practices and changing urbanisation patterns in the city. We also analyse the social, economic and psychological consequences of these fires on the lives of ordinary township residents. What does fire mean for ordinary people in Duncan Village? How is it experienced and understood? What impact does it have on the vectors of social power and the dynamics of urban social relationships at the local level? By addressing these questions, we aim, firstly, to deepen public knowledge and understanding of the problem of residential fires in high-density, low-income urban areas and, secondly, to present urban policy makers with a glimpse of the long-term consequences of unmanaged urbanisation and unsafe fuel-use practices in over-crowded metropolitan areas.

THE ANATOMY OF FIRE

Duncan Village is a highly congested and impoverished township with over 100,000 residents situated within a few kilometres of the East London city centre. It is the only African township in the city with easy access to the city centre. This has made Duncan Village a target of intense and continuous population influx. It is estimated that between 30,000 and 50,000 new residents have set up home in the township since 1986 (Bank 1996). This influx has been tolerated and managed by the Duncan Village Resident's Association (DVRA), a civic body which seized control of the township from the former Gompo Town Council in 1986. One of the explicit aims of DVRA has been to reverse apartheid urbanisation planning in the city, which since the 1960s had been responsible for forcibly displacing between 60,000 and 80,000 Duncan Village residents from the city to the Ciskei dormitory township of Mdantsane, some 40 kilometres away (Reintges 1992).

From the outset, DVRA argued that the long history of forced removals made it impossible for them to deny Africans access to land in the township. The civic organisation claimed that it would have failed in its duty to the 'oppressed people of the Eastern Cape' if it had not created opportunities for settlement near the economic hub of the city. As a result, DVRA permitted 18,000 new shacks to be erected in Duncan Village between 1986 and 1996 without any new land being added to the township. This meant that population densities sky-rocketed, reaching over 3,000 people per hectare in some areas by 1995. This process was heavily criticised by the

East London municipality who urged the civic body to halt further urbanisation until such time as an orderly urbanisation strategy had been devised for the township (Nel 1990; Reintges 1992). Suspicion and mistrust between the DVRA and the white-dominated municipality, however, ran too deep for any political agreement to be reached before the 1994 elections.

One of the consequences of this was that it delayed infrastructural development in the township. Between 1962 and 1983, very little investment was made in Duncan Village because it was official policy that the entire township would be demolished (cf. Bank 1996; Nel 1990). When this policy was finally rejected by the municipality in 1983, and the forced removals were stopped, new political struggles broke out between DVRA and the African (i.e. black) local authority, the Gompo Town Council. The political violence associated with DVRA's rise to power culminated in the Duncan Village uprising of August 1995. This took a heavy toll on the township infrastructure as electrical installations, schools and government offices were destroyed or damaged. Most of these installations have still to be repaired. After forty years of systematic neglect, it is not surprising that three-quarters of the population live in wood-and-iron shacks with no access to on-site water, sanitation or electricity.

The combination of exceptionally high residential densities, the use of highly flammable materials in shack construction and the virtually total dependence on paraffin as a domestic fuel has made Duncan Village extremely susceptible to fire disasters. Prior to 1986, there were never more than ten residential fires in a given year. After 1986, the number of fires per annum rose steadily from twenty-four in 1986 to forty-seven in 1995, with an average of thirty-six fires a year over that period. The East London Fire Department records reveal that 57 per cent of these fires occurred in one section of the township, Duncan Village Proper. Only 43 per cent of fires occurred in the other two residential zones, C-Section and Duncan Village Extension. A breakdown of the distribution of fires by area is shown in Table 10.1.

The table shows an uneven, but steady escalation in the number of residential fires over the decade. This escalation has been accompanied by increasing residential densities. As a result, individual fires have also become more destructive over time. This is demonstrated in Table 10.2 below, which measures the number of housing units destroyed by fire per year since 1986. Between 1991 and 1995, 1,776 houses were destroyed in 191 fires at a rate of 9.2 homes per fire, whereas only 565 homes were destroyed in 168 fires at a rate of 3.3 homes per fire in the previous five years. To use a more specific case, in 1995, forty-seven fires claimed 416 homes, while approximately the same number of fires (45) claimed only 119 homes in 1988. Due to the increased population densities, residential fires in Duncan Village have become three times more destructive in the 1990s than they were in the 1980s.

Table 10.1 Distribution of fires by residential area in Duncan Village, 1986–1995

Year	DV proper	C–section	DV extension	Total
1995	29	4	14	47
1994	25	4	8	37
1993	19	3	10	32
1992	24	5	9	38
1991	19	6	9	34
1990	21	2	14	37
1989	21	6	16	43
1988	27	10	8	45
1987	13	8	6	27
1986	10	7	7	24
Total	208	55	101	364

The source for information in Tables 10.1 to 10.3 is the East London Fire Department, Fire Reports, 1986–1995

Table 10.2 Total number of dwellings destroyed by fire, by year, 1986–1995

Year	Number of dwelling units destroyed by fire					Total Fires	Total Units
	1–3	4–6	7–10	11–50	50+		
1995	35	4		5	3	47	416
1994	23	6	4	3	2	38	294
1993	23		2	6	1	32	290
1992	22	8	3	4	2	39	526
1991	22	2	3	7	1	35	250
1990	20	6	5	3		34	190
1989	34	7	2			43	98
1988	35	7	2	1		45	119
1987	18	5	1	1		25	115
1986	17	1	2	1		21	43
Total	249	46	24	31	9	359	2341

Table 10.3 Causes of fire by fuel-use activity in Duncan Village, 1986–1995

Year	Lighting	Cooking	Open fire	Malicious	Unknown	Total
1995	19	10	1	2	15	47
1994	19	4	1	2	11	37
1993	18	3	2	2	6	31
1992	21	9	2		5	37
1991	24	4	1	1	3	33
1990	19	2	6		9	36
1989	29	9	2	1	3	44
1988	19	10	5	3	2	39
1987	15	10	1	1	1	28
1986	8	3		8	3	22
Total	191	64	21	20	58	354

In addition to these linear progressions, the fire statistics also revealed distinctive cyclical patterns. Residential fires, for instance, have followed a predictable seasonal pattern. The figures reveal that 42 per cent of the fires occurred in the winter months (May to August), while only 24 per cent were recorded in the summer months (November to February). The greater use of domestic fuels, especially for heating, during the colder winter months is the major reason for this variation. It should, however, be noted that a large number of fires (34 per cent) broke out 'between seasons' (East London Fire Department Records). This appears to be associated with the high wind speeds experienced in the city, especially in August. Significantly, the most fire prone shack areas in Duncan Village are situated on an unprotected hillside which is exposed to these powerful northwesterly winds.

An assessment of the timing of fires also reveals that, contrary to expectations, relatively few fires occurred at meal times. The majority of fires occurred at night when people were asleep; 57 per cent or 205 of the 360 fires occurred between 8 p.m. and 4 a.m. During the day, fires were less frequent and usually broke out when a paraffin appliance was left unattended. We also found that high levels of alcohol abuse was another factor which contributed to the timing of fires. When men had been out drinking at night, they would often arrive home drunk and hungry. In their haste to prepare a meal, they would use paraffin appliances carelessly or would fall asleep next to a flame stove or candle. Table 10.3 provides a detailed breakdown of the fuel-use activities associated with fire.

This table convincingly demonstrates that the majority of fires in Duncan Village were caused in the course of people going about their daily domestic activities; cooking, lighting and heating their homes. The heavy reliance on cheap, unsafe paraffin appliances in shack areas is one of the major causes of fire. With unemployment rates in many shack areas exceeding 40 per cent of the adult population (Bank 1996: 19), household heads are always keen to economise. This has led to the purchase of cheap, unsafe appliances. The reliance on technically inferior flame stoves, for instance, contributes to the high incidence of fire. Another problem is the use of *ufinya-futhi* (naked paraffin lights) and candles for lighting in shack areas. Both options are much cheaper than the standard gas or paraffin lamps on the market, but neither has a glass cover to protect the naked flame. This makes them extremely dangerous to use. DVRA has tried to reduce the use of these devices by banning candles in many shack areas. However, very few people in Duncan Village Proper follow DVRA's directives.

THE FEAR OF FIRE

Phumeza Nono is a domestic worker in East London who lives on Sandile Street in Duncan Village. She arrived in East London from the rural location of Mooiplaas in 1987 and, after working for a period as a live-in domestic in the white suburbs, she purchased a backyard shack in Dunga Street. Phumeza's first experience of fire occurred in 1989 when she lost her shack and all her possessions when a paraffin pressure stove burst in a neighbour's house and burnt out thirty-five shacks. The fire left Phumeza destitute and she was forced to return to the white suburbs as a live-in domestic. By 1990, she had saved enough money to purchase a second shack in Duncan Village – this time on Sandile Street where she felt her small family would be safe. However, in June 1993, fire once again ripped through her neighbourhood and destroyed her home. For a second time, Phumeza had lost all her possessions. On this occasion she was fortunate because welfare assistance was forthcoming and she was soon able to rebuild her shack.

For two years, Phumeza Nono was spared the tragedy of fire, but then suddenly in October 1995 a massive fire broke out again on Sandile Street. When we arrived on the scene, she was sitting on a wooden bench staring at her charred home. She was crying. She explained that she had been woken at about 3.00 a.m. by the familiar acrid smell of smoke and had immediately sprung to her feet, grabbed her one-year old daughter and fled. She said that the intensity of the heat was so great that she did not even think of trying to salvage any possessions, and that she had assumed that her other children had already left the shack. However, when she emerged from the dense smoke, she realised that her other two children were still trapped in the blaze. Instinctively, she had rushed back into the fire, amidst cries from onlookers that she would be burnt to death if she went back in. A few minutes later she emerged with the remaining members of her family in tow. She had saved her children, but lost her home. Phumeza Nono explained that she was not crying about her lost possessions. Her tears, she said, were for the children that she had so nearly lost. In despair, she proclaimed: '*siyatsha yile parafini sihlala kuyo*' (we burn in this paraffin in which we live).

The human tragedy of fire, as the above case shows, is clearly immense. Fire tends to pick on the poorest of the urban poor. It destroys their homes and claims their possessions. These people are seldom left with more than the clothes on their backs and the money in their pockets. Many fire victims have no way of replacing what they have lost. They are thus totally dependent on welfare organisations for support and survival after fires. In some cases, such as the Dunga Street fire of 1989 referred to by Phumeza, where such support was not forthcoming, those who did not have savings to rebuild their shacks were forced either to find shelter with relatives and friends, or to leave the area. In Duncan Village we were struck by the number of people who, like Phumeza, had been victims of more than one fire. One informant explained at a fire site in 1996:

> This is the third time that I have experienced fire here and again all my belongings have been burnt out. It seems to be me that this fire is hungry for my soul; it claims my salary and eats up my possessions.

The European cultural historian, Simon Schama, argued in his book *The Embarrassment of Riches* that Dutch social, political and cultural life during the Golden Age was dominated by an overwhelming fear of flooding. The titanic struggle during the seventeenth century to keep the sea from erasing their coastal villages and farmlands had been a major preoccupation of Dutch life. In fact, Schama suggests that so pervasive was this fear of flooding that it became a central metaphor for the construction of Dutch identity. For the Dutch, the struggle against flooding was perceived to be part of their divine calling as the 'chosen people' and their ability to endure floods became central to their notions of freedom and survival. Like Noah, they came to believe that they had been called on by God Almighty to overcome the calamity of flood. To achieve this objective, they felt that it was imperative to be disciplined, industrious and devoutly religious. The wild forces of nature, it was believed, could only be tamed through the trilogy of prayer, psalms and self-sacrifice (Schama 1991: 27).

Schama's fascinating account of the construction of Dutch identity during the Golden Age provides a compelling account of how physical hardship and environmental constraints provide far more than a material context for existence; they provide a set of social and cultural texts and symbols through which people construct images of themselves and others. For Schama, the most poignant image of the Dutch obsession with flooding was the so-called drowning cell at the Heiligeweg House of Correction in Amsterdam. This penal device, erected for the most dangerous felons in Dutch society, exposed criminals to the experience of flooding by incarcerating them in a waterproof cell which was slowly filled with water. The only route to survival was for the inmates to use their labour on a wooden treadmill to expel the incoming water. Schama (1991: 5) maintains that this penal device captured the central moral lesson of Dutch life: 'to be wet was to be captive, idle and poor, to be dry was to be free, industrious and comfortable'.

A similar equation might be applied to the impact of fire on the urban poor of Duncan Village. For these people, the trauma of fire went far beyond the ordeal of lost possessions and dragging frightened children from burning shacks. It hit at the very fabric of this urban society and at people's perceptions of themselves and of the city. Because fires were frequent, uncontrollable and random, people actually became conditioned to think of themselves as victims, caught up in powerful and destructive forces over which they had no control. Like many of the other mysterious aspects of the urban system, fire was too ubiquitous to be ignored – it had to be explained to address people's fear and alleviate their sense of powerlessness. In Duncan Village, such explanations have taken various forms, but the most immediate metaphor used for the understanding of fire and its destructive potential is that of witchcraft. This is not surprising given that the use of fire has long been implicated in Xhosa witch beliefs. Fire (*umlilo*), used in the form of *uvutha*, is one of the malevolent forces used by witches to perpetrate their evil deeds. To suspect witchcraft where fire is involved does not demand a great leap in the imagination in Duncan Village (Mayer and Mayer 1961; Wilson 1951).

Moreover, the appearance of fire carried with it all the hallmarks of witchcraft activity. Fires, it was said, were like witches. They struck in the small hours of the morning when people were least prepared to deal with them. They tore through entire neighbourhoods with the speed of lightning and caused havoc and mayhem in their paths. They always arrived unannounced and disappeared unexplained. Moreover, the devastation wrought by fire, like the action of witches, seldom only affected the lives of one person. Fire challenged people's perceptions of social and community life as orderly and stable. Like witches, it appeared to embody a selfish and gluttonous desire to destroy the lives of others. Fire offered no ordinary threat to this beleaguered community. To use Monica Wilson's phrase, it represented 'the standardised nightmare of the group' (1951: 313). It is not thus surprising that people so often dealt with fire within the idiom of witchcraft by refusing to focus on the structural conditions of life in the slum which caused their misfortune, but rather attributing its arrival to individual causation. In Duncan Village, it was often assumed that fire was driven by malice and that, if there was evidence to suspect direct nefarious intent, those who started fires should be pursued as if they were witches.

The most famous witchcraft case in the recent history of this township occurred in 1986, when a leading political activist died in a motor accident on the same day that a residential fire destroyed his shack in the township. The two events were quickly connected in local interpretations that started to circulate in the neighbourhood. A version of the incident soon became widely accepted in the township as a whole, in which it was believed that the sister of the activist had conspired with two other women to bewitch her brother. In the week that followed, a people's court was arranged for the women to stand trial. The court hearings were held in public and attended by thousands of people. According to eye witnesses, these women first denied that they had anything to do with the fire, but as public pressure mounted on them to admit their culpability, they capitulated, and were summarily burnt to death in one of Duncan Village's most famous 'necklace' cases.

The dramatic fate of the three women was determined largely by the coincidence of two connected disasters on a single day. It seemed incomprehensible to local people that these incidents were not connected. They demanded that they be explained and that proper retribution be exacted for the threat these deeds presented to the integrity of community life and to the political struggle of the people of Duncan Village. In the decade of fire between 1986 and 1995, countless others have been accused of causing fire and of maliciously destroying property through selfish and anti-social behaviour. In the vast majority of these cases, people have not been necklaced or even pursued as witches. But the fact remains that the idiom of witchcraft has been an enduring metaphor through which people explain and deal with the consequences of fire on their lives. This was powerfully brought home to us on Sandile Street on 3 July 1995. The press report of the incident we witnessed read as follows:

> Armed police prevented an enraged crowd from meting out mob justice to a sixteen year old girl who allegedly caused a fire which left 200 people homeless in Duncan Village yesterday ... While the fire was raging residents caught and bound the alleged culprit whom they claimed has started a fire twice before and shouted that they wanted to hold a people's court, police said.
>
> Police Internal Instability Division members who were on the scene to assist firemen fired rubber bullets to disperse hundreds of angry residents and rescued the girl. The mob who were wielding sticks and throwing stones again tried to attack the girl as police escorted her to an armoured vehicle with her arms held behind her back and bundled her inside. She was guarded by police clad in bullet proof vests and holding tear gas canisters at the ready. (*Daily Dispatch* 1995)

As the police escorted the girl away, we watched as the crowd bayed '*makatshiswe, makatshiswe*' ('let her burn, let her burn'). There was no doubt that they meant what they said. Had the police not arrived on the scene, this girl would have been burnt by the mob. So intense was the fear of fire that those who caused it, like the inmates of the horrific *Heiligeweg* House of Correction in Amsterdam, were made to endure it. In Duncan Village, those accused of causing fires for selfish reasons were not taken through the slow and arduous process of the state legal system and penal institutions, but were exposed to the full wrath of popular justice on the street.

One of the interesting aspects of the pattern of witchcraft accusations in cases of fire is that they were often directed at women, especially single women, and other social marginals, such as epileptics or mentally retarded people. This distinct pattern of implicating women in witchcraft accusations is, of course, not unique to Duncan Village. Recent research throughout Africa (cf. Auslander 1993; Bastian 1993; Schmoll 1993), shows that this is the trend across the continent, especially in urban areas. Men in Duncan Village caused fires, especially when they were drunk or fighting with their wives, but they were seldom exposed to the wrath of stick-wielding mobs baying for their blood. Our evidence suggests that where men did cause fires, local interpretation of their actions tended to, at best, blame them for 'carelessness' or attribute their actions to the resolutions of inter-personal politics. Thus, when a middle-aged man started a fire on Florence Street during October 1995, it was suggested that the fire might have been caused by the man's involvement in the ongoing taxi feuds in the township. The explanation of the fire consequently became submerged in a well-known discourse about male business politics.

At worst, however, men were accused of using sorcery in domestic quarrels or in altercations with their lovers to start fires. In such cases, men were blamed for consciously manipulating medicines to harm other people, but these actions were not generally seen as morally depraved or aimed at undermining the integrity of the entire neighbourhood or community. Township women, on the other hand, it seems, were believed to have a natural propensity for evil. In considering the gender politics of witchcraft accusations in Duncan Village, it must be remembered that the popular justice system in this township was dominated by men. People's courts were open to every man and woman in the neighbourhood over eighteen years old, but the sentences administered by these courts were decided upon and passed down by men. This is why women have found it so difficult to press charges of domestic violence against men and why many of them are suspicious of the popular justice system in Duncan Village.

In reflecting on the widespread implication of women in witchcraft activities in Africa more generally, the Comaroffs (1993) suggest that the targeting of women as witches may have a great deal to do with the increasingly ambivalent position of women in contemporary African societies, especially in the urban areas, where they have acquired new roles as accumulators of wealth, bearers of independence, and enemies of custom. The Comaroffs argue that, just because women now bear the brunt of witchcraft accusation in Africa, we should not think that this has always been the case. Ritual, they argue, is not only about affirming past practices; it is also about enforcing new regimes of power. This kind of analysis has direct bearing on the Duncan Village situation where, during the decade of fire, women have poured into the township in unprecedented numbers, have made considerable headway in the urban job market, and have come to dominate the township informal sector completely. In short, in no other period in the history of Duncan Village have women threatened the patriarchal power and economic networks of men more directly than they do today.

The fear of fire in Duncan Village is a generalised fear, yet it is also a particularly feminised fear. This is not only because women are socially and demographically dominant within shack neighbourhoods where most fires occur, but also because they are so often viciously hunted down to take responsibility for the havoc it wreaks. The saying, 'we burn in this paraffin in which we live' clearly carried particular meaning for women. It ensured that women were considerably more vigilant in their use of fuel and in their concern for safety than men. Local rituals of witchcraft accusation and the fear that they provoked served to discipline women. The selection of younger women who were mainly new arrivals in the city for special treatment seems to suggest that the gender dimension of these accusations were overlaid by an 'insider/outsider' dynamic. In Duncan Village, the older migrants and long-standing townsfolk tended to live in formal houses or in backyard shacks. The new arrivals and the younger households dominated in the fire-prone shack areas (see below). These people were less well known and therefore more vulnerable to accusations of social deviance. Fire and the ritualised forms of punishment that sometimes accompanied it acted as powerful reminders to women of the dangers of challenging male domination, on the one hand, and helped to warn new arrivals against undisciplined behaviour, on the other.

FIRE, PATRONAGE AND COMMUNITY CONFLICT

When the DVRA took control of Duncan Village in 1986, they immediately set out to challenge the old influx-control laws by opening up new areas in the township for settlement. The aim of the DVRA was to try to accommodate larger numbers of Africans in the township without allowing the urbanisation process to become disorderly and uncontrolled. To achieve this, DVRA insisted that new arrivals be registered with the civic body before being allocated a site. Only site applicants who genuinely required accommodation in the city and could show (via a letter from the civic body in their places of origin) that they were 'good citizens' were supposed to be considered. In theory, the DVRA had devised a sound basis for managing urban influx. In practice, the system was less easy to implement. One of the major problems was that residential fires frustrated DVRA's planning efforts, undermined their ability to control the local population, and often ignited deep community divisions. Some of these problems are highlighted in the case of Area 7, a fire-prone, unplanned informal settlement in Duncan Village Proper.

In 1992, this shack area was a strip of vacant land, occasionally used for the planting and harvesting of maize. The land was not occupied because DVRA believed that the gradient was too steep for safe settlement. This changed in June 1992, when a massive fire broke out in Gwijana Street and destroyed over 400 backyard and free-standing shacks. The fire, which left 1,500 to 2,000 people homeless (*Daily Dispatch* 23 June 1992), was one of the largest ever to hit Duncan Village and attracted widespread publicity. On the same weekend as this fire disaster, the DVRA executive were away at the funeral of an MK(*Mkhonto we Sizwe*)-cadre in the Cambridge township. As a result they were not available to manage the fire victims. This angered the homeless who decided among themselves to settle illegally on unoccupied maize gardens. A deal was struck with the gardeners in the area, who agreed that the fire victims could use the land.

On Monday morning, the DVRA ordered the fire victims to move. They refused and petitioned local East London ANC and ANC-Youth League structures for support. The powerful city ANC branch was sympathetic to their request and urged them to continue building their shacks. The DVRA responded to the ANC initiative by denying all fire victims in the new area access to welfare assistance. The divisions between the DVRA executive and the ANC-supporting residents deepened in 1993 when DVRA excluded people from the new area from access to a massive food relief scheme organised by foreign aid donors in Duncan Village as a whole. In response, local residents strengthened their alliance with the local ANC branch, which managed to pressurise the discredited Gompo Town Council to install taps in the new shack area. The taps were installed, but the project was never completed, allegedly because DVRA intervened to stop it. In August 1995, when several shacks burnt down in the area, the fire victims again received no welfare assistance from DVRA. By 1996, DVRA's persistent pressure was beginning to pay off. Many now said that they feared that, if they did not resolve their tensions with the DVRA executive soon, they would be excluded from the benefits of the R140 million presidential RDP (Reconstruction and Development Programme, now the Growth, Employment and Redistribution Programme) project in the township.

In Duncan Village Proper, fires also proved to be extremely divisive in individual neighbourhoods. The fires that initiated the most conflict were those which received sizeable amounts of welfare assistance. The Sandile Street fire of July 1995 provides a good example. After this fire, truck loads of food, clothing and building materials were brought to the fire site. According to the local press:

> about eight truck loads of timber had been received from Mercedes Benz South Africa, while more timber, doors and window frames worth about R15,000 had come from D&A Timbers. (*Daily Dispatch* 4 July 1995)

The arrival of these materials caused conflict. On the one hand, allegations were made that the donations were not reaching fire victims and were being siphoned off by local DVRA representatives. On the other hand, those who had not been affected by the fire became envious of the amount of assistance given to the victims. Many were asking questions like: 'Why had so much arrived for so few?' or 'Why did we not receive the same treatment when our houses burnt down?'

To compound matters, a decision was taken by DVRA to create spaces of 1.5 metres between all shacks in the area. This meant that a third of those who had lost their homes would not be able to build in the same area. However, many realised that, if they did not build immediately, they could loose out on the donated materials at the site. The question soon became: who would be entitled to build and who not? This generated fierce debate, even physical fights, among the residents. Some argued that mature adults should be given first choice to build because they were 'not careless with fire' and that young people 'living together' or children who lived in shacks without adult supervision should be asked to move elsewhere. On the other hand, there were those who argued that many of the older people should leave the area because they were approaching retirement age. As the debate raged, the internal divisions grew and, when no consensus was reached, everyone – young and old, men and women – began rebuilding their shacks exactly where they wanted. DVRA's attempt to replan the area had failed, as it did at most of the other fire sites we visited during 1995.

DOMESTICITY AND URBAN INSECURITY

While fire has had a profound impact on community and neighbourly relations, it has also left an indelible imprint on domestic groups. Social research in Duncan Village in the 1950s revealed that multi-generational households were the norm in the township, especially in the old wood-and-iron shack sections of the location (cf. Mayer and Mayer 1961; Pauw 1963). The dominant trend in the 1990s has been towards much smaller households. The reasons for the changes in domestic group composition are highly complex, but fire has played a decisive role in fragmenting and dispersing larger domestic units in Duncan Village Proper. Young adults have been particularly attuned to opportunities created by fire to break away from their parental homes. They have capitalised on the abundance of free building materials to carve out their 'own places', especially in the free-standing shack areas.

This dispersal of domestic groups across space did not, however, always imply that these groups disintegrated socially. Young adults who moved out of their parents homes did not always have jobs and often returned to their parental home for meals, recreation, or to borrow money, appliances and other items. Often they even continued to participate in household decision-making, despite being physically located in other areas. This meant that domestic life in Duncan Village was highly diffuse and that there were high levels of inter-household mobility. To be sure, we found that some parents were happy to part company with their children. As one mother explained:

> It is not good for my son to live here anymore. He is old enough to work now and must support himself. There is also the problem of privacy in these shack areas and it is better that he takes his girlfriends to his own place.

Household fission associated with fires, however, loosened social bonds within township families, increased generational conflict and undermined the ability of parents to exert control over their children. The fragmentation of domestic groups in Duncan Village Proper weakened families as economic units and exposed them to intense internal conflicts and divisions. However, this process also left a mark on the spatial configuration of the settlement as a whole. In the struggle for space that followed fire, established male household heads usually got first choice of the available space while new households and, especially, young or female-headed ones had to wait in line.

The disadvantages experienced by female-headed households were compounded by the gendered distribution of welfare aid. At all fire sites, building materials were distributed to men and food and blankets to women. Female household heads, who could not afford to purchase their own materials or did not have male kin to queue for them, tended to lose out. Young couples were also at a disadvantage because the principle of seniority was applied in the welfare queues. In spatial terms, this meant that the new shack areas created as a result of fires tended to be dominated by women and young unmarried couples.

The other consequence of fire on domestic organisation in Duncan Village was that it encouraged new arrivals in the city to maintain active connections with their ancestral homes in rural areas. In Duncan Village Proper, 26 per cent of all households heads have retained a house elsewhere: 14 per cent of these have municipal houses, 46 per cent have free-standing shacks prone to fire, while the rest keep homes in the country. The retention of a second home and, in some cases, even the acquisition of a country home in the former Ciskei or Transkei among urban-born residents, was at least partially a product of the insecurities wrought by fire (Bank 1996: 31–4). Even more common in Duncan Village was the practice of sending children out of the city to be socialised with close kin in the countryside. Over 50 per cent of households in Duncan Village Proper have children living outside of the city (Bank 1996: 34). Many women who discussed this practice highlighted their desire to protect their children from the threat of fire.

CONCLUSION

The case material presented here leads us to a number of conclusions about the social impact of residential fire in this urban setting. Firstly, we have seen how incidents of fire derailed the plans of DVRA to control urban growth and shack development. At most fire sites, DVRA tried to impose some restrictions on the rebuilding of shacks, but these directives were ignored with the result that more rather than fewer shacks were rebuilt. In Duncan Village, fires have clearly been one of the driving forces behind urban densification.

Secondly, we noted fires generated a culture of fear and fatalism. The horror of fire was so immense that the people of Duncan Village often turned on themselves to purge the community of 'evil forces'. The use of witchcraft as an idiom to identify and deal with fire is symptomatic of acute social stress and strain engendered by these disasters. Since fire appeared as random, uncontrollable and constant in people's lives, it is not surprising that local people began to see themselves as victims, that they believed in their own powerlessness, and came to view the city as insecure, unstable and violent.

Thirdly, feelings of insecurity and anxiety were entrenched through a network of local-level social relations of dependency and patronage that emerged around fire. In the 1980s and 1990s, the DVRA jealously guarded its role as community gatekeeper. It set itself up as the only conduit through which outside agencies, like the Red Cross, could interact with local people. This gave DVRA officials enormous power to control and direct welfare aid. More importantly, it allowed DVRA to use fire relief as a means of rewarding loyal supporters and of punishing critics. This was seen in the case study of Area 7. We have seen that the conflicts that surrounded welfare assistance and other resources associated with fires, tend to undermine community solidarity and weaken people's capacity to deal with disaster.

Fourthly, at the level of domestic organisation, fires put enormous pressure on domestic groups to split and disperse. This enabled young adults and school-going teenagers to break away from their parents' home and set up their own shacks. This undermined family solidarity and encouraged inter-generational conflict in fire-prone areas. The social pressure created by fire has also been reflected in the internal shifting and sorting of domestic groups between shack areas. We observed that vulnerable domestic groups, such as female-headed households and young, unmarried couples, were often pushed out onto the fringes of the settlement. In the intense competition for space that always followed fires, only those with local-level social influence and power were guaranteed sites. This constant competition and infighting for space further eroded urban social fabric and encouraged social disintegration and inertia.

In Duncan Village, fire is clearly no mere epiphenomenon which delays real urban development and temporarily disrupts the normal functioning of urban social relations. It is an extremely powerful social force in its own right which has left an indelible mark on the social fabric of this urban community. In view of the analysis presented here, we would argue that it is essential that local stakeholders and government officials begin to recognise the social power of fire and acknowledge the long-term social and economic damage that can be done if it is allowed to take hold in densely settled, metropolitan shack areas. Urgent attention needs to be given to identifying high-risk areas and arriving at strategies that will contain shack densities and improve fuel safety.

NOTE

1. The author is grateful to the Department of Mineral and Energy Affairs (DMEA) for funding the research reflected in this article. The views presented here are, however, not necessarily those of the DMEA. The author would like to thank Bongani Mlomo, Phumeza Lujabe and Mandisi Jekwa for their assistance in gathering some of the material presented in this chapter.

THE IMPACT OF NATIONAL POLICY ON RURAL SETTLEMENT PATTERNS IN ZIMBABWE

Two broad sets of factors have influenced the evolution of rural settlement patterns in Zimbabwe during the past century (Zinyama 1988). The first lies in the political history of the country from the late nineteenth century when it was colonised from South Africa by European settlers led by the British South Africa Company. Land was subsequently divided between the majority black population and the minority white settlers. The blacks were assigned to the agriculturally more marginal areas with lower rainfall and light infertile sandy soils. The higher altitude land along the central water-shed of the country, enjoying cooler temperatures, more fertile soils and higher rainfall, was alienated for white settlement. The zone of white settle-ment subsequently evolved into the economic heartland of the country, with all the main urban centres and more developed economic infrastructure and services, while the black areas became an exploited labour reserve for the modern sector. Unlike the black reserves, now called the communal lands, the white areas were, and are, sparsely populated. Since attaining political independence in 1980, the black-majority government has sought to redress some of these inherited colonial imbalances in the distribution of land through the resettlement of black peasant farmers on former white-owned farmlands. Thus, both colonial and post-colonial government policies and legislation regulating land have influenced the evolution of settlement patterns in the rural areas of Zimbabwe.

The second, and related, factor that has influenced settlement patterns in rural Zimbabwe is the rapid growth of population during the past few decades, with a growth rate of over 3 per cent per year. But some areas of the country, especially the communal lands and, more recently following the removal of colonial influx-control measures, the urban areas, have carried much of the burden arising from rapid population increase more than the commercial farming areas. This uneven growth and distribution of popula-tion has resulted in considerable pressures on resources and environmental degradation in the affected rural areas, adding to the pressure on government

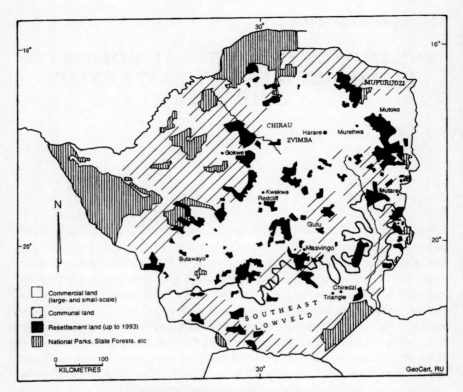

Figure 11.1 Zimbabwe: Major land divisions

for land redistribution and population resettlement on the one hand and fuelling rural-to-urban migration on the other. Growing population pressure and land shortages have also led to the expansion of settlement and cultivation into areas that were previously designated for grazing within the communal areas.

This chapter examines the origins and evolution of settlement patterns within the rural areas of Zimbabwe from the 1920s. It is shown that the colonial division of land on racial lines from the end of the nineteenth century produced several distinct systems of tenure that have persisted to this day. Different settlement patterns evolved within each of these tenure categories, reflecting the impact of state policies that were applied to each area to regulate rural land use and settlement. Although state policies may alter to meet changing circumstances or as a result of a change of government, settlement patterns tend to be more persistent over time, even in the face of increased population densities. The chapter begins by presenting the four agricultural (and underlying tenurial) sub-sectors. The next section discusses the historical division of rural land by the state from the end of the nineteenth century, the resulting settlement patterns within each tenure category, and the effect of population growth on settlement changes. The third section examines the impact of the post-independence programme of land redistribution on settlement patterns within the resettlement areas. The final part of the chapter discusses the development of rural service centres within the communal lands and the emergence of new urban-type settlements in areas where none had previously existed.

THE FOUR SUB-SECTORS IN RURAL ZIMBABWE

Rural Zimbabwe today comprises four agricultural sub-sectors that are divided on the basis of land tenure, resulting in distinct variations in settlement patterns, population densities, agricultural production, living standards and engagement in the wider national economy (see Figure 11.1). The first is the large-scale commercial farming sector which occupies some 11.2 million hectares, or about 28.7 per cent of the national land area of 39.07 million hectares. The sector comprises some 4,400 individual farming units held under freehold or leasehold tenure which range in size from smallholdings of less than 200 hectares to extensive ranches in excess of 10,000 hectares. Generally, farms are smaller in the vicinity of large urban centres and in the higher rainfall regions in the north and east of the country. The largest properties are found in the drier south and west where extensive livestock and game ranching are more viable land uses than crop cultivation. Until independence, the land was owned exclusively by whites. According to the results of the 1992 census, the large-scale commercial-farming areas had a population of 1.17 million people, or 11.3 per cent of the national population of 10.4 million.

The second is the small-scale commercial farming sector which comprises some 10,600 farming units held by blacks, under leasehold (from the state) or freehold tenure. These farms were originally established by the colonial government in the 1930s to compensate blacks for the loss of their right to acquire land in open competition with whites following the enactment of the Land Apportionment Act of 1930 (Floyd 1962). The farms are generally less than 100 hectares each, with larger units of up to 500 hectares in the drier western and southern parts of the country. The sector covers 1.4 million hectares, or 3.5 per cent of the total land area. At the 1992 census, there were 170,170 people, or 1.6 per cent of the national population, within the small-scale commercial farming sector.

The third is the communal farming sector which occupies some 16.4 million hectares (41.8 per cent of the country), largely under subsistence agriculture. It supported directly from agriculture 5.35 million people, or 51 per cent of the national population in 1992, in about one million households. When migrant workers who, for reasons of low and declining real wages and lack of long-term security in urban areas are compelled to maintain their rights to rural agricultural land are included, the communal lands are home to as much as 70 to 80 per cent of the national population (Potts and Mutambirwa 1990; Government of Zimbabwe 1994). The farmers have traditional freehold tenure which guarantees ownership rights to arable and residential land for the family. The average size of arable landholding per family is about 2 hectares. Households also have access to communal grazing land, forests and other resources.

The fourth sector, the resettlement land, is a post-1980 development, being the outcome of the government's attempts to redress the colonial inequities in the distribution of land between the races and to relieve some of the population pressure and land shortages within the communal areas (Zinyama 1986). By 1994, some 56,000 families had been resettled on 3.3 million hectares throughout the country under the land redistribution programme. A total of 426,690 people were recorded within the resettlement areas at the 1992 census. The question of tenure within the resettlement areas is only now being addressed following the recommendations of a commission appointed by the government in late 1993 to inquire into appropriate agricultural tenure systems for the country (Government of Zimbabwe 1994). To date, the settlers reside as tenants of the state under a set of three permits authorising them to reside, cultivate land and pasture livestock on the scheme. The settlers are subject to much closer supervision in their utilisation of land and the siting of settlements by government officials, notably land use planners, as well as resettlement officers and agricultural extension staff who are normally resident on each scheme.

STATE POLICIES AND RURAL SETTLEMENT PATTERNS

The apportionment of land, which started in 1891 with the establishment of the first two reserves for the defeated Ndebele people in the northwest of the country, was enshrined into law under the Land Apportionment Act of 1930 (Christopher 1971; Floyd 1962). It was replaced by the Land Tenure Act of 1969, which in turn was only repealed in 1978 shortly before independence. Under the Land Tenure Act, the country was divided equally between the blacks and whites (the latter including Asians and people of mixed race), each group allocated 46.6 per cent, while the remaining 6.8 per cent was designated national parks and forest lands. The notion of parity in the distribution of land espoused by the colonial government ignored the wide disparities in the quality of the land and the numbers of people each sector was required to support. Even at their largest in the early 1970s, whites never constituted more than 5 per cent of the total population. Much of the land that was allocated for blacks was situated in marginal areas where the light sandy soils derived from granitic parent rock are inherently infertile. and the rainfall is both inadequate and unreliable for crop cultivation (Roder 1964; Vincent and Thomas 1962). But the role of the state was not confined to the broad allocation of land between the different racial groups. A number of laws and policies pursued during the past seventy years has shaped the patterns of rural settlements within each of the major rural land categories.

In both large- and small-scale commercial farming areas, settlement patterns are determined in the main by the conditions of freehold or leasehold tenure, while the density or proximity of the farmsteads to each other depends on the size of the farm holdings in the area (see Figure 11.2). In addition, current regulations governing the subdivision of large-scale commercial farmland are too restrictive and outdated (Government of Zimbabwe 1994). This has inhibited even those farmers who would want to subdivide their holdings. This is quite anachronistic in a country with an acute racially defined land shortage and has perpetuated low population densities in these farming areas. In the large-scale farming sector, settlements are generally widely dispersed. On each farm are normally found spacious farmsteads and associated outbuildings as well as clusters of huts to accommodate the farm labourers. Although settlements in the small-scale commercial farming sector are also dispersed, densities are higher because of the smaller size of the farms. On each farm will generally be found the homestead of the farm-owner and the immediate family. Most farmers in this sector rely on family labour rather than on permanent paid labour, except during peak labour-demand periods when they may hire some temporary workers. Settlement patterns in the two sub-sectors have therefore tended to change little over time.

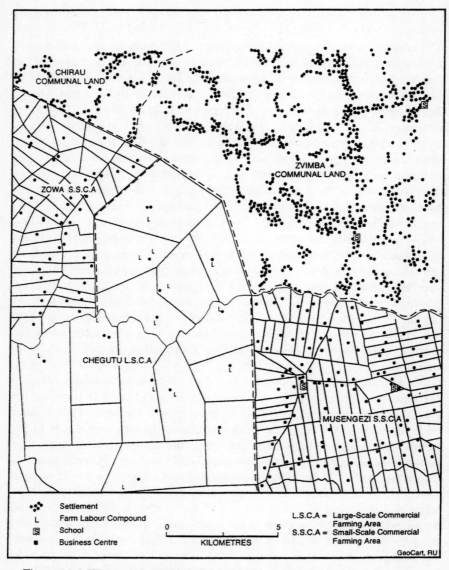

Figure 11.2 Three agricultural sub-sectors and associated settlement patterns
northwest of Harare

The population within the reserves increased from 1.99 million in 1962 (when the first full enumeration of blacks was conducted) to 2.91 million in 1969 and 4.28 million by 1982. During the 1950s and 1960s, increasing numbers and densities in some of the reserves were due to the relocation of black families being evicted from lands that had been alienated for white settlement. Some of these displaced people were resettled in the dry, tsetse-infested, and hitherto sparsely populated regions in the northwest of the country (Zinyama and Whitlow 1986).

The increasing population densities precipitated land degradation within the reserves. The looming environmental crisis did not go unnoticed by the colonial authorities. However, the official view was that land degradation was the result, not of growing land shortage and increasing population pressure within the reserves, but was due to backward and wasteful farming practices on the part of the inhabitants. In 1926, an American missionary-cum-agriculturist, D. E. Alvord, was appointed the first director of the newly created Department of Native Agriculture, a position he was to hold for twenty-three years until his retirement in 1949. More than any other person, Alvord's policies have remained imprinted in the settlement patterns of the reserves to this day. In 1929, he launched a programme to rationalise settlement and land uses within the reserves with the intention of putting a stop to the practice of shifting cultivation. The effect of the rationalisation programme, or 'centralisation' as it was officially known, was to replace the traditional dispersed and clustered village settlements with a uniform pattern of linear settlements that separated large consolidated blocks of arable and grazing lands on either side throughout the reserves in the country. The long lines of villages usually ran parallel to rivers and water-courses, with the arable lands above and the seasonally wet grazing areas below the homesteads. This way, crops would be better protected against stray livestock during the growing season (November–April); in the dry season, the animals are allowed to roam freely grazing on the crop residues in the croplands. The re-organisation of land uses, or centralisation, con-tinued for the next two decades and was ultimately embodied into law under the Natural Resources Act of 1941 and the Native Land Husbandry Act of 1951 (Beck 1960; Floyd 1959; Yudelman 1964). Among other things, the Native Land Husbandry Act proposed to change the system of land tenure from the traditional communal to Western-style private owner-ship, whereby land would become a market-exchangeable commodity, and to deny non-residents such as urban migrant workers access to land within the reserves. Implementation of the Act began in earnest in 1955, including the re-allocation of land only to eligible resident cultivators and the reor-ganisation of settlements. It was to continue into the early 1960s when the government was compelled to abandon the programme because of moun-ting political opposition from the burgeoning black nationalist movement.

In the years following the Unilateral Declaration of Independence (UDI) by the white minority government in 1965, attempts were made to further entrench racial separation, with traditional black leaders being assigned new powers to run their local areas (Bratton 1978; Mutizwa-Mangiza 1985). One such responsibility was the allocation of land in the reserves which was transferred from government-appointed district commissioners and agricultural extension staff to chiefs and local Tribal Land Authorities under the Tribal Trust Land Act of 1967. In practice, land allocation by the chiefs was not always based on sound ecological and conservation principles. Chiefs and members of the Tribal Land Authorities were also often accused of corruption and favouritism in the allocation of land for residential and cultivation purposes. On the other hand, a few traditional leaders, not wanting to be associated with the implementation of unpopular land policies by a repressive regime, made little attempt to prevent the encroachment of settlements into areas that had previously been designated grazing land due to mounting land shortage.

The mid-1960s were therefore a turning point in the state-guided evolution of settlement patterns within the reserves (Whitlow and Zinyama 1988; Zinyama 1988). The period marks the beginning of the partial disintegration of, and departure from, the strictly regulated and planned linear settlement pattern that had been implemented by Alvord since the late 1920s. Unauthorised cultivation and settlement became more widespread from the mid-1970s as the war for political independence intensified in the rural areas. Both the traditional leaders (some of whom were viewed as collaborators of the regime by the nationalist guerrillas) and the civil district administrators found it increasingly difficult to retain control over land use and settlement within the communal areas. Given the increasing population pressures on the land, a local administrative structure that was preoccupied with the anti-guerrilla campaign rather than with routine civil administration, and overworked and impoverished soils within the designated arable lands, many landless families chose to clear grazing areas for cultivation and settlement, thereby breaking away from the existing linear villages.

For a short time after independence in 1980, it was not clear who was responsible for land allocation within the reserves, now renamed communal lands. On the one hand were the largely discredited and ineffectual Tribal Land Authorities set up in terms of the Tribal Trust Land Act of 1967. On the other hand, there were the newly established popularly elected district councils set up under the District Councils Amendment Act of 1980. But the latter Act only prescribed that district councils would act as conservation committees and be responsible for natural resources conservation within their respective areas of jurisdiction. Legally, therefore, land allocation was still the responsibility of the Tribal Land Authorities. The Tribal Trust Land Act was finally repealed in 1982 following the enactment of the

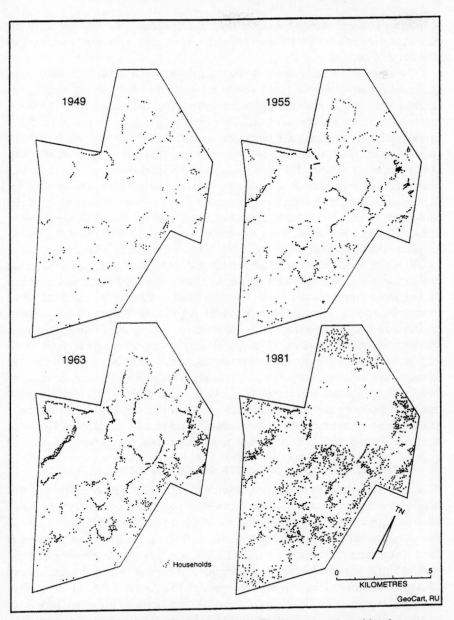

Figure 11.3 Changes in settlement patterns in Zimunya communal land, eastern Zimbabwe, 1949–1981

Communal Land Act. This latter legislation transferred responsibility for the allocation of communal land for agricultural and residential purposes to the district councils.

The transfer of responsibility for the allocation of land to elected local political functionaries did not, however, solve the problems of settlement encroachment and resource degradation that had developed over the years in the communal areas as a result of growing land hunger. Instead, conflicts over land use and responsibility for its allocation are reported to have worsened throughout all the communal areas (Government of Zimbabwe 1994). In most areas today newly established households have the choice of either remaining landless or settling in areas that were previously used by the community for livestock grazing and other areas of unsuitable land. In most communal lands, although vestiges of the old linear pattern established during centralisation in the 1950s are still present, there has been considerable dispersal since the mid-1960s, resulting in a landscape comprising a mixture of linear, dispersed and clustered settlement patterns (Whitlow and Zinyama 1988; Zinyama 1988). Figure 11.3 shows changes in settlement patterns between 1949 and 1981 in Zimunya communal land twenty kilometres south of Mutare, with a population density of 162 persons per square kilometre at the 1982 census, the third highest for any rural area in the country. Centralisation had been implemented in this area by 1949 and subsequent changes in settlement patterns have been influenced by changes in government policy, increasing population pressure, as well as local relief/physical conditions (Whitlow and Zinyama 1988). It is in part to meet the pressing land hunger that the government embarked in 1981 on a programme to redistribute under-utilised land within the large-scale commercial (former whites only) sector to black peasant families.

RURAL LAND REDISTRIBUTION AND SETTLEMENT CHANGES

The resettlement programme represents a significant redistribution of the population and alteration of rural settlement patterns by the state in areas that had previously been alienated for white agriculture. The government has sought to avoid the problems that arise from unplanned and haphazard land resettlement. Instead, from the outset, formal procedures were instituted for the land redistribution programme. These involve the identification and purchase of blocks of land large enough to accommodate at least a few hundred farming families to make the provision of social infrastructure (e.g. schools, clinics) viable. This is followed by an assessment of appropriate agricultural land uses for the area, the identification and planning of village sites, arable and grazing lands, roads, service centres and so forth. As a result, the low population densities and dispersed settlements of the former white commercial farmlands have, upon resettlement, been transformed into higher densities with nucleated village settlements, especially under the

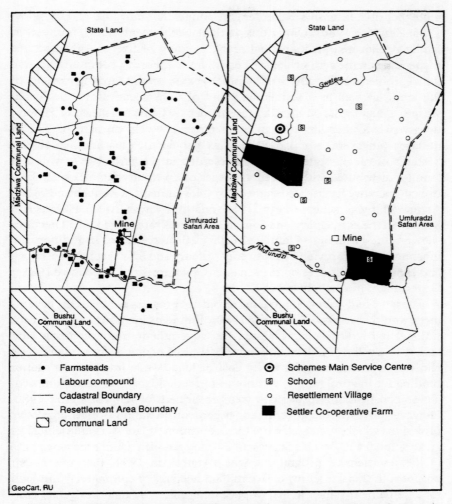

Figure 11.4 Settlement patterns before and after resettlement in Mufurudzi,
northeast of Harare

more popular Intensive Resettlement Model A (Zinyama and Whitlow 1986; Zinyama 1986). Under this particular settlement model, each settler family is allocated an individual arable holding of five to eight hectares (depending on the agro-ecological conditions of the area), communal grazing for a specified small number of livestock (based on the carrying capacity of the area), as well as a residential stand of 0.25 hectares in a nucleated village. Thus, in the Mufurudzi resettlement scheme northeast of Harare, twenty-two former large commercial farms covering an area of 35,823 hectares (an average of 1,628 hectares per farm), plus another 18,889 hectares of vacant state land, were resettled in the early 1980s with 563 families distributed within twenty villages of up to fifty families each, plus two co-operative farms (see Figure 11.4) (Government of Zimbabwe 1981a). At the Chinyika scheme near Headlands mid-way between Harare and Mutare in the east, eighty-one commercial farms totalling 11,3752 hectares were resettled with 3, 984 families in 103 nucleated villages. In addition, the inhabitants were provided with twenty primary and four secondary schools, and eight service centres on the scheme (Government of Zimbabwe 1981b; Government of Zimbabwe 1987).

The land-redistribution programme did not progress as well as the government would have liked during the 1980s. Problems included certain constitutional barriers which prohibited the government from acquiring land except on a willing-seller willing-buyer basis, lack of money for land purchase and development, and the rising cost of land, while international donor funding for the programme was not as forthcoming as had been promised. These constitutional provisions were enshrined for ten years after 1980. However, in 1989 the government began consideration of new legislative provisions which would expedite the acquisition of land for resettlement of an additional 110,000 black peasant farming families. Under the new phase of the resettlement programme which started in 1991, the government proposes to transfer a further five million hectares of commercial farmland for resettlement (albeit at a slow pace determined by tight budgetary constraints), plus another 1.2 million hectares for urban expansion and other public uses. The size of the large-scale commercial farming sector will ultimately be reduced from 11.2 million hectares in the early 1990s to five million hectares at the end of the programme. The resettlement areas in turn will occupy some 8.5 million hectares. Full implementation of the programme will entail substantial diminution in the area of widely dispersed rural settlements and higher population densities in the former large-scale commercial farmlands.

The government-appointed commission of enquiry into appropriate land-tenure systems made several recommendations for the reduction of individual farm sizes in the large-scale commercial sector (Government of Zimbabwe 1994). These recommendations, which have already been accepted by government as part of its efforts to achieve a more equitable distribution of land, will entail changes in settlement patterns and population densities in the sector. The recommendations include the streamlining and relaxation of regulations governing the subdivision of large farms into smaller units for sale to others (including prospective black commercial farmers). Other proposals are the introduction of a progressive land tax on farms in excess of the maximum size stipulated for each agro-ecological region, and the principle of one farm per individual entity (person, family or company). In the end, it is hoped that commercial farms in Zimbabwe will become smaller, which in turn will result in higher population and settlement densities.

DEVELOPMENT OF RURAL SERVICE CENTRES

Since independence, the government has pursued several strategies aimed at improving living standards within the rural areas of Zimbabwe. These include the land-redistribution programme which aims to reduce population pressures in the communal areas, the improvement of agricultural production and household incomes through the provision of the necessary supporting economic, social and technical services and infrastructure. Attempts have also been made to create rural off-farm employment in order to reduce the rate of migration to the major urban centres such as Harare and Bulawayo. Both service provision and employment creation are manifest in the policy to develop rural service centres in both the communal and resettlement areas. These places not only serve as the local administrative centres for their communities, but also as points for the location of a variety of economic and social infrastructure and services provided by the government, non-governmental agencies and private investors (Gasper 1988; Wekwete 1989).

The government had hoped that small manufacturing enterprises would develop at these centres to provide jobs for the large numbers of young unemployed who are entering the labour market each year. Unfortunately, economic activities being established at most of these rural service centres are dominated by small scale general retailing, diesel-operated grain-milling plants, butcheries and informal sector artisanal activities (Wekwete 1988a). However, there are a few centres located in areas of high agricultural potential and incipient peasant cash cropping that have begun to attract investment by large urban-based commercial organisations which are seeking to capture some of the growing annual inflows of cash from crop sales by peasant farmers (Zinyama 1990). The principal such centres are Gokwe which is located in the main peasant cotton-growing region to the northwest of Harare, Murehwa in the northeast, and Gutu-Mupandawana in the south of the capital. As shown in Table 11.1, these few relatively successful communal sector service centres have grown since the early

Table 11.1 Population growth of selected small centres in (a) the large-scale commercial and (b) communal farming areas: 1969–1992 censuses

Centre	1969	1982	1992	Growth rate 1982–1992 per annum
Commercial lands				
Gwanda	2,050	4,920	10,565	7.9
Chivhu	1,670	3,426	6,909	7.3
Mvurwi	1,500	3,378	6,026	5.9
Plumtree	2,040	3,250	6,228	6.7
Dete	2,470	2,895	3,427	1.4
Nyanga	730	2,893	3,442	1.7
Concession	3,120	2,783	4,035	3.8
Nyazura	1,760	2,500	2,513	0.1
Communal lands				
Gokwe	n.a.	n.a.	7,418	–
Mutoko	1,190	5,106	5,380	0.5
Murehwa	650	2,666	4,719	5.9
Gutu-Mupandawana	520	2,500	6,197	9.5
Tsanzaguru	n.a.	n.a.	2,562	–
Sanyati	n.a.	n.a.	2,902	–

Note: List includes only those centres that are predominantly service centres with no mining activities and had a population of 2,500–4,999 at the 1982 census. 2,500 is the minimum cut-off for an urban centre in Zimbabwe.
n.a. = Less than 2,500 people at the time of the census.
Sources: Government of Zimbabwe (1984) '1982 Population Census A Preliminary Assessment'. Central Statistical Office: Harare; Government of Zimbabwe (1994) 'Census 1992: Zimbabwe National Report'. Central Statistical Office: Harare.

1980s to levels comparable with much older centres situated in the large-scale commercial farming areas.

These emerging urban centres within the communal areas have been particularly attractive to private-sector investment because of the provision by the state of the necessary infrastructure such as electricity, wide all-weather roads and telecommunications. The presence of a large complement of middle-level administrative and service employees with regular incomes is an additional attraction to private investors. Thus, in a slow and at present geographically uneven manner, the government's rural service centre programme is assisting in the diffusion of urban development in the country. Whereas before independence, urban centres were confined to the areas of white settlement alone, the programme is bringing a new form of settlement within the communal areas which had previously been far removed from any urban places.

CONCLUDING REMARKS

Rural settlement patterns in Zimbabwe today bear the heavy imprint of state policies that have evolved since the late 1920s. While in areas of leasehold or freehold tenure state policy has been to provide an enabling environment for free enterprise in agriculture to prosper, in the communal sector the state has historically followed a more regulatory approach towards settlement patterns. It has also been shown that while policy may change over time, the settlement patterns that emerge from implementation of these policies tend to be more enduring such that the new are superimposed on the older patterns. At the same time, increasing population pressure has also affected settlement patterns not only within the communal sector, but also in the large-scale commercial farmlands as government responses to the growing land shortage by way of the land redistribution programme.

THE IMPACT OF NATIONAL POLICY ON URBAN SETTLEMENT IN ZIMBABWE

The evolution of settlement in Zimbabwe has been influenced by political, administrative and economic factors during both the colonial and post-colonial periods. Pre-colonial Zimbabwe was predominantly agrarian with scattered nuclear and village settlements spread across the country. The scattered settlements were largely located to service an agricultural economy with limited trade and manufacturing, except for limited barter of goods and home manufacture of implements such as hoes and spears. The levels of specialisation were few and therefore the settlements had limited physical and social infrastructure. Except for the Great Zimbabwe monument and other relics of early pre-colonial settlements, there is no evidence of urban development until the colonial period. The settlement system tended to be semi-permanent as the population practised shifting cultivation.

During the early period of colonialism, up to approximately 1890, new settlements were established largely to serve as military and administrative centres, for example, Fort Salisbury, Fort Charter and Fort Victoria. These settlements were part and parcel of the colonisation process. After the European conquest at the end of the nineteenth century, new permanent forms of settlement were developed, together with the establishment of physical infrastructure linking them: railways, roads, telegraph. This process was vital to the establishment of the spatial system which exists in Zimbabwe today. The process was elaborated through a massive process of land alienation which effectively divided the country into European and African areas through the Land Apportionment Act of 1930 and the Land Husbandry Act of 1952.

By the end of the Second World War, Zimbabwe had experienced a rapid process of urbanisation and industrialisation, which effectively consolidated the settlement system. The main urban settlements benefited from significant infrastructure investment from government through the establishment of all the major parastatal and utility companies. Indeed by the beginning of the 1960s, Zimbabwe had a relatively well-developed spatial system despite the prevailing racial segregation which created racial and economic imbalances in terms of overall development.

The colonial inheritance in 1980 was therefore clearly much more significant than some other African countries had inherited in the 1960s. There was a strong settler European imprint which has been difficult to restructure. In spite of the government efforts since 1980 to engineer structural changes to promote equity in terms of distribution of social and physical infrastructure, the core of the economy has continued to increase its dominance, thus marginalising the rural periphery further. For example, new investments have all continued to be attracted to the main urban centres and particularly Harare.

The purpose of this chapter is to analyse the complex factors which constitute national policy and how they have influenced the settlement pattern. The chapter emphasises the need for in-depth analysis of historical influences on policy, which is sometimes overlooked by those who want to promote new changes. In Zimbabwe, history has had an indelible mark on the nature, function and distribution of settlements. Whilst it is possible to apply the classical economic and location models, in most cases they provide post-facto rationalisation of processes deeply embedded in historical and behavioural factors. Whilst the location of industries can be explained in terms of proximity to raw materials and markets, in Zimbabwe it is clear that the first decision of locating Fort Salisbury [Harare] was not influenced by the concern of industrialists.

Ultimately government policy has a decisive influence but only when there is both political will and financial commitment. Both the colonial and post-colonial administrations have been pro-active in public sector policy and investments, and have therefore sought to significantly influence settlement patterns. Zimbabwe also has a strong infrastructure investment tradition which has been a positive force for settlement development. There is therefore a high degree of connectivity which exists between and within settlements.

CONCEPTUAL FRAMEWORK

In developing a conceptual framework for the location of manufacturing industries in Zimbabwe, Wekwete (1982) outlined a model which highlighted the articulation of the colonial mode of production, in particular the interaction between the capitalist agrarian–mining–industrial sector and the indigenous peasant sector which provided cheap and controlled labour. This framework was initially elaborated in a seminar paper by Arrighi (1967) and it was consistent with the regional development perspectives of the neo-marxist dependency paradigm. Unlike the traditional location models which began with the entrepreneur seeking to maximise advantages and shaping the location of activities and settlements, colonial settlements and

economic activities were a product of total space manipulation to achieve
specific political outcomes.

Indeed the argument by Soja and Tobin (1975: 158) captures the essence
of this type of spatial manipulation when they argue that processes of
migration, urbanisation, industrialisation and social mobilisation assume a
spatial dimension in two fundamental ways:

> First they are space-forming in that they work to shape and structure human
> interaction in space – in the development of transport and communication net-
> works, in the growth of urban and administrative systems, in the territorial
> distribution of political authority, in the evolution of a differentiated and inte-
> grated space economy. At the same time they are space contingent in that their
> space-organising influence is itself shaped by the existing spatial framework. The
> decision to locate a modern factory, for example, or an administrative centre,
> both powerful and persistent forces in the organisation of space, will depend in
> large part upon earlier localised decisions.

The above argument is important in understanding the interaction
between policy decisions and space, and particularly the interrelated nature
of policy decisions in shaping settlement distribution, nature and functions.
In the settler colonial systems which prevailed in Zimbabwe, South Africa
and to some extent Kenya, settlement patterns were strongly influenced by
the political economy of colonialism which carved out 'Africa of the labour
reserves' (Amin 1972). Amin forcefully argues that the African social
systems were distorted and impoverished and lost even the semblance of
autonomy. Indeed 'the unhappy Africa of *apartheid* and the Bantustans was
born, and was to supply the greatest return to central capital.' (519).

At independence, most African countries argued for restructuring their
economies to reduce colonial imbalances and to benefit the largely disadvantaged indigenous majority. In Zimbabwe this urgency was highlighted
in the first major policy statements including: 'Growth with Equity' (Government of Zimbabwe 1981c) and the 'Transitional National Development Plan
1981–1982, 1984–1985' (Government of Zimbabwe 1982). Conceptually,
however, the policies did not depart from the dominant modernisation
paradigm whose main objective was to transform the periphery of the economies and to allow capital (through industrialisation) to structurally transform the economies. This modernisation paradigm was however subjected
to major stresses with the adoption of a monolithic one-party system with an
extensive bureaucracy to direct the development processes. There was also
a strong socialist influence on the development paradigm adopted in
Zimbabwe which is currently being blamed for disturbing economic processes and the role of the market. The blame is coming as part of the economic structural-adjustment critique which is projecting the predominant role
of the market in economic development.

Policy is the broad framework which guides development processes and
the type of policy will vary depending on the ideology and role of the state,

institutional structures, the scope of statutory provision, the sectors of intervention and the extent to which policy is supply or demand driven. Indeed there are many types of policy operating at different levels, national or supra-national, and they have different implications for institutional and management structures. Policy tends to be prescriptive and seeks to determine and measure the impact of change on social and economic conditions, and usually represents the political consensus prevailing. Many countries have economic policy, social policy and a variety of other sectoral policies emanating from the broad socio-economic policy. Policy determines the type of legislation adopted and generally influences the direction of development.

In many African countries, including Zimbabwe, economic structural-adjustment policies have completely transformed the direction of socio-economic development. First, the role of the developmentalist state has been completely reversed as the laissez-faire neo-liberal thinking has come to dominate economic policy. The market has been given a prominence in economic decision-making, reinforcing the 'rolling back' of the state. Secondly, the social welfare policies have been removed and more and more service provision is left to the private sector. Finally, with economic structural adjustment policies, there has been a strengthening of the globalisation trends as the nation states have lost control of the basic parameters of development policy. Some commentators have pointed to the negative impact of the prevailing dominance of finance capital and the growing prominence of speculators. In the current structural adjustment paradigm it is argued that settlements will grow or decline depending on their comparative advantage, and that market forces should determine where new activities will locate. For many developing countries, including Zimbabwe, the major result will be increasing the primacy of the major centres and the limited growth of the small peripheral cities. In Zimbabwe the dominance of Harare is clearly evident and more recently it has been consolidated by the establishment of Ruwa industrial satellite as a growth point on the outskirts of Harare.

POLICY IN ZIMBABWE

This section will highlight the influence of policies during the colonial and post-colonial periods, and will demonstrate the underlying continuity of structures established by the early policies. The starting date is set at 1890 when European settlers began to systematically colonise Zimbabwe. Before then, there were traders and missionaries who did not establish any significant infrastructure.

1890–1930: Establishment

Firstly, there was the 1890 to 1930 period, which was characterised by land apportionment on a racial basis culminating in the Land Apportionment Act 1930 and the significant displacement of the African population from

areas which were designated 'European'. The history of land has been well
documented by Riddell (1978) and Palmer (1977). Indeed the politics of
land has dominated the Zimbabwe development debate to the present day
(Moyo 1995). In 1995 the report of the Land Tenure Commission was
published and adopted by government. Whilst the report does not make any
major radical proposals, it highlights the need for further reform of the
tenure system and underlines the need for active state intervention in the
process.

Land tenure and distribution have been the major determinants of
settlement patterns in rural and urban areas. The land-distribution pattern
(by race) influenced the definition of what was urban i.e. a settlement
located in what were designated European areas with twenty-five white
residents engaged in non-agricultural activities. Indeed there were no urban
settlements in areas which were designated for African settlement (Tribal
Trust Lands). Urban settlements developed on the basis of privatisation of
both state and municipal land and the bona-fide urban residents on this
land were Europeans. Africans were classified as temporary sojourners who
came to provide labour to the mines, commerce, industry and services.

During the period 1890–1930 the basic physical infrastructure for
Zimbabwe was established – the railways, roads, telegraph, electricity and
all the major towns. This infrastructure effectively linked all the European
areas and developed the capitalist core of the economy. Of significant
importance was the consolidation of commercial European agriculture, and
the setting up of supporting extension and marketing services.

1930–1950: Consolidation

The period 1930 to 1950 witnessed the consolidation of European settler
dominance, infrastructure and the manufacturing industry sector. This
period was marked by significant state intervention in organising economic
activity. The following highlights some of the key interventions by the state:

1. 1931, Maize Control Act, which regulated both domestic and export marketing of maize and thwarted African competition. This eventually resulted in the
   setting up of the Grain Marketing Board and related infrastructure in different
   centres;
2. 1936, Tobacco Marketing Act, which improved the bargaining powers of
   European tobacco farmers against the monopoly power of the United
   Tobacco Company. The state actively supported the local tobacco farmers
   and provided public sector funds to improve infrastructure;
3. 1936, establishment of the Electricity Supply Commission, to generate and
   supply power nationally. This consolidated the national power grid and
   ensured power supply for industry and commerce;
4. 1937, establishment of the Cold Storage Commission, which became responsible for domestic and export marketing of meat, and resulted in the setting-up
   of abattoirs nationwide. In some small towns – Masvingo and Marondera –
   the meat-processing industries became the key economic activities;

5. 1942, Iron and Steel Industry Act, which gave the state authority to develop the industry, beginning with agricultural extension right up to finished products. This resulted in the development of Kwe Kwe and Redcliff as the hub of the steel industry;
6. 1945, Industrial Development Corporation was established to give technical and financial assistance to emerging industries. This was particularly important to support the large influx of European settlers who came to Zimbabwe after the war. (Wekwete 1982)

These various forms of state intervention demonstrated government policy which was highlighted in the second report of the Industrial Development Advisory Committee (1941–44) which stated:

> The government policy is to nationalise, under commissions of government, utility companies, basic industries such as iron and steel and cotton spinning, the object being to make semi-finished products so that private enterprise can obtain semi-manufactured materials at the lowest prices, and so enable them to compete with imported manufacturers. This will also prevent monopolies from being established by the cornering of semi-manufactured products. The government believes that all creameries, bacon factories and meat processing should be done on a cooperative basis or by a commission or utility company. (Wekwete 1982: 121)

Government therefore took an active role in setting up and directing economic activities which had a major impact on the nature and distribution of settlements. In all cases activities were designated to specific settlements, for example, iron and steel at Kwe Kwe and Redcliff; cotton industry at Kadoma; sugar industry at Chiredzi and Triangle. The rural peasant sector (African Tribal Trust Lands) was ignored in the process and shaped to supply and reproduce cheap labour for the capitalist enterprises. The rural settlement pattern continued to be dominated by villages and small administrative centres with very limited commercial activities.

1950–1965: Federation
The third period from 1950 to 1965 witnessed the formation of the Federation of Rhodesia and Nyasaland (Zimbabwe, Zambia and Malawi). The Federation significantly expanded the domestic market for Zimbabwean industry, which was more developed than both Zambia and Malawi combined; and Zimbabwe, as the focal point of the Federation, significantly benefited from the Zambian copper revenues (Stoneman 1976: 25–8).

However, there were no significant changes in the settlement system in Zimbabwe except for increasing the dominance of Harare as the capital of the federation, and expanding the physical infrastructure, particularly with the construction of the Kariba Dam and the increased capacity to supply power.

1965–1971: UDI
The final colonial period spanned from 1965 to 1979 and was characterised by the break up of the federation, the gaining of political independence of

Zambia and Malawi (1964), and the isolation of Zimbabwe (then Rhodesia) after the unilateral declaration of independence (UDI) in 1965.

Of significant importance was the adoption of a strong import-substitution policy to safeguard the capitalist interests of the European settlers. Government supported import control and linkages of local industries through infrastructure investments. The then Rhodesian authorities intensified the opening up of new resource zones, e.g. South East Lowveld, which benefited from the water development investment in the Sabi-Limpopo basin and supported the growth of the sugar industry with the development of crops under irrigation. New towns were established which became a focus for agro-processing industries – Chiredzi and Triangle.

However, in spite of these developments, there was also increased pressure on land in African areas and attempts were made to promote the urbanisation of these areas through designation of growth points. The colonial government established the Tribal Trust Land Development Corporation (TILCOR) to spearhead the development of designated growth points. Sanyati, located in the Midlands cotton-growing region, became a prototype settlement where the basic principles of growth centre planning were applied. The underlying principle was to support the development of a resource which became the economic basis of the centre's growth. Meanwhile the political contradictions of colonial development intensified and were being transformed into military conflict and, therefore, there were limited achievements of the new policy. It, however, laid ground for the post-colonial strategy of rural growth centres, although the basic principles somewhat shifted from a focus on resource centres to administrative or services centres (Wekwete 1987).

POST-COLONIAL POLICY

From 1980 to the present day, post-colonial government policy was clearly committed to redressing the colonial imbalances as stated in the Transitional National Development Plan of 1982–5 (Government of Zimbabwe 1982: i).

This plan clearly marked an important shift in terms of public-sector investment which was now to be targeted towards the rural areas (formerly African areas) which were underdeveloped and lacked both social and physical infrastructure. The new policy direction was therefore to designate new centres and provide them with infrastructure investment which would stimulate local economic development. Wekwete (1987) elaborated the theoretical underpinnings of policy and highlighted some of the specific infrastructural investments created in the designated centres which were mostly small business centres serving the commercial needs of the peasant communal farmers.

The impact of this policy has been to expand the urban settlement system and to create some opportunities for decentralised development. Whilst the growth of most of the centres has been driven by public-sector investment and benefited from the de-concentration of government activities, there are some centres which have attracted significant private-sector investment and created local employment.

Another major policy thrust was directed at the land resettlement programme. The cornerstone of the Lancaster House Agreement in 1979 was political independence and a land resettlement programme which would acquire up to one million hectares of land to settle the landless and war refugees, and redress the colonial imbalances (Government of Zimbabwe 1983: 2).

The consequences of the resettlement programme for the overall settlement policy are wide ranging in terms of population movements from what were formerly African areas to European areas. By mid-1989, up to 50,000 families had been resettled on 2.64 million hectares of what were previously European farms. This is below projected targets, but it still represents an important geographical shift of population. Whilst there were no designated settlements in the resettled areas, the movement of population to what were commercial farming areas created new nodes for service provision and even stimulated the urbanisation of some small centres. However, there remains a problem of the tenure system as the resettled farmers have remained tenants of the state, creating a level of uncertainty.

There was a strong commitment by the state to planning and directing the post-colonial economy. Beyond the socialist rhetoric, however, there was significant continuity with the past, and the core of the European settler economy continued to exert the dominant influence. It is clear that fifteen years since the Transnational Development Plan, the colonial land-tenure system and categories have largely remained intact. The spatial system continues to revolve around a core of the main urban centres and commercial farming areas.

CONCLUSION

An important conclusion about the post-independence policy is that it shifted the direction of development from the core of the colonial economy. Some key structures have been established which should form an important basis for the long-term development of rural areas. However, a decade of such policies is not likely to reverse ninety years of systematic colonial policy (Mutizwa-Mangiza and Helmsing 1991).

There is no doubt that national policy in Zimbabwe has played a crucial role in shaping the settlement system during both the colonial and post-colonial periods. There are many forms of policy which have been adopted and implemented since 1890 when European settlers moved to Zimbabwe. The two most significant and crucial elements which have shaped the settlement system have been the land policy and public-sector investment programme in infrastructure, which established the spatial system segregating European land from African land. This in turn had an impact on the policy of land resettlement which was part of the post-colonial political arrangements agreed at Lancaster House in 1979. In all cases the post-colonial state has been strongly pro-active, influencing, through the public-sector programme, where investments have been located and providing infrastructure to settlements. The colonial state was particularly effective in opening up new areas of settlement, particularly through investments in water infrastructure in the drier lowland regions.

The post-colonial focus on rural development in former African areas has been important in the extension of services through the private sector to the majority of the population. However, the new settlements have not received as much investment to make a significant contribution to the provision of new employment. Most of the new settlements have been based on the provision of administrative infrastructure for both local and central governments. This means the majority of population living in these settlements are directly employed by local government or the sector ministries.

More recently however the adoption and implementation of structural-adjustment policies, has resulted in limited state intervention in terms of public-sector investment, and in placing more emphasis on the role that the private market plays. It has been observed that this scenario is leading to a greater concentration of activities in the primate city of Harare, consistent with private capital seeking advantages of agglomeration economies of the major metropolitan centre. This is likely to result in the increasing primacy of the capital city.

On balance, the Zimbabwe settlement system will continue to have a strong legacy of state intervention at the local and national levels. The relatively strong local-government system will continue to play a key role in determining infrastructure investments and their maintenance. There is probably, however, a need to look at the traditional instruments of regional development which can help to direct investments in a significant way to the disadvantaged regions and help create new settlements.

THE INFLUENCE OF GOVERNMENT POLICIES ON THE DEVELOPMENT OF RURAL SETTLEMENTS IN BOTSWANA

This chapter looks at change in Botswana's settlement patterns since independence in 1966 when approximately 95 per cent of the population was in rural areas or large villages. Since independence, one of the major changes in settlement patterns has been the growth of modern towns following the implementation of certain development programmes.

The redistribution of population in space has received considerable attention (Clarke and Kosinski 1982). People have always moved from one area to another in search of opportunities and have brought with them skills and other forms of capital. Opoko (1990) has shown how the Western Region of Ghana has experienced an increase in cocoa production and a rise in literacy as a result of in-migration. Wood (1982) has studied the spontaneous migrations by peasants from congested rural areas of Ethiopia to the unused (or underutilised) lands, transforming agricultural production in their new home areas.

The awareness of population issues by governments has increased significantly since the 1974 World Population Conference. At an intergovernmental meeting organised by the Economic Commission for Africa (ECA) in 1977, African governments made a number of suggestions regarding the policy measures to be adopted with regard to population distribution and internal migration. In the same year, many African governments considered the spatial distribution patterns to be unacceptable and with regards to policies of internal migration, most African governments 'desired to either decelerate or even reverse the existing trends' (Clarke and Kosinski 1982: 13).

African countries have in varying degrees consequently experimented with a series of programmes that were designed explicitly or implicity to influence existing population distributions, especially in rural areas (Adepoju 1982). The main motivation behind these programmes has been the desire to stem the high rates of rural–urban migration by stimulating development in the rural areas. One of the major impediments to rural development has

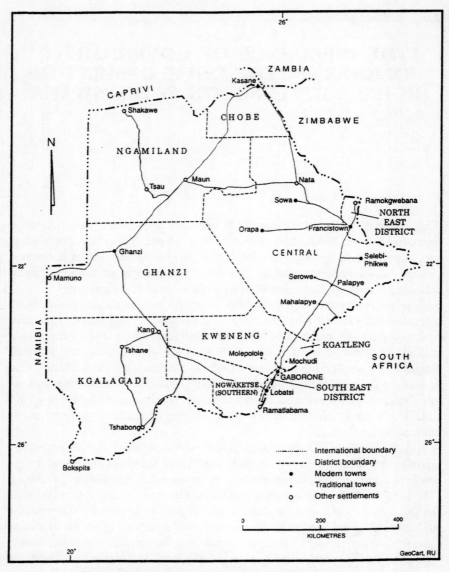

Figure 13.1 Botswana: Major settlements and districts

often been perceived to be the distribution of population in small and scattered settlements.

Most policies have not been explicit as regards population redistribution or settlement changes, although some have formulated rural development strategies, entailing resettlement schemes and the creation of new growth centres to stimulate development in low density regions and the provision of social amenities in more concentrated areas.

Adepoju (1982) has reviewed a number of resettlement programmes, e.g. the settlement of landless peasants (Kenya), commercial agriculture development schemes (Zambia, Kenya), sedentarisation of nomads (Somalia, Ethiopia), villagisation (Tanzania) and resettlement schemes for the unemployed youths (Somalia, Zambia, Nigeria). The best-documented resettlement programme is the Ujamaa villagisation scheme in Tanzania (e.g. Mascarenhas 1979; Maro and Mlay 1982). However, there have been similar experiments in other countries, such as Zambia, (Jaeger 1981) entailing the relocation of farmers at resettlement schemes and grouping and concentrating of villages around service centres. There are also situations where services provided to improve the living conditions of the people may lead to population re-distribution by encouraging settlement (e.g. Khogali 1981: 309).

SETTLEMENT PATTERNS IN BOTSWANA

Silitshena (1982a) has identified five types of settlement in Botswana; namely, the seasonally changing settlements, the agro-towns, dispersed homesteads, farmsteads and the modern commercial and industrial towns. Before independence, the first four types were more prevalent. In 1964, only 4 per cent of the total population lived in the tiny urban centres of Francistown, Lobatse and Gabarone. Currently about 25 per cent of the population lives in the modern commercial and industrial towns (Figure 13.1).

Seasonally changing settlements are traditionally found among the hunter-gatherer Basarwa (or Bushmen). Originally concentrated in eastern Botswana, and indeed found all over the wetter parts of Southern Africa, the Bushmen are now generally confined to the marginal areas of the Kalahari semi-desert. According to Barnard (1979: 132): 'Bushmen groups aggregate and disperse according to custom and social circumstance, the availability of plant and animal foods and, most importantly, the availability of water' (cf. Barnard 1995).

The mobile life-style of Basarwa has been threatened by the spread of other population groups into this area. In the Ghanzi district the colonial government demarcated ranches, which were sold to some white settlers, transforming Basarwa into squatters on their original land (Childers 1976; Russell and Russell 1979). The drilling of boreholes in the area after the Second World War has enabled the Tswana pastoralists to establish their grazing stations (cattleposts) in this area (see Hitchcock 1978). These developments have contributed to the depletion of both game and vegetation, the two basic resources on which Basarwa depended.

It is therefore becoming difficult for Basarwa to pursue a hunting and gathering existence. They have developed permanent settlements around boreholes, increasing their subjugation to their technologically superior compatriots. In some districts, they have been experiencing land hunger, exacerbated by the National Policy on Tribal Grazing, which has leased ranches to wealthy Batswana cattle farmers, while Basarwa suffer from neglect, indifference and even prejudice from some Government officials. Basarwa are thus at the bottom of the social ladder (Hitchcock 1978; Wily 1979).

Dispersed homestead settlements are traditionally found in the North East District among the Kalanga-speaking people, in Ngamiland among the Herero, in the Kalahari among the Bakgalagadi and in the Southern District among the Barolong. They are now also prevalent in areas that were traditionally characterised by nucleated settlements. There are many explanations for the existence of dispersed settlements. In social terms the dispersed settlements are prevalent among the groups with weak central political organisation. In economic terms, they reflect a land-use system where agriculture, both arable and livestock, is practised close to the settlement. Indeed both the Kalanga and the Barolong have resisted regrouping on grounds that this would disrupt their agriculture (Silitshena 1982b).

Settlement patterns among the Setswana-speaking people, who comprise the majority of Botswana's population were generally nucleated. The large nucleated villages, or agro-towns, comprising populations of 1,000 to 30,000, have been well documented (e.g. Schapera 1943, 1953, 1955; Silitshena 1983; Tlou 1974). This settlement type was also prevalent among the Batswana of South Africa but disappeared after the imposition of colonial rule (Dachs 1975; Pauw 1960).

The agro-towns were part of a land-use system that comprised concentric rings around the village with arable agriculture ('lands') being closest, followed by livestock agriculture ('cattleposts') and finally hunting (Silitshena 1983). Everybody was expected to live in the village and visit the lands and cattleposts to carry out agricultural activities. Where lands were distant, people built 'temporary' seasonal homes near their fields, and increasingly so as the fields near the village became exhausted, moving to the lands, at the start of the rains and returning to the village after harvest. Failure to return to the village incurred the wrath of the chief who might forcibly evict the culprits (Schapera 1943). The same measures were taken against individuals who tried to settle permanently at the cattleposts. As chiefs saw it, the system of living in villages was not only customary but it also facilitated administration and formed a better basis for the development of social and economic adaptation to changing circumstances (Schapera

1943: 270–2). The persistence of large nucleated settlements among the Tswana stemmed the extensive power enjoyed by the chiefs bolstered by the colonial regime (Silitshena 1983).

POST–COLONIAL GOVERNMENT POLICIES WITH IMPLICATIONS FOR RURAL SETTLEMENTS

British colonial rule in Bechuanaland was indirect with chiefs as the local agents responsible for the welfare of their people and with control over the movement of both settlements and their people (Schapera 1943). No individual could change his residence or go to the lands without the permission of the chief. It can be argued that settlement changes in areas with agro-towns could not possibly have taken place as long as the chiefs wielded a lot of power.

An array of legislation was enacted starting in 1965 to take away some of the powers of the chiefs, vesting them in new institutions. The Chieftainship Law of 1965 and the Chieftainship (Amendment) Act of 1970 placed the appointment and removal of chiefs at the discretion of central government. Other legislation concerned the power to levy taxes, to dispose of stray cattle and to regulate the social and economic life, transferring these to the democratically elected district councils, and transferring control over land allocation to elected Land Boards. The chiefs' main functions are now mainly concerned with judicial matters and they no longer control the spatial organisation of society. Curbing of the powers of the chiefs created a framework in which people were free to move and settle wherever they desired. Indeed a survey carried out in the late 1970s revealed that more than 60 per cent of households that had settled in lands had done so since 1966 (Silitshena 1983).

The development of permanent settlements at the lands and cattleposts must also be understood in the context of rural development policies. At independence in 1966, Botswana was too poor to contemplate the dramatic expansion of services. The policy was to consolidate and improve the existing facilities (Government of Botswana 1968: 60; 1970: 9). This favoured the existing villages. Indeed one of the reasons for the attachment to the villages was the services they offered. Children normally stayed behind in the village and joined their parents at the lands during weekends or school holidays. Permanent water supplies were available only at the villages. At the lands, people depended on temporary water supplies from the rain.

At independence, agriculture was the backbone of the economy and the government needed to improve productivity in order to raise incomes. The traditional system involving seasonal movements to the lands was seen as an impediment to productivity (Khama 1970: 5).

The key to encouraging permanent settlement on the lands was the development of dams to improve water supply and irrigation possibilities (Government of Botswana 1966: 18; 1991: 266). The 1971 census had revealed that at least 44 per cent of the total national population were settled at the lands, cattleposts and other areas with dispersed populations. The policy with respect to the provision of education and health services changed in 1972 with the adoption of a formal policy on rural development. In the early 1970s the government adopted a policy of providing social services for areas outside the villages as part of a formal rural development policy (Government of Botswana 1972, 1973). The Ministry of Health in 1971 encouraged the health personnel to make occasional visits to areas outside villages to provide preventive aspects of medicine. In 1973 there was a definite policy shift, extending health-care facilities to all settled communities (Government of Botswana, n.d.: 285; 1977). In the case of development of schools at the lands, the policy has been a rearguard action in response to the spontaneous actions of the people (Silitshena 1983: 134–8). Once settled at the lands, people put up their own primary schools, in most cases poorly constructed sheds and not staffed with professionally qualified teachers. The people then put pressure on the district council through their local councillor or Member of Parliament to take over the schools. In 1979 the Ministry of Education formulated guidelines on the location of schools at the lands.

In 1974 the government introduced the Bushmen Development Programme, later extended to other remote populations. The policy aimed to create special settlements for Remote Area Dwellers, providing each settlement with a package of services, notably a borehole to provide potable water, a school, a health facility and income generating activities. There was also a component concerned with the promotion of leadership (Government of Botswana 1990a, 1990b; Saugestad 1994). However, social activities and economic opportunities in the villages remained strong attractions (Fortmann and Roe 1982: 113).

The concern with ensuring accessibility to social services has prompted the adoption of a regrouping policy in districts with dispersed settlement patterns, particularly in the North East District where costs of providing services was high and social facilities were being enjoyed by only the few people who happened to live nearby and the district council set about regrouping the population around identified key villages (Kwele 1975: 3; Silitshena 1982b).

Government policies are, however, not always consistent. The policy of providing services to the population at the lands and cattleposts has encouraged migration from the major villages and is in direct conflict with the policy of regrouping dispersed settlements, although both were concerned with improving the provision of services. Towards the late 1970s, the government, which had earlier perceived large villages as a stumbling block to rural development, realised that these settlements could be used as instruments of development or growth centres and this has led to investment in community infrastructure and services (Government of Botswana 1997: 197; Swedeplan 1990).

In the early 1990s a National Settlement Policy was adopted to provide a framework for the distribution of investment in an equitable way in order to upgrade the infrastructure of some of the large traditional towns to the level of those provided in modern towns (Government of Botswana 1992). The idea is to 'enable these villages to become alternative locations for commercial and industrial investment' (Government of Botswana 1991: 44). The policies of curbing the powers of the chiefs and of providing medical and educational facilities at the lands and cattleposts areas were not explicitly aimed at changing settlement patterns. However, those concerning Remote Areas Development and National Settlement Policy are more explicit.

SETTLEMENT CHANGES AND THEIR IMPLICATIONS

The previous section has outlined some of the policies that have helped in shaping settlement in Botswana, and although government policies may not be the only factor at work in settlement changes, the influence of the policies of the Ministry of Agriculture on settlements at the lands is widely recognised (Fortmann and Roe 1982; Hitchcock 1978; Swedeplan 1994a: section 4–18).

The development of settlements at the lands and cattleposts is taking place all over the country and poses a number of problems that stem from the uncontrolled growth of the settlements and failure to enforce development covenants (Government of Botswana 1990c: 33). The major concern is the cost of providing services to scattered settlements of small villages (Swedeplan 1994b: 60; Silitshena 1983: 154–8). The Government of Botswana (1977: 67) declared in the name of social justice that all Botswana 'should have equal access to services that Government provides ... such as education, health and water supplies'. The government has, however, found it difficult to sustain the provision of services to dispersed populations. In the North East District where regrouping was attempted, it failed mainly because people did not want to live far from their fields, compounding the 'problem' of the scattered settlement pattern (Government of Botswana 1990d; Silitshena 1982b).

The government recently decided that only minimal services will be provided to settlements that qualify for village status, with a minimum of 500 people in the more densely populated eastern part of the country, or 250 people in the sparsely populated western part of the country; and such a settlement must qualify in other respects (Government of Botswana 1991: 424).

The National Settlement Policy has categorised settlements into primary, secondary and tertiary. The primary centres comprise the large settlements with a minimum of 20,000 people including both the modern towns and large traditional towns. There are ten settlements in this group. These

Table 13.1 Location criteria for infrastructural services – summary table

Facility	Primary centres	Secondary centres	Tertiary I	Tertiary II	Tertiary III
Location and Population Coverage	20,000	10,000–20,000	5,000–10,000	1,000–5,000	500–1,000
	Health hospital national referral hospital	Health centre (with at least a doctor)	Clinics (maternity wing) (30 km radius)	Clinic within 30 km radius	Health post (with 15 km radius)
	District hospital				Population coverage 1,400–8,000 in towns and major villages
	Private practitioners	Private practitioners			
Education	University, vocational training institutions; teacher training college; brigade centre; adult education centre; secondary schools	Senior secondary school (based on needs assessment)	Community junior secondary school, senior secondary school provided there are five CISS in the area.	Primary school	Primary school (15 km radius)
Community	District office	Other headed by senior community development officer;	Community development officer; VDC	ACDO	Mobile or subject to need assessment; VDC

Source: Government of Botswana 1992: 87–9

settlements are supposed to provide the highest order of goods and services. Secondary centres include an amalgam of settlements – some small modern towns and some traditional towns, which are either district or subdistrict headquarters. These intermediate centres (population 10,000–20,000) are expected to act as central places for their immediate hinterlands and offer the same range of functions as primary centres but at a lower level.

The tertiary centres fall within the minimum definition of a village and comprise 'settlements and communities of a size and distribution that bridge the gap between agricultural needs of each family to live on its own land areas and farm, and the need to bring people together to provide them with services' (Government of Botswana 1992: 18, 87–9). There are three levels of tertiary centres (Table 13.1).

Each district is working out its own settlement strategy to resolve the tussle between the economic needs of agriculture, which favour dispersed patterns, and the social needs, which favour nucleation. The Ministry of Agriculture has consistently been critical of large nucleated settlements and was critical of the regrouping policy noting: 'in general it seemed from the point of view of agricultural productivity there were more serious disadvantages than advantages associated with village regrouping' (Silitshena 1982b: 205).

The major challenge facing government is the creation of a viable rural economy in drought-prone Botswana where crop farming is unproductive. In addition to low and variable rainfall, agriculture is constrained by poor soils, pests and diseases, poor credit facilities and inadequate marketing infrastructure (Government of Botswana 1991: 242). The long drought of the 1980s (1981–7) appears to have encouraged many people to migrate to modern towns or to congregate in larger rural settlements, where water, drought relief, services and non-agricultural employment could be found. The tendency to migrate to the lands and cattleposts is thus counteracted by migrations to larger settlements, and many rural dwellers have developed a dependency on drought relief especially in remote areas (Government of Botswana 1990a: 30).

CONCLUSION

To conclude, at independence, because of the need to increase agricultural production, the government encouraged settlement dispersion and declared itself willing to provide high quality social services to the communities in dispersed settlements. However, this has proved rather costly and the government is now trying to find a compromise between the needs of economic production and social provision. But creating a viable rural economy underpinning community livelihood in all the settlements is proving intractable. The experience from Botswana shows that changes have often been initiated by one sector. The pendulum has swung between agriculture and the ministries providing services. The development of Remote Area Settlements has suffered from the lack of coordination between various departments, 'some population clusters have to be relocated either because the location conflicts with other developments or land is too limited' (Government of Botswana 1990a: 18).

The implementation process is greatly assisted by lack of bureaucratic red tape, but this often creates a wide gap between formulation and implementation of government policies and poor linkages between the centre and the regional offices and schemes have often failed because there was no attempt to involve the people in the planning processes (Adepoju 1982).

DEVELOPING SETTLEMENT POLICY ALTERNATIVES: THE ROLE OF RURAL SERVICE CENTRES IN AFRICA

This paper presents some of the results of a research project carried out by the United Nations Centre for Human Settlement (UNCHS) in four African countries – Côte d'Ivoire, Malawi, Nigeria and Tanzania (UNCHS 1993), and a fifth, Zimbabwe, is also considered here.

Rural service centres can be defined as those central places at the bottom end of the central place hierarchy which contribute directly to the basic economic and social needs of agricultural producers (Economic and Social Commission for Asia and the Pacific [ESCAP] 1979: 64). In performing this function, rural service centres concentrate on provision of infrastructure; collecting and marketing agricultural produce from the surrounding rural areas; providing and distributing agricultural inputs, basic agro-processing facilities, social services, and low/middle-order consumer goods.

In most African countries, these services are offered at district capitals and at many central places below this level, down to the village service centres, which are sometimes known as 'locality towns' (ESCAP 1979: 65). In many African countries, such centres usually serve populations below 20,000, and offer basic services directly to agricultural producers in the hinterland and generate non-agricultural employment.

DEVELOPMENT IN FIVE AFRICAN COUNTRIES

Côte d'Ivoire

Côte d'Ivoire has no specific policy on rural service centres. Instead, the development and management of rural service centres takes place partly within the framework of national urban policy. One of the main objectives of Côte d'Ivoire's urban policy adopted in the 1970s was to counteract what was considered to be the excessive size and economic dominance of its capital city, Abidjan. This objective was to be fulfilled through two strategies: firstly, the creation of regional centres; and, secondly, the development of a network of small towns, including those which can be classified as rural service centres.

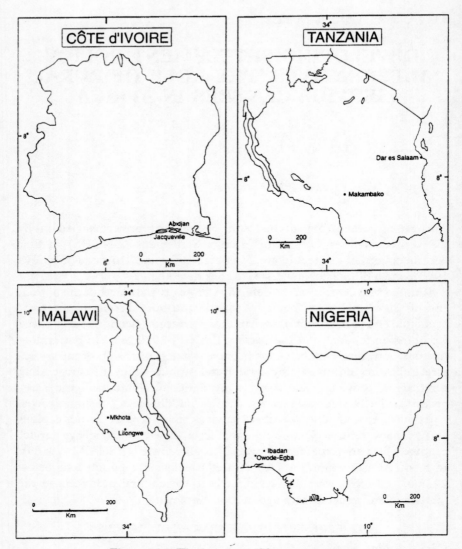

Figure 14.1 The locations of four case studies

Table 14.1 Jacqueville Centre, Côte d'Ivoire: Infrastructure and functions

---

Jacqueville is the principal town of both the sub-prefecture and the commune. It covers an area of 376 hectares. In 1988, Jacqueville centre had a population of 7,614 inhabitants.

The centre has the following *infrastructural facilities*: a running water system; electricity supplied from the national grid; and telephone system (with only twenty subscribers). Transport facilities between the centre and its hinterland as well as with Abidjan are limited because of unsuitable topography.

The *administrative functions* existing in the centre are: offices of the sub-prefecture, commune offices (the town hall), and police station. There are also offices of the following ministries and departments: Agriculture Water and Forests; Primary Schools Inspection; Ministry of the Environment, Building and Town Planning; and Ministry of Youth and Sports. Parastatals with offices in the centre include: Electricity Company of Côte d'Ivoire; Water Company of Côte d'Ivoire; Palm industry; Postal Services and Banking; and Telecommunications of Côte d'Ivoire.

Social service functions in the centre include: a hospital with sixty-seven beds, including a maternity ward; a dispensary; a laboratory; a mobile medical team responsible for endemic diseases over the whole of the sub-prefecture; a women's group with antenatal care and child health facilities; a post office (with 360 postal boxes, of which only twenty are rented); six primary schools; a municipal secondary school; and a technical college specialising in electrical engineering studies (which draws students from the whole country).

Commercial and retail functions include: a central market with twenty-six kiosks; a bank; a hotel; eight restaurants; a bar with dancing facilities; four commercial establishments which supply staples; about 115 retail shops, including butchers who slaughter an average of three cattle per week; about twenty cassava grinding windmills; sixteen tailors' shops; eight masons; five joiners; and 3 house painters.

There is only one *industrial* establishment of significance, SICOR, which employs 830 people.

Source: Saint-Vil (1993).

Another national policy which contributed towards the development of rural service centres was the communalisation policy adopted in the 1980s, which aimed at more effectively meeting local development needs through the transfer of some central government functions to local authorities. The policy accelerated the restructuring of sub-national government. By 1985, there were fifty departments, 183 sub-prefectures and 136 communes – compared to the 1950 figures of four departments, nineteen sub-prefectures and eight communes (Saint-Vil 1993). In 1991, twelve regions were also created, and these became the largest sub-national administrative units in the country. This reorganisation and strengthening of sub-national government has enhanced the status and growth of many rural service centres, some of them (such as Jacqueville) becoming capitals of sub-prefectures and communes.

The government has also encouraged industrialisation in small towns and rural service centres through an investment code which gives advantages to investors wishing to establish themselves in the interior of the country. In addition to Abidjan, two other interior fiscal zones were created.

New enterprises established in the latter two zones qualified for exemption from taxes on industrial and commercial profits for their first seven years of operation. Some specific categories of enterprises located outside Abidjan, such as consumer cooperative societies, also received preferential treatment (Saint-Vil 1993).

A specific measure adopted for the enhancement of the development of small towns and rural service centres was the creation of the Fund for Regional and Rural Development (FRAR) to provide capital for investment in infrastructure and human settlement services in small towns, rural service centres and villages (Saint-Vil 1993). In addition, the Ivorian government has set up organisations for the promotion of industrial development particularly outside Abidjan. Among the organisations created are: CAPEN (the Centre for Assistance of the Promotion of National Enterprises); OPEI (the Office for the Promotion of Ivorian Enterprise); and BIDE (the Fund for Insurance and Credit for Ivorian Enterprises).

Malawi

Malawi is one of the few African countries where the spatial dimension has been systematically integrated into national development policy. The emphasis within Malawi's national development plans is on the improvement of living conditions of rural people, who are the vast majority of the national population. The National Physical Development Plan, formulated in 1986, provides the overall framework for rural service centre development. A key dimension of the National Physical Development Plan is the six-tier central place hierarchy ranging from the national centre to rural market and village centres, which provide a direct link to the rural population within about fifteen kilometers of the centre (Matope 1993). In 1979, the Malawi Government embarked on the implementation of the Rural Growth Centres Project (RGCP) on a pilot basis which expanded in a modified form into a nationwide rolling programme known as the National Rural Centres Programme (NRCP), placing greater emphasis on the service functions of rural centres (as opposed to their growth functions).

Of the countries covered in the UNCHS (1993) study, only Malawi's local government legislation makes specific provisions for the management of rural service centres. District councils, which consist of elected and appointed councillors and operate through standing committees, are responsible for the management of rural service centres through the Rural Growth Centres Committee, which has responsibility over all rural service centres in the district, and Centre Management Committees, located at the individual centres.

Another national policy relevant to the development of rural service centres in Malawi is the National Rural Development Programme (NRDP) to improve the performance of smallholders through the provision of basic

Table 14.2 Mkhota Service Centre, Malawi: Infrastructure and functions

---

Mkhota centre has a total population of 2,250 people. It covers an area of seventy-three hectares and was specifically designed and developed on virgin land as part of the first ten centres in a pilot Rural Growth Centres Project (now transformed into a National Rural Centres Programme).

Infrastructural facilities available in the centre include: all weather road connection; bus service; two boreholes; four shallow wells; telephone service; and cattle dip tank.

Administrative functions in the centre include: agricultural extension service; community development extension service; Mkhota Centre Management Committee offices; Malawi Congress Party office; and traditional court.

Social service functions include: one health centre; one primary school; one post office; a mobile library service; a multi-purpose community hall (including classrooms, library, bar and demonstration kitchen); and a sports field adjacent to the community hall.

Commercial and retail functions in the centre are: Agriculture Development and Marketing Corporation temporary market; permanent produce market with kiosks; one slaughter slab; thirty-one trading shops, grocers and canteens; two tinsmiths; four carpenters; two bicycle repairers; one ox-cart workshop; one bakery; and two tailors' shops.

The only existing *industrial functions* are in the form of purpose-built industry workshops. Non-agricultural employment in the centre amounts to ninety-eight, with central government, Save the Children Fund (USA), and the private sector accounting for 47.7% (forty-nine people), 24.5% (sixteen people) and 33.7% (thirty-three people), respectively.

Source: Matope (1993).

agriculture related services (Matope 1993). A complementary programme known as the Secondary Centres Development Programme was initiated in 1985 to manage the development of secondary centres.

Nigeria

Nigeria has no specific rural service centre development policy. Instead, rural service centres have been developed within the general framework of local government decentralisation. In 1976, the then military government issued a decree designed to restructure and standardise the local government system throughout the country (Adalemo 1993; Adamolekun and Rowland 1979; Gboyega 1981, 1983; Olowu 1986; Smith 1982; Smith and Owojaiye 1981). The decree required all state governments to establish local governments and prescribed the basic conditions under which they should operate, including their composition, functions, staffing and finance. As part of this process, numerous rural settlements were designated as local government area capitals, and these have since become some of the most vibrant rural service centres, and others can now be classified as small towns rather than rural service centres (Adalemo 1993; UNCHS 1991). The physical growth of rural service centres and the related infrastructures has also greatly benefited from implementation of the National Integrated Rural Development Policy (Adalemo 1993).

Table 14.3 Owode-Egba Centre, Nigeria: Infrastructure and functions

---

Owode-Egba became the capital of the newly created Obafemi-Owode Local Government Area in 1976. In 1988, it had an estimated total population of 11,205.

Infrastructural facilities at the centre include: radio-telephone; electricity; piped water system; borehole. The centre is well connected by tarred roads and has excellent accessibility from all parts of the Local Government Area.

The only *administrative function* at Owode-Egba is the Local Government offices.

Social service functions at the centre include: general post office; clinic; maternity home; dispensary; traditional healing clinic; community centre; viewing (audio-visual) centre; adult education centre; a primary school.

The following *commercial and retail functions* exist at the centre: two banks; rural market; agro-service centre; hotel; number of general retail dealers; number of blacksmiths.

The only *industrial activities* at the centre are a number of small agro-based cottage industries involved in cassava and rice preparation.

Source: Adalemo (1993).

It is important to note here that many of Nigeria's rural service centres have evolved over a long time under the management of traditional authorities. These authorities continue to provide a human settlements management system parallel to formal local government. In Yorubaland, towns were under the administration of *obas*, the Yoruba traditional kings. The *oba* administered the town through a board made up of chiefs, each chief representing a ward or sector of the town. A ward chief also had authority over the rural lands outside the town wall, including rural service centres, and over any new towns emerging in his sector of the rural hinterland. This strong traditional system has continued to provide a framework for community investment in rural service centre development (UNCHS 1991).

In Nigeria, there are no specific financial allocations for rural service centre development. However, as earlier indicated, the Directorate of Food, Roads and Rural Infrastructure has injected a lot of capital into rural service centres. Much of the physical development in rural centres designated as local government area capitals has been on the basis of normal annual capital investment by the responsible local authorities, using direct and indirect federal and state financial allocations (Adalemo 1993).

Tanzania

Tanzania does not have a nationwide policy dealing exclusively with rural service centres. Instead, rural service centre development is handled through a number of policies and plans, some of them sectoral in orientation. One of the plans prepared was the Zonal/Regional Physical Plan covering Mbeya, Iringa (including Njombe district), Morogoro and Coast Regions and incorporating the fast growing Uhuru Corridor. The Uhuru Corridor Zonal Physical Plan provided for the creation of a five-tier hierarchy (Lerise 1993).

Table 14.4 Makambako Centre, Tanzania: Infrastructure and functions

The centre had 15,489 people (or 5,147 households) in 1988. Although it should have been reclassified as a class 1 township with its own local authority (the population range for this status is 9,000 to 18,000), it is still functioning as a rural trading centre, and most rural centres, including district centres are in the same position. It was the headquarters for the division, as well as for four wards. The centre covers an area of about 432 hectares.

Infrastructural facilities at the centre include: telephone service (with sixty-five connections); rail and road connections (making the centre a very accessible local collection and transportation centre); piped water supply (with a capacity to serve 40,000 people); electricity (supplied from the main national grid).

The centre's *administrative functions* include: police camp; primary court; military camp; Trunk Road Maintenance camp; Revenue Office (central government); Tanzania Electricity Supply Company office; Tanzania Coffee Board office; Tanzania–Zambia (Tanzam) Railway office.

Social service functions at the centre include the following: two nursery schools; three primary schools; one secondary school; one health centre with twelve beds, catering for about 300 patients and 50 maternity cases per day; two dispensaries.

The centre has the following *commercial and retail functions*: one branch of the National Bank of Commerce; one crop produce market; one farm implements sales outlet; one fertiliser sales outlet; one cement sales outlet; 160 retail shops; five sub-wholesale shops; three grocers; six soft-drink retail outlets; two cigarette agents; one stationery and photocopying shop; four petrol stations; four automobile garages; seven butchers' shops; five hardware shops; four motor vehicle spare-parts shops; six timber shops; one insurance agent; two cinema halls; fourteen guest houses; seven charcoal dealers; seven beer-wholesale dealers; twenty-two *pombe* (local brew) bars; one photographic studio; one hotel; six tailors' shops; and five shoe-making and repair shops.

Industrial and other non-agricultural enterprises include: eighteen grain mills; ten furniture-making enterprises; and storage go-downs with the capacity to handle 15,000 tonnes.

Source: Lerise (1993)

The hierarchical and spatial organisation of Tanzania's rural service centre system is closely tied to the country's local government and central government field administration systems through a policy of decentralisation (1972–82). Other related policies include the regional growth centre strategy, recommended by the First National Five Year Development Plan (1964–9), and the villagisation resettlement programme (1968–75). The idea of villagisation was partly based on the assumption that compact spatial arrangement of individual villages would minimise infrastructure costs and improve access to basic services. For this purpose, the establishment of village centres, the lowest tier in the rural service centre hierarchy, was recommended.

The Integrated Rural Development Plans (1972) also had some implications for rural service centres to identify development projects and programmes to be incorporated in the Third Five-Year Development Plan (1976–81).

The final policy of relevance is the National Agricultural Development Policy, introduced in 1983. This recommended the establishment of 'zonal centres' whose purpose would be to receive and distribute agricultural inputs to farmers in the surrounding areas and to provide storage facilities for the 'National Strategic Grain Reserve' programme (Lerise 1993).

Zimbabwe

During Zimbabwe's colonial period, the entire network of urban centres was located within areas reserved exclusively for the white settler population then called 'European Areas'. Virtually all small towns and rural centres were designed to serve the needs of white commercial farmers and mining companies. In comparison, black rural areas, then known as 'Tribal Trust Lands', were served by small townships and business centres that generally had very poor infrastructure and were functionally dominated by rather impoverished general dealer stores. Correcting this imbalance was one of the most urgent development objectives of independent Zimbabwe's first government which assumed power in 1980. An additional motive was the rehabilitation of rural infrastructure which had been destroyed during the liberation war in the 1970s. To this end, the Ministry of Local Government and Town Planning released a document in 1981 entitled 'Programme for the Development of Service Centres in the Rural Areas of Zimbabwe' and this was implemented through the Transitional National Development Plan, focusing on the Communal Areas, formerly Tribal Trust Lands (Government of Zimbabwe 1981d; 1982). It was not until 1985 that the Ministry of Local Government and Town Planning proposed a national hierarchy of human settlements ranging from cities to rural service centres, rural business centres, and consolidated villages. Each rural service centre is designed to serve up to 10,000 people residing within a maximum radius of twenty kilometres.

Implementation of the growth and rural service centre policy has focused on the provision of funds for the establishment of basic physical and social infrastructure in all of the fifty-five district service centres in the country (one in each district), some of them designated as growth points. (Mutizwa-Mangiza 1992; Wekwete 1991).

CONCLUSION

From the above discussion, it is clear that there has been considerable effort in developing rural service centres in Africa, even within countries which have no specific rural service centre policies.

Evaluations of the implementation of the national rural service centre programme in Malawi have generally been positive. Monitoring is being undertaken as part of the implementation process. The success of the pilot project resulted in its extension into a national programme. In Tanzania, evaluations of other related policies and programmes, in particular the villagisation programme, have indicated some positive results. Most of these services have been provided at village centres, the lowest tier of Tanzania's rural service centre hierarchy. In Nigeria, the designation of some rural service centres as rural local government area capitals has led to rapid improvements in the provision of public facilities, which has boosted the vibrancy of rural market centres (Adalemo 1993). In Côte d'Ivoire, many small centres have been accorded commune status with a much higher level of infrastructure and service endowment (Saint-Vil 1993). In Zimbabwe, the rural growth and service centre policy has vastly improved the infrastructure within the formerly neglected communal lands, and this has contributed to the significant growth of smallholder and peasant agricultural production (Mutizwa-Mangiza and Helmsing 1991).

There remain significant policy and implementation problems. Côte d'Ivoire and Nigeria have no specific rural service centre development policies or programmes except through the creation of rural local authority capitals, and development in Tanzania has focused on areas of rapid economic growth. As a result, coordination of rural service centre development activities continues to be a problem in these countries (Lerise 1993). In Malawi and Zimbabwe, with explicit rural service centre policies, the planning and implementation of these centres has largely followed a top–down approach, with little involvement of rural local authorities and local communities (Matope 1993). In Malawi, this resulted in over-planned provision, high maintenance cost, and some unneeded services which are grossly underutilised. In Côte d'Ivoire, many rural service centres are poorly connected with their hinterlands and with larger centres in the central place hierarchy.

While the justification for rural service centre development is the reduction of imbalances between rural and urban areas, this has not been achieved in most African countries. Local employment opportunities remain low in the rural areas and the maintenance of infrastructure and services at the centres is generally poor (Matope 1993; Lerise 1993; Saint-Vil 1993). They provide an inadequate geographical coverage and require a more equitable spread through a larger number of smaller centres and the establishment of periodic markets and mobile services (Matope 1993).

Rural development in developing countries, including those in southern Africa, can be greatly enhanced through the adoption of clear national rural service centre policies. Rural service centres are part of a wider network within a national hierarchy of central places from the smallest rural service centre to the capital city and should be coordinated with adequate means to implement these policies. Rural service centre policies should be flexible to accommodate both service and growth oriented centres and local needs, through a more mobile service where necessary. In general, road networks are inadequate to cope with the transportation of agricultural produce to the markets. The whole issue of transport is often either ignored or treated lightly, and yet it is essential for integrating rural service centres more closely with the regional and national economy. The majority of the world's poor reside within rural areas, and raising farm productivity and generating non-farm rural employment through community participation in rural service centre infrastructure are essential for tackling rural poverty.

NOTE

I am grateful to UNCHS (Habitat) for allowing me to use the results of the project reported in this paper. However, the interpretations and views expressed here are my own, and not of UNCHS (Habitat).

URBANISATION STRATEGY IN THE NEW SOUTH AFRICA: THE ROLE OF SECONDARY CITIES AND SMALL TOWNS

The spatial pattern of population, and the concomitant spatial arrangement of human settlement, constitute the most essential geographical expression for the distribution which provides human geography with its starting point. This distribution both reflects and influences a nation's social, economic and political organisation. It defines to some extent the problems a society faces in attempting to guide the pace and direction of change, and fundamentally influences the opportunities for and constraints on future development (Rondinelli and Ruddle 1978). Small wonder, then, that most governments have attempted to modify or mould the distribution of population and settlement to a greater or lesser degree.

Past South African governments have been no exception with population policies during the apartheid era geared to maximising the proportion of the black population living in Bantustans located on the periphery of the national space-economy. South Africa's first democratically elected government of 1994 has inherited an urban system which reflects the country's history of colonisation, white settlement and apartheid policies. With the removal of restrictive legislation and more permissive urban planning, changes in both the volume and spatial patterns of urbanisation are to be expected. Urban–rural disparities in incomes, actual or perceived job prospects and service provision are likely to fuel migration flows. Given the already high concentration of population in metropolitan areas, especially Gauteng, together with high levels of unemployment (Rogerson 1995) and large housing backlogs (Lupton and Murphy 1995), the desirability and possible form of a national urbanisation strategy must clearly be considered. The government's white paper on urban development (Government of South Africa 1995a) largely fails to address this issue. It categorises South African urban settlements into a four-level hierarchy with dividing points at populations of 100,000, 500,000, and 2,000,000, following classification used by the United Nations in the developing world.[1] This crude classification conceals more than it reveals, leading to the assertion in the white paper that South Africa's urban hierarchy is 'not an unbalanced one, with the relative sizes of urban settlements from the largest to smallest corresponding with international norms' (Government of South Africa 1995a: 17). However a recent analysis of the urban hierarchy suggests otherwise (Lemon and Cook 1994), as will be seen below. The white paper also takes no account of the very considerable variations in the nature of the existing hierarchy.

The question of an urbanisation strategy should not be viewed only, or even primarily, in the context of metropolitan growth, but also that of rural and regional reconstruction. The government's Reconstruction and Development Programme recognises the need to address both rural–urban and regional inequalities, and an urbanisation strategy is potentially relevant to both problems. Of particular importance in the context of rural reconstruction is the role of small towns, which pose distinctive problems in post-apartheid South Africa (Dewar 1994a).

It is not without some trepidation that these questions are posed. Regional and spatial planning in developing countries has an unhappy track record (Dewar *et al.* 1984a; Rogerson 1989a, 1989b; Simon 1990, 1992a), and is generally in retreat. This trend has been underpinned both by the return of growth as the dominant World Bank approach to development, and by the widespread adoption of Structural Adjustment Programmes (Simon and Rakodi 1990). The ensuing section of the chapter draws on the now considerable literature on spatial planning in developing countries with a view to learning lessons from past failures and understanding both the nature and limitations of such strategies. The South African situation will then be considered in the context of international experience.

PLANNING URBAN SYSTEMS: LESSONS AND LIMITATIONS

Most governments have achieved less than they expected (or purported to expect) from the application of national urbanisation strategies. One reason is simply geographical inertia. Historical settlement patterns are generally quite resilient: in England, place-name evidence quickly reveals that most towns and villages date from the Anglo-Saxon period. Such historically evolved settlement patterns therefore constrain subsequent development. In theory at least, radical changes may be easier for countries with a low level of urbanisation (Renaud 1981; Richardson 1976), although resource constraints and other factors may belie this. For most countries, including South Africa with its relatively developed urban system, attempts to work with the existing pattern of cities and towns are likely to be more effective than trying to create new growth poles.

Theories of spatial planning in developing countries have been abstract and elusive. They have invariably been based on Western models which were either inappropriate, or which needed careful adaptation to local circumstances. During the 1970s in particular there was a spatial element in the five-year plans of most developing countries, generally focusing on some variant of growth-pole or growth-centre strategy. Regional planning became a state tool of redistribution, or apparent redistribution, from core to periphery, through conspicuous investment: a top–down strategy which contrasted with the bottom–up character of much of the development activity undertaken by NGOs and local social movements (Simon and Rakodi 1990).

Even in high-income countries, growth-pole policies have enjoyed mixed success. They have often reduced disparities between cities in different regions, but tend to have increased disparities between these centres and other localities within peripheral regions. Thus it is hardly surprising that Mabogunje (1981: 213) warned: 'The developmental significance of a growth centre in an underdeveloped country is thus predicated on a prior restructuring of the spatial economy – without this, it will simply create a dual economy.' Whereas in developed countries like France, with its 'metro-poles d'equilibre', growth poles sought to reactivate and develop existing productive structures, in developing countries it is often necessary to create new ones. In practice, growth poles in these countries generally failed to promote economic growth either of the cities selected or of the surrounding regions; at best, they became enclaves of modern activities with few if any linkages to their hinterlands (Rondinelli 1981). Failures were often compounded by instability of policy, rendering urbanisation strategies totally ineffective.

Underlying growth-pole policies was a belief in processes variously described as modernisation, diffusion, 'trickle-down' and 'spread' (Lemon 1977). Hirschmann (1958) argued for massive investments in central locations, recognising that this would accentuate core-periphery differences, but arguing that 'trickle-down' would take over, as growth impulses spread slowly over the periphery. Myrdal's (1957) model of cumulative causation might have been taken as a warning: his 'spread' effects only became active at a late stage of economic development, and then in part due to government intervention. Developing countries were by definition at a much earlier stage of development, and in any case lacked an adequate spatial structure to promote and spread development.

In Western countries, as Johnson (1970: 171) pointed out 'the varied hierarchy of central places has not only made possible an almost complete commercialisation of agriculture but facilitated a wide spatial diffusion of light manufacturing, processing and service industries'. The absence of such hierarchies in developing countries, and the weakness of transport systems, maximises distance–decay effects, and encourages concentrated development (Logan 1972). To promote increased production and exchange between urban and rural areas, the development of places at the lower end of the settlement hierarchy is needed. Unless the economies of secondary cities are integrated with those of their regions, their growth may generate strong 'backwash' effects that drain their hinterlands of resources (Rondinelli 1983a: 14). Rondinelli argues that the strengthening of secondary cities and the linkages between them and smaller cities and towns can stimulate equitable, bottom–up development without necessarily creating a classical urban hierarchy or log normal rank-size distribution.

Not all agree with such prescriptions. Richardson (1981: 269) argued that in many developing countries, the easiest way to raise rural incomes and welfare is to absorb surplus rural population in the larger towns. More recently, he showed that claimed savings in per capita costs for providing infrastructure, shelter, education and health facilities outside the metropolitan areas are partially offset by increasing costs with distance from the core region (Richardson 1987). Likewise Dewar *et al.* (1984a: 132) have argued the case for investment in large cities:

> in countries where large numbers of people are being forced off the land through abject poverty to seek survival elsewhere, and where the national priority is the creation of jobs and survival chances, the degree to which governments can afford not to capitalise on every opportunity they have is questionable. In these situations, the largest cities represent a considerable resource and it may make sense relatively to concentrate urban investment on them.

The circumstances described here will be all too familiar to South Africans. Certainly the provision of infrastructure and services to a concentrated urban population will be far cheaper than to a dispersed rural population; the practical and very urgent question for policy makers concerns the relative advantages of locating surplus rural population in large cities or small towns.[2] This will be addressed further below.

This reference to the specific problem of surplus rural population may usefully carry the discussion to questions of context and goals. It has often been the case in developing countries that the goals of spatial-planning policies have not been clearly enunciated, or that too many (sometimes contradictory) goals are stated, and altogether unrealistic expectations are placed on the policy tools available. The development of policy needs to start from a particular development problem, and to be based on an understanding of the social and economic processes underlying it, in order to formulate clear goals and strategies. Thus Gasper (1988), in his study of rural growth points in Zimbabwe, emphasised the need for a more thorough knowledge of the constraints imposed by the structures of retailing, marketing and manufacturing, including the dominance of markets by large-scale manufacturers and the need to compete with established traders. Instead, spatial strategies have tended to view settlement in isolation from its socio-economic context. Too often they have treated symptoms rather than the underlying causes of poverty and inequality (Simon and Rakodi 1990).

A settlement strategy should be developed only as one element of a country's overall development planning. If this is not the case, other elements of national economic development policy may have unintended spatial effects which undermine the supposed benefits of spatial policies (Renaud 1981). Examples include trade protection and industrial incentives, agricultural policies, regulation of economic activities such as energy, transport investment and regulation, the centralisation of the state and concentration of decision-making in the capital, institutional structure and policies concerning public enterprises and government procurement.

Settlement strategies are thus appropriate only if spatial and settlement issues are contributory factors in the development problem. It may well be the case that spatially uneven development and an atypical settlement hierarchy result from economic and political forces which lie beyond the scope of settlement policy (Dewar et al. 1984a). Spatial policies are innately conservative, in that they do not seek to affect the underlying processes of social and economic change. In this sense they may appeal to governments wishing to be seen to be tackling problems of poverty and inequality (Gore 1984; Richardson 1976; Simon 1992a), leading Simon and Rakodi (1990: 258) to conclude that 'continued widespread development of regional policy has been functional to the state and allied segments of capital'. The pervasive obfuscation in spatial planning between place and people, settlement and income, may thus be a conscious one in many countries, explaining the degree to which discredited policies continue to be promoted.

Spatial planning viewed in a wider development context raises related issues of 'top–down' versus 'bottom–up' approaches, local economic development initiatives, and the devolution of power from central government. Although there may be inherent contradictions in some instances, the dichotomy between top–down and bottom–up strategies is essentially artificial: both approaches are needed, the former to create an appropriate framework for the realisation of the latter (Dewar et al. 1984a). Top–down strategies have failed not so much because they are top–down as because they suffer from weaknesses already discussed. Where small and intermediate centres are concerned – the level where they may interact with bottom–up strategies – there has been an over-emphasis on physical planning, neglecting social and economic relations, and too little account has been taken of local conditions. Simon (1992a: 43) calls for a 'people-centred focus sensitive to indigenous values' and Todes (1993: 25–6) calls for a more socially sensitive regional planning which facilitates greater control by the poor over the nature and path of development in particular regions, building on aspects of bottom–up strategies including basic needs, eco-development and community participation approaches. Ærøe (1992) favours a Scandinavian approach focusing on the interplay between the individual entrepreneur and his business environment; he argues from the example of Makambako, Tanzania that local regional development does not depend on the selective spatial closure demanded by the agropolitan approach, but may happen within open systems.

Whereas bottom–up approaches are essentially concerned with rural and agricultural development (but require supportive development at the lower end of the urban hierarchy and other national or regional policy elements), local economic development (LED) is an essentially urban concept which may be associated with places at all levels of the hierarchy from small towns up to secondary cities. Tomlinson (1993a) and Rogerson (1994) argued that spatial planning in South Africa should follow experience elsewhere, moving not from national to regional scale but to LED planning which promotes economic growth and job creation, and contributes to the local tax base. Tomlinson (1993b) suggested alternatives to the municipal marketing of cities most commonly associated with LED, including entre-preneurial, progressive, community-based and private-sector-led initiatives (Tomlinson 1993b). LED has produced some dramatic success stories, but is not without its critics (Bovaird 1992). If the pool of business and industrial expansion is seen as finite, LED is open to the objection that it is a zero-sum game, leading to wasteful competition. The initiatives of local governments may suffer from inadequate analysis, weak implementation and insufficient coordination. Some may be at variance with national priorities. Many of these criticisms could apply equally to programmes led by the private or voluntary sectors. The solution would seem to be for national policy to encourage diversity and innovation at local level, harn-essing local energy and resourcefulness, but within a strategic framework of national objectives and priorities.

Revenue sources pose a critical question for LED, and indeed for the success of bottom–up forms of rural development too. In most developing countries, the scope for local governments to raise their own revenue is limited (by national policy as well as by the limitations of the local revenue base), yet support from central government may be meagre and irregular. To capitalise on local initiative and drive, local governments need the financial autonomy to initiate and implement policies without being subject to long delays or rejections from central government.

In larger developing countries, meaningful local autonomy should ideally coexist with an effective provincial level of government which is able to execute nationally formulated strategies and to identify priorities and policies appropriate for each region. Fiscal resources are again crucial: since lagging regions generally have the weakest resource base, revenues based on the principle of derivation will not suffice: a redistributive formula based on development priorities is needed, allocating central government revenues (or revenues earmarked for regional governments but raised centrally).

This necessarily brief review of the experience of spatial planning in developing countries has, it is hoped, demonstrated both its limitations and its potential value if sensitively used as part of a wider developmental strategy. In turning to the South African case, attention is focused on two specific aspects of the issues discussed so far: small towns and secondary cities. Limitations of space decree that the discussion will focus particularly on the role of these settlements in a national urbanisation strategy, but it should be remembered, first, that they represent only two levels in the overall hierarchy of settlement (albeit arguably the most critical in the South African context); and secondly, that policies relating to these groups of settlements should be worked out in conjunction with broader national, provincial and local development policies.

THE DISTRIBUTION AND SIZE OF URBAN SETTLEMENTS IN SOUTH AFRICA SINCE 1910

During the present century, metropolitan areas have overshadowed other towns, limiting their growth. In the period 1911–36, 77 per cent of the positive net shift in South Africa's population occurred in the eight largest metropolitan areas plus Kimberley (Fair 1965: 65), notwithstanding the establishment of several new towns during this period, based on railway development (De Aar), agricultural intensification (Eastern Free State), coastal tourism (Margate) and resource development (Nigel) (Lemon and Cook 1994: 334). Between 1936 and 1960, 74 per cent of the positive net shift was still in the same nine areas, but there was evidence of some spilling out into areas immediately adjacent to the Witwatersrand, Cape Town and Durban (Fair 1965: 65). In the 1960s the upward shifts of African population were more widely distributed (Board 1973), reflecting, *inter alia*, both recent industrial development and new mining developments on the eastern highveld. African shifts to the Western Cape were relatively small, reflecting the stringency of the coloured (mixed-race) labour preference policy in that region until its abolition in 1984. All new towns established between the mid-1930s and 1970 were resource based.

This continuing pattern of urban concentration, albeit with a gradually widening base, was reflected in the 1960s in a distinctive urban hierarchy (Table 15.1). South African metropolitan areas appear considerably larger than the size predicted by Christaller's k=3 central place model, whilst there are fewer places than might be expected at the lower levels of the hierarchy (Davies 1967; Davies and Cook 1968). This reflects both the low population densities and extensive farming patterns characteristic of 'white' rural areas and the virtual absence of a modern economy in most of the black rural areas.

Lemon and Cook (1994) have attempted to update earlier studies of the South African urban hierarchy using data from the 1985 census. The position of settlements in a central place hierarchy would ideally be

Table 15.1 The South African hierarchy of central places in the 1960s as compared with Christaller's k=3 model

Order number of towns	South African number of towns	K = 3	South African average size of towns	K = 3 average size of towns
1. Primary metropolitan areas	1	1	2,180,914	1,000,000
2. Major metropolitan areas	3	2	754,352	300,000
3. Metropolitan areas	8	6	197,040	100,000
4. Major country towns	19	18	30,136	30,000
5. Country towns	57	54	11, 131	9, 000
6. Minor country towns	173	162	3,538	3,500
7. Local service centres	140	486	1,364	1,500
8. Low order service centres	200	1,358	1,047	800

Sources: Davies (1967), Davies and Cook (1968)

Table 15.2 The South African urban hierarchy in 1985

Metropolitan areas	Population 1985
Witwatersrand	3,395,286
Greater Cape Town	1,911,521
Durban	1,482,127
Greater Pretoria	1,034,572
Port Elizabeth	501,804
Vanderbijlpark/Vereeniging	462,242
Greater East London	431,973
Greater Bloemfontein	328,609
Free State Goldfields	320,319
Pietermaritzburg	236,463

Table 15.3 The South African urban hierarchy by size categories

	Total urban population	Number of towns	% of total urban
Metropolitan areas	10,074,196	10	72
Towns over 100,000	530,226	4	4
Towns over 50,000	889,507	13	6
Towns over 20,000	968,551	31	7
Other urban settlements	1,636,776		11

Source: Lemon and Cook (1994: 334–5)

measured in terms of functions, using data on service provision and on retail turnover and/or floorspace if it were available in an acceptable form. Population does, however, provide a crude surrogate. Lemon and Cook have overcome one serious limitation of census data by combining figures for parts of contiguous urban areas where these are given separately in the census (often on an ethnic basis where black areas had acquired the status of independent local authorities). The figures in Table 15.2 and 15.3 and Figure 15.1 thus represent urban systems rather than single local authority areas, although they are still far smaller in many cases than the functionally urbanised populations of the country since these included many people living in informal settlements outside local authority boundaries.

Ten metropolitan areas are recognised, using the big gap between Pieter-maritzburg and Newcastle to justify the cut-off point. Some 80 per cent of urban dwellers in towns of over 20,000 were found in these ten areas, indicating a very high degree of concentration; 39 per cent lived in South Africa's megapolis, the combined metropolitan areas Pretoria–Witwatersrand–Vereeniging, an area which generated 40 per cent of South Africa's GDP.

The overshadowing effect of metropolitan areas is clearly apparent in Table 15.2 and 15.3. Only four secondary cities had more than 100,000 people, and together they accounted for a mere 4 per cent of urban dwellers.

At a magisterial district level, the distribution of districts with an urbanisation level of 40 per cent or more in 1985 divided the country into a relatively more urbanised southwestern part and a less urbanised north-eastern part (van der Merwe *et al.* 1991). This appears surprising at first sight, given the much greater density of urban settlement in the north-eastern half of the country. The explanation rests in the semi-arid nature of much of the southwestern half, which supports only extensive grazing outside the winter rainfall area around Cape Town. All the former Bantu-stans except western Bophuthatswana were in the better watered half of the country, although topography and soils limit their agricultural potential over wide areas. In 'white' farming areas too there is a denser rural population in these northern and eastern areas, thus it is these areas which are potential reservoirs for future urbanisation (Lemon and Cook 1994: 336).

The high degree of metropolitan concentration has long been used by South African governments to justify successive industrialisation policies, although the relationship of these to apartheid ideology, and in particular the concentration of as high a proportion as possible of the black population in the Bantustans, has always been apparent. The urban hierarchy shows that industrial growth points have made a minimal contribution to the redis-tribution of the urban population: in 1985 only 15 per cent of the urban population lived in the fifty-nine deconcentration and industrial develop-ment points earmarked in the 1982 strategy, many of which had enjoyed incentives under previous decentralisation programmes (van der Merwe *et al.*

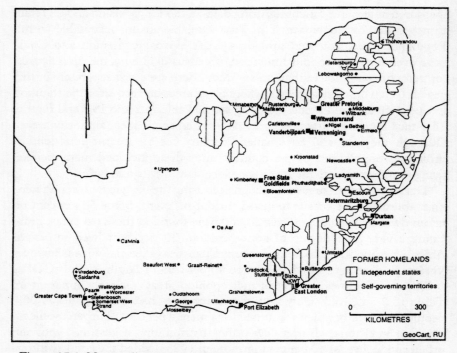

Figure 15.1 Metropolitan areas and main urban centres. Former bantustan areas

1991). Umtata, the Transkeian capital, was the only free-standing growth point in the Bantustans with a population of more than 50,000 in 1985 (Figure 15.1). Along with Butterworth, the second largest growth point, it was an established urban centre with a rail connection long before apartheid decentralisation policies were pursued. There were only four other free-standing urban settlements of over 20,000 in the Bantustans in 1985. Three (two in Ciskei and the Qwaqwa capital Phuthaditjhaba) began life as resettlement camps – thus people were dumped there long before a degree of very poorly paid employment was induced to follow. The fourth, Kanyamazane in KaNgwane, is unusual for its dependence on white farm employment (Lemon and Cook 1994: 336).

South Africa's distinctive urban hierarchy poses important questions for post-apartheid planners. Should they attempt to reduce metropolitan dominance by concentrating on secondary cities? At lower levels in the urban hierarchy, how far should planners seek to increase the numbers of smaller central places? And how far should the future of Bantustan urban centres, which owe their very existence to apartheid planning, be sustained by further assistance or allowed to decline?

SECONDARY CITIES IN A SOUTH AFRICAN URBANISATION STRATEGY

Perhaps in reaction to failed apartheid policies of decentralisation to the periphery of the South African space economy, several authors have suggested that regional policy should emphasise the stimulation of secondary cores with strong potential for regional growth (Bos 1989; Lemon 1989; Lemon and Cook 1994; van der Merwe 1990). Secondary city strategies are a popular alternative for middle-income countries such as South Africa (Tomlinson 1993a), where they aim to reduce the perceived bias to large cities in taxation and public spending, and to implement economic policies that move the terms of trade in favour of secondary cities. Rondinelli (1983a) argues that in developed countries, cities of 100,000–200,000 people can supply all but the most specialised services efficiently, and that cities of this scale can offer economies of scale for efficient investment in public utilities, infrastructure and social services.

Various reasons may be advanced for secondary city strategies, and it is essential that those who frame a specific strategy are clear about its aims. All the reasons noted by Rondinelli (1983a) could apply to South African circumstances:

1. alleviation of problems in larger cities;
2. reduction of regional inequalities;
3. the stimulation of rural economies (which will also require the strengthening of linkages between secondary cities and smaller towns);
4. increase in administrative capacity to help secondary cities to absorb rural migrants and themselves initiate programmes to stimulate rural economies;
5. the reduction of urban poverty within the secondary cities themselves.

Some believe that a reorientation in the location of investment will occur by moving from import substitution, which steers investment to the largest cities, towards export promotion (Rondinelli 1983a). In South Africa, such a shift to export-oriented manufacturing is widely regarded as desirable (Black 1992; Rogerson 1991, 1995), but is likely to favour the port cities which already enjoy metropolitan status. This is indeed already the case with the 1991 Regional Industrial Development Programme, which aimed to neutral-ise the policy distortions (including cross-subsidisation favouring transport of raw materials rather than finished goods, and industry-wide wage bargaining) which favour the establishment of industrial firms in the PWV region and to a lesser extent in the Durban–Pinetown area (Wilsenach and Lighthelm 1993).

Although they are not secondary cities in terms of the urban hierarchy defined in this chapter, there are strong arguments to favour policies which will strengthen coastal metropolitan areas, especially Port Elizabeth and East London which have been themselves economically depressed and which head the urban hierarchies of depressed regions. It has already been noted that successful urbanisation policies are likely to be those which look to existing cities with growth potential, and the identification above of only four secondary cities in the existing urban hierarchy clearly poses problems in this regard. As Dewar *et al.* (1986: 158) observe, 'spatially uneven develop-ment and an atypical settlement hierarchy may in fact be and usually are the result of economic and political forces which lie beyond the scope of settlement policy'.

This is the difficulty with suggestions such as that of van der Merwe *et al.* (1991) who, noting the relative absence of higher-order centres over large areas such as the Western Karoo and Northern Cape, stress the need for strong regional centres to be identified. The only true secondary city in the whole of this region is Kimberley (Figure 15.1), whose eccentric position on the eastern edge of the new Northern Cape region makes it far from ideal as a provincial capital or secondary city intended to strengthen the regional economy. Upington is far better located, but much too small to perform the role of a secondary city; this would remain true even if the functions of a provincial capital were transferred there, given the small population and economy of the province in question. What this points to is that even towns of over 20,000 are so few in the arid western half of South Africa that it is no great research task to identify regional centres, strong or otherwise: the coastal town of George, with nearby Mossel Bay, has the greatest potential; Beaufort West, Graaff Reinet and De Aar are virtually the only inland possibilities, and these are all in the southeast of the region. Much of the western half of the country simply lacks an urban hierarchy altogether, and no urbanisation strategy can be expected to change this.

Whilst the eastern half of the country is much more densely settled, serious candidates for promotion as secondary cities are again few. The least controversial is Newcastle, which meets the qualifications in terms of size and the potential to serve a considerable region with no other city of similar size. In the northern Transvaal, Pietersburg, although well below 100,000 people at present, is not inconceivable as a future secondary city; it has already benefited from the effective leadership of a former town clerk (Tomlinson 1993a: 337). Much more problematic long-term candidates are Umtata and Mmabatho for Transkei and Western Transvaal/Northeastern Cape respectively. In the Free State, it is existing metropolitan areas rather than secondary cities – Bloemfontein and the Free State Goldfields – whose regional role will continue to be important.

A nationwide secondary city strategy does not appear to meet South Africa's needs. Rather it appears that a flexible, regionally sensitive approach is required. This will confirm the growth of some of the smaller metropolitan areas, strengthen the growth of well-located secondary cities, especially Kimberley and Newcastle, and promote the growth of a few towns with potential in less urbanised or less densely settled areas.

To name specific towns is bound to provoke controversy, and this brief excursion into consideration of particular places is necessarily superficial. It is also vital, however, if only to demonstrate that the alternatives in South Africa are few, and that an expensive research project to identify candidates for a secondary-city strategy is not required.

What is important is that South Africa's urbanisation strategy responds to the specific characteristics of its urban hierarchy, and to its marked regional variations. This suggests that a national framework should be purely indicative; the provinces should have the power to pursue appropriate strategies within this framework, while individual cities should have the autonomy and the resources to pursue local economic development paths consistent with the provincial strategy.

THE ROLE OF SMALL TOWNS

The relative deficiency of smaller urban settlements in the South African urban hierarchy has already been noted. It is doubtful, however, that the attempted creation of new lower order central places would be a wise use of limited resources in most of the country. What is at issue here is primarily the strengthening of existing small towns. The government's urban development strategy recognises the need 'for more systematic action to enhance the prospects of small towns in particular' (Government of South Africa 1995a: 17). As with secondary city strategies, it is important to clarify the purposes of such policies. Referring to the work of Dewar, cited below, the strategy recognises that 'the fate of small towns and cities often rests on the unpredictable and unstable condition of the agrarian economy'. In the South African context, there are essentially two justifications for a focus on small towns: as instruments of rural development, and as a means of holding and employing population rather than leaving it to swell migration flows to metropolitan areas.

The rapid population growth of South Africa's major cities is well known, but it is less widely appreciated that all except Cape Town have been experiencing an economic decline greater than that in South Africa as a whole, with growth in business and financial services only partially compensating for sharp declines in manufacturing employment (Tomlinson 1993a). This clearly questions the common assumptions of regional policy, that cities have a surfeit of economic activity and resources which can be redistributed to achieve greater equity. It also means that continuing flows of migrants – an estimated 600,000 a year in the 1990s according to the Urban Foundation (1990) – together with continuing high levels of natural population increase, are seeking jobs, shelter and services in a context of decline: fewer formal opportunities and a decreasing demand for informal sector goods and services (Tomlinson 1993a). This grim reality has a dual significance for small towns: it underlines the need for them to provide employment opportunities and act as holding points which will reduce migration flows to already overcrowded cities; but it also brings the unpalatable message that they cannot expect substantial handouts from national or provincial government to achieve this role, given current pressures on metropolitan areas.

There is widespread agreement that rural development in developing areas demands direct investment in small rural centres. Whether the approach is one of rural modernisation or a more integrated, locally controlled development strategy such as that embodied in the agropolitan development approach, small towns are perceived as providing a number of functions for their hinterlands.

Agropolitan development envisaged each district as centred on a town of 10,000–25,000 people, with a commuting radius of not more than five or ten kilometres, and forming a local government unit coinciding with a genuine community-of-interest area (Friedmann and Weaver 1979, Friedmann 1981/2). In much of South Africa, rather smaller towns would need to be used, and the radii would be necessarily greater. This in turn makes improved access to markets a critical issue in a situation where many rural producers are immobilised through poverty and able only to sell on foot (Dewar et al. 1984a: 143).

The functions of small urban centres include marketing, innovation diffusion, the 'capture' of income leakage to higher levels of the urban hierarchy, employment (including small-scale industry) and service provision. Whilst valid as a model, such statements are inadequate and potentially dangerous as the basis for top–down policies applied to whole countries or regions. The distribution of small towns and the population in their hinterlands is far from even, and their sizes far from uniform. The varying range of different services may invalidate the concept in the wrong conditions. Nor is it any good providing services or production facilities for which there is no demand: this underlines that policies of small town development cannot succeed in isolation from those more directly concerned with land and agriculture. This is particularly the case in the former Bantustans (Dewar *et al*. 1983), where there are structural obstacles to increased rural productivity arising from their historical functions as labour reservoirs and, in more recent years, dumping grounds for surplus labour.

In many areas of these former Bantustans, the best option may be to take the town to the countryside. Thus the government's white paper on rural development proposes the setting up of 'rings of periodic markets' (Government of South Africa 1995b: 10, 24–5). Government services such as pension distribution, mobile post offices and the health clinics could, it suggests, be arranged to coincide with these markets. The hope would be that these nodes would become more permanent central places eventually; whether or not this occurs, they could be a very effective way of reducing spatial imbalances and contributing to the development of South Africa's poorest regions.

The Bantustans also include two other groups of problem towns: industrial growth points and former Bantustan capitals. Both were essentially artificial creations sustained by apartheid policies. Those growth points which formed part of wider urban functional regions, such as Babelegi and Garankuwa in Bophuthatswana, may have sufficient locational attraction to retain much of their industrial employment, but since the introduction of a less politically determined regional industrial policy in 1991 industries have already begun to close down or leave as subsidies expire. Many of the former Bantustan capitals face severe economic decline unless they are allowed to retain significant administrative functions (Drummond and Parnell 1991).

Small towns in commercial agricultural areas display a different set of problems (Dewar 1994a). Changing transport technologies and the operation of cartels which control marketing have weakened connections between these towns and their hinterlands. They still provide some social and commercial services to the local regions, but they have lost what manufacturing functions they once possessed to larger towns. However the economic decline of these towns, which endangers the continued provision of essential services, has taken place in the context of rapid growth in their populations, swollen by loss of jobs on commercial farms. Increasing poverty and unemployment is the inevitable result.

The critical issue facing these towns, and those of the former Bantustans too, is, thus, job creation and income generation, without which few if any other forms of development are realistically possible. Dewar (1994a) and Nel (1994) draw attention to the success story of Stutterheim in the Eastern Cape, where talented local leaders from the black and white communities formed a joint forum in 1990 to tackle local disputes and build a common future. Subsequently, with the aid of the Development Bank of Southern Africa (DBSA), the forum established a company to oversee the development process, which it did with considerable success. The emphasis on job-creation schemes is particularly noteworthy, with the award of building and site-provisioning and servicing contracts to local black contractors who used labour-intensive practices. Also important is the fact that the money raised in Stutterheim has been largely retained within the community.

However, this success has depended on external finance from the DBSA, the Regional Services Council and the Independent Development Trust. The question, as Nel (1994: 374) acknowledges, is whether the initiative is replicable in other towns or even sustainable in Stutterheim in the long term without continued financial support. One can only agree with Nel's comment: 'The poorest areas cannot be expected to be self-funding and, as international experience indicates, making available loans and funds to the poorest regions is part of a government's social responsibility.' But how many small towns can realistically expect to gain such assistance, and which ones should have priority? Those in the commercial areas whose problems are less acute may perhaps be able to find most of the necessary resources themselves. Most towns within the former Bantustans will require substantial external help, and by no means all will be capable of providing the local leadership and initiative which were so critical in Stutterheim; many have little tradition of civic involvement under the erstwhile Bantustan administrations. Only if the national and/or provincial governments feel able to make them a priority commitment as part of a wider rural development policy can they hope for significant change.

Stutterheim represents an intermediate category; although in a commercial farming area and containing better infrastructure than most ordinary Bantustan rural centres, much of its hinterland consists of the former Ciskei Bantustan. Its transformation from desperate economic and political circumstances undoubtedly demonstrates the potential for local development initiatives. Where promising local leadership does emerge, it certainly deserves strong encouragement: there is little doubt that limited funds are most effectively used when targeted at responsible local groups who know what is needed for their communities. The government's rural development strategy stresses the importance of capacity building (Government of South Africa 1995b: 24, 44–6) 'so that individuals can take control of their own destinies', but makes clear that communities will have to manage with limited resources, supplementing them from the private sector where possible and targeting them well (24).

CONCLUSION

South Africa faces daunting development problems in both major cities and smaller towns. Employment and income generation must be priorities in both, because without them little else can happen. Urbanisation strategies at national and provincial level must be framed firmly within this context if they are to be meaningful, and local leadership, initiative and enterprise must be allowed maximum autonomy in framing solutions. Except perhaps for rural centres in the former Bantustans, they will at least begin with considerable advantages over their counterparts in most of southern Africa in terms of communications, infrastructure, services and human resources.

NOTES

1. In an end note, the White Paper notes the government's intention to provide a uniform classification system consistent with South African realities.
2. The government's urban development strategy implicitly recognised this, stating that there is no justification for interventionist policies which attempt to prevent urbanisation (Government of South Africa 1995a: 17). The rural development strategy is more explicit, acknowledging the greater costs of infrastructural development in the rural areas and the low incomes of the new rural councils. It concludes that poverty will limit the level and type of services developed, and that rural councils must seek to provide basic services to as many people as possible rather than high quality services to a minority (Government of South Africa 1995b: 38).

SOME ISSUES IN DEVELOPING SETTLEMENT POLICY ALTERNATIVES IN SOUTH AFRICA

There has been a long history of interference with settlement patterns in South Africa: the evolution of the settlement system has been profoundly influenced by direct settlement policies tied to the changing face of the political economy. Indeed, settlement policies and programmes have arguably been the main planks of what has passed for national and regional planning in this country. More recently, however, in the face of turbulent political change, and informed by planning tendencies internationally, this focus on settlement planning has largely disappeared as has a concern with, and confidence in, regional planning generally.

As South Africa's attention turns slowly towards tackling the daunting development issues it faces, this is a timely moment to return to the question of whether or not there is a case for national or regional settlement policy and, if the answer is in the affirmative, what are the issues which should inform this? My focus in addressing this question is not on urban and rural settlement policies *in toto* but rather on concentrations of settlements – on the desirability or efficacy of policies relating to national and regional urban settlement systems.

My approach to the question is structured into five parts. The first reviews the historical record of settlement policy in South Africa. The second scans this record, as well as the international experience of settlement policy, in order to extract some major lessons. The third reviews contextually the argument for settlement policy and planning. The fourth returns to the main lessons in order to identify an appropriate philosophic approach to the task. The final section identifies the primary roles that national and regional settlement policy and planning should play and some of the issues it must address.

HISTORICAL SETTLEMENT-BASED POLICY INTERVENTIONS

Although there is a common tendency to regard the historical experience of South Africa as being unique (and, indeed, in some respects, particularly the single-mindedness with which it pursued objectives of racial separation, it is), it is important to recognise that there are marked similarities with other southern African countries with a significant scale of settler penetration (for example, Namibia, Zimbabwe, Malawi and, to a lesser extent, Angola and Mozambique) (Dewar 1994b) with respect to settlement-based policies. This review, therefore, of South African policies is initially cast in the broader southern African perspective.

Historically, urbanisation in southern Africa did not originate 'naturally' in response to indigenous economic pressures and responses. It was manipulated consciously, through the displacement of peasant farmers, by a variety of colonial powers seeking to fuel the needs of embryonic settler economies, initially at least, in the form of labour to work commercial ranch and plantation farms and the mines. The extent of peasant displacement was directly proportional to the scale of settler economic penetration. As the settler economies became more diversified, policy shifts reflected attempts to resolve often conflicting settler requirements. On the one hand, there was an economic need for cheap labour reserves in the towns and cities. On the other, there was a strong social and political will to prevent a build-up of African people in the urban areas.

Similarly, while there was a strong political desire to keep the indigenous African population in economic and political subjugation, there was a growing need to develop an African urban middle class (to provide markets, a supply of increasingly skilled labour and a source of industrial capital, and to contribute to urban stability) and a progressive peasant-farming class (to contribute to meeting the consumption needs of the urban population and to expand the local market). Many policy shifts reflected a desire to distinguish between urban 'insiders', whose absorption into the urban system should be assisted, and 'outsiders' who should be excluded.

The policies applied have generally been strongly anti-large-city in thrust and can be grouped into a number of types.

1. Displacement policies, aimed at forcing peasant farmers off the land (for example, involuntary land seizure, expropriation, hut taxes).
2. Influx-control policies, aimed at preventing the free flow of people to the cities. These policies took two forms: direct measures (such as pass laws and forcible repatriation to the countryside) and indirect measures (of which anti-squatter laws, coupled with the limited state supply of housing, were the most common).
3. Deflective or diversionary measures, aimed at diverting urban flows away from the largest urban settlements to smaller towns and cities. Policies were frequently couched in the international rhetoric of growth-pole theory and primarily entailed decentralisation incentives that were aimed at making it cheaper for industries to move to, and operate from, smaller centres than from the largest cities.
4. Incentive measures, aimed at improving conditions in the source areas of migration – the rural areas. These primarily took the form of rural development and social investment programmes directed mainly at the commercial small-farmer sector, particularly via top–down organised nodal agricultural schemes (Dewar et al. 1986).

5. Urban absorption measures, to accommodate continuing urban growth and absorb insiders into the system. These measures had a number of characteristics. Patterns of urban expansion were informed primarily by the desire to separate poorer, particularly African, people from the settler town or city and urban growth took the form of sprawling, scattered pockets of development around the original settlement.

Significantly, settlement-based policy formation in South Africa has been informed by a number of different, and sometimes contradictory concerns, within the general rubric of concerns outlined above. Frequently, the policy rhetoric employed reflected international concerns and planning directions: always, however, there have been racial overtones. The main concerns have been:

1. racial separation, both regionally and intra-urbanly;
2. the (perceived excessive) growth of the largest cities;
3. regional economic development in underdeveloped regions (particularly, the need to establish an economic base for the homelands);
4. greater regional economic convergence and particularly combatting the economic polarisation of the PWV.

Frequently, the same policies or policy instruments have been used to pursue these very different objectives and this has contributed in no small measure to their relative failure. The main direct policies which have affected processes of settlement formation in South Africa are described in the following sections.

Influx control
Apart from the huge social, economic and fiscal costs imposed by this policy, and its long-term failure to achieve its objectives of controlling rapid (African) urbanisation, some of the main negative consequences in terms of settlements were very rapid rates of urbanisation in the large cities as controls began to crack, making urban management even more difficult; increased overcrowding in the rural homeland areas; high degrees of uncertainty, which negatively affected ongoing investment policies (this is particularly true of identified 'black spots' in white areas which were earmarked for removal – almost no investment occurred in these areas for over forty years, although populations frequently continued to grow); the promulgation of a mind-set in urban areas that Africans were temporary urban sojourners, which again led to investment neglect; and the creation of 'resettlement' areas in the homelands, where people removed from the white areas were relocated – frequently, the location of these settlements had no economic rationale and they often became remote islands of poverty and social misery.

Betterment programmes
'Betterment planning', common in many parts of Africa (it has been estimated that some 22 million people have been villagised in Africa in pre-

and post-independence periods through schemes of this kind (de Wet 1991, 1995)) has long been practised in South Africa. The term refers to successive schemes by various central and bantustan governments to rationalise small-scale agriculture, *inter alia* to combat the deterioration of natural resources and to contribute to agricultural development in black-occupied rural areas. Some have argued that the real motives underlying its implementation have less to do with environmental conservation and agricultural development than with ensuring a steady supply of migrant workers to the mines and industries of white South Africa and, later, with the control of rural populations (McAllister 1991).

Betterment programmes essentially involve four main steps:

1. The proclamation of a given area as a 'betterment' area;
2. The development of a land-use plan which divides the area into three zones (residential, arable and grazing), mainly on the basis of soil quality;
3. The relocation of people from their previous (usually widely dispersed), homestead sites to new, more compact villages ('compact' in order to promote the more efficient use of land and more convenient access to social and utility services);
4. The fencing of residential areas and grazing camps (McAllister 1991).

The consequences of the programmes have not been encouraging and they have frequently been negative (de Wet 1995; Yawitch 1981). They have resulted in considerable relocation which has had profoundly negative consequences in terms of social and kinship ties and local political structures; they have reduced local autonomy; they have failed to improve agricultural efficiency (primarily because they have not been undertaken as holistic rural development programmes) and have frequently reduced it (particularly through decreased flexibility in arable patterns as a result of the rigid separation of grazing and arable uses); they have failed to increase convenience significantly (primarily because the programmes most commonly have not had a service component); and they have failed to combat ecological decline (primarily because they have not changed the practices which underpin this).

Reactions to this system are occurring. In parts of the Transkei, people are reported to be leaving the residential areas of their betterment villages and re-establishing homesteads on or near their former pre-betterment sites. Similar processes have been taking place from the Ujamaa villages of Tanzania (McCall 1985).

Industrial decentralisation programmes
Historically, South Africa has pursued the goal of industrial decentralisation with considerable vigour and the form of the programme has changed on a number of occasions. The rhetoric associated with these policies indicates that a number of different (frequently conflicting) objectives have underpinned these programmes and the emphases of these objectives, too, have

shifted over time. The objectives have included, *inter alia*, the creation of an industrial economic base for newly emerging 'nation–states' (the bantustans); reducing economic polarisation and, particularly, slowing the growth of the largest cities; diverting black migrants away from the 'white' parts of metropolitan areas; promoting greater regional economic convergence and reducing inter-regional disparities; stimulating rural development through increasing rural incomes and creating a demand for agricultural products; and (primarily rhetorically) increased efficiency in rural social service delivery through rural service centres.

The programme has gone through a number of phases (Dewar *et al.* 1986). The initial phase in the 1950s and 1960s was related to the development of the bantustans. The original intention was to provide an industrial base within the bantustan areas, but this was, for political reasons, quickly diluted into the border industry policy. In the second phase, dominating the early and mid-1970s, the concerns were broadened, particularly in relation to the perceived 'hyper-urbanisation' of the largest cities (largely equated with the rapid growth of the black population). Numerous industrial decentralisation points were established, along with direct controls on the absorption of black labour in the white cities. The bantustan areas were primarily favoured in the selection of decentralisation areas.

In the third phase, focused on the late 1970s and early 1980s, the emphasis broadened beyond the bantustan areas. The rhetoric, although not the practice, of growth-pole theory was appropriated (growth points and centres replaced decentralisation points), associated with stated concerns about stimulating greater economic convergence; deconcentration points (points nearer, but still some distance from, the main metropolitan areas) were included in the settlements nominated for incentives, in a pragmatic attempt to pursue diversionary objectives while realising some economies of scale, if not agglomeration; and more indirect controls on metropolitan labour absorption (particularly through housing) replaced direct influx-control measures. In the final phase, following the Good Hope Conference in 1982, the nature of the programme changed. The need to reduce the number of points, to graft onto existing centres of agglomeration (the target changed from all large cities to the PWV, and the rhetoric increasingly included arguments for secondary city programmes), to target incentives, and to build on local strengths and local resources, were all recognised, at least rhetorically. However, very little has happened following this rhetorical acceptance: the programme began to fall into increasing disuse from this time, as increased questioning about its objectives took root (in particular, its racial overtones, the assumption that the large cities were 'too large' or 'too primate', the possibility or even the desirability of seeking to achieve regional economic convergence and the possibility of stimulating self-sustaining viable alternatives to existing centres of economic agglomeration).

There is widespread agreement amongst commentators that industrial decentralisation policy over the years has been a resounding failure (Bell and Padayachee 1984; Coetzee 1986; Dewar *et al.* 1984a, 1984b; Greyling 1983; Louw 1984; Maasdorp 1985; McCarthy 1985; Rogerson and Kobben 1982; Tomlinson and Addleson 1987; Wellings and Black 1986). *Inter alia*, it achieved little in terms of altering the regional pattern of economic activity and employment over the period of its existence; it failed to slow the growth of the largest cities significantly; it failed to bring about greater regional convergence; even in places where some decentralisation occurred, few backwards or forwards linkages into local hinterlands were achieved and the local impact of growth centres was therefore minimal; it resulted in transfers of jobs rather than the creation of new jobs and this damaged the economic infrastructure of many existing towns; it distorted the settlement pattern; it seldom resulted in self-sustaining development; it promoted large-scale corruption; and the cost has been enormous – there is general agreement that, in terms of the opportunity cost of capital employed, the programme resulted in a net loss of jobs.

The reasons underpinning this failure are complex but the most important include:

1. the spatial policy of decentralisation was diametrically opposed to the spatial dynamics generated by international and national macro-economic forces (for example, import substitution policies, transport tariff structures and the like all favoured the largest cities);
2. economies of agglomeration and scale proved stronger than anticipated;
3. the location of many growth points was informed more by political motives than by issues of economic efficiency;
4. it proved impossible to resist political pressures in the awarding of incentives: there were simply too many growth points and this diffused the resources available for the programme;
5. in most cases, little economic planning accompanied the programme. Although the rhetoric of growth-pole theory was appropriated, scant attention was given to the critical issue of backward and forward linkages in seeking propulsive growth;
6. too many, and confused, objectives underpinned the policy instruments;
7. policy instruments (and particularly incentives) were insufficiently targeted: the programme was too general.

The bantustan development policy

The demarcation of bantustan boundaries, which defined the limits of areas where large numbers of black people could legally stay, has had a profound effect on the South African space economy. Particularly it has led, in cases where the border is within commuting distance of large centres of employment, to the emergence of 'closer settlements': the damming up of large numbers of people in settlements which are functionally part of the metropolitan area or large city but spatially far removed from it. The system, which is extraordinarily inefficient, is underpinned by large scale, long distance commuting (frequently people spend three to four hours a day travelling in each direction at considerable cost in terms of time and money). The system is maintained by state transport subsidies which represent a continual, large, drain on the public *fiscus* and which are currently being increasingly questioned politically.

The Group Areas Act
The Group Areas Act (1966, as amended) entrenched the principle of rigid separation within towns and cities. It is included in this review because, in the case of the small towns in 'white' areas, this frequently resulted in considerable spatial disparity. The 'town' is in reality a system of settlements, consisting of a white core which contains the economic centre and most social services, surrounded by a number of disparate, racially discrete and far-spread, dormitory areas or 'locations' often of considerable size. This raises particular problems for any programme of reconstruction for small rural towns.

Two basic, interrelated, conclusions emerge from this review. Firstly, the urban settlement pattern in South Africa is grotesquely distorted and inefficient. Secondly, overt settlement policies have achieved little positive in developmental terms. Indeed, they have contributed considerably to the distortion and inefficiency and have resulted in a massive waste of fiscal, human and other resources. In the face of this record, there seems to be a strong local case for arguing that the country may be better off without regional or national settlement policies at all. Indeed, there appears to be a total lack of confidence in policy-making circles. For the first time in a long period there are effectively no overt regional or national settlement policies in operation, although the emergence of certain 'wish list' documents may be heralding a renewed burst of policy-making activity (Government of South Africa 1995a, 1995b).

SOME LESSONS FROM LOCAL AND INTERNATIONAL EXPERIENCE

At this point, it is useful to reflect on international experience of settlement policy and planning over the last few decades, in order to identify some of the main lessons which can assist in answering the question of whether or not there is a case for national and regional settlement planning and, if so, how it should be approached. I believe there are five lessons which are particularly important.

The first lesson
International record of direct settlement policies has at best been mixed–settlement patterns have been far more affected historically by sectoral economic policies than they have been by overtly spatial policies.

Particularly important are agricultural pricing policies, transportation tariff structures and trade policies (for example, international shifts away from import-substitution economic policies towards export-based policies have recently led to significant 'polarisation reversal' in a number of countries – a reversal of growth away from the major metropolitan markets favoured by import-substitution policies towards smaller centres with a comparative advantage in terms of export products).

This realisation has further implications. One is that goals relating to economic policy and to the management of settlement systems need to be compatible and synergistic - there needs to be a national urbanisation policy which fuses national economic and spatial imperatives. Historically, implicit goals have frequently been diametrically opposed. Thus, for example, in the passion to achieve national spatial decentralisation of economic activities which marked the period from the 1960s through to the 1980s internationally, many countries, including South Africa, were investing substantial finance (through industrial incentive schemes and the like) in the pursuit of decentralisation while at the same time, and equally vigorously, pursuing import-substitution policies which favoured the largest cities over all others.

Another implication is the realisation that an important reason for much of the relative failure of settlement-based policies over the last three decades has been that they have been excessively spatial in orientation. The emphasis has been on the physical growth of towns, their position in the settlement hierarchy and their spatial location rather than on the stimulation of their economic development through nationally consistent policies and, in particular, through consciously forging their linkages with their surrounding hinterlands. The physical entity of the settlement, rather than functions, has been the focus of endeavour.

Thirdly, that policies directly aimed at settlements need clear objectives: it is seldom possible to achieve very different objectives (for example, combatting polarisation or promoting rural development) through the same policy instrument. This, too, has contributed to the relative failure of many settlement-based programmes in South Africa and elsewhere.

Finally, it is not possible, in policy terms, to fly in the face of economic realities. Attempts to do so consistently fail to achieve their objectives, result in a wasteful use of resources and frequently have directly negative outcomes.

The second lesson
Regional settlement dynamics, as well as factors affecting central spatial organisational concepts such as range and threshold, are complex. By definition, static blue-print approaches to settlement planning, such as the inducement of clearly defined, static, national settlement hierarchies or attempts to stimulate artificially the emergence of rural service centres or

growth points in places where economic and social forces promoting agglomeration are not already in operation, will inevitably fail. There are examples: Zimbabwe (Mutizwa-Mangiza 1992) and Malawi (Government of Malawi 1984). Sensitive, contextually specific analyses are required before decisions are made on issues such as economic programmes, social service delivery and so on.

The third lesson
The potential of different settlements to grow and develop is not the same (for example, the propensity for towns to grow and develop is affected by factors such as the natural-resource base and the prosperity of the rural hinterland; the availability of local resources to which value can be added; the availability of skills; the presence of entrepreneurial initiative; the leadership and the strength of local organisation; and location – for example, settlements near major cities tend to be more economically propulsive, as do those located on nationally or regionally significant transportation routes and some towns are more centrally located than others in terms of social service delivery). If policy exists, therefore, its emphasis should be on realising and mobilising full economic and social potentials, rather than treating all settlements the same.

The fourth and fifth lessons
Fourthly, endogenous, locally driven, bottom–up initiatives stand a better chance of success than centrally driven, top–down programmes although top–down support is usually necessary. And the fifth and final lesson is that restrictive policies (policies which attempt to encourage certain things to happen in some places by preventing them from happening elsewhere) almost inevitably have negative consequences and should not be used.

IS THERE A CASE FOR NATIONAL AND REGIONAL SETTLEMENT POLICY?

Given the largely negative consequences of interferences in the settlement system historically in South Africa, and the weak record of policy in achieving developmental objectives internationally, the question which must be asked is whether or not there is a case for national or regional settlement policy at all. There are a number of grounds for suggesting that, despite these difficulties, it should form an important dimension of planning in South Africa.

Firstly, it is important to coordinate economic, social and environmental objectives with spatial objectives: failure to do so can create severe distortions and inefficiencies and result in a wasteful use of public finance. At the heart of this issue is the complex concept of 'balance' and central to this debate in South Africa, in turn, is the availability and distribution of water: the cessation of inter-basin water transfers, for example, would undoubtedly have significant, spontaneous, impacts on Southern African regional settlement patterns and on the pattern of economic activity in the longer term. Ironically, the central regional debate in southern Africa – water policy – has never occurred within any developmentally holistic, publicly transparent, framework.

Secondly, demographic growth will continue to be high in the short to medium term and the phenomenon of unmanaged settlement raises the spectre of serious environmental degradation. An important dimension of settlement planning, therefore, is determining where development should not go, in the interests of environmental protection.

Thirdly, an outcome of historical settlement intervention is a highly distorted, inefficient settlement system. One of the priorities of the next decade will be to begin to manage the system back to greater economic rationality and new growth provides the primary resource to achieve this (for example, the resettlement of households via small farmer programmes requires the close coordination of these programmes with urban settlements, which can provide markets and essential economic and social support systems as well as with public transportation routes). The management process will involve hard investment decisions about which settlements get and which do not, but the issue cannot be shirked. The issue of rural and regional restructuring is as relevant as urban restructuring.

Fourthly, developmental experience shows that the impact of public investment is greatest when the investment forms part of a complementary net of investments: the issue of investment coordination is one of considerable significance (Dewar 1995a). Finally, resources available for the provision of social and utility infrastructure will be in short supply relative to demand. One implication of this is that the issue of social service delivery needs to be considered at a regional or inter-settlement scale. It is necessary to think systemically about how best to deliver systems of service and to trace analytically the implication of this for different settlements, rather than assign roles to settlements *a priori*.

A PHILOSOPHIC POSITIONING

Given that a case can be made for an emphasis on regional settlement policy and planning at this time, there are a number of lessons which can be drawn from the developmental experience internationally about how the task should be approached. The eight main ones are listed below.

1. Policy should be based on concerns of dynamic balance, efficiency and equity, not ideology;
2. It is necessary to work with dominant forces within the political economy to achieve these objectives, rather than attempting to fly in the face of those forces;
3. Policies and programmes should be proactive and enabling, thereby increasing choice, rather than reactive and prescriptive;

4. Policies should not be based on 'anti' motives (for example, anti-large-city): rather they should seek to optimise the full potentials of all settlement strata and forms;
5. Policies should be positive rather than restrictive. In particular, non-voluntary population relocations should be avoided to the greatest degree possible;
6. Policies and plans should be directed towards releasing the potentials of settlements, rather than treating them all the same;
7. New growth should be used strategically and structurally, to bring about a more efficient settlement system;
8. Policies and programmes should mesh top–down support and bottom–up initiatives.

THE CENTRAL FOCUS OF SETTLEMENT POLICY AND PLANNING

More specifically, a number of central roles of national and regional settlement planning can be identified:

1. The development and application of strong policies relating to where development should not go, informed by environmental issues and analyses, and by understandings about the language of regional landscapes and the making of place. Enhancing uniqueness and reinforcing the 'placeness of place' are not romantic concerns: they are highly relevant, socially, ecologically and economically;
2. The sensitive locational integration of small-farmer programmes with the existing settlement system, in order to maximise synergies and to promote local economic diversification. The great danger is that they will be pursued in isolation (not as rural development programmes but simply as farming) in the deep periphery, where they have a limited chance of success;
3. The implementation of a national small-towns programme. Small towns have a vital role to play in rural reconstruction (Dewar 1995a). The programmes should be directed at promoting local economic development and improved living conditions. The programmes should reflect the following characteristics: they must be initiated locally; they should be individually designed to maximise the potential of the town and its hinterland – they should not all be the same; they should include the surrounding rural hinterland and should consciously seek to strengthen urban–rural linkages; they should be entrepreneurially based (they should promote entrepreneurial attitudes and should be driven from the bottom–up – initially, at least, this means that their focus must be on small-business promotion); they should seek to meet local needs locally; they should seek to add value to local resources; they should promote the use of locally relevant skills and technologies; and they should apply labour-intensive methods to the improvement of the living environment. While they should be locally initiated, owned and controlled, therefore, it is clear that, given the usually tiny revenue bases of small towns, they cannot operate exclusively on locally generated finance: they require national financing assistance (Dewar 1995a). However, national assistance should be mobilised only by the demonstration of strong local organisation, ideas and commitment – the process of rewarding winners would encourage local communities to organise, in order to address their own futures.
4. A particular problem in many parts of the ex-bantustan areas, where settlement patterns are expansively diluted, is that many people do not live within convenient range of urban centres supplying functions and services: many are

trapped in space. Here, periodic markets may have an important role to play. The principle of the periodic market ring is to bring goods and services closer to the people (as opposed to bringing people to the services) albeit on a non-permanent basis. In effect, these markets operate as incipient small towns: indeed, if demand builds up sufficiently, one or a number of these may become permanent. The markets perform a number of functions: marketing; service delivery (for example, libraries, health services, banking, credit, post office, pension payouts, telecommunications and so on); manufacturing; information; and culture and entertainment.

5. Spatially, when taken in conjunction with initiatives to coordinate line services (such as roads, piped water, electricity), point services (such as schools, hospitals, etc.) and existing towns, the periodic market system offers an important way of restructuring the countryside and thus encouraging economic reconstruction (Figure 16.1). This diagram is conceptual and should not be interpreted statically. Basically, it seeks to identify the elements of indicative planning and relationships between these. Centrally, it seeks to emphasise three points: the importance of achieving logical, synergetic coordination in public investment, for this will send unambiguous signals to private decision-makers and investors, thereby resulting over time in an increasingly rational pattern of investment and settlement; the importance of line as an ordering element, particularly for social service delivery, and the need to allow settlement to respond to the line (something which is already beginning to happen spontaneously in many rural areas), thereby creating the preconditions for more efficient rural public transportation and higher levels of convenience and access to services; and the importance of using time (periodicity) as a central planning instrument:

6. The coordination and organisation of social service delivery. It is clear that conventional approaches to social service delivery are failing in the face of increasing financial constraints and increasing demand. The issue needs to be considered regionally, for not all settlements can have a full range of services; deeper hierarchical forms need to be developed which best achieve a balance between taking people to services and taking services to people; greater use must be made of the principle of periodicity; and innovative forms of back-up need to be provided. Particularly important in the rural areas, for example, is the establishment of rural resource centres. A vital factor determining the success of small town and rural development initiatives is the quality and capacity of leadership. Local leadership therefore needs to be 'grown': there needs to be a purposeful programme of equipping people (and particularly community leadership) with the full range of skills necessary for them to realise their potential. Rural resource centres, therefore, are places where small groups of people engage, over relatively short periods, in a range of skills programmes (e.g. community organisational skills, entrepreneurial and small-business training and advice, technical skills directed towards adding value to local resources – such as building, wood and metal working, weaving, brick-making – and life skills). The centres should be venues, not bureaucracies – the programmes themselves may be organised by NGOs. They are also places where people can access information and advice about other forms of available support (for example, information about housing-policy assistance and how to access this, accessing credit and so on): they therefore become loci through which national, regional and local government can diffuse information and assistance to grass-roots levels.

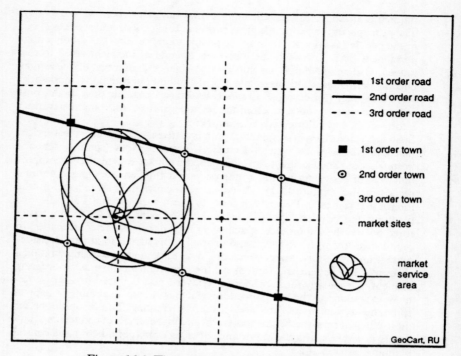

Figure 16.1 The conceptual ordering of regional space

CONCLUSION

South Africa is at a watershed. The overarching imperative is to move from
ideologically-based to developmentally-based policies and programmes.
Ironically, the country is losing confidence in its ability to determine positive
outcomes precisely at the time when the need for pro-active planning and
action at all scales is greatest. There is a powerful case to be made for
vigorous, sensible settlement policy and planning at this time. It is clear,
however, that static, standardised, prescriptive approaches to the task (such
as central place programmes, the creation, *de novo*, of rural service centres,
growth poles, industrial decentralisation programmes, and so on) will
achieve little. The central task of policy and planning is to work with existing
forces in the political economy to unleash energies, to create opportunities,
to remove barriers to entry, to coordinate initiatives and to provide
appropriate forms of back-up and assistance to individuals and groups. This
chapter, while not attempting to be comprehensive, has attempted to
outline some forms of these.

EIGHT MAIN RISKS: PREVENTING IMPOVERISHMENT DURING POPULATION RESETTLEMENT[1]

Impoverishment is the central issue in development-caused population displacements and resettlement. Historical experience shows that, more often than not, the risks of impoverishment and social disruption turn into grim reality. In India, for instance, resettlement researchers found that development programmes have caused the displacement and involuntary resettlement of close to twenty million people over roughly four decades, but that as much as 75 per cent of these people have *not* been 'rehabilitated' (Fernandes 1991; Fernandes *et al.* 1989). That means that the vast majority of resettlers in India have been impoverished and made worse off.

Similar findings about impoverishment and the *de facto* lack of equity in resettlement come from many other countries. Another serious consequence is the political tension surrounding forced relocation. The socio-cultural and psychological stress induced in people who are forcibly uprooted lingers long and shapes their subsequent individual and group behaviour. Therefore, targeted economic, technical, financial, legal and cultural measures must be taken to prevent or mitigate the impoverishment risks in each and every development programme that entails displacement.

SOCIAL JUSTICE AND PLANNING WITH AN EQUITY COMPASS

Understanding the mechanisms that cause impoverishment under government *planned* developments is a key prerequisite for mitigating the risks intrinsic in displacement. Studies that I carried out in 1985–6 (Cernea 1986) and in 1989–90 (Cernea 1990) identified the main 'impoverishment risks' inherent in processes of involuntary resettlement. Subsequently, during 1993–4, I led a Task Force established to review all 1986–93 World Bank-financed projects involving involuntary population displacement, a review that also covered many projects not financed by the Bank (Cernea 1995b; World Bank 1994b).

We determined that in the 1990s about 10,000,000 people were being displaced *annually* by infrastructural development programmes in some key sectors (dam construction, urban development, highways and roads). This amounts to some 90–100 million people for the decade, a number much larger than the total numbers of refugees caused by wars and natural disasters. We also focused a large part of our study on how impoverishment happens during resettlement and how it can be avoided, in line with the World Bank's policy to protect and restore the livelihoods of people involuntarily resettled (World Bank 1990). In this chapter I elaborate on some findings from this set of successive studies.

Development programmes that provide irrigation water for thirsty fields, energy for expanding industries, hospital buildings and schools in residential areas, or wider roads in clogged city centres are indisputably needed. They improve the livelihoods of vast numbers of people and develop the national and local economies. But such developments also make certain rearrangements in human settlements inevitable. Historically, involuntarily displaced people have suffered losses and traumas, and have shared more in the pains than in the gains of development. However, while some degree of population territorial rearrangement is unavoidable, such inequitable distribution of benefits and losses is neither mandatory nor inevitable. It should not be accepted in resigned fashion.

'Social justice' and 'social injustice' are not concepts frequently employed in the development discourse, but they should become so. Recently, these concepts have been brought into the public forum in authoritative statements. In the words of the President of the World Bank:

> We must act so that poverty will be alleviated, our environment protected, social justice extended, human rights strengthened ... Social injustice can destroy economic and political advances. (Wolfensohn 1995)

Certainly, a domain to which the call for social justice and equitable distribution of benefits surely applies, is involuntary resettlement. Redressing the inequities caused by displacement and enabling affected people to share in the benefits of growth is imperative.

Although development makes relocation unavoidable as *a class* of social processes, not every single case of proposed displacement is inevitable or justified. There are ways to fully avoid or minimise specific instances of involuntary displacement, or their disproportionate adverse impacts on resettlers. In poorly planned and handled displacements, severe social disintegration affects many people. Conversely, socially responsible resettlement – that is, resettlement guided by an equity compass – can prevent impoverishment and can generate benefits for the regional economy and host populations. Ensuring that involuntary resettlement is avoided or reduced – and when unavoidable, is carried out without impoverishing the people displaced – is necessary on both economic and ethical grounds.

Our research found that the worst consequences of displacement – impoverishment and violations of basic human rights – happen most frequently when national resettlement *policy* guidelines are absent; when, consequently, equitable action strategies for socio-economic re-establishment are not pursued, and there is no independent professional monitoring and evaluation of outcomes. In plain terms, this means that tens of thousands of people are undergoing unnecessarily amplified losses and hardships, that otherwise could possibly have been avoided or mitigated. This is the irrefutable argument for adopting *national policies and legal frameworks* for resettlement in all developing countries, yet it is an argument resisted by many governments. As Ismail Serageldin (1995: 102–3) noted:

> Bank experience shows that if a government adopts its own national policy to reintegrate displaced people into the national economy, resettlement is successful for more than just Bank-financed projects ... The key to sound resettlement is to adopt a people-centred development policy, not a property-compensation policy.

Without equitable resettlement policies, the technicians and economists who plan specific programmes entailing displacements are deprived of a much needed compass for allocating financial resources equitably, in a manner able to prevent or mitigate impoverishment risks (Cernea 1996a). Indeed, the planning approach that had produced programmes resulting in many people resettled but only in few 'rehabilitated' has not proven itself wise enough and effective enough to prevent impoverishment. Such repeated failures of resettlement *without* rehabilitation point to profound fallacies and failures in the planning system itself, which need to be corrected. As Victor D'Souza wrote in his sharp and insightful sociological analysis of development planning in India,

> Gigantic social problems ... cast serious doubt on the suitability of the current mode of planning ... They call for a drastic change in the method of setting the goals of planning; it is not the rate of growth of the economy per se, but the degree of fulfilment of human needs and the elimination of glaring inequalities in society which should be the yardstick of success in planning. (D'Souza 1990: 202)

THE RISK AND RECONSTRUCTION MODEL FOR RESETTLERS' RE-ESTABLISHMENT

How does impoverishment through displacement occur and how can it be prevented?

To identify the basic socio-economic mechanisms set in motion when people are forcibly displaced, I compared the empirical findings of many field monographs and examined a massive body of data. The comparison revealed several common characteristics that these cases share, beyond the enormous diversity of individual project-specific or country-specific situations. Thus, I found *a pattern of eight general sub-processes or trends, whose cumulative effect is the onset of impoverishment* (Cernea 1995a). As long as the resettlement operation has not yet started, these recurrent processes must be regarded as impending *social risks*. These discrete risks, taken in their interconnection, form an *overall risk matrix* that must be carefully considered *before* any such operation is undertaken. The risks and losses are not only to the people directly affected: they are risks and losses incurred by the local economy as well. The present chapter explains these impoverishment risks as the first part of a broader conceptual model which deals with the *risks* and with the *reconstruction of livelihoods* in an integrated manner. I call this the 'risk and reconstruction' conceptual framework or model, which has been more fully developed in a subsequent piece of writing (Cernea 1996b).

As a conceptual construct, this risk and reconstruction model captures not only the economic but also the social and cultural dimensions of impoverishment. It shows that during displacement people lose:

- natural capital;
- man-made (physical) capital;
- human capital;
- social capital.

It also shows that during re-establishment they must regain this capital. Before describing this model, however, I will emphasise two elements that reflect not only the model's *cognitive value*, but also its very important *operational* usefulness.

First, by synthesising lessons from many past processes, this model is able to accurately predict future outcomes, *if* the warning offered by the model is ignored. Therefore, the risk model provides a matrix directly usable for planning, more specifically *for preventive planning*. Indeed, these eight potential risks – in fact, high-probability risks – will undoubtedly become painfully real deprivation processes, if unheeded. But they can be purposively counteracted. Knowledge about these risks can influence social planning and practice. As Robert Merton (1979) brilliantly argued, a conceptual–predictive model can successfully act as a 'self-destroying prophecy'. In other words, such a risk model is maximally useful when, as a result of it being acted upon, the risks are diminished or destroyed, and the consequences predicted by the model do not occur.

Therefore, I propose the risk and reconstruction model described below as a *working tool* for preparing resettlement plans and monitoring their impacts. This model is built around the *fundamental variables identified as present in virtually all displacement situations:*

- land;
- employment;
- housing;
- the status of individuals;
- health;
- nutrition;
- common property; and
- the status of communities.

Attempts to use this model as such have been initiated recently in some cases in India (Thangaraj 1996). Planners who use it as a guide may thus 'destroy' its prophecy. Risk recognition and analysis are crucial for the *practice of sound planning* and for the argument that *impoverishment through displacement can be counteracted*.

Second, and most important, this conceptual construct of impoverishment through displacement is therefore not just a model of gloom, but contains in a nutshell the *model for the socio-economic re-establishment of those displaced*. Indeed, if we *reverse* this model, it suggests precisely what kind of positive action must be initiated to restore the livelihoods and incomes of those displaced and, whenever possible, to improve them. Stood on its head, the model offers a strategic framework and pragmatic guidance for governmental and individual action to be taken towards the rehabilitation that must follow displacement.

Overall, this *impoverishment–reconstruction* model provides, in my view, a more comprehensive image of the content and essence of the displacement–resettlement process than other models suggested in the social science literature – for instance, the *stress-centred model* proposed by Scudder and Colson (1982). As a comprehensive socio-economic model, it encompasses the stress dimension and goes farther and deeper, conceptualising more fully the essence of displacement and recovery. It also offers a broader frame of reference both for resettlement research and resettlement practice (see also Cernea 1995a, 1996b). Chris de Wet (1988) has also analysed the Scudder and Colson stress-based model from a broader, spatial/environmental explanatory perspective. The risks and reconstruction conceptual framework helps understand and explain more fully the multi-faceted behaviour of displaced populations as a response to economic, cultural and social impoverishment, rather than to 'stress'. And further, the socio-economic model zeroes in precisely on what must be the heart-of-the-matter in any resettlement operation: preventing impoverishment and reconstructing livelihoods.

Eight impoverishment processes

The eight sub-processes that converge in impoverishment are not the only processes of economic and social deprivation, but rather the most important ones. In different locations, they occur with variable intensities. These are:

Landlessness

Expropriation of land removes the main foundation upon which people's productive systems, commercial activities and livelihoods are constructed. This is the principal form of de-capitalisation and pauperisation of displaced people, as they lose both physical and man-made capital.

Selected empirical evidence. Unless this foundation is reconstructed elsewhere, or replaced with steady income-generating employment, landlessness sets in and the affected families are impoverished. In the Kiambere Hydro-power project in Kenya, a sociological study found that farmers' average landholdings after resettlement dropped from thirteen to six hectares; their livestock was reduced by more than a third; yields per hectare decreased by 68 per cent for maize and 75 per cent for beans. Family income dropped from Ksh. 10,968 to Ksh. 1,976, a loss of 82 per cent (Mburugu 1988). Lassailly-Jacob's (1996a) several studies on Kossou Dam and other major reservoirs in Africa have empirically documented resettlers' loss of land and the insufficiency of the land-development remedies adopted. In Indonesia, the Institute of Ecology of Padjadjaran University carried out a social survey several years after reservoir families were given cash compensation in the early 1980s; it was found that their land ownership had decreased by 47 per cent and their income was halved. Impact studies for the Cirata dam, also in Indonesia, found that while 59 per cent of the poor households improved their incomes after relocation, about 21 per cent were worse off primarily because of loss of land, with a 25 per cent decrease from their previous income levels (Padjadjaran University 1989). Similar evidence is available from Brazil (Mougeot 1988). Findings from sociological and anthropo-logical field studies show that for farm families, loss of farm land has generally far more severe consequences than the loss of their house.

Joblessness

Loss of wage employment occurs both in urban displacement and in rural areas, and those losing jobs are landless labourers, enterprise or service workers, artisans and small businessmen. But creating new jobs is difficult and requires substantial investments. Resulting unemployment or underemployment among resettlers lingers long after physical relocation.

Selected empirical data. For several categories of people whose liveli-hoods depend on jobs – including landless labourers in reservoir areas; employees of local service enterprises, or other enterprises; and shopkeepers and small businessmen – job loss due to displacement causes painful econo-mic and psychological effects that last as long as employment is not re-established. The employed landless, rural or urban, may lose in three ways: they lose access to land owned by others and leased or share-cropped; they lose job opportunities, primarily in urban areas; and they lose the use of assets under common property regimes. In the Madagascar Tana Plain project, private small enterprises being displaced in 1993 – workshops, food-stalls, artisan units – were entitled to no compensation, and lost their place of trade and their customers (personal observation 1993). Vocational retraining, offered to some resettlers, can provide skills but not necessarily jobs. Similar findings come from developed countries: in the Churchill-Nelson Hydro project in Manitoba, Canada, the economic activities of resettled indigenous people – fisheries, waterfowl capture, fur processing –

were curtailed; field studies found a significant increase in non-productive time in the community. Joblessness among resettlers often surfaces with some time delay, rather than immediately, because in the short run they receive employment in project-related jobs. However, the sustainability of these jobs is limited. Evidence compiled from several non-Bank financed and some Bank-financed dam projects[2] shows that the employment boom created by the new construction temporarily absorbs some resettlers but severely drops towards the end of the project, compounding the incidence of chronic or temporary joblessness, among the displaced population.

A particular form of joblessness risk occurs in China (e.g., in relocation under the Yangzhou Thermal Power Plant project, in 1994–5, and in other similar projects) in the case of displaced farmers converted to wage employment in enterprises in townships and villages (some such enterprises are created with compensation funds for lost land). New enterprises have high failure rates, are often unable to pay salaries for months in a row, or soon go bankrupt; thus, such 'jobs' do not provide resettlers with the expected income recovery and they are left without both jobs and land. The long-term sustainability of jobs given to resettlers is, therefore, a critical characteristic.

Homelessness

> Loss of housing and shelter may be only temporary for many displacees, but for some, homelessness remains a chronic condition. In a broader cultural sense, homelessness is also placelessness, loss of a group's cultural space and identity, or cultural impoverishment, as argued by Downing (1994) and by students of 'place attachment' (Low and Altman 1992). And in a socio-spatial sense, as argued by de Wet (1995), placelessness is often perceived, albeit at a lower intensity, by populations subjected to compulsory villagisation schemes.

Selected empirical data. If resettlement policies do not explicitly provide improvement in housing conditions, or if compensation for demolished shelters is paid at assessed value rather than replacement value, the risk of homelessness is increased. A 1990 Bank report on the Cameroon–Douala Urban resettlement completed in 1989 found that over 2,000 displaced families were hindered in their efforts to set up new permanent houses; less than 5 per cent received loans to help pay for assigned houseplots. From the Danjiangkou reservoir (not Bank-financed), China has reported that about 20 per cent of the relocatees became homeless and destitute. (This sad experience and the results of China's Danjiangkou and Sanmenxia dam displacements, led to the adoption of new and better resettlement policies in China, policies that attempt to transform resettlement into an opportunity for development.) Violent destruction of houses of people labelled as 'squatters' is a procedure still used in some places, to speed up evictions. The 'emergency housing centre' or temporary 'relocation camps' used as fall-back solutions in poorly planned resettlement tend to make homelessness chronic rather than temporary. When resettlers cannot meet the time and labour costs involved in rebuilding a house, they are compelled to move into 'temporary' shelters, which then tend to become long-term shelters. In the Foum-Gleita irrigation project in Mauritania, only 200 out of the 881 displaced families reconstructed their housing, the rest living precariously for two years or longer in tents or under tarpaulins (Ngaide 1986). A Bank field review of a large-scale resettlement found that prolonged lack of support made the temporary shelters into permanent residences, in which resettlers shared common sleeping spaces with their animals. Yet homelessness – like joblessness, marginalisation, morbidity, or other social risks – is not un-avoidable in involuntary resettlement.

Marginalisation

> *Marginalisation occurs when families lose economic power and slide on a 'downward mobility' path: middle-income farm-households do not become landless, but become small landholders; small shopkeepers and craftsmen are downsized and slip below poverty thresholds. Relative marginalisation may often begin long before the actual displacement; for instance, when lands are condemned for future flooding and are implicitly devalued, new public and private infrastructural investments are prohibited, and the expansion of social services is undercut.*

Selected empirical data. Resettled families very often cannot fully restore lost economic capacity. For farm families, partial but significant loss of farm-ing land to reservoirs, roads or canals may make their farm economically non-viable. High productivity farmers on fertile valley-bottom land are marginalised when moved uphill to marginal, infertile soils, even though they may be given the same area of land. In the Nepal Kulekhani Hydroelectric project, an independent study found the majority of displaced people worse off socially and economically, due to lower productivity of new land, and less diversified production. Marginalisation also occurs through the loss of off-farm income sources; in Sri Lanka's Kotmale project, financed by a European donor, a field study assessed that marginalisation occurred because opportunities for non-farm income generation were lost or limited through displacement, increasing the economic differentiation between evacuees and hosts (Soeftestad 1990). For urban resettlers, marginalisation is some-times gradual and occurs after relocation, as in the case (described above) of resettlers given jobs (instead of land) that prove to be temporary and unsus-tainable in the long run as income sources. Marginalisation of resettlers is also implicitly and tacitly accepted in all cases when governments or project agencies consider it a matter of course that those displaced cannot be provided re-establishment at their prior standard of living.

Increased morbidity and mortality

> *Serious decreases in health levels result from displacement-caused social stress, insecurity, and psychological traumas, and from the outbreak of relocation-related diseases, particularly parasitic and vector-born (malaria, schistosomiasis). Unsafe water supply and poor sewerage systems heighten vulnerability to epidemics and proliferate diarrhoea, dysentery, etc. The weakest segments of the demographic spectrum – infants, children, and the elderly – are most affected.*

Selected empirical data. People forced to relocate have a higher degree of exposure and vulnerability to illness, and to comparatively more severe illness, than those who are not. At Akosombo in Ghana, the prevalence of schistosomiasis around the reservoir rose from 1.8 per cent prior to resettlement to 75 per cent among adult lake-side dwellers and close to 100 per cent among their children, within a few years after impoundment in the 1960s. In the Foum-Gleita irrigation project, in Mauritania, the predicted increase of schistosomiasis was exceeded, reaching 70 per cent among school children; farmers' health worsened from contaminated drinking water and agrochemical intoxication. An outbreak of gastroenteritis occurred along the Victoria dam reservoir in Sri Lanka (Rew and Driver 1986). At Nam Pong dam in Thailand, monitoring confirmed that local rates of morbidity – from liver fluke and hookworm infection – were higher than provincial levels, the result of deteriorated living conditions and poor practices of waste-disposal. Overall, direct and secondary effects of involuntary dislocation without preventive health measures range from psychosomatic diseases and diseases of poor hygiene, such as diarrhoea and dysentery, to outbreaks of parasitic and vector-borne diseases such as malaria and schistosomiasis caused by unsafe, insufficient water supplies and inadequate sanitary waste systems. Increased mortality rates are also reported as a result of epidemic outbreaks of malaria around new bodies of water and of accidents associated with new reservoirs. Lack of proper information and precautionary measures resulted in 106 deaths by drowning at Saguling Lake (Indonesia) during the first fourteen months of operation; at Cirata reservoir (Indonesia) ten people drowned in the first ten months after impounding (Padjadjaran University 1989).

Food insecurity

> *Forced uprooting increases the risk that people will fall into chronic undernourishment and food insecurity, defined as calorie–protein intake levels below the minimum necessary for normal growth and work.*

Selected empirical data. Sudden drops in food crop availability and/or incomes are predictable during physical relocation, and hunger or undernourishment tend to be lingering long-term effects. Undernourishment is both a symptom and result of inadequate resettlement. Forced uprooting increases the risk that people will fall into chronic food insecurity, defined by the Bank as calorie–protein intake levels below the minimum necessary for normal growth. In addition, rebuilding food-production capacity at the relocation site may take years. At the Foum-Gleita irrigation project, in Mauritania, when multiple cropping and animal husbandry were replaced with paddy-rice monocropping, diets and cash-crop income deteriorated. In 1986 at the Victoria dam project in Sri Lanka, financed by a European donor, some 55 per cent of resettled families were still receiving food stamps after a considerable period of time, compared to a much lower rate in the country as a whole. Because the area of cultivated land per capita in the Bailiambe reservoir in China (not Bank-financed) decreased from 1.3 mu to only 0.4 mu after relocation (15 mu = 1 hectare), local food production became insufficient and 75,000 tons of food relief annually had to be provided for several years.

Loss of access to common property

For poor people, particularly for the landless and assetless, loss of access to common (non-individual) property assets belonging to communities that are relocated (forested lands, water bodies, grazing lands, etc.) represents a major form of income and livelihood deterioration. Typically, such lost resources remain uncompensated by government relocation schemes, with only few positive exceptions – mainly in China.

Selected empirical data. Empirical evidence shows that fruit and other edible forest products, firewood and deadwood for use and sale, common grazing areas, and use of public quarries, account for a significant share of poor households' income. For example, in semi-arid regions of India, 91 to 100 per cent of firewood, 66 to 89 per cent of domestic fuel, and 69 to 80 per cent of the grazing needs of the poor households are supplied by lands under common property regimes (Sequeira 1994: see also Gopal 1992). Losing the use of such natural resources under common property, displaced people tend to encroach on reserved forests or increase the pressure on common property resources of the host area population – a source of social tension and increased environmental deterioration. Secondary adverse effects of resettlement on the environment also occur when oustees who do not receive cultivatable land move uphill in the reservoir watershed, intensify deforestation and cultivation of poor soils, and accelerate erosion and reservoir siltation.

Social disintegration

Forced displacement tears apart the social fabric and the existing patterns of social organisation. Production systems are dismantled, kinship groups and family systems are often scattered, local labour markets are disrupted, and people's cultural identity is put at risk. Life-sustaining informal social networks of mutual help among people, local voluntary associations, self-organised service arrangements, etc., are dispersed and rendered inactive. This unravelling represents a massive loss of social capital incurred by the uprooted people, yet a loss that remains unquantified and uncompensated. Such 'elusive' disintegration processes undermine livelihoods in ways uncounted by planners.

LOSSES CAUSED BY THE DISMANTLING OF
INFORMAL SOCIAL NETWORKS

A research project, unrelated to resettlement, documented how essential the informal
networks among households are in the daily economic life of the poor. During
resettlement such networks are dismantled and dispersed, a net loss to their members.
Household networks help cope with poverty through informal loans; exchanges of food,
clothing and durable goods; mutual help with farming, building houses, and caring for
children. 'Household networks pass around large amounts of money, goods, and
services, and may substitute for public subsidies ... But recognition of the importance
of private transfers for economic policy is relatively recent' (Cox and Jimenez 1990:
205). Such transfers flow from better-off to poorer households and help equalise the
distribution of income.

Bank economists, measuring and quantifying the contribution of such informal social
networks, have documented what anthropologists and sociologists have long described
in qualitative terms. Research has found that in developing countries 19 to 47 per cent
of people report recurrent transfers, representing as much as 20 per cent of household
incomes, compared to only 5 per cent in the United States. In the Philippines, for
instance, private transfers among households in the lowest quintile boost their income
by more than 75 per cent. Such support can reach high levels: in Peru, the pre-transfer
income of households that are net givers of transfers is 60 per cent higher than recipient
households. Such private transfers also function as informal credit arrangements and as
mutual insurance mechanisms. Simulation analysis shows that in Colombia such
transfers contribute up to 40 per cent to stabilising incomes in households experiencing
unemployment.

The dismantling of such multifunctional, yet virtually 'invisible', social networks
through displacement acts as one of the 'hidden' but real causes of impoverishment
through displacement. This is a loss of social capital. It is difficult, and it takes time, to
reconstitute similar social structures and networks among resettlers and their hosts,
capable of exercising similar support functions at the new relocation sites.

Figure 17.1 Losses caused by the dismantling of informal social networks

Selected empirical data. Dismantled forms of social organisation that
mobilise people for actions of common interest and for meeting pressing
needs are hard to rebuild (Figure 17.1). Such loss is higher in projects that
relocate people in a dispersed manner rather than in groups and social units.
Field studies have documented that such disarticulation processes deprive
the displaced people of 'goods' such as mutually rendered help and services,
labour exchanges, reciprocal informal credit and are part of the complex
causes of impoverishment and power loss.

In the Rengali dam project in India (not World Bank-financed), a
sociological study found various manifestations of social disarticulation at
the kinship system level, such as the loosening of intimate bonds, growing
alienation and anomie, the weakening of controls on interpersonal behaviour
and lower cohesion in family structures. Marriages were deferred because
dowry, feasts and gifts became unaffordable. Resettlers' obligations and
relationships towards non-displaced kinsmen were eroded and interaction

between individual families was reduced. As a result, participation in group action decreased; leaders became conspicuously absent from settlements; post-harvest communal feasts and pilgrimages were discontinued; daily informal social interaction was severely curtailed; and common burial grounds became shapeless and disordered (Nayak 1986: 50).

A monograph on the Hirakud dam in Orissa, India, found that displaced households whose 'economic status had been completely shattered as a result of displacement' were not 'properly integrated' in the host villages many years after relocation (Baboo 1992). Overall, if poverty is more than the absence of material means or basic services, such as shelter, means of work, food, health or education, in as much as it is also lack of power and greater dependency and vulnerability, then the disorganisation of communities and voluntary networks is also a loss of power and a greater vulnerability.

There are also other kinds of counter-developmental effects, that can vary from one project situation to another, being dependent on the specific circumstances of each project. Also, the main risks discussed above affect various categories of people differentially – rural and urban, children or elderly, tribal and non-tribal groups, women or men. More severe impacts of involuntary resettlement on women are documented by significant findings revealed in the recent literature (Feeney 1995; Koenig 1995). Such differences are very important in practice, and call for targeted responses.

WHEN SOME SHARE THE GAINS AND OTHERS SHARE THE PAINS, OR THE FALLACY OF MACRO COST–BENEFIT ACCOUNTING

The above analysis has focused on the essential and general processes, in other words – on the *paradigm of impoverishment* through forced relocation.

Findings about adverse effects are not entirely new, even though it is always unexpected and disturbing to see destruction arriving on the wings of progress and to find poverty striking within programmes designed to help alleviate poverty. Development is not a linear-growth process: conflicts and contradictory outcomes are bound to appear at many junctures. What is surprising, however, is not that adverse consequences occur, but that in many countries they continue to be widely overlooked in planning, underestimated and not thought through in advance. Thus, even though they are predictable, they become 'unanticipated' in particular situations or programmes. *As a result, growth strategies and development programmes are often ill equipped with safety-net measures designed to prevent, mitigate and compensate for risks and actual counter-developmental effects.*

In certain projects, adverse social effects are anticipated conceptually, but in practice they are dealt with only in a perfunctory manner: plans and projects mention them, but do not really build barriers against them as meticulously as they build up the technical elements of the projects (Cernea

1988). Technocentric biases in projects mean that the physical components (e.g., civil works) are addressed first while people are put last; detailed social planning and execution are not done and necessary resources are not allocated; and misguided and non-monitored implementation compounds the negative socio-economic effects. That justifiably raises the fundamental question asked by a respected Indian scholar who has devoted much analysis to resettlement: 'Development for Whom?' (Mahapatra 1991).

The justification usually offered by many decision-makers and planners to the criticism of such counter-developmental impact is that the sum of their many benefits outweighs the sum of their costs and negative effects. Arithmetically, this may be so in many (but not all) cases. A quantified 'justification' of this sort may, at first glance, appear rational. Upon closer analysis, however, this answer is neither legitimate nor convincing. It implies that the harm caused to the individuals subjected to displacement is compensated by the *aggregate* benefits of development, *independent of the allocation of these benefits*. This kind of desk macro-accounting of costs and benefits, rather crude, is morally and practically fallacious when one cannot predict with reasonable certainty the allocation of the future benefits of a programme.

The fallacy is even more obvious where – as in the case of upstream displacement vis-à-vis downstream development – the programme randomly generates benefits for *some,* while it inflicts negative effects upon *others*. When certain development projects are poorly conceived and managed, they result in situations in which *some share the gains, while others share the pains*.

The fact that planned programmes often produce long-term improvement gains and development for those labelled 'project beneficiaries' does not make the hardship any lighter for those suffering the immediate misfortune of being uprooted. In real life the negative effects are not fully subtracted from the benefits, or shouldered by the project's beneficiaries, but are compensated only partly by the state and in large part are borne by the population that is being victimised in the name of the 'greater good for the greater numbers'. *This kind of spurious rationality plagues rather than serves development philosophy and planning practice,* because it distracts planners from seeking alternative approaches and solutions. It is responsible for tolerating or even magnifying some of the ill effects of such programmes, which otherwise could be counteracted – either prevented, or mitigated.

Worldwide resettlement experiences converge in showing that *the single most damaging factor* to the quality and outcomes of resettlement is the absence in many countries of *policy and legal frameworks* that define the rights and entitlements of people affected by development-related, state-imposed displacements. Within such policy vacuums standards are disregarded, arbitrariness sets in, and the powerless are victimised once again, rather than being enabled to share in the benefits of the development for which they incur sacrifices. Relevant in this respect is the World Bank's general counsel observation:

> lessons derived from Bank-assisted projects involving resettlement [show] that in many countries the national legal framework of resettlement operations is incomplete ... Resettlement legal issues [are treated] as a subset of property and expropriation law. For various reasons, these national laws do not provide a fully adequate framework for development-oriented resettlement ... New legislation often must be introduced, or existing laws must be modified, in order to plan and carry out involuntary resettlement adequately. (Shihata 1991: 181)

This is why the World Bank has recommended policy reform in this area to all governments whose projects entail involuntary resettlement, together with the build up of their institutional capacity for resettlement. The enunciation of national policy guidelines and legal frameworks for resettlement, embodying principles of equity and social justice, should be seen as one of the strategic steps towards generally beneficial development.

THE 'HOW TO' OF SOCIO-ECONOMIC RE-ESTABLISHMENT

As emphasised at the outset, the eight characteristics of impoverishment described above, taken together, could help such prevention efforts, because they provide a warning model that captures the lessons of many real processes and clearly points to what must be avoided. The predictive capacity of such a model informs about the main social risks intrinsic in population dislocation and helps adopt timely counteracting or compensating measures for risk management.

The basic policy message embodied in the above model is that these intrinsic socio-economic risks must be brought under control through an *encompassing strategy* and by allocating *adequate financial resources*. They can not be tamed through *piecemeal* random measures, based simply on cash compensation for lost assets, but only through concerted multi-sided action.

Standing the matrix model on its head provides the second part of our full 'risks and reconstruction model' and thus incorporates an action matrix for the constructive re-establishment of those displaced (Cernea 1996b). In other words, landlessness risks should be met through planned land-based re-establishment; homelessness – through sound housing programmes; joblessness – through alternative sustainable employment; increased morbidity – through adequate prevention, education, and improved health care assistance; community disarticulation – through purposive community reconstruction and host-resettler integrative strategies. One way to accomplish such reconstruction is to enable those displaced to directly *share in the specific benefits* generated by the programme which pushed them out in the first place.

The 'how to' answers to these risks consists both in a policy response – of the type embodied in the World Bank policy regarding resettlement (World Bank 1990) – and in operational measures, through a vast spectrum of practical options for reconstructing the livelihoods of displaced and resettled people. Describing this vast arsenal of available measures is not the subject of this chapter, but it is encouraging to note that the literature documenting positive experiences in reconstructing livelihoods in various countries is growing.[3]

The usage of the risk concept proposed above is not limited, however, to the initial stages of the project cycle – preparation and project planning – in resettlement operations, but should be extended to the project implementation stage, particularly to *the monitoring of early outcomes*. It is a necessity to initiate *early* monitoring studies focusing whenever possible on the initial cohorts of resettled people in each large project to assess whether or not their income is being restored, improved, or remains below pre-project levels. Such monitoring studies[4] can be structured in terms of the eight elements of the model, and would produce implementable recommendations tailored to the project's circumstances.

In conclusion, it is crucial to emphasise that *impoverishment through displacement is not inevitable* in resettlement. After having done much field research and operational work on resettlement, I am left with no illusion about the major difficulties associated with preventing and mitigating these risks. But the advantage of forecasting trends is that the forecast offers the possibility to take policy and project counteractions. There is no doubt that failure to acknowledge the inherent social risks will allow them to unfold unimpeded, in every case. Conversely, equitable policies and improved planning, financing, and implementing of resettlement are apt to transform the production of the risk of impoverishment into a self-destroying prophecy and are apt to facilitate the socio-economic reconstruction and re-establishment of resettlers' livelihoods.

NOTES

1. The author has continued to elaborate the topics he addresses in the paper presented at the Grahamstown Conference, benefitting from the suggestions he has received; in particular, he has further developed that part of his conceptual framework that deals with post-relocation reconstructive activities. Interested readers are invited to see the article, 'The Risks and Reconstruction for Resettling Displaced Populations', in *World Development* (1997) 25. 10: 1–9.
2. E.g., the China-Gezhouba dam, Brazil-Tucurui dam, and Turkey-Ataturk dam, which were all not Bank-financed; or the Togo-Benin Nangbeto Hydropower dams, and Korea-Chungju dam as Bank-financed projects.
3. An international conference devoted primarily to analysing and synthesising such field experience in 'the restoration of livelihoods' of displaced people took place in September 1996 under the auspices of the Refugee Studies Programme, University of Oxford, England (see Cernea 1996b).
4. One of the first of such ongoing monitoring studies on income restoration has

been started in China's Ertan Hydroelectric Project. It is carried out by local researchers under the methodological guidance of Professor Fredrik Barth and Professor Thomas Williams, the social science members of the project's international monitoring panel. The interesting feature of this study is that it does not wait for all the people to be resettled, but rather focuses on the first cohorts of resettlers and their income; in this way, the midstream findings will be used for improving the resettlement of the subsequent cohorts, before the end of the project (see Barth and Williams, 1995).

RECONSIDERING SETTLEMENT
STRATEGIES FOR SOUTHERN AFRICA

Theories, policies and plans for settlement and resettlement in southern Africa are changing, but are they changing fast enough? Are such changes properly informed by the southern African and global experience with land settlement, and with increasingly serious environmental constraints, of which the most important are inadequate rainfall, surface flows and ground water? Are they sufficiently imaginative and innovative?

In regard to an awareness on the part of academics and policy makers of the experience within southern Africa and elsewhere, I think, if anything, that there is too much awareness of difficulties – to the extent that discussion of disappointing results, and reasons for those results, may be discouraging, rather than improving, further settlement planning, including strategies based on smallholder activities. That awareness is exemplified by the attention paid to settlement issues at the World Bank/UNDP organised November 1992 workshop in Swaziland on the international experience with various agricultural and rural development issues and the possible relevance of that experience for the New South Africa. It is also exemplified by a 1993 special issue of World Development based on revised versions of some of those workshop papers, including that of Kinsey and Binswanger on 'Characteristics and performance of resettlement programs: a review'.

Additional papers were also contracted by the World Bank in connection with its involvement in attempts to restructure South Africa's rural development policies. They include Chris de Wet's 'Resettlement as an aspect of a land reform programme in South Africa: some issues and recommendations' (1993a), and documents, including mine on 'Poverty reduction and gender issues', prepared for the June–July 1994 Land and Agricultural Policy Centre (Johannesburg) conference that dealt with a range of options for land reform and rural restructuring in South Africa.

In this chapter, I wish to emphasise three points that I believe are critically important for the success of such programmes as the Reconstruction and Development Programme (RDP).[1] The first, made by a number of international experts including Michael and Merle Lipton (1993) but still viewed with some scepticism in South Africa, is the essential role that tens of thousands of small-scale households involved in both on- and off-farm activities, could play in both rural and peri-urban localities. I comment on that point in the next two sections of the chapter that deal with the settlement process and smallholder development. The second point, rather paradoxically it might seem, addresses the increasingly serious water constraint by emphasising the need for small-scale irrigation of high value crops, not just in river basins but especially in peri-urban locales. The third point suggests a wider range of strategies, from joint ventures to community trusts, which have been insufficiently considered in the past. Throughout, my analysis will apply to South African conditions in the hope of influencing current policy debates on poverty alleviation, conservation and development.

THE SETTLEMENT AND RESETTLEMENT PROCESS INVOLVING SMALL-SCALE DIVERSIFIED PRODUCTION SYSTEMS

Resettlement/settlement theory

In recent years, analysis of the settlement and resettlement process has become almost a separate sub-field of anthropology to which other social scientists including human geographers have made major contributions (see Guggenheim 1994 for a lengthy and partially annotated bibliography dealing solely with involuntary resettlement). Theorising continues to be largely influenced by the four- or five-stage conceptual framework that I have developed over the years (Scudder 1981a, 1993a, 1997a, 1997b; Scudder and Colson 1982). Though based on comparative analysis of over 100 schemes involving land settlement (Scudder 1981b, 1984, 1991; World Bank 1985), the evolution of this framework has been particularly influenced by Elizabeth Colson's and my longer-term study of Kariba resettlement/ settlement in Zambia (Colson 1971; Scudder and Colson in press) and by Kapila Vimaladharma's and my 1979–89 monitoring of Sri Lanka's Accelerated Mahaweli Project (Scudder 1993b), as well as by the three-stage frameworks proposed by Robert Chambers (1969) and Michael Nelson (1973).

Critiques of this framework by Partridge *et al.* (1982) and de Wet (1993b) have correctly emphasised that its emphasis on settlement process similarities is at the expense of explaining the range of variation presented by specific cases. Nonetheless, more recent analyses continue to draw on it. Hence, while Cernea and Guggenheim do not specifically refer to it in the introductory section to their book, *Anthropological Approaches to Resettlement: Policy, Practice, and Theory* (1993), the authors of more than two-thirds of their case studies have found it useful, as has McMillan (1995). That usefulness, however, has tended to over-emphasise the constraints that land settlement imposes on settlers as opposed to potential opportunities. Stated differently, more reference has been made to the difficult stage of adaptation/coping that accompanies movement of a majority to new lands and production systems as opposed to the stage of economic development and community formation than can follow if adaptation restores living standards and if opportunities exist for raising those standards in a fashion that is sustainable environmentally, economically and institutionally.

Policy and planning constraints

The greatest constraint to successful settlement remains a policy and planning constraint and not a capacity constraint on the part of settlers. That point is critical in trying to assess the role that settlement could play, for example, in the New South Africa. In good part the policy and planning constraint is due to the difficulty that sponsored settlement schemes present to the planner. As Cernea emphasised: 'Agricultural development through new land settlement is socially the most complex of all development interventions, both to design and implement' (1985: 119). At the time both he and I believed that to be the case. While today we might want to equivocate a bit before making such a strong statement, clearly great difficulty is involved in any attempt to plan and implement new production and sociopolitical systems in what frequently are problem-prone environments – which is often why they are not fully settled in the first place.

Lack of knowledge and political will, as well as inflexibility, on the part of policy makers, is part of the problem, along with the predisposition of so many planners to plan production systems for people as a top–down approach, as opposed to encouraging people to plan production systems with government assistance. Politicians fear the latter approach as transferring too much empowerment from central government to community levels. As for planners, too frequently they plan a scheme based on a single technology (irrigation, for example) or crop (such as cotton) for low income people whose preference is to diversify their production systems, not just to reduce risks, but also as a means for shifting labour to more productive activities.

As for working with people, difficulties there also tend to be under-estimated. That is because of contemporary trends away from more cooperative social systems, not just toward nucleated families but toward divided families (Dwyer and Bruce 1988) and single-parent families as well. For reasons that are not entirely clear, countries such as Botswana, South Africa and Lesotho are world leaders in regard to the increased proportion of female-headed households.

My emphasis in this chapter, therefore, is less on new land settlement schemes than on reformulating household production systems on existing schemes and increasing the number of participants on such schemes, and on developing production systems for aggregates of households (with special emphasis on female-headed households), rather than for communities, in

peri-urban locales. While communities will not be totally neglected, I agree
with Norman Reynolds that their development requires the institutionalisation of new approaches (Reynolds 1981), such as community trusts
(Maema and Reynolds 1995), or the revolving funds that were so successful
in the initial development of the Lake Kariba fisheries and the correction of
problems remaining with China's Danjiangkou resettlement. Nor will
schemes be omitted entirely, for opportunities do exist, I believe, along the
Orange River and its tributaries (such as the Caledon), the Pongola and the
Komati.

Settler-household initiative

I continue to be impressed by the initiative that settler households show,
even on the least successful settlement schemes. As a recent example, in July
1995 Lisa Cliggett and I spent nearly six hours trying to track down a Kariba
family who had migrated from the increasingly degraded (due largely to
poorly planned settlement in the 1950s) Middle Zambezi Valley to the
Zambian Plateau adjacent to the Kafue National Park. Our journey took us
to a government-sponsored settlement scheme west of Mumbwa in Zambia's
Central Province, where settlers on 1,000-hectare holdings had received
none of the requisites for development aside from their land. Feeder roads
were mere traces impassable during the rains, with the only marketing
services provided by the Lonrho-run cotton ginnery near Mumbwa.
Appropriate research-based extension was unavailable, as were primary
schools and clinics. The family that we were seeking, we found as labourers
on a holding whose lessee had 'loaned' them a several hectare portion. Years
after land settlement's pioneer phase should have ended, that household
continued to meet more than its subsistence needs, while the household for
which it worked continued to produce a significant surplus. Too few studies
have been undertaken of the later stages of land settlement projects. Those
that have been undertaken suggest, however, that settlers have the potential
of showing more enterprise and initiative, and hence being more productive, on their new holdings than if they had remained in their old homes
without the resettlement project. Kariba resettlement is one example, but
only between 1962 and the mid-1970s. During that time living standards
for the majority of the resettlers rose significantly for at least three apparent
reasons that span psychological, economic and wider cultural variables. On
a psychological level, people who expected the worst when forced to move,
may have gained a greater appreciation of their abilities and control over
their destinies when the majority not only survived but, after the adaptation/
coping stage, raised their living standards to a previously unrealised extent.
Though clearly 'fuzzy', such a possibility does warrant more careful
research. The same applies to the effects of an initial reduction of cultural
inventory that tends to follow settlement, with settler households being less

constrained by previous patterns of land distribution, and political and ritual organisation.

In this chapter, however, what I wish to emphasise is the economic reason, i.e. the potential provided to government, donors, NGOs and the private sector for providing households and communities with new economic opportunities for raising living standards, and the capacity of those households and communities to respond to, and experiment with, those opportunities. Due both to the Kariba Dam scheme and national independence, new opportunities arose that were not previously available. At the scheme level, the Middle Zambezi Valley was incorporated within a wider political economy in which an improved system of communication enhanced the export of agricultural produce as well as the sale of several thousand tons per annum of fish from the new reservoir.

The fishery was especially important between 1962 and 1964 in generating capital which villagers invested in cattle, schooling and, in the more successful cases, in such small commercial enterprises as stores, taverns and tea shops. Sale of village produce and beer brewing in the fish camps also accelerated the incorporation of previously isolated Gwembe women into a wider national economy, while helping to sanction women's marketing role. Though improvement of living standards not only stopped in the mid-1970s but was reversed, that was not due to lack of local initiative, but rather to detrimental national policies, including adverse rural/urban terms of trade, and a pre-independence resettlement process which was neither environmentally nor economically sustainable over the longer term, i.e. the carrying capacity of the land under the prevailing system of production being exceeded at the time of removal.

To date most implemented settlement schemes have met neither the expectations of the planners nor of settler households in regard to increased productivity and living standards. Granted such a discrepancy between successful and unsuccessful land settlement, the majority of scholarly works on the land settlement process have dealt with 'unsuccessful' schemes, and hence with reasons for lack of success. Emphasis on constraints also results from lack of understanding of the settlement process. In the World Bank's Issues Paper on 'Agricultural Land Settlement', the author wrote, 'Typically, evaluation of settlement projects three to five years after the start of implementation shows economic rates of return at least 50 per cent below those in project appraisal documents' (1978: 16). That is hardly surprising since a majority of settlers at that time may well still be in the relatively low-production stage of adaptation/coping.

In the above case we are dealing with an inadequate monitoring process tied to donor disbursements which themselves tend to be tied to a three to five year project cycle. Especially when dealing with complex government sponsored schemes, success, where achieved, tends to take a longer period of time. That is the conclusion from an analysis of the relatively small number of successful settlement schemes. Interestingly enough, examples exist in all major areas, suggesting that generalisations are possible which supersede ethnic, technical and geographical factors. Those examples include Kenya's Mwea and million-acre settlement schemes and at least one of Burkina Faso's onchocerciasis control land settlement schemes, as well as Abis in Egypt, Minneriya in Sri Lanka, Metro in Indonesia, various FELDA (Federal Land Development Agency) plantation schemes in Malaysia, Northern Parana in Brazil and San Lorenzo in Peru. In such cases, as at Kariba through 1974, a majority of settlers, finding themselves within a relatively favourable policy and opportunity environment, tend to follow the same investment and consumer strategies.

Initial settler emphasis is on achieving food security through the production of food crops if allowed; otherwise through sale of cash crops. That is the strategy during the adaptation/coping stage, during which a majority of settler households tend to be risk-averse. What is most interesting, however, and has been inadequately researched, is the remarkably similar series of investment strategies that a majority follow once they believe they have achieved food security and have come to terms with their new habitat, including environment, neighbours and scheme administration. What evidence is available suggests that a very rapid shift can then take place, during which a dynamic process of economic development and community formation can proceed.

With regard to consumption, it is fascinating to observe how similar upwardly mobile settler households are as consumers. Also an investment, improved housing typically is furnished with glassed-in cabinets, similar sets of stuffed chairs and sofas, calendars and wall clocks, regardless of location in Africa, Asia, Latin America or the Middle East. With regard to economic development, a shift within a matter of months can take place from a risk-averse to a risk-taking stance. What evidence we have suggests strategic shifts to higher value cash-crops, as well as investment in livestock and education of children and other dependents. Somewhat later labour is re-allocated into a range of on-scheme non-farm occupations whereby rooms in improved housing are rented out and women open on-site boutiques or other small businesses (e.g. sewing clothes). Men begin investing in a wider range of activities including artisanal skills, transport and fixed-site commercial activities. A small minority then begin opening businesses in scheme service centres and towns while the most successful expand their activities to cities, including national capitals, where they trade, open businesses and buy real-estate. African examples include Kenya, Sudan, Egypt and Burkina Faso. In the sections that follow I address situations which would appear to couple such household initiatives to enhanced opportunities for enterprise development and employment generation while reducing the various constraints associated with the previous stage of adaptation and coping.

WATER SCARCITY AND SMALL-SCALE IRRIGATION

Water scarcity

Regardless of whether or not global warming has begun, water is southern Africa's scarcest natural resource. In South Africa, average annual rainfall (at 500 mm per annum, only 60 per cent of the world average (Government of South Africa 1994a)) is the absolute minimum required for rain-fed agriculture. It is, however, poorly distributed throughout the country, 65 per cent of which receives lower amounts. Furthermore, distribution during the cropping season is often inadequate, drought becoming an increasingly serious problem since the 1981–2 rainy season and worsening during the 1990s – the 1994–5 drought being the worst recorded to date. Further loss of moisture, adversely affecting surface run-off, is caused by high rates of evaporation that annually exceed rainfall throughout most of southern Africa.

Water availability is worsened because the predominant basement complex, as well as Karroo sediments and Karroo sandstones, are poor aquifers. Hence in South Africa, ground water provides only about 15 per cent of accessible supplies (Government of South Africa 1994a: 33). Granted inadequate rainfall and ground water supplies, countries in southern Africa are especially dependent on surface waters. This is particularly the case in South Africa where the need for inter-basin water transfers rivals that of western North America. The two major transfer systems involve the mainstream of the Orange River and the basin of the Vaal. Diversions from the Gariep Dam flow into the Eastern Cape Province's Great Fish and Sundays Rivers, which provide municipal water to coastal areas and to various irrigation schemes. Gauteng is the major recipient of water via the Vaal. Producing over 50 per cent of the country's GNP, water demands in that province already exceed Vaal River catchment resources, hence requiring inter-basin transfers from the Tugela and the Komati Rivers. Even those have proved insufficient, resulting in water restriction and planned transfers from upper tributaries of the Orange River via the Lesotho Highlands Water Project, which in turn will prove insufficient by the second decade of the twenty-first century.

South African planners, as well as the public, also look longingly at the Zambezi. Hence in a May 1992 editorial and later article *The Star* announced 'But there is new water: the Zambezi has enough for all of southern Africa's future needs' and 'tapping into the virgin waters of the Zambezi could do the trick'. Those waters are hardly virgin. Furthermore, Zambezi flows since 1981–2 have been only about half those of the preceding twenty years, while the only water spilled at Kariba is through the turbines, and, even there, current supplies are insufficient. If present trends continue, there will not be sufficient water to meet the needs of the riparian states. Mozambique is especially at risk and already is complaining to South Africa and Swaziland about receipt of reduced Komati flows.

In South Africa the situation is made worse by the fact that large quantities of what water is available are controlled by a small proportion of the farming population under an archaic system of rights that does not separate land and water issues. Clearly the situation is serious and will require more than demand management and recycling efforts. As intended by the current Government, the 1956 Water Act must be revised and updated.[2] But what is really needed are pricing mechanisms that not only reflect the true value of existing supplies, but also, through economic pricing, the cost of future projects. Such pricing, recommended by the World Bank and other advisers, must be directed at all uses, including not just higher-income urban gardens (which consume up to 60 per cent of middle and upper income residential use as opposed to 'the lower income and informal areas where approximately 5 per cent is estimated to be used for garden watering' (BKS 1995: 9–5)), but also commercial irrigation.

Restructuring irrigation to benefit smallholders

As in so many water-deficit areas, prices paid by irrigators for water fall far below the cost of providing that water. The situation is made worse in South Africa by the extent to which the previous government subsidised the commercial community of rain-fed and irrigation farmers. According to the World Bank (1995c), approximately 35 per cent of the annual flow of the Vaal River (approximately 2,200 million cubic metres or MCM) was used for irrigation, with nearly two-thirds of the farmers working land on government schemes, the biggest of which was the Vaalharts scheme. Used primarily for growing low-value cereal crops, annual demand there was nearly 20 per cent of the Vaal's average flow (425 MCM in 1992 according to BKS 1995).

Economic pricing of water will bring an end to such cropping systems, but not to irrigation as such, which will continue to play an important role in South Africa. One of three outcomes can be forecast. As in rain-fed areas, the land of some farmers will be acquired by the Land Bank for sale and redistribution. Other farmers will switch to high-value crops and/or participate in water auctions and water rights trades to mining, industrial and municipal users.

The extent to which South Africa's low-income majority is intended to benefit from such restructuring remains to be seen. Aside from suggestions from international advisors and experts, I have come across few policy statements that go beyond domestic use of scarce water supplies for the low-income majority. One major exception is contained within the executive summary of the Reconnaissance Phase Report of the Orange River Development Project Replanning Study (BKS/Ninham Shand 1995). According to that report's section on agricultural development, current irrigation demand for Orange River water is at least 2,153 MCM, or not quite 20 per cent of the Orange's average annual flow. One third of that irrigation water is diverted for cultivation of approximately 45,000 hectares along the Great Fish and Sundays River in the Eastern Cape. At least 7,000 hectares of that amount is labelled as 'social irrigation'. That includes consumption cropping, 'food plots and community gardens', which received a higher rating than larger scale commercial irrigation during a study team workshop. More specifically, with the RDP in mind, along the Lower Fish River 'pressures exist for the present irrigation scheme supplying small-scale farmers to be expanded to its fullest capacity to maximise its opportunities for Black farmers' while on the Middle Fish River 'initiatives are underway to develop urban agricultural opportunities in towns like Cradock, Somerset East and Cookhouse, based around irrigation and intensive food crop cultivation' (BKS/Ninham Shand 1995, Eastern Cape Social Study Section 2).

I would like to generalise those Eastern Cape suggestions to suitable areas near and within all South African cities as development strategies with some potential for increasing production, raising living standards and generating employment – in particular for low-income female-headed households. Though Webb (1996) cautions against over-emphasising the potential based on his own Eastern Cape research, and inadequate research elsewhere, the reference to 'urban agricultural opportunities' is particularly interesting, especially if emphasis is placed on peri-urban rather than urban locales. Those I see as less problem-prone than small-scale irrigation schemes. What is involved is a smallholding within a home lot or a subdivided set-aside area serving a community of users. Though more research is needed on size for different crop and livestock mixes, less than 500 square metres need be involved. Irrigation could be provided by water from a tap that is then sprinkled from a watering can, or a hose-attached rainbird.

In such cases, experience elsewhere in southern Africa points up a number of prerequisites which appear to apply equally well to small-scale irrigation schemes. First, to motivate gardeners, high-value crops must be grown, primarily for sale, as well as for home consumption. Second, a mixture of high-value crops should be grown, including especially relishes (greens) for complementing the stable cereal (porridge) dish. Annual crops should be mixed with less water-demanding fruit trees. Third, regardless of what crops are involved, such gardens should be planned, to the extent possible, as part of a diversified household-production system based on both farm and non-farm activities, rather than as a sole economic activity. In regard to the farming component, a logical complement would be for family members also to market what they grow, or to raise small animals (caged rabbits and turkeys for example, or several pigs, sheep and goats, or dairy cows such as one finds in garages and small household open spaces in Mexican cities).

An excellent example of how to combine marketing with gardening characterises the 'green belt' surrounding Maputo in Mozambique. There women have brought under irrigated cultivation small plots, the produce of which they sell in Maputo markets (Little and Lundin de Coloane 1992). Another example comes from Lesotho. Country-wide, the proportion of women in households producing and selling cabbages, for example, increased from 15.7 per cent in 1970 to '43 per cent and 57 per cent in 1980 in two different surveys' (Sechaba Consultants 1994: 32). While most of that production was in rural areas, the importance of peri-urban and urban home gardens in Maseru has been increasing over the years. Increased productivity and incomes are a major reason. According to the same Sechaba report,

> crops from home gardens are worth 16.9 times the amount per hectare as those from dryland cereal crops ... In the urban areas, where there is also a thriving business in home gardens, 62 per cent of the sales are directly to the consumers while 38 per cent is to vendors ... Home gardens are the largest source of domestic supply of vegetables. (216–17)[3]

Given the opportunity, it should be possible for home gardens to help raise the living standards of tens of thousands of low-income South Africans. That cannot happen, however, without government participation. Especially important would be the design of metered water delivery systems to low-income urban and peri-urban communities that would permit home gardens, and the education of Local Water Committees (at least 30 per cent of whose members are supposed to be women) to advise home gardeners on appropriate water usage in a water-scarce environment. Participation of agricultural and public-health staff would also be needed.

As for small-scale irrigation schemes, as along the Sundays and Great Fish Rivers, careful RDP/GEAR (Reconstruction and Development/ Growth, Exployment and Redistribution Programme), Ministry of Lands and other agency involvement is needed to assess the extent to which Land Bank and other government-acquired lands can be adapted to small-scale use, or to which willing seller–willing buyer transactions can be facilitated through appropriate credit and extension policies. Considerable forethought and knowledge will be required on the part of planners so as to avoid the unsatisfactory experience with African irrigation, including the Makathini irrigation scheme on the Pongola River in South Africa. Without neglecting the potential for new schemes along such rivers as the Orange, Pongola and Komati, special emphasis should be paid to restructuring and expanding existing facilities, as in the Eastern Cape. With regard to the difficult resettlement problems that can be expected at the beginning of the twenty-first century, should the governments of Lesotho and South Africa decide to go ahead with Phase Two of the Lesotho Highlands Water Project (LHWP), new resettlement options should consider acquiring, subdividing, and irrigating as smallholdings a number of Trans-Caledon, Land Bank-acquired, Free State farms that currently are rain-fed. Several such farms could provide for hundreds of resettlers if irrigated holdings were kept small (certainly less than two hectares and probably less than one) and were planned, as should be the case with most similar schemes, as part of a household-production system based on a number of diversified activities as opposed to just one, and linked to marketing networks that bring services as well as providing opportunities for sale of produce (written communication from Norman Reynolds in Scudder *et al.* 1993).

OTHER STRATEGIES

This section briefly discusses two strategies for facilitating settlement initiatives in ways that have been under-utilised in the past. The first, evolved by Norman Reynolds for rural development situations in southern Africa, including settlement/resettlement, involves community trusts combined with decentralised marketing arrangements. The second relates to contract farming involving large numbers of individual farmers, joint ventures or both.

Community trusts

Growing out of his thinking on social contracts for local communities (Reynolds 1981), Reynolds originally proposed the community trust idea for Zimbabwe's CAMPFIRE Programme during the 1980s. Though yet to be implemented there, a key component of the trust concept was subsequently successfully implemented in South Africa in various communities adversely affected by the 1991–2 drought. That component was to empower communities by providing them with a budget which they, working with government agencies, NGOs or other outsiders, could utilise. In that case, the monies financed work on community development projects at below minimum wages so as to gain as much employment and as many multiplier effects as possible.

Currently, the full community trust idea with associated periodic markets (that combine provision of government and other services with sale of produce) has been proposed for the local resettlement-with-development component associated with Phase IA of the Lesotho Highlands Development Project (Maema and Reynolds 1995; SMEC/Price Waterhouse 1995). According to the 1986 Lesotho Highlands Water Project (LHWP) Treaty, the Highlands Development Project has three major goals. The third, in addition to water transfer to South Africa and hydropower generation for national self-sufficiency within Lesotho, is to ensure that project-affected people are sufficiently 'enabled' eventually to restore what were their living standards at the time of 'first disturbance'. Owing to structural problems and major delays in implementing the project's rural development plan, the SMEC/Price Waterhouse report concludes that current planning approaches will fail. As an alternative they suggest that the entire budget available for rural development be placed in a 'Highlands Trust' which will empower impacted-upon communities to plan, manage and implement their own development under the watchful eye of a Board of Trustees composed of community, government and other appointed and elected personnel.

Since 1989 I have been on the LHWP's independent Panel of Environmental Experts. Annual visits since then have familiarised me with the complexity of the resettlement-with-development component. While I can see problems associated with the implementation of the Trust idea, I too have become frustrated with structural and other factors constraining implementation of the Phase 1A rural development plan. Since these may be insurmountable, I see the Highlands Trust idea as an attractive option.

Obviously, Trust implementation problems exist. In Phase 1A of the LHWP, the construction of hundreds of kilometres of road and transmission lines has required more physical removal of households than reservoir inundation. On the other hand, loss of livelihood is more critical than physical removal and in the reservoir basin affects far more households within discrete communities than those scattered along roads and transmission lines. Though the latter might fall between the cracks, the Trust idea would still apply to the large majority of affected communities and households.

A second constraint relates not just to community factions but to the extent to which large-scale river-basin development projects increase stress, including stress arising from conflict within communities. Though the Snowy Mountain Engineering Corporation Ltd (SMEC) report provides examples of how the Trust idea can overcome intra-community conflict, the Lesotho Highlands Development Authority (LHDA) situation presents 'a hard nut to crack' due to the lack of available land and employment, national poverty and structural constraints associated with large-scale engineering projects.

Thirdly, application of the Trust idea to Phase 1B must deal with a situation where perhaps 50 per cent of project-affected people (numbering several thousand) may have to move from their current rural highland habitat to rural and peri-urban lowland habitats. It remains to be seen how well aspects of the Trust concept, such as individual female and male rights to work and rights to training, can be adapted to such dispersal.

Notwithstanding constraints, I think that every effort should be made to institutionalise the Highland Trust as soon as possible. Institutionalisation, however, need not lead to an attempt to implement the Trust simultaneously in all affected communities, whose citizens number nearly 20,000. Rather, as a first phase, the Trust could be implemented in the Muela Catchment where the hydropower station will be installed and a small reservoir created that will inundate the more fertile arable land. Not only are there less than 3,000 people there, but they live in six villages that fall under one respected chief, whose brother is not only the MP from the area but is well-disposed towards working with villagers and the Lesotho Highlands Development Authority (LHDA). This convergence of a manageable area with the political will to proceed is of crucial importance, granted the unwillingness of so many southern African politicians and government officials to share empowerment with communities. Already, with the encouragement of the chief and the LHDA staff, village dairy and poultry groups have commenced meeting. In discussing possible development projects with them in October 1995, a range of opportunities were mentioned that could be expedited through the Highland Trust, including a dairy collection point and a community cooperative combining livestock feed with foodstuffs and clothing.

Contract farming

Little and Watts (1994) define contract farming as a futures market in which a willing buyer, in agreeing to purchase a given hectarage or volume of agricultural produce, may also provide technical assistance and various inputs. While such contracts frequently link commercial farmers with government parastatals or commercial firms in southern Africa, Little and Watts' concern, as is mine, is with smallholders. Such smallholders may constitute an aggregate of sellers linked to a processor and/or marketing agency, as in the case of Kenya, where green beans are processed locally and other vegetables are exported to Europe for Asian consumers (Jaffe 1994). Or they may be articulated in a joint venture as outgrowers to a nuclear estate/processing facility, as is the case with cane in Zambia and cotton in Zimbabwe.

Unlike the Community Trust idea which has very broad applicability, contract farming as a settlement/resettlement strategy should be limited to more isolated areas or special situations, such as when utilisation options are considered for lands acquired by the Land Bank. Limiting contract farming to isolated areas makes sense for two reasons. First, as a development initiative it reduces marketing networks and hence employment for low-income people. Hence, restricting supply of vegetables, for example, to parastatals or other contractors would adversely affect over three thousand vendors, the large majority of whom are poor women, in Harare (Horn 1988) and over one thousand vendors in Maseru (Sechaba Consultants 1994). For similar reasons, in South Africa's Eastern Cape Province, the option for produce grown on smallholder plots along the Great Fish or Sundays Rivers should be promoted. Second, contract farming, in articulating producers to outsiders, is at the expense of their independence as decision-makers, in contrast to the Community Trust idea. But in isolated areas with poor infrastructure, as with cotton in the Middle Zambezi Valley, or smallholder crops in the Komati and Pongola River basins, contract farming could provide market outlets not otherwise available. Another possibility in South Africa would be merging rain-fed farms acquired in the Free State to create a large enough holding, subdivided into smallholdings, to service a central processing facility.

SUMMARY

For smallholder development strategies based on land settlement to be effective in southern Africa, they must come to grips with two major constraints. The first, still strong in South Africa in particular, is the erroneous belief of too many development planners that smallholder agriculture is inefficient in comparison with large-scale commercial agriculture. The second, all too common unfortunately, is the failure of far too many smallholder land settlement schemes to meet settler household, government and donor expectations in terms of increased productivity and higher living standards.

In regard to both constraints, a major problem lies with planners' inaccurate understanding of the complexity of the settlement processes, and especially with their unrealistic expectations as to the rapidity with which project success can occur. On the other hand, while the more successful settlement projects demonstrate the willingness of a majority of settler households to respond to new opportunities, contemporary changes in the nature of the family, including increased spousal conflicts and an increase in the proportion of female-headed households, pose new problems that must be addressed, including labour constraints.

Against the background described above, there is a need to reconsider how land settlement can better contribute to local and national development. Granted water constraints in much of southern Africa, the relationship between rain-fed and irrigated smallholder agriculture must be carefully reconsidered, with more emphasis placed on provision of supplemental water for higher value smallholder crops, especially during the current restructuring of agriculture in South Africa.

While the rethinking and rehabilitation of existing projects, as along the Great Fish and Sundays Rivers in the Eastern Cape Province, deserves priority, experimentation with new approaches is also required. Each restricted to specific situations, three are emphasised. One is small-scale horticulture and small animal production for market as well as household consumption, in peri-urban areas. Though too high expectations have been rightly critiqued by Webb (1996), nonetheless, the potential is there. The second is the use of Community Trusts as advocated by Norman Reynolds (1981 and in SMEC/Price Waterhouse 1995). And the third is based on the type of smallholder contract farming that Little and Watts (1994) have analysed in sub-Saharan Africa.

NOTES

1. The RDP has been restructured into the Growth, Employment and Redistribution (GEAR)Programme.
2. The new Act (the National Water Act No 36 of 1998), which does indeed separate land and water rights, has subsequently come into effect (the editors).
3. A somewhat more guarded view emerges from a nationwide survey in 1992 (see Phororo, this volume), which suggests that, of 21,800 tons of vegetables produced in the 1991–2 season, only 2,600 tons (i.e. 12 per cent) were sold.

MIGRATION, SETTLEMENT AND THE POPULATION DEBATE IN SOUTH AFRICA

BACKGROUND: THE ONGOING POPULATION DEBATE

Population policy in South Africa has had quite an unfortunate history. For a long time population policy under the auspices of the apartheid regime was used as a political instrument to achieve certain apartheid ideology aims, including *inter alia* reducing population growth among black people to limit the *swart gevaar* (i.e. 'Black Peril'). Even today, many population theorists inside and outside South Africa still claim that the population growth rate among blacks is too high and that there should be a concerted effort to reduce it (Barker 1995; Jordaan *et al.* 1991; Mostert *et al.* 1991). By focusing so strongly on population growth among blacks, serious population problems in respect of whites are ignored and unaddressed, i.e. that whites in general over-consume and take up a disproportionate area of land in South Africa to the detriment of the advancement, empowerment and development of other population groups (Government of South Africa 1995: 19–20).

In the past there have been several endeavours to formulate suitable population policies and programmes for South Africa. Such programmes mostly focused on a single population aspect, namely *fertility*. In so doing, other population aspects such as mortality and migration have received comparatively little attention. The Population Development Programme (PDP), which was instituted during 1984, emphasised a broad range of policy measures and programmes to improve the quality of life of people, but stressed that the main demographic objective of the PDP remained the realisation of a total fertility rate (TFR) of 2.1 by 2010 (Government of South Africa 1993: 23). Because the TFRs of the Asians and the whites are already at or near the population replacement level of 2.1, PDP programmes were mostly targeted at coloureds and blacks whose TFRs are still higher than the population replacement level (1995 black TFR projection was 3.7).

With the political transition during the first half of the 1990s came the realisation that existing population policies and programmes needed to be adapted or replaced to cater for new social and political realities. To start this process, a discussion document on population policies and programmes was drafted by Klugman (1994) and distributed for discussion by the stakeholders in the population debate. In Klugman's document (1–24), several issues were raised which are important for the purposes of this chapter, namely:

- the theoretical models used in the past to analyse population processes and dynamics in South Africa were originally developed to describe historical population trends in Western countries (and especially Western Europe, Britain and the United States) and can thus hardly be directly applied to describing and explaining the present and future population processes and dynamics in South Africa. There is a need to find a more applicable theoretical framework to account for population issues and trends in South Africa;
- there is an overemphasis on overpopulation and population control in South Africa, and too little emphasis on population distribution and quality of life. The former emphasis is based upon a belief among many participants in the population debate that there is a direct linkage between the population growth rate and poverty levels. This view often finds its expression in efforts to reduce the levels of population growth by 'quick-fix' measures such as promoting contraception and limiting in-migration, without addressing development problems among the population which often give rise to high fertility, i.e. poverty, underdevelopment, disempowerment, inequalities, unemployment and illiteracy (Ashford 1995: 38–40; World Commission on Environment and Development 1991: 29–31);
- there has in recent years been a shift in international thinking away from addressing 'overpopulation' to focusing on 'population concerns', such as the environment, economic development and human rights. This shift has come about in response to international research, experience and discourse regarding the efficacy of various population and development programmes implemented from the 1970s in many developing countries (Johnson 1994: 325–46; World Commission on Environment and Development 1991: 27–41). This shift in thinking should, according to Klugman (1994), have an impact on the formulation of population policies and programmes in South Africa;
- the apartheid system limited urbanisation in South Africa, which would have been a positive response to industrialisation. Furthermore, draconian migration control measures (i.e. influx control and the Group Areas Act) and forced removals to a significant degree determined the demographic profile of South Africa. The migrant labour system has also given rise to a large number of widespread social and socio-economic problems. In light of this, the expediency of policies which may make for further socially engineered migration and settlement (urbanisation) trends and patterns in South Africa is questionable.

The International Conference on Population and Development (ICPD), held in Cairo during September 1994, had a marked influence on international thinking about population issues. For the purposes of this chapter, some of the conclusions arrived at during the ICPD Conference (Ashford 1995: 15, 16 and 31) need to be kept in mind:

- it appears that population growth and poverty are linked in a complex way, such that high population growth leads to poverty, while poverty in turn leads to higher levels of population growth;

- there are already half a billion people in developing countries who are either unemployed or under-employed. To ensure sufficient levels of job creation for their growing populations, developing countries need to create about 30 million jobs per year just to maintain their current employment levels;
- poverty goes hand in hand with low literacy levels, poor health, low status of women, exposure to environmental hazards and environmental degradation;
- population movements (both international and internal migration) are usually an intrinsic part of the process of economic development because people tend to move from areas of low to high economic opportunity;
- migration results because of a wide array of economic and demographic factors. The rapid population growth in developing countries resulted in a large number of new labour market entrants in economically stagnant areas having to migrate to and settle in areas where more economic opportunities are available. As the rural–urban economic differential grows and labour demand in the rural areas declines, people are forced to move to settlements in areas where there is a greater demand for labour;
- in Africa urban growth is primarily brought about by high levels of rural-to-urban migration. Because of the higher levels of fertility in rural as opposed to urban areas, the large number of people who are not able to find jobs in the stagnant rural labour markets are forced to migrate to and settle in urban areas. Because of the rapid urbanisation that results, the ability of urban authorities to provide housing, sanitation, public safety and other services and jobs to new settlers, becomes strained (see also Gelderblom and Kok 1994a: 221–30).

Based on the views expressed in the Klugman document, the Reconstruction and Development Programme (RDP), the Population Development Programme (PDP) and the ICPD documents, the Ministry for Welfare and Population Development in 1995 formulated a Green Paper for public discussion on a population policy for South Africa. The Green Paper does not make specific recommendations regarding population policies and programmes, but rather suggests some possible approaches to the three population processes of fertility, mortality and migration. These approaches reflect the ideas about migration and settlement issues being discussed in the wider population debate in South Africa.

This chapter focuses on these matters with respect to macro-level aspects (i.e. migration and settlement patterns and trends), meso-level aspects (i.e. community and cultural influences on migration and settlement) and micro-level aspects (i.e. migration and settlement decision-making).

The current population debate emphasises a demographic perspective, as against the economic and sociological perspectives often used when focusing on migration and settlement. With the main emphasis in the current debate on enhancing the quality of life through sustainable human, social and economic development and ensuring human rights, the challenge is to formulate policies and programmes that would ensure that migration and settlement patterns and trends facilitate the realisation of a better quality of life in practice.

POPULATION-RELATED PERSPECTIVES ON MIGRATION AND SETTLEMENT

In government discussion documents on population policy in South Africa released by the Government of National Unity in the mid 1990s, the question is raised concerning the expediency of developing specific strategies to influence migration and settlement trends in South Africa as part of a national development strategy that integrates population trends. There is, however, no clear indication from government as to what such 'specific strategies' should encompass. This vagueness about a 'national or even regional economic development strategy' to influence the distribution of the population is symptomatic of the population strategies of large governments. Issues such as population concentrations in the cities, uncontrolled migration, informal settlement and brain drain overlap with so many other issues, interpretations and ramifications, that any attempt at a comprehensive strategy paradoxically often results in policy fragmentation. Government administrations become frustrated at the dispersion of a problem across different offices and agencies. Often they try to solve the problem of 'big government' by making it even larger.

The various possible approaches to migration and settlement being considered in the current population debate seem to be underpinned by different demographic perspectives on migration and settlement. These perspectives are:

1. *The population growth and distribution perspective.* According to this perspective, migration and settlement will not be regarded as problems as long as migration, urbanisation and informal settlement formation are perceived to be at acceptably low levels. However, as soon as a large number of migrants enters a country, region or urban area and significantly contributes to population growth, or when high levels of internal migration dramatically upset the present population distribution, or when rapid urbanisation puts pressure on the existing urban infrastructure and/or when informal settlement formation goes along with large-scale land invasion, then migration and settlement become perceived as problem areas. In such cases more stringent measures are adopted or called for to ensure migration and settlement control.

2. *The population displacement perspective.* This approach stresses the importance of ensuring a high level of stability in respect of migration and settlement patterns in a country. As long as no large-scale rural-to-urban migration movements or large-scale displacements are taking place, there are no significant migration and settlement problems. Protagonists of this approach emphasise the necessity of rural development as a measure to effect a rural–urban turnaround and to ensure stability of settlement in rural areas.

3. *The population profile perspective.* This approach emphasises that migration and settlement policy should lead to gains in terms of skilled people, entrepreneurship, industrial development and the improvement of rural and urban infrastructure in order to improve the population profile. Those population movements and patterns of settlement formation that do not lead to such an improvement, should be actively discouraged, while those that do give rise to such an improvement, should be encouraged.

4. *The labour market skills mix perspective.* In terms of this approach, positive migration and settlement patterns improve the skills mix in the labour market so as to ensure that labour supply becomes more congruent with labour demand in a specific geographical area. Migrants with skills in demand in a specific labour market, should be encouraged to settle at or near that labour market to ensure that they obtain employment and that the specific labour market benefits by the skills that they supply. However, this often leads to a situation where migrants who initially had scarce skills may find that by the time they actually migrate and settle in an area, their skills may be in over-supply because of other people with similar skills who have already migrated to and settled in the area.
5. *The population and development perspective.* This approach focuses on the impact that migration and settlement have on development. Should people who settle in an industrial growth area become involved in the expansion of the economic cake through their productive efforts in such an area, they are seen to be contributing towards development. However, should a large number of people migrate to and settle in an area where they are not able to obtain employment, and/or start up new informal settlements in places where few economic opportunities are available, they often live in abject poverty, thus becoming a burden instead of being a boost to development.

The so-called 'overpopulation theorists', who emphasise the negative effects of rapid population growth, have been dominant in discourse about population issues, since Malthus originated this approach in 1798 until the 1960s (Samuelson 1976: 30–9). During this period it was seen as an 'econo-mic fact' that countries with small populations are wealthy while those with large populations live in poverty. Because of economic stagnation being viewed by the overpopulation theorists as the result of high population growth, it was postulated that rapid population growth leads to impover-ished communities, high levels of economic migration (because of people being forced by poor economic circumstances to leave impoverished communities in an endeavour to find economic opportunities elsewhere) and a high level of informal settlement formation (because of impoverished people not being able to afford formal housing in the areas they migrate to) (Gelderblom and Kok 1994a: 171–94 and 221–30).

The overpopulation perspective, however, came into disrepute during the 1960s when more and more researchers demonstrated that in many countries rapid population growth went hand in hand with high levels of economic growth and stable forms of migration and formal settlement forma-tion (i.e. in Western European countries, Japan and the United States). With the realisation that rapid population growth can facilitate either econo-mic growth and development (as characterised by high levels of job creation and poverty reduction) or economic stagnation and underdevelopment (as characterised by high levels of unemployment and poverty), a greater emphasis has been placed on the profile of the population. The term 'popu-lation profile' here refers to the level to which a developed population (as characterised *inter alia* by high literacy levels, a high per capita GDP and a relatively equal income distribution) is found in a specific country. The population-profile theorists in general indicate that a large, highly educated and entrepreneurially minded population facilitates economic growth and development, while a large, illiterate population who are not entrepreneurially minded will contribute towards economic stagnation and underdevelopment. This realisation among population scientists gave rise to an emphasis on the importance of comprehensive human development in large populations to ensure optimal participation in the generation of national wealth and economic development. From the 1980s onwards there has been a growing emphasis, not only on effecting such human development in large populations, but also on empowering individuals, communities and populations to develop themselves. In respect of migration and settlement issues, the implication of this would be that people should be empowered to make good migration and settlement decisions by providing them with the necessary information on the labour market and economic empowerment, and teaching them how to make good decisions by weighing-up available information.

Although the various population perspectives discussed above provide some explanation for migration and settlement issues in post-apartheid South Africa, a lot of pressing issues (i.e. informal settlement formation and migration to areas where very few economic opportunities are available) are left unexplained. In the rest of the chapter I supply the broad outline of an alternative population perspective which could be used to account for some of these issues in South Africa.

MACRO–LEVEL APPROACHES TO MIGRATION AND SETTLEMENT MOOTED IN THE CURRENT POPULATION DEBATE

There is no clarity in the current population debate on the level to which government should become involved in influencing migration and settlement trends and patterns in South Africa. As an argument against government intervention it could be said that these patterns are the inevitable product of economic opportunities and that, given the history of influx control in South Africa, it is perhaps questionable whether government should seek to influence migration and settlement patterns at all through the policy, legislative and/or executive means at its disposal. On the other hand, there may be several pragmatic reasons compelling government to influence these patterns, e.g. the present large-scale inflow of people from the poverty-stricken rural areas to the peri-urban, semi-urban and urban areas, and the resultant high level of informal settlement formation (sometimes linked to land invasion).

There are several ways in which government can influence the inflow of people to urban areas, including forced resettlement in the countryside, influx control, the creation of balancing growth poles or rural development (Gelderblom and Kok 1994b: 173). Of these measures, forced resettlement in the rural areas and influx control may be counter-productive, because people who are forcibly resettled or whose inflow to urban areas is prevented, will, in all probability, migrate to urban areas at a later date when such migration is possible. Furthermore, such measures are potentially in conflict with the letter and spirit of the South African Constitution.

Although it may not be expedient for government to influence migration and settlement patterns directly, there may be a strong case for it to prevent the depopulation of the rural areas by focusing more strongly on the crisis of rural under-development. Ideally, the depopulation of the rural areas could be limited by creating economic opportunities there and developing rural infrastructure to limit rural-to-urban migration. However, one should not be overly optimistic about such possibilities, remembering the limited success and the problems of the government subsidised regional decentralisation policies of the apartheid era.

There is evidence (Government of South Africa 1995c: 25) to suggest that urbanisation is an inevitable part of the process of economic and social development. If this is true, it will be incumbent upon government to put major infrastructural and economic development efforts into preparing for and handling the flow of people from the rural areas. However, merely condoning rapid urbanisation as a necessary part of development may not be wise. Several South American governments have had nasty experiences in using rapid urbanisation as a development instrument, when they found to their horror that they could not supply urban infrastructure rapidly enough for the 'inevitable' inflow of people (Gelderblom and Kok 1994a: 216–30). Even where they succeeded in supplying infrastructure rapidly enough, the new city dwellers could in many cases not afford urban infrastructure such as sanitation, electricity and housing, leading to land invasion, squatting, high levels of urban poverty, high unemployment rates and high crime levels.

Because a large part of the South African population is still staying in the rural areas, economic infrastructure and economic opportunities need to be improved in both rural and urban areas, in order to create economic opportunities in rural areas and to effect a more balanced population distribution. Financial constraints may however limit the effective use of development as an indirect measure to influence migration and settlement patterns.

Other policy instruments which are used by some governments to influence migration and settlement patterns and trends, include:

1. *Persuasion through IEC (Information, Education and Communication) programmes.* Through IEC, prospective migrants and settlers could be informed about the availability of economic opportunities in areas to which they want to migrate or in which they want to settle. However, even educating prospective migrants and settlers about the limitations in terms of jobs and development opportunities in possible areas of destination or settlement poses a moral dilemma to government, given the relative poverty in the rural areas from which they

want to escape. Some governments simply by-pass this dilemma by leaving it to people to make their own migration decisions without supplying them with the necessary information.

2. *The principle of a tort system whereby damages are compensated for.* This might form part of the re-allocation of land to the formerly disenfranchised to halt rural-to-urban migration, but is a cumbersome way to motivate migration movements.

3. *Regulations backed up by police power.* For example, in the case of land reform that places a ceiling on the amount of land an individual may own or stronger action against illegal squatting. However, such moves are at odds with the more humanitarian approach to population and development which is advanced by the ICPD.

4. *Taxes or other charges and a set of disincentives* which can also become coercive.

5. *Subsidies* which can be put to good use in agricultural development.

6. The *establishment of a market in rights* where people can, for example, bid for the right to move to a certain area and settle there, can be used to place a ceiling on the inflow of the unskilled and the outflow of the skilled, but may result in many abuses of individual freedom.

Policy instruments such as persuasion through IEC and a tort system are viewed in the current population debate as possible options to use in conjunction with rural development, while more coercive measures (i.e. influx control, police power, taxes and regulations) are not viewed as appropriate. It is however ironic that when speaking to community organisations in various urban and rural communities, the wide-scale introduction of such coercive measures is often described as the 'only way' to bring about stability with respect to migration and settlement patterns.

MESO- AND MICRO-LEVEL APPROACHES TO MIGRATION AND SETTLEMENT MOOTED IN THE CURRENT POPULATION DEBATE

One of the fundamental population decisions to be taken in South Africa is whether to encourage or discourage higher levels of *fertility*. Should South Africa decide on pro-natal policies, the already high fertility rate in the rural areas will increase, thus leading even greater numbers of people in the rural areas to migrate to and settle in the urban areas where more economic opportunities are available. On the other hand, policies and programmes discouraging high fertility, together with the rapidly aging population in South Africa, may limit migratory movements and may lead to more stable settlement formation over the long term (Government of South Africa 1995a: 26–8).

High fertility leading to rapid population growth will also aggravate the already acute housing crisis in South Africa. Greater numbers of people will be constrained to stay in informal settlements where there is insufficient infrastructure (i.e. water, sanitation, economic opportunities and electricity). However, high fertility is not necessarily only negative as the overpopulation theorists would have us believe. High fertility could lead to better economies of scale that would open up opportunities for entrepreneurs, and more

labour-intensive manufacturing and construction concerns could start up to
serve the rapidly growing population that would in turn open up a lot of new
job opportunities. The factors that will determine whether high fertility will
have an overall positive or negative socio-economic impact will be:

1. the ability of the country to educate and train the rapidly growing population;
2. the level to which wide-scale entrepreneurship is realised;
3. the success of the economy in generating wealth, linked to the ability of
   government and other societal institutions to ensure economic opportunity
   (wealth) transfer to the growing population;
4. the level to which the populace as a whole is allowed to participate freely in
   economic activities

The consequence of an inability to educate/train and to ensure sufficient
wealth transfer would be that large parts of the population will migrate to
and settle in or near large urban centres where there are still jobs, housing
and economic opportunities available. Enabling people to provide for themselves economically, irrespective of where they stay, through training them
and through ensuring sufficient wealth transfer, will improve the chances of
both economic development and of an urban–rural balance being realised.

In the current population debate, the importance of ensuring sound
development planning, is emphasised. Improving development planning may
over the medium- to long-term have a significant impact on migration and
settlement decision-making in South Africa. To improve development planning we need to determine the most effective way to gather relevant data on
population trends. To address this issue it would be important to guarantee
coordinated efforts to ensure the generation of high-quality data and research
on population issues in South Africa. This would enable us to identify those
communities from which large-scale migration and displacement is taking
place because of poverty and a lack of economic opportunities. Based on such
research, development funds could be more accurately aimed at meeting
basic needs in poverty-stricken communities, alleviating the plight of those
people, and lessening the pressure to migrate from such communities.

Women's legally, politically and economically inferior position in many
rural areas, has meant that they have not been free to decide for themselves
whether they wish to migrate or settle elsewhere. This has impacted upon
patterns of migration and settlement formation. This inferiority is reflected
in the fact that women often bear disproportionate burdens of illiteracy,
landlessness, poverty, unemployment and limited social mobility. However,
the rapid urbanisation going on at present could give impetus to greater
gender equality, as with urbanisation women tend to get easier access to
educational and economic opportunities, leaving them more scope to make
their own migration and settlement decisions (Boserup 1985: 383–9; Todaro
1994: 203, 257–8, 370–1).

To make informed migration and settlement decisions (i.e. to know where there is a high demand for labour and/or entrepreneurs), it is important for people to have the necessary *development and population information*. They need to be informed of over-concentrations of people in certain urban areas, and of the economic development levels of different areas. Information about economic development in the rural areas may make for a situation where people, who had migrated to the urban areas, might return to the rural areas when economic opportunities become available there (see Groenewald 1989: 256–7). Although the need for development and population information to ensure informed migration and settlement decisions is evident, there is no clarity as to who should be responsible for gathering and disseminating such information. Possible institutions who could provide such information include *inter alia* the Department of Health, the Department of Home Affairs, the Department of Education, the Department of Welfare and NGOs.

CONCLUDING REMARKS

A large number of possible approaches to aspects of migration and settlement are being considered in the current population debate. An heuristic model can be formulated that summarises these various possible approaches by means of a diagram (Figure 19.1). This model is based on two dichotomies regarding policy options to deal with migration and settlement issues, namely: *direct versus indirect policy measures*; and *general versus specific policy strategies*.

Four types of possible approach to migration and settlement may be identified, based on the above dichotomies, namely:

1. *Direct general strategies*, which are used to regulate migration and settlement directly in a general manner, by *facilitating migration flows and settlement formation trends* by encouraging or discouraging migration and settlement through subsidies and creating new industrial growth centres.

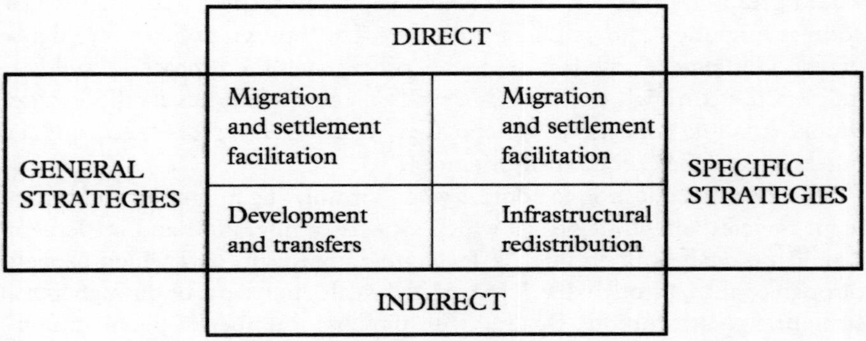

	DIRECT		
GENERAL STRATEGIES	Migration and settlement facilitation	Migration and settlement facilitation	SPECIFIC STRATEGIES
	Development and transfers	Infrastructural redistribution	
	INDIRECT		

Figure 19.1 An heuristic model of possible approaches to migration and settlement

2. *Direct specific strategies*, where there is an endeavour to regulate migration and settlement directly in a specific manner, through *controlling migration and settlement formation* by border patrols, influx control, forced removals, resettlement and displacement.
3. *Indirect general strategies*, aimed at regulating migration and settlement indirectly in a general manner, through *development and wealth transfer* by developing rural areas to effect a rural–urban turnaround in migration and settlement patterns.
4. *Indirect specific strategies*, which are formulated in an effort to regulate migration and settlement formation indirectly in a specific manner, through *the redistribution of infrastructure* by helping migrants to return to the rural areas, resettling them there and involving them in the development of infrastructure in such areas to create economic opportunities for them.

Direct general and direct specific strategies are often used in a reactive manner to cope with rapid urbanisation, as is evident from case studies of migration and urbanisation in some South American countries. It appears that such strategies initially showed good results, which motivated governments to use such measures over the longer term. However, over time such measures often back-fired because people were compelled to find ways around policy instruments and patrols to migrate to and settle in large numbers in areas which were not deemed suitable for more settlers by the government concerned. On the other hand, indirect general and indirect specific strategies are usually used as pro-active measures to influence migration and settlement patterns. Although such measures might be effective over the longer term, they are costly to introduce and maintain, and often do not show significant short-term results. Because of the more humanitarian nature of such measures, governments are often pressurised by the international community to use such indirect approaches to deal with acute migration and settlement problems, where direct measures could have been more effective.

Any successful migration and settlement strategy should encompass aspects of the various possible approaches discussed above. In practice this would mean that policies and strategies should in respect of certain issues address migration and settlement directly (i.e. through policies on migration and settlement), while in respect of other issues the approach should be indirect (i.e. through policies on development). Strategies in this regard should in some aspects be general (i.e. wealth-transfer oriented) and in others be specific (i.e. control-oriented).

The essential question to address when formulating migration and settlement policies and strategies is: which aspects of migration and settlement should be dealt with through a facilitative approach, and which aspects through control, through development and wealth transfers, or through infrastructural redistribution? Dealing with the large number of people migrating from neighbouring countries and the large number of people taking part in land invasions might require migration and settlement control, although there are many political sensitivities to take into account in this regard. On the other hand, migration control might not be the desired mechanism to deal with rural–urban migration and informal settlement formation practices, given the influx control and forced removals history of this country. Development, wealth transfer and infrastructural development may be more acceptable and more effective mechanisms to deal with such issues.

What would be the correct mix of control, facilitation, development and infrastructural redistribution? There is no simple answer to this question. However, with the increasingly strong emphasis being placed on people-centred policies and strategies, it can be expected that facilitation and development will feature more strongly than control and redistribution. Should this be the case, it needs to be kept in mind that the pay-offs of facilitation and development would be over the medium to longer term, rather than over the short term, because of the financially intensive and time-consuming nature of development and facilitation. So what should be done in the short term? One answer may be that migration and settlement control is the short term answer and facilitation and development the long-term answer. However, migration and settlement control may impede the creation of an environment conducive towards facilitation and development. If we however do nothing over the short term regarding migration, we may find that mass inflows and haphazard (informal) settlement formation occurring in the short term obliterate any positive effects resulting from facilitation and development. Obtaining the correct mix between control and redistribution on the one hand (as short-term measures) and development and facilitation on the other hand (as medium- to longer-term measures) is therefore one of the major challenges in formulating workable migration and settlement policies and strategies for South Africa.

It is also important to ask where such policies and programmes should be located, i.e. should they be dealt with in development policies, in population policies, in housing policies, in rural and urban development policies, in departmental policies of state departments, in migration and settlement legislation or in population programmes? A possible answer in this regard may be that different aspects of migration and settlement policy issues could be dealt with via different policy instruments, i.e. migration and settlement control could be dealt with through legislation and state department policies, while development aspects could be dealt with through RDP/GEAR and population policies. Such policy instruments should also ensure effective coordination of migration and settlement policies, programmes and strategies, to ensure a coordinated and holistic framework to deal with migration and settlement issues in South Africa.

EQUITABLE AND SUSTAINABLE URBAN FUTURES IN POST-APARTHEID SOUTHERN AFRICA

As with the basic term sustainability itself, the professed concern with sustainable urbanism has become something of a cliché in the 1990s. While such popularisation is a vital element in the process of getting the issue onto political agendas, the simplifications and abstractions involved often diffuse essential meanings. Expedient or cynical hijacking of popular slogans like sustainability have sometimes served to conceal status quo arguments and to reduce or prevent substantive change. It is now widely accepted that existing urban areas and forms of urbanism are generally unsustainable in the sense that they are highly energy intensive, polluting and waste generating, are often inefficiently structured and organised, and (apart from newly industrialising countries) are characterised by increasing social inequalities to the point where long-term viability and the ability of future generations to meet their needs and aspirations (e.g. in terms of an equivalent quality of urban life) cannot be guaranteed. I would argue that an acceptable level of equitability is essential to sustainability, because the latter can be achieved only through general legitimacy, acceptance, empowerment and participation.

The issues have now been accorded international recognition at the highest level. For example, Chapter 7 of Agenda 21, adopted at the United Nations Conference on Environment and Development in Rio de Janeiro in 1992, deals specifically with 'promoting sustainable human settlement development' (Middleton *el al.* 1993). In mid-1996, Habitat II, the second UN City Summit, was held in Istanbul, Turkey. The draft 'Global Plan of Action' to be agreed at Habitat II contains two key national commitments for governments to endorse, namely 'adequate shelter for all' and 'sustainable human settlements in an urbanising world' (Church 1995). In support of these activities and commitments, the UN Centre for Human Settlements (UNCHS/Habitat) and United Nations Environment Programme (UNEP) have launched a Sustainable Cities Programme. This is a technical cooperation and capacity building programme for 'the development of a sustainable urban environment, founded on broad-based and meaningful public participation' (UNCHS 1995).

In the academic and professional literatures, at least two books with the title *Sustainable Cities* (Haughton and Hunter 1994; Stren *et al.* 1992) and a range of shorter works on this topic have appeared recently. One important feature of these developments is that the broad problems are recognised as being universal, not the particular preserve of any one region or continent. Although the precise nature and balance of issues is naturally context specific, we do now have a clear sense of broad considerations to be addressed in making cities and urban life more environmentally and socially sustainable.

That said, however, it is certainly true that many authors concerned principally or exclusively with countries of the North see the way forward in relatively modest reformist terms. Thus, the 'problem' for cities and national economies has generally been conceived in terms of the need to refine neoclassical economic tools to establish 'economic values' for pollution, resource degradation and the like. In other words, environmental and associated problems are held to arise from 'market imperfections' in that no or inappropriate monetary values have been placed on such externalities. If these can be more accurately imputed and then incorporated into private and public resource accounting, market mechanisms will become self-correcting and yield more sustainable outcomes (e.g. Pearce *et al.* 1989; Turner 1988).

However, this approach is too limited because it fails to address the basic flaws and limiting assumptions of neoclassical economics, relating to profit maximisation, individual benefit, the divisibility of factors of production, etc., together with the failure to account for structural, politico-economic processes (e.g. Redclift and Sage 1994; Simon 1989a). Much of the relevant recent literature on Third World cities emphasises management problems, structural inequalities, the implications of globalised economic production and consumption processes, flexible specialisation, information and communications technology and capital mobility (e.g. Armstrong and McGee 1985; Devas and Rakodi 1993; Ginsburg *et al.* 1991; Rakodi 1990b; Simon 1992a; Stren and White 1989). This complex set of issues should be taken together; exclusive concern with (mis-)management, for example, has sometimes become an oversimplified agenda of agencies like the World Bank. Urban problems and the pressures for greater urban sustainability cannot be addressed purely or mainly in terms of conventional urban management issues.

The aim of this chapter is to elaborate this argument with particular respect to southern Africa, where inherited patterns and processes of urbanisation have been particularly unsustainable and inequitable but where the current transitions and restructurings provide very real opportunities to break with the past and to adopt more sustainable development strategies.

Table 20.1 Rural–urban service indicators – southern Africa population with access to services (%)

HDI rank	Urban population (as % of total)	Health		Safe water		Sanitation		Rural–urban disparity in services 100=rural–urban parity: see note		
		Rural 1985–93	Urban 1985–93	Rural 1988–93	Urban 1988–93	Rural 1988–93	Urban 1988–93	Health 1985–93	Safe water 1985–93	Sanitation 1985–93
74 Botswana	25	85ᵃ	100ᵃ	77	100	41	91	85	77	45
95 South Africa	50									
108 Namibia	33	60ᵃ	92ᵃ	35	98	11	24	65	36	46
121 Zimbabwe	30	80ᵃ	96ᵃ	80	95	22	95	83	84	23
124 Swaziland	29									
131 Lesotho	21			45ᵃ	59	23	14		76	164
136 Zambia	42	50ᵃ	100ᵃ	28	70	12	75	50	40	16
157 Malawi	12			50ᵃ	97ᵃ	81	30		52	270
64 Angola	30			20	71	15	25		28	60
167 Mozambique	30	30ᵃ	100ᵃ	17	44	11	61	30	39	18

Note: The figures in the last three columns are expressed in relation to the urban average, which is indexed to equal 100. The smaller the figure the bigger the gap, the closer the figure to 100 the smaller the gap, and a figure above 100 indicates that the rural average is higher than the urban average.
ᵃ Data refer to a year or period other than that specified in the column heading, differ from the standard definition or refer to only part of the country.
Source: UNDP (1995) *Human Development Report 1995*. New York: Oxford University Press

While cities will form my principal subject, no policies addressing them exclusively can succeed since cities do not exist in isolation. They form integral parts of wider national and regional systems, both reflecting and shaping political, economic and social relations. Since access to urban services and basic needs is generally better in urban than rural areas of southern Africa (Table 20.1), pressure on this infrastructure and these services has been intense, not least through net migration, a trend unlikely to change much in the foreseeable future unless and until the costs and difficulties of urban living exceed those to which many city dwellers retain access in their rural areas of origin (Potts 1995).

THE BURDEN OF THE PRESENT: URBANISM IN SOUTHERN AFRICA

Historically, the dominant parameters of urbanisation and urban settlement on the subcontinent were established by European colonisation and the discriminatory policies pursued in the process. Indigenous centres did exist in parts of the region, e.g. among the Zulu (Umgungundhlovu, Ulundi) and Ndebele (Bulawayo), but these were generally destroyed or marginalised. Moreover, the ruins of Great Zimbabwe and similar settlements bear testimony to well-established polities which dominated substantial territories but which had disappeared by the time of the European conquest. Along the east coast, Arab–Swahili traders and slavers had established settlements from the tenth to fifteenth centuries; these were captured by, or co-existed with, the Portuguese from the sixteenth century onwards. Angoche, Ihla de Moçambique and Sofala are probably the historically most important examples, linked to Mombasa, Zanzibar and other networks further North (Torp 1989). Indigenous Tswana nucleated villages, or agro-towns as they are now generally called, had populations of up to 30,000 people. Whereas these disappeared under colonial rule in South Africa, they have survived in Botswana and some have retained their historic importance (Silitshena 1996).

Simultaneously mirroring and reinforcing the external dominance–dependence relations characteristic of colonialism, the towns and cities established under European rule in southern Africa catered primarily for settler needs. Indigenes were either excluded altogether or accommodated as subordinate providers of labour, initially in slave quarters and subsequently in segregated 'locations' of grossly inferior quality (O'Connor 1983; Simon 1992b). Although the earliest European settlements in the region were established by the Portuguese and Dutch from the late sixteenth to early eighteenth centuries (e.g. Luanda 1576, Benguela 1617, Cape Town 1652, Stellenbosch 1679, Lourenço Marques/Maputo 1721), most urban centres date from the nineteenth and early twentieth centuries. Racial discrimination was universal, even where not embodied in formal legislative practice, as in the former Portuguese colonies of Angola and Mozambique.

Despite a legitimising myth propagated from the early 1950s by the fascist
dictatorship in Lisbon that these were 'overseas provinces' and not colonies,
the under-development and exploitation indicated otherwise. These 'overseas provinces' had to be self-financing and to contribute to the development of metropolitan Portugal. There was a strong social hierarchy based
on phenotype (skin pigmentation), with the small proportion of mixed-race
or *misteco* people occupying an intermediate position between whites and
the tiny minority of Africans who were permitted to 'assimilate'. Apart from
these *assimilados*, most *indigenas* had to live on the fringes of the formal, so-
called cement city (*cidade cemento*), principally in flimsy dwellings
constructed from cane (*caniço*) in Mozambique and sand/mud in the urban
slums (*musseques*) of Angola. Such a structural distinction was every bit as
clear as that between the segregated African townships and white areas of
former British and German colonies.

The colonial experience of urbanism across southern Africa, therefore,
left the successor states with an inheritance at independence of physically
and socially structured urban inequality. Formal town planning, imbued
with the ethos of creating clear and healthy order out of the perceived unhealthy pre-modern urban chaos, was applied through inflexible development
control mechanisms like building codes, zoning regulations and health ordinances to create increasingly monofunctional land-use zones and segregated
residential areas. This legacy has generally persisted to the present, except
that class has largely replaced imputed 'race' as the principal basis of distinction
and segregation where access to housing occurs to a large extent through
private property markets (Cumming 1990; Simon 1989b, 1992a). During
the socialist period (approximately 1975–90), central allocation by the state
or its property agencies occurred in Angola and Mozambique. Increasingly,
however, this process was characterised by corruption and illegal sub-letting
(Simon 1992a). In three of the region's former settler colonies, European
numbers declined substantially during or immediately after the transition to
independence – in Zimbabwe by about half to perhaps 100,000 today, and
in Angola and Mozambique by over 95 per cent from their peaks of over
200,000 and 300,000 respectively. In Namibia, a quarter of the 100,000
whites – many of them South Africans on contract – left during the 1980s, but
numbers have remained constant since independence. South Africa retains
a white population of some five million today. It is worth noting that South
Africa has been independent since 1910, but that institutionalised segregation
and then apartheid were enforced by white minority regimes. In its current
transformation therefore, the problems and issues now posing such formidable challenges have much in common with newly independent states.

As in other parts of sub-Saharan Africa, the principal urban changes in
the region since independence – which, of course, was quite recent in several
cases – have been:

1. rapid urban growth, with accretion principally at the urban fringe;
2. the inability of formal official and private housing delivery systems to cater for more than a small minority of new residents, with the result that informal/irregular shelter, including in backyard shacks, now houses a substantial proportion[1] of urban residents;
3. some densification through plot subdivision in middle- and upper-income areas;
4. rapid expansion of the civil service and some categories of industrial employment in the 1960s and 1970s but generally static or declining formal sector employment since the mid-1980s;
5. and the increasing importance of informal sector activities.

The 1980s, in particular, proved a harsh decade for the subcontinent. South African destabilisation and the related conflicts raging in Angola and Mozambique have reduced much infrastructure and most urban centres in those countries to ruins, killing vast numbers of people in the process. Inside South Africa, resistance campaigns and political feuding became increasingly violent, undermining apartheid local authority structures and services, depriving them of revenue, and precipitating death and widespread destruction in urban townships and rural areas, especially in parts of Gauteng and KwaZulu-Natal. These continued right up to the 1994 elections and are still persisting in the last-mentioned province. In Zambia and increasingly also in Malawi, Zimbabwe and Mozambique over recent years, the impact of prolonged recession and structural adjustment programmes (whether externally imposed or home-grown) is being felt in terms of rising urban poverty and unemployment levels – with civil services and certain industrial sectors making heavy retrenchments – reduced rates of formal shelter construction, urban upgrading and infrastructural expansion. Prospects for urban sustainability may have been enhanced in the narrow sense of state finances but few urban residents would claim that their situations have improved of late; indeed, the ability of the urban poor to meet their basic needs is frequently now under threat (Comissao Nacional de Plano et al. 1993; Simon 1994; Tevera 1993, 1995).

Thus, although the particular issues and problems vary in origin, extent and detail across southern Africa, there is a general need for urban reconstruction, not simply in ways which replicate past structures and processes, but in accordance with prevailing conditions on the one hand, and the need to promote more sustainable urban futures on the other. Rates of growth, patterns of energy consumption, modes of organisation and control (including planning) have become increasingly unsustainable, as well as remaining generally inappropriate and highly inequitable.

The end of the Cold War, Namibian independence, the end of apartheid and emergence of a legitimate, democratic government in South Africa, peace in Mozambique (and hopefully now also in Angola) and the related transformation of regional interstate relationships since the start of the 1990s have provided unprecedented opportunities for cooperation and increased resource allocation to development. Urban areas need to be considered within this context.

Nevertheless, the challenges remain formidable. The Reconstruction and Development Programme (RDP) (African National Congress 1994; Government of South Africa 1994b) provides ambitious targets for South Africa in terms of shelter provision and urban upgrading, but a coherent urban policy is still required. Namibia's National Development Plan (NDP1) (Government of Namibia 1995) is focused very much along traditional sectoral lines, with line ministries retaining effective power over the National Planning Commission or regional councils to promote integrated development. Under the new non-racial local authority system, municipalities retain a high level of autonomy within their boundaries, while town councils and village councils have more limited functions and financial resources, remaining in effect dependent on the Ministry of Regional and Local Government and Housing. There is also no clear urban policy in NDP1 or other documents. Much the same holds for other countries in the region, whatever the nature of their specific urban initiatives and shelter programmes. In Angola and Mozambique, even basic upgrading and rebuilding of the urban fabric – whether suffering neglect and overcrowding as in Luanda, Lobito, Benguela, Maputo and Beira, or comprehensive destruction as in Huambo, Moxico, Malange and most other provincial and district centres – will require levels of resourcing far beyond their countries' means. Long-term decline and neglect in Lusaka must also be reversed, while Zambia's Copperbelt towns have also been increasingly affected by recession and reduced mining activities. Cities like Gaborone and Maseru (and from 1990 also Windhoek), which attracted some foreign investment, diplomatic and NGO activity as a result of the situation in South Africa, are likely to find themselves more marginal through relocations to the PWV metropolitan area (Gauteng Province) or Cape Town.

Against this background, the rest of this chapter explores the options and alternatives for more sustainable urban futures, drawing where possible on local resources and traditions, experience elsewhere and current debates on sustainable cities in the context of contemporary southern African conditions, including access to international donor funding and the potential role of external agencies. Importantly, though, the achievement of more equitable and sustainable cities appropriate to the new order in the region requires more than technical or financial adaptation. Substantial changes in attitudes and approach are necessary, geared to the longer-term aims of sustainability thinking and also to people-centred perspectives and procedures capable of ensuring wide legitimacy by meeting widely different, even conflicting, aspirations and senses of identity and rationality.

TOWARDS EQUITABILITY AND SUSTAINABILITY

General issues

In a broad survey such as this, it is clearly possible only to formulate a general argument, indicating the principal processes, forces and considerations to be addressed in respect of individual cities, as well as the parameters for doing this. Relevant examples will be used to illustrate appropriate points. In essence the challenge facing those concerned with achieving more sustainable urban futures in southern Africa can be summarised in terms of the relationship between two contradictory assertions. First, as indicated in my introduction, seeking to promote sustainability by refining existing tools – as exemplified by current efforts within conventional environmental and urban economics – and procedures is an inherently limited approach. Waste may indeed be reduced and efficiency increased, but such 'tinkering around the edges' offers little prospect of achieving more fundamental changes in approach which, I would argue, is necessary. Indeed, such 'reformism' is often cast as a conscious strategy to pre-empt more fundamental change. As I will elaborate below, enhanced urban sustainability requires that the underlying structures and processes such as land-tenure systems, relations of production, basis of access to employment and other bases for accumulating social power, urban planning and management processes, the nature of the energy supply and the appropriateness of technologies being utilised need to be examined and addressed.

The second assertion is that prospects for more far-reaching transformation or reconstruction – at the national or urban level – seem dim. This applies especially in the present international climate favouring 'democratisation', 'good governance', 'economic responsibility' – for which read political and economic conditionalities on official development assistance, structural adjustment and economic recovery programmes (Simon 1995). In the particular southern African context, as mentioned above, some very real and dramatic positive changes have recently occurred. These do give ground for measured optimism, although it is important to appreciate the substantial compromises negotiated in the course of securing Namibian independence, the Mozambican settlement and the transition to non-racial rule in South Africa, for example. Radical, 'socialist' and other often longstanding demands for concerted action to redress inherited inequalities to the bases for accumulating social power, perhaps most importantly in relation to land, have been abandoned or dramatically toned down. The sanctity of private property and market mechanisms has been enshrined in the recent political transitions in Namibia, Mozambique and South Africa, providing an effective curb on both rural and urban redistribution or reform. In Zimbabwe, government attempts to accelerate rural land redistribution through wider powers after the ten-year guarantees of the independence constitution lapsed in 1990, have proved politically charged and controversial, not least because of evident corruption. Pressure to revert to market-led procedures is accordingly strong.

What I am therefore arguing is that while, ideally, the attainment of sustainable urbanism requires some quite fundamental changes to thinking and procedures, the present international and regional climate indicates that for the time being, at least, the way forward in southern Africa seems to lie with negotiation, compromise and accommodationist (reformist) strategies. In an urban context, moreover, it is impossible to conceive of comprehensive redesign and rebuilding of entire towns or cities unless they have been well-nigh destroyed by war. Bricks, mortar and concrete generally prove extremely durable symbols of accumulated investment, vested interest and inertia (Simon 1992a). The inherited urban fabric of previously segregated and apartheid cities in southern Africa is a particularly potent symbol of exploitation and unsustainability. Ethical and moral issues of such policies and design standards aside, they have produced gross inefficiency, often greatly exacerbating energy-intensive and time-wasting mass commuting over long distances within the urban areas and from Bantustan or communal area boundaries. The costs of urban design and management have been greatly increased, while poverty and hardship have been exacerbated.

In war-ravaged centres such as Huambo, comprehensive redevelopment may provide a rare opportunity to introduce more appropriate and sustainable urban designs, environments and lifestyles, as currently being attempted in entire districts of Beirut following the end of hostilities in the Lebanon. For most southern African cities and towns, however, the challenge will therefore be how best to enhance equity and sustainability by adapting and modifying existing structures with limited resources and against strong vested interests, while simultaneously assuaging popular expectations. This will be no mean feat. However, the need is widespread, even where the end of apartheid or of devastating wars has not created unprecedented demands and pressures. For example, Carole Rakodi concludes her study of Harare by contrasting the continuing strict control over illegal development and the maintenance of infrastructure and services there, with the situation in South Africa and other African countries. Even though urban protest has been largely defused up to now, problems are looming:

> For the moment, the city works. However, as the pressures arising from population growth, inflexible and traditional administration and planning, and economic hardship and liberalisation build up, it is becoming a little like a pressure cooker. If Harare is to continue to provide economic opportunities and a pleasant and healthy environment for its residents in future, more responsive urban administrations, implementing more realistic and innovative policies, are needed quickly. (Rakodi 1995: 275)

Urban decision-making, management and financing
It might seem unusual to commence with this sub-heading, but appropriate institutional frameworks and procedures are probably the most important prerequisite for achieving meaningful progress. For, as Church (1995: 8) rightly observes, '... improving our urban environments is almost entirely a matter of political will. The techniques and technologies exist.'

In southern Africa, as elsewhere in Africa and beyond, post-colonial governments have generally been authoritarian and centralised in nature. Local authorities have struggled to fulfil their responsibilities with inadequate resources and frequently also curtailment of their powers by central government. Paradoxically, whatever their specific ideology, national governments have sought the role of developmental states but, for well-known reasons, have nevertheless proved to be weak states in many respects. The perceived lack of legitimacy, the unresponsiveness, top–down and often also repressive nature of governance have all contributed to domestic and external pressure for democratisation and change (Simon 1995).

The extent to which this has happened or is still occurring across the region differs substantially, but the often protracted negotiations over the interim and final constitutions, the RDP and local authority boundaries (especially the so-called metropolitan sub-structures) in South Africa serve as models of broad participation and negotiation. Inevitably, though, such processes are time consuming and often highly politicised contests, which may not be satisfactorily resolved. As in Namibia in 1990–2, the transition has created an unusual, short conjuncture where what has been at stake is not simply power within existing institutions but the power over those institutions, how they are to be constituted and what powers and responsibilities they are to have. Nevertheless, the fundamental nature, organisation and powers of 'new' local authorities in South Africa, as well as in Namibia and virtually all the other countries of the region, bear a close resemblance to those inherited from the colonial and/or previous post-colonial orders (Grest 1995; Simon 1996). This may in time serve to undermine the new-found spirit of public participation and responsiveness.

For example, the competing views and interests articulated in the political 'struggle for the cities', as we might term the recent negotiations over boundary delimitation in South African metropolitan areas and their constituent substructures, were articulated in terms of existing, apartheid era territorial entities and boundaries. Perhaps it is inevitable that people still perceive themselves, their identities and those of the 'others' they seek to exclude, out-flank or reassure with reference to so recent and defining an exercise in discriminatory social engineering. In other words, it is significant that the alternative urban visions articulated by representatives of both the old and new orders participating in those negotiations,[2] projected geographical amalgamations of suburbs, townships, commercial and industrial areas that would best serve their respective interests. These can be summarised as securing existing privilege (i.e. producing defended and defensible spaces) versus providing the resource base – epitomised by the anti-apartheid slogan 'one city one tax base' – to redistribute resources and help overcome spatial inequalities (ie. producing more open and empowering spaces). Both strategies are highly spatialised. Despite their conflicting visions and intentions, the future challenges and envisaged roles of local authorities in each case are seen as essentially modernist and modernising. Even in ANC-dominated structures and councils, the degree to which heterogeneity and difference can or will be accommodated remains unclear. Replication of the accommodationist politics being pursued at national level could prove facilitatory but could also fail to satisfy competing or contradictory interests. Homogenisation is a strongly modernist impulse, which may not accord with the conceptions (e.g. of urban structure and spatially referenced identities), objectives or aspirations of hitherto alienated and marginalised groups. In other words, the dominant political discourses and institutional agendas at present remain firmly modernist, in sharp contrast to the growing evidence that disjuncture, contradiction and diversity of form and practice – which comprise the essence of post-modernity – are widespread, inevitable and perhaps also necessary in Third World urbanism (Simon and Parnell 1996).

This raises very different questions and issues regarding urban futures. For this chapter, it is also essential to link them with notions of equitability and sustainability. As mentioned above, the characteristics of participation, transparency and responsiveness are essential if sustainability is to be achieved. National blueprints and top–down processes cannot substitute for widespread legitimacy and acceptance of what must be participatory processes. Marginalised, dispossessed or unempowered people cannot or will not share dominant values and procedures; their responses will be apathetic, hostile and/or undermining. Moreover, issues of empowerment are most meaningfully expressed and experienced first and foremost at the local level (Friedmann 1992; Wisner 1988).

It is precisely for this reason that UNCED's Agenda 21 envisages local action as an essential component. As a first step, in terms of Chapter 28, most local authorities should have reached consensus on a local Agenda 21 by 1996 through a consultative process with their inhabitants. Although no hard information is available, I suspect that this has not happened in most southern African cities. In a similar vein, and unlike most conventional national development plans, South Africa's RDP and subsequent policy developments see local authorities as crucial implementing agencies of individual projects and galvanisers of public involvement. Progress to date has been slow, although some infrastructural upgrading projects are underway. Now that the local elections have been held in most of the country, political commitment should hopefully increase.

Because of the need for a local and participatory focus, the UNCHS/ UNEP Sustainable Cities Programme operates at the individual city level, where 95 per cent of its resources are disbursed. At least three cities in the region, namely Lusaka, Maputo and Durban have recently requested inclusion in this programme.

Another promising commitment to appropriate change was the adoption of the Dakar Declaration, 'Environmental Strategies for African Cities', by urban and national representatives from twenty-one African countries on 30 June 1995. Held under UNCHS auspices as part of the build-up to Habitat II, it recommends widespread adoption of participatory approaches to urban environmental planning and management. Each of the four approaches identified is based on the identification of stake holders, strengthening broad-ranging consultative processes, capacity building of all so-called stake holders and institutions, and the establishment of political commitment to the strategies (see Table 20.2). This declaration was then incorporated into Habitat II preparations at the African Ministerial Meeting in Johannesburg in October 1995. Although it would be naive to expect such chapter commitments to be translated rapidly or fully into practice across southern Africa, the nature of the document and its contents, to which so many countries have now signed up, is significant in itself. If necessary, this can be used as a lever by NGOs to secure fuller roles and to open up new windows or 'political spaces' and to accommodate greater diversity of vision and practice.

Although the recent political transitions in several countries of southern Africa have brought new elected representatives into municipal councils, which now have broad legitimacy, these councillors vary greatly in experience and expertise. Some are taking time to adjust their practices from the days of exile and/or resistance, while others are quickly finding the rewards of office seductive and/or are assuming positions little different from those of their predecessors on key issues. Conversely, there is already evidence of resistance to new, more accountable and responsive procedures from some vested interests among long-serving councillors, some powerful municipal officials and local business interests with whom they may have close relationships. In other words, merely creating legitimate institutions and mechanisms provides no guarantee of substantive change: genuine participation, responsiveness and permissive procedures are and will need to be achieved and defended through contest and negotiation. The same applies to adequate levels of funding to ensure that policies and programmes can be implemented appropriately (*Mail and Guardian* 1995). In the words of an international comparative study on the subject,

> The cornerstone in ensuring the maximum contribution of the human settlements sector to national economic development is the establishment of a viable and stable human settlements finance system capable of mobilising both

Table 20.2 Environmental strategies for African cities – The Dakar Declaration

We Ministers, together with the mayors and other national and local government officials concerned with the urban environment, and the development actors from the private sector, NGOs, community groups, universities and research institutes and international development agencies participating in the international workshop on Environmental Strategies for African Cities.

Recalling the declaration of African Ministers responsible for human settlements made in Nairobi, Kenya, on March 30, 1994, and the declarations of the region's Ministers made in Dakar, Senegal, on October 3, 1994, in Kampala, Uganda, on February 28, 1995:

Recognising the important contributions that African cities make to social and economic development at local and national levels:

Aware that environmental problems in our cities pose serious threats to these contributions and achievements of sustainable development:

Acknowledging the need to rely on local technical and financial resources for resolving urban environmental problems:

Understanding the critical importance of urban environment planning and management for mobilizing and effectively applying available local resources:

Supporting the Habitat II preparatory process: and

Based on an exchange, during the Workshop, of the lessons of operational experience from 21 African countries as well as a detailed review and discussion of twelve case studies of specific urban environmental planning and management (EPM) initiatives:

Recommend the wide-spread adoption of the following approaches for planning and management in African Cities:

1 *Identifying priority urban environment issues and involving the stakeholders* through:
   - preparation of environmental profiles;
   - identification of stakeholders;
   - establishment and utilisation of consultative processes;
   - formulation of criteria for prioritisation; and
   - capacity building of all stakeholders.

2 *Formulating urban environmental management strategies* through:
   - formulation of appropriate objectives;
   - establishment of processes for consensus building;
   - focus on issue-specific strategies;
   - identification of resources; and
   - establishment of frameworks for coordination strategies

3 *Formulating and implementing environmental action plans* through:
   - consultative meetings of stakeholders and their involvement in planning and implementation;
   - definition of activities and priorities for intervention;
   - establishment of political commitment to these strategies;
   - mobilisation of resources;
   - analyses of impacts and costs and benefits; and
   - strengthened cross-sectoral and inter-institutional coordination

4 *Capacity-building and institutionalizing an environmental management routine* by:
   - strengthening of institutions at all levels;
   - up-dating of policies and legislation;
   - capacity-building for financial resource management including cost-recovery;
   - institutionalisation of concerns for gender and for poverty;
   - strengthening of the facilitator and support role of governments; and
   - establishment of monitoring and evaluation.

Commit ourselves, in our respective capacities and contexts, to promote the application and further development of these approaches at the local, national and regional levels through:

- local EPM Programmes and projects;
- national follow-up and application in other urban areas; and
- regional sharing of know-how and technical resources.

Request the organisers of the Workshop to widely disseminate the Dakar Declaration to urban environmental planning and management practitioners in Africa and to international development organisations for their information and support.

Recommend that the Dakar Declaration be incorporated into the preparatory processes of Habitat II at national and regional levels, and be presented to the African Ministerial Meeting to be held in Johannesburg, South Africa, in October, 1995.

Adopted in Dakar, Senegal, 30 June 1995 *by 111 government decision makers and development practitioners from 21 African countries, including fifteen Ministers, as well as representatives from international development support agencies list on file with Sustainable Cities Programme United Nations Centre for Human Settlement (Habitat). P.O. Box 30030, Nairobi, Kenya. Telephone–254 (2) 623225. Fax–254 (2) 624264. E-Mail gochen.eigen@unep.no or eleanor.cody@unep.no*

---

public- and private (household)-sector savings for channelling into human settlements development. (UNCHS 1990a: 51)

Significant elements of such a strategy include:

1. strengthening financial institutions such as mortgage and housing funders in order to increase investment resources;
2. accessing additional sources of funds that can be used in this sector, e.g. from insurance, pension and provident funds. The Singaporean experience in utilising the Central Provident Fund is particularly noteworthy (Pugh 1987), although this must be taken in context;
3. greater use of savings and loans schemes to raise additional funds from individuals and the community;
4. strengthening property valuation and taxation systems, together with the implementation of cost-conscious service charging by local authorities, in order to secure their financial position and ability to fund new developments and to maintain existing infrastructure and services. (UNCHS 1990a: 51–6)

If all this can be achieved to a reasonable extent, however, the nature of urban governance, planning and management (what might be called urban social reproduction) will have been dramatically altered. In practice, this will signify that the urban poor, their interests (including community based organisations) and residential areas – which have generally been partially or wholly excluded from official processes and resources – will have been legitimately incorporated and that significant resource redistribution will occur in their favour (cf. Friedmann 1992; Turner 1990; Wisner 1988). The importance of political will can therefore not be over-estimated (Aina 1990).

Urban design

In view of the inherent inequities and inefficiencies of current urban designs and layouts, it is necessary to consider potential changes to these areas as well as in the design of new urban extensions. Inevitably, though, there are numerous common issues, many of which will require amendment and adaptation of the existing planning system and design/building standards. The continued adherence to often inappropriate colonial practice and reliance on expatriate consultants and Northern-trained planners, unwilling or unable to adapt to very different planning contexts, has been well documented (Knox and Masilela 1989, 1990; Simon 1992a; Wekwete 1988b). This applies very much across southern Africa, in terms, for example, of conventional zoning regulations and development control, and building standards, as will become clear below.

Densification and residential integration. Along with some leading South African urban planners (Dewar 1995b; Dewar and Uytenbogaardt 1991), the World Bank urban-sector mission to South Africa perceived the principal strategy for dealing with low urban densities in middle-income areas and the high overall cost of service and infrastructure provision, as being densification (e.g. World Bank 1992). In other words, by encouraging or requiring the subdivision of large plots and greater vertical development (i.e. the construction of double-storey homes, duplex or town-house schemes, and blocks of flats), more people can be suitably accommodated and supplied with infrastructure within existing developed suburbs or townships, and at lower unit cost. There is certainly scope for this in many areas (not only in South Africa), but some middle-income areas in major South African cities have been experiencing considerable market-led densification of these types since at least the late 1970s (Simon 1992a). Measures to encourage densification, and the development of vacant plots of urban land held for speculative purposes could include modifying zoning density limits, and introducing differential property rates which discriminate proportionately more heavily against undeveloped plots or those with low bulk–density ratios.

However, such intervention cannot alone address the scale and magnitude of the problems facing southern African cities, particularly as regards the needs of the urban poor and those previously suffering discrimination in access to urban spaces and opportunities. A more comprehensive approach is required. One crucial issue to be addressed is whether market-led property redistribution and residential integration can or will change the complexion of urban areas substantially. The evidence from post-colonial cities in southern Africa and beyond is negative on this, as the class character and associated characteristics of existing residential areas are generally maintained. In Johannesburg's inner-city Mayfair suburb, the rapid inward movement of Asians (many of them returning to an area from which they had been forcibly evicted under the Group Areas Act) in the late 1980s and early 1990s has actually resulted in substantial refurbishment and upgrading (Parnell and Pirie 1991: 140). It is, after all, only those with adequate financial means who are able to 'buy into' better quality housing in more desirable or suitably located areas (Cumming 1990; Simon 1992a, 1995; Yahya 1990). As mentioned above, the same limitation applies to rural land redistribution. Class is thus becoming the basis of residential organisation rather than imputed race, but the legacy of apartheid and colonial segregation policies will ensure that a substantial overlap between the two remains for a considerable period.

Other mechanisms and processes. So how, then, can different changes be effected? I will suggest several elements of a strategy.

1. Generally, the most substantial residential opportunities for black and poor people within the former colonial or white cities have been where and to the extent that down-market accommodation becomes available. Such properties are found especially in and around central business districts, in older cottages and blocks of flats. The recent transformation of the Joubert Park–Hillbrow–Berea area in Johannesburg into 90 to 95 per cent black occupancy is undoubtedly the most dramatic example in South Africa, on account of its size and the rapidity of the process (Crankshaw and White 1995). Since the late 1960s whites had been suburbanising at an increasing rate, precipitating a survival crisis for many flatland rentlords and for shops and offices in and around the central business district. Just as the clientele of these businesses became increasingly black, so landlords, managing agents and sectional title companies accepted black tenants in order to secure rents. Indeed, when the Group Areas Act was still in force (i.e. until mid-1991) higher rents could be charged on account of the illegality and attendant risks; at the same time, the need to provide formal leases could be avoided. Banks and other financial institutions 'red-lined' the area, refusing to provide mortgage bond funds out of a mixture of racial prejudice and fear that property prices would fall substantially.

In order to help meet such rentals, and to assist relatives or friends lacking housing or facing the long, expensive commute from the townships, tenants began taking in sub-tenants. Multiple occupancy became common, services and infrastructure were overloaded and landlords reduced or ceased to undertake maintenance. Tenants sometimes responded by withholding rent payments. Evictions were sought and occasionally carried out. Since most lacked formal leases, they were technically illegal residents. In some areas, conditions deteriorated rapidly, and crime increased. The term 'slum' is used regularly by municipal officials and politicians, although the

City Council took little action (Crankshaw and White 1995). People occupying several blocks of flats effectively abandoned by their owners were faced with evictions in what became a celebrated case of resistance organised by community based organisations, known as the Seven Buildings Project. Residents are organised into groups with responsibility for cleaning, maintenance and security. In January 1996 ownership of the blocks of flats was to be transferred from the existing landlord to a company owned by the Project. The tenants would become sectional title shareholders, paying rent to the company, on the board of which one representative from each of the buildings with serve as a director. With a R5 million subsidy from the National Housing Forum, affordable, income-related rents can be charged (*Mail and Guardian* 1995). If successful, this innovative scheme could serve as a model not only for the rest of what is colloquially dubbed Johannesburg's 'lost city'[3] but inner city areas of other conurbations as well. It provides a mechanism for managed transition, giving poor black people a stake in accessible parts of the existing urban structure, and avoiding the downward spiral of living conditions and quality which would otherwise result.

2. The second way forward is to encourage multi-functional land-use and different urban designs. Current zoning and development control practice throughout the region still has an acutely modernist thrust. It is very restrictive, favouring single functions in given zones, except within very clearly defined limits for the number and variety of convenience and other shops permitted in residential areas. Although certain office functions are now sometimes permitted within homes or entire houses, e.g. medical, architectural, accountancy and other professional practices, industries are almost entirely banished from residential areas. Greater flexibility should be exercised in permitting non-disturbance causing industries, e.g. cottage industries, small-scale upholsterers, picture framers, repairers.

Redevelopment, development on vacant land (e.g. on disused railway shunting yards and reclaimed mine dumps provided that the ground is not toxic) and in new areas should also make explicit design provision for a fuller mix of activities overall rather than on an exceptional permission basis. Cape Town's District Six, Durban's Cato Manor and Johannesburg's Pageview, inner city areas which suffered celebrated enforced population removals under the Group Areas Act and where the former communities are now seeking to reclaim their land (Desai 1995; Maharaj 1996), could become important symbolic and practical experiments in this respect. Fortunately, these broad principles, together with their potential contribution to enhanced urban sustainability, have been adopted in the South African government's draft urban development strategy (Government of South Africa 1995a: 24). While not advocating a romantic return to pre-industrial or colonial urbanism, it is worth noting that earlier forms of multi-functional land-use, e.g. the 'home above the shop or workshop' have largely been eliminated through rigid application of modernist town planning. Apart from providing a boost to municipal revenue from increased rates and taxes, change in this respect would diversify the geography of employment, reduce commuter traffic pressure (and the associated energy, pollution and time costs[4]) and also provide greater convenience for local residents. As their unit costs, installation and operating costs decline, new information and communications technologies can also play a role in reducing the need for travel and face-to-face contact. Overall urban efficiency would thus be enhanced.

More appropriate and sustainable urban designs and standards can more readily be incorporated into new township developments or new settlements. These should aim to reduce the need for travel, especially by means of motorised transport, utilise appropriate energy sources and technologies (including new information technologies), improve the living environment and be designed to accommodate often diverse existing social structures and senses of identity. This would mean innovation in terms of street layouts and the creation of diversity.

By contrast, conventional town planning has generally sought to erase such diversity in favour of an assumed modern norm, namely geometric street grids and crescents. At least one recent author has advocated drawing lessons from the design principles of pre-colonial African towns and cities, albeit in a somewhat romantic conception (Amankwah-Ayeh 1995). As argued above and elsewhere (Abu-Lughod 1987; Simon 1985, 1992a), the future lies rather more in developing hybrids able to draw on appropriate traditions and principles of urban design but adapting them to current urban and social realities. In this regard, it is worth noting that the permitting of indigenous dwelling forms and materials in low income urban settlements, hitherto forbidden in terms of existing town planning regulations in anglophone countries and beyond, but which I have argued for on the basis of cost, construction materials and social appropriateness (Simon 1985, 1992a), became a reality in Katutura, Windhoek's former African township, in 1992. Over time they should be upgraded or replaced. Rich (1995) also highlights valuable aspects of traditional Ndebele housing design and construction, which have potential in this context.

3. Thirdly, a crucial way in which socially more diverse cities can be encouraged is to break the tradition of residential zoning in terms of plot size and associated dwelling density, which is a surrogate method of institutionalising class segregation through the property market. Instead, more diverse mixes of residential types and densities within individual residential areas can and should be encouraged. This will undoubtedly generate substantial

opposition from high-income groups, fearful of the unknown and probably disguised in rhetoric of social difference and thus conflict, rising crime and falling property prices. The positions adopted by the National Party, Freedom Front and Conservative Party during the mid 1990s negotiations over metropolitan sub-structures in South Africa represented strategies designed precisely to defend suburban territory defined increasingly in class terms now that apartheid's demise has enabled residential integration in accordance with financial resources (see above). Nevertheless, given adequate political will by new local authorities, the problem should not be insurmountable and a greater mix of housing styles, sizes and densities would form an important means of assisting people to transcend inherited social prejudices and cleavages between 'them' and 'us', in other words, the fear of 'alien' racial, cultural and poorer 'others'. Again, no single or uniform blueprint can or should be imposed; local circumstances must be taken into account in determining an acceptable and appropriate mix of densities, 'income groups' and urban designs within each area. The 1991 draft Written Statement based on the Harare Combination Master Plan actually proposes encouraging more 'socially mixed housing' and higher residential densities in low density areas, although no specific policy measures or instruments were mentioned (Rakodi 1995: 97). Similar points are also taken up in the South African draft urban-development strategy (Government of South Africa 1995a). In any event, the scope for implementing change within many established suburbs in any town or city is limited by the availability of open space, large plots suitable for subdivision and dwellings in poor condition which might be demolished.

The one major exception here is in allocation or divestiture policies (in the case of privatisation) pursued by state or parastatal bodies with respect to their existing housing stock, where social policies could have a significant influence. This is relevant to many cities across the region, but Mozambique provides perhaps the best example. The government's State Property Administration, APIE (*Administração do Parque Imobiliário do Estado*), inherited the formal housing and blocks of flats abandoned by the emigré settlers in the mid-1970s and other investment property in the 'cement cities' nationalised thereafter. Although allocation criteria based on need were established, over time the bureaucratic process became increasingly corrupt and subject to informal bypassing, while maintenance was negligible. Today these units are in an appalling state, especially with respect to infrastructure and services, and a major structural survey was undertaken to assess refurbishment needs (*Notícias* 1995a).

Privatisation has been commenced, with current tenants supposed to have first option, although some properties (or substantial compensation) are being claimed by *retornados* (returning emigrés). To date the state has issued several assurances that such repossessions will not be granted.

Nevertheless, access to and control over such properties, and the resource they represent in a situation of chronic housing shortage, have become highly contested in ways which reflect the nature of economic liberalisation in this impoverished peripheral ex-socialist state and the effective recolonisation by foreign capital (*Notícias* 1995c; Sidaway and Power 1995; Simon 1992a). Privatisation was now beginning to move rapidly. By the end of September 1995, requests for purchase had been lodged in respect of 16,000 of the total national APIE stock of 56,500 dwelling units. 11,500 of these had been authorised, over 61 per cent of them (i.e. 9,847) in Maputo city. Another 1,823 were in the rest of Maputo province and 1,526 in Sofala province, including Beira, the country's second city. No other province registered more than 600 (*Notícias* 1995b). Details of the purchasers and their relative social positions are unavailable, so it is currently impossible to ascertain the extent to which existing tenants, as the desired beneficiaries, are actually able to purchase their homes.

4. Finally, we need to mention the well-known imperative of upgrading townships, shanty settlements and similar areas occupied principally by low-income households. Various such programmes have been undertaken in numerous cities within southern Africa since the early 1970s, perhaps most notably Lusaka. Some of the issues raised in the preceding paragraphs apply here too, not least the question of planning for diverse income groups in areas from which higher-income households have departed. The objective should be to achieve improvements in living standards and conditions, not merely in shelter quality through *in-situ* upgrading or some other form of aided self-help (cf. Hardoy *et al.* 1993; Main and Williams 1994; Ramphele and Greal 1991; Wekwete 1992). Infrastructure, employment opportunities, recreational spaces and environmental improvements should all be included, through participatory processes.

The Government of National Unity's draft urban development strategy (Government of South Africa 1995a: 24) prioritises the rebuilding of the townships as a key element of urban reconstruction and integration:

> The dormitory role of low-income areas must finally be terminated. Specific attention will be focused on these low-income areas: townships, informal settlements, and low-income inner city residential zones. These areas represent an under-utilised resource for the future. They have to be transformed into productive, habitable, environmentally healthy and safe urban environments, free from crime and violence. Rebuilding the townships is unquestionably the single most important urban development challenge facing the country.

Arguably the largest township upgrading programme in the region was launched in Soweto, Gauteng, which is home to 1.5 to 2 million people. Dubbed 'The World in Soweto', it aims to attract foreign donors to provide funds for specific upgrading projects. Contemporary press reports suggest that donors will have wide discretion and will even 'be allowed to imprint their own cultures if they wish' (*Mail and Guardian* 1995); this sounds extremely top–down, even patronising, and could prove problematic, and, if done insensitively, could create new alienating spaces and projects. Tight oversight is necessary. This could turn out to be a counterproductive exercise redolent of donor- and market-led conventional wisdoms which remain powerful – and arguably dominant – in current South African housing debates (Lupton and Murphy 1995), and in which sustainability still takes a back seat. This illustrates the potential pitfalls if the government's evidently sincere commitment to rapid upgrading leads it to embrace ill-conceived, inappropriate projects, which may be designed to further commercial or donor interests, without due care and prior consideration.

Resource use

Substantial progress has been made in recent years in developing principles and criteria for more sustainable energy and resource use (especially of water), waste reduction and recycling, pollution control and the use of more appropriate local construction technologies and materials. In each case, the origin, nature, efficiency and sustainability implications need to be addressed. Detailed coverage of these important issues will not be provided here on grounds of length and because useful existing reference sources exist (Hardoy *et al.* 1993; Haughton and Hunter 1994; Main and Williams 1994; McRobie 1990; Ramphele and Greal 1991; Simon 1992a: 173–7; Stren *et al.* 1992; UNCHS 1990b). These themes feature prominently in the list of four sustainable development criteria suggested by the UNCHS for judging human settlements:

1. the quality of life it offers to its inhabitants;
2. the scale of non-renewable resource use (including the extent to which secondary resources are drawn from settlement by-products for reuse);
3. the scale and nature of renewable resource use and the implications for sustaining production levels of renewable resources;
4. the scale and nature of non-reusable wastes generated by production and consumption activities and the means by which these are disposed of, including the extent to which wastes impact upon human health, natural systems and amenity. (UNCHS 1991: 4)

Although some require concerted institutional intervention, others can appropriately be addressed through local community action and participation. Resource mobilisation and the transmission of international experience as a basis for local adaptation or adoption are very important support activities which can involve both official and NGO structures and channels at local and supra-local levels in complementary ways.

All too often, however, official commitments on environmental issues and sustainable resource use remain just that, being vague if not contradictory, and lacking any specific or clear mechanisms for implementation. For example, the 1992 Written Statement based on the Harare Combination Master Plan usefully proposes the execution of environmental impact assessments for major development proposals, the strengthening of pollution control agencies, the maintenance of buffer zones along rivers and around ecologically valuable areas, and the zoning of land for urban allotments to encourage cultivation in designated areas. However, the last-mentioned proposal may be undermined in part by bureaucratic procedures and by efforts to prevent cultivation along river banks 'the need for which is not clearly proven'. A further proposal to institute a green belt to limit urban sprawl is not supported by 'any evaluation of the potentially positive or negative outcomes of such a designation or of the results of green belt policies elsewhere' (Rakodi 1995: 98). Greater clarity, specificity and consistency will be required if such policies are to be implementable and to achieve their apparent objectives. Pressure groups, professional associations and interested NGOs can all play roles in encouraging official bodies to amend and improve their policies and practice.

CONCLUSION

In this chapter, I have sought to articulate a coherent set of ideas about the closely linked objectives of enhancing equitability and sustainability in southern Africa's towns and cities. Conventional efforts to promote such goals tend to be inherently limited in conception, seeking to achieve more efficient resource utilisation through attaching real economic values to waste, resource depletion, conservation and the like. Such measures may be seen as precluding or even pre-empting the need for more far-reaching change. By contrast, I argue that current urban processes and planning/ management practices need to change substantially. Although planning is inherently concerned with long-range futures, the methods and objectives of inherited modernist town planning and urban management are increasingly inappropriate to the pressing tasks of post-apartheid reconstruction in South Africa and the rest of the region. Concerns with homogenising and standardising, especially within individual urban segments, often militates against substantive change to the underlying character defined in terms of unifunctional zoning, plot size, housing density, building lines and the like. These have generally served as surrogates for racial exclusivity, but the process of market-led post-colonial or post-apartheid residential integration is producing increasingly class-based social and spatial cleavages, which nevertheless mirror their predecessors to a remarkable extent. Such developments will do little if anything to change the fundamental realities of unsustainable urbanism and urban social reproduction.

By contrast, promoting greater equity and sustainability, as well as accommodating (in both the physical and metaphorical senses) the multiple, increasingly diverse, and even antagonistic social groups with distinct identities and agendas, will require very different visions and processes. These will need to be more participatory, decentralised, flexible and empowering, capable of providing local access and accountability within a framework offering strategic metropolitan-wide integration. Such notions do borrow from concepts of agropolitan development, urban villages and such like but, importantly, also from certain indigenous traditions as well as from contemporary debates in social theory about sustainability, post-modernism, post-colonialism and development.

Equally important, however, is to offer practical guidelines for operationalising the grand concepts and goals. I set out some clear examples of how existing as well as new settlements and suburbs/townships can be adapted or conceived in accordance with these ideas. What these measures have in common is the promotion of various forms of diversity and better functional, spatial, social and technological integration, so as to reduce energy consumption, pollution generation, travel time loss, both within and between parts of the urban mosaic, and to promote use of renewable resources, recycling and more varied forms of human and social interaction. Interestingly and importantly, many of these concepts find resonance in the South African government's draft urban development strategy, published for comment at the end of 1995 (Government of South Africa 1995a: 24–40).

There will undoubtedly be numerous obstacles and concerted resistance from those who stand to lose effective power or control over resources, or who feel participatory processes to be excessively time consuming and inconclusive. Ultimately, however, the (local or regional) state may need to resolve deadlocks which persist after negotiations have run their full course, including attempts at mediation or compromise. This necessarily implies the retention of sufficient implementational capacity to intervene, to take necessary actions and to enforce laws 'in the public interest'. Especially in heterogeneous societies with fractured histories of inequality and exploitation, and where the powers and institutions of the developmental state have traditionally been (ab)used to further sectional interests, clear rules and procedures for such interventions will be necessary. Nevertheless, this position runs counter to current donor pressures – felt most acutely in small peripheral countries – for a minimalist state which limits its role to facilitation.[5]

The current privatisation initiatives in Mozambique, Zambia, Zimbabwe, Malawi and increasingly now also Angola, create new opportunities for local interests to take economic initiatives at one level but are ultimately likely to reduce the space for the agendas outlined here in favour of increasingly market-led and foreign-controlled outcomes. On the other hand, if the traditions of mobilisation among civic associations in South Africa and equivalent community based organisations and NGOs elsewhere are not harnessed within such a facilitatory framework, and if expectations and basic needs are not at least partially met, the results will be renewed alienation, division and resistance.

NOTES

1. In the cities and towns of Angola and Mozambique, the majority of inhabitants live in such circumstances (see below).
2. We need to recall here that many grass-roots groups and perspectives, especially within black communities, were excluded by the particular process through which the Local Government Negotiating Forum and the Local Government Transition Act emerged. These may well have provided different scenarios, given the militant tradition of local anti-apartheid mobilisation achieved during the late 1980s and early 1990s within civic associations, street committees and the like. On the other hand, it is unclear whether and to what extent their conceptions of alternative futures and urban identities extended beyond the individual communities and townships.
3. This term not only refers to the 'loss' of the area from the rest of Johannesburg through urban decline but represents an ironic contrast with the over exuberant kitsch of The Lost City, Sol Kerzner's ruritanian resort in the former Bophutatswana Bantustan.
4. In Bangkok Metropolitan Area, for example, it has recently been estimated that the monetary cost alone of vehicle fuel wasted through idling in the chronic traffic congestion in one of the world's fastest developing metropolises, amounts to at least US$500 million and possibly as much as $2.92 billion annually (Setchell 1995: 9–10).
5. I am grateful for Michael Cernea's intervention in the Seminar discussion to emphasise this point.

BIBLIOGRAPHY

Abu-Lughod, J. L. (1987), 'The Islamic city – historic myth, Islamic essence and contemporary relevance', *International Journal of Middle East Studies* 19: 155–76.

Abrahams, R. G. (1985), 'Introduction', in Abrahams, R. G. (ed.) (1985), *Villagers, Villages and the State*. Cambridge African Monographs 4: 1–15. Cambridge: University of Cambridge African Studies Centre.

Adalemo, I. A. (1993), *Improving Rural-regional Settlement Systems Management: A Case Study of Rural Service Centres in Nigeria, with Special Reference to Obafemi-owode Local Government Area*. Nairobi: UNCHS (Habitat).

Adamolekun, L. and Rowland, L. (1979), *The New Local Government System in Nigeria: Problems and Prospects for Implementation*. Ibadan: Heinemann.

Adepoju, A. (1982), 'Population redistribution: a review of governmental policies', in Clarke, J. I. and Kosinski, L. A. (eds), *Redistribution of Population in Africa*. London: Heinemann.

Ærøe, A. (1992), 'The role of small towns in regional development in South-East Africa', in Baker, J. and Pedersen, P. O. (eds), *The Rural-Urban Interface in Africa*. Uppsala: Scandanivian Institute of African Studies.

African National Congress (1994), *The Reconstruction and Development Programme*. Johannesburg: ANC.

Aina, T. A. (1990), 'The politics of sustainable Third World urban development', in Cadman, D. and Payne, G. (eds), *The Living City: Towards A Sustainable Future*. London: Routledge.

Akwabi-Ameyaw, K. (1990), 'The political economy of agricultural resettlement and rural development in Zimbabwe: the performance of family farms and producer cooperatives'. *Human Organization*, 49: 320–38.

Alcock, R. (1994), 'Evictions and land hunger in Msinga/Weenen districts', in Minnaar, A. (ed.), *Access to and Affordability of Land in South Africa: The Challenge of Land Reform in the 1990s*. Pretoria: Human Sciences Research Council.

Allen, T. and Morsink, H. (eds) (1994), *When Refugees Go Home*. Geneva: United Nations Research Institute for Social Development, in association with London: James Currey and Trenton, NJ: Africa World Press.

Allen, T. and Turton, D. (1996), 'Introduction', in Allen, T. (ed.), *In Search of Cool Ground*. Geneva: United Nations Research Institute for Social Development, in association with London: James Currey and Trenton, NJ: Africa World Press.

Amankwah-Ayeh, K. (1995), Planning environmentally sustainable cities in Africa, *Africa Insight* 25 (1): 37–47.

Ambrose, D. 1995. *Maseru: An Illustrated History.* Lesotho: Morija.

Amin, S. (1972), 'Underdevelopment and dependence in Black Africa – origins and contemporary forms', *Journal of Modern African Studies* 10 (4): 503–24.

Anderson, B. (1983), *Imagined Communities: Reflections on the Origin and Spread of Nationalism.* London: Verso.

Andrew, M. (1992), 'A geographical study of agricultural change since the 1930s in Shixini Location, Gatyana District, Transkei'. Unpublished MA thesis. Grahamstown: Department of Geography, Rhodes University.

Appadurai, A., (1995), 'The production of locality', in Fardon, R. (ed.), *Counterworks – Managing the Diversity of Knowledge.* London: Routledge.

Ardington, E. and Lund, F. (1995), 'Pensions and Development: How the Social Security System Can Complement Programmes of Reconstruction and Development'. Midrand: Development Bank of Southern Africa, Halfway House.

Armstrong, W. and McGee, T. G. (1985), *Theatres of Accumulation: Studies in Asian and Latin American Urbanization.* London: Methuen.

Arrighi, G. (1967), *The Political Economy of Rhodesia.* The Hague: Mouton.

Ashford, L. S. (1995), New perspectives on population: lessons from Cairo. *Population Bulletin,* 50 (1): 2–40.

Auslander, M. (1993), 'Open the wombs! The symbolic policies of Modern Ngoni witchfinding', in Comaroff, Jean and Comaroff, John (eds), *Modernity and its Malcontents: Ritual and Power in Postcolonial Africa.* Chicago, IL: University of Chicago Press.

Baboo, B. (1992), *Technology and Social Transformation. The Case of the Hirakud Multi-Purpose Dam in Orissa,* New Delhi: Concept Publishing Company.

Baker, J. and Pederson, P. O. (eds) (1992), *The Rural-Urban Interface in Africa: Expansion and Adaptation.* Uppsala: Scandinavian Institute of African Studies.

Bank, L. (1996*)*, 'Poverty in Duncan Village: A Qualitative Assessment'. Development Studies Unit, Working Paper 69. Grahamstown: Institute of Social and Economic Research, Rhodes University.

Barker, F. S. (1995), *The South African Labour Market: Critical Issues for Reconstruction.* Pretoria: J. L. van Schaik.

Barnard, A. (1979), 'Kalahari Bushmen settlement patterns', in Burnam, P. and Ellen, R. F. (eds), *Social and Ecological Systems.* London: Academic Press.

—— (1995), 'The state of the art in Anthropology and Sociology', Keynote Address, Basarwa Research Workshop, University of Botswana, 24–5 August 1995.

Barth, F. and Williams, T. (1995), *Third Monitoring Project on Resettlement in the Ertan Hydropower Project, Ertan.* Washington, DC.

Bassett, T. and Crummey, D. (eds) (1993), *Land in African Agrarian Systems.* Madison, WI: University of Wisconsin Press.

Bastian, M. L. (1993), 'Bloodhounds who have no friends: witchcraft and locality in the Nigerian popular press', in Comaroff, Jean and Comaroff, John (eds), *Modernity and its Malcontents: Ritual and Power in Postcolonial Africa.* Chicago, IL: University of Chicago Press.

Beavon, K. S. O. (1972), 'The intra-urban continuum of shopping centres in Cape Town'. *South African Geographical Journal* 54: 58–71.

Beck, J. H. (1960),'Yafele's kraal: a sample study of African agriculture in Southern Rhodesia', *Geography* 45 (1–2): 68–78.

Bell, T. and Padayachee, V. (1984), 'Unemployment in South Africa: trends, causes and cures', *Development Southern Africa* 3/4 (1): 16–25.

BKS Incorporated Consulting Engineers (1995), 'Vaal Augmentation planning study: further water demands and return flows'. Pretoria: BKS for Department of Water Affairs and Forestry.

BKS/Ninham Shand (1995), 'Orange River Development Project Replanning Study: Executive Summary, Reconnaissance Phase Report'. Pretoria: BKS/NS for Department of Water Affairs and Forestry.

Black, A. (1992), 'Industrial strategy: lessons from the newly industrialized countries' in Abedian, I. and Standish, B. (eds), *Economic Growth in South Africa: Selected Policy Issues*. Cape Town: Oxford University Press.

Board, C. (1973), 'Population concentration in South Africa 1960–1970: a shift and share analysis', *Standard Bank Review supplement*, September: 5–13.

Bonner, P. and Lodge, T. (1989), 'Introduction', in P. Bonner *et al.* (eds), *Holding Their Ground – Class, Locality and Culture in Nineteenth and Twentieth Century South Africa*. Johannesburg: Ravan Press.

Bos, D. I. (1989), 'Prospects for the development of intermediate cities as part of a decentralization programme for South Africa', *Development Southern Africa* 6: 58–81.

Boserup, E. (1985), 'Economic and demographic interrelationships in sub-Saharan Africa', *Population and Development Review* 11 (3): 383–98.

Bovaird, T. (1992), 'Local economic development and the city', *Urban Studies* 29: 343–68.

Bowen, M. L. (1992), 'Beyond reform: adjustment and political power in contemporary Mozambique', *The Journal of Modern African Studies* 30 (2): 255–79.

Bratton, M. (1978), *Beyond Community Development: The Political Economy of Rural Administration in Zimbabwe*. From Rhodesia to Zimbabwe Series No. 6. Gwelo: Mambo Press.

Bruce, J. and Migot-Adholla, S. (1994), *Searching for Land Tenure Stability in Africa*. Madison, WI: University of Wisconsin Press.

Bureau for Refugees (1993), 'Mozambican refugees in South Africa', Southern African Catholic Bishop's Conference.

Butler-Adam, J. F. and Venter, W. M. (1984), 'The Present Residents of Cato Manor: gathered fragments of a dispersed community'. Institute for Social and Economic Research Occasional Paper 11. Durban: University of Durban-Westville.

Cato Manor Development Association (1994), 'Annual Report'. Durban.

Cato Manor Development Association (1995), 'The Cato Manor Annual Business Plan 1994–1996'. Durban.

Centre for Community and Labour Studies (1992), 'Cato Manor Project'. Progress report prepared for the Greater Cato Manor Development Forum. Durban.

Cernea, M. M. (ed.) (1985), *Putting People First: Sociological Variables in Rural Development*. New York: Oxford University Press for the World Bank.

—— (1986), 'Involuntary resettlement in Bank-assisted projects. A review of the application of Bank policies and procedures in FY79–85 projects'. Agriculture and Rural Development Department. Washington, DC: The World Bank.

—— (1988), 'Involuntary Resettlement in Development Projects: policy guidelines in World Bank-financed projects'. World Bank Technical Paper No. 80. Washington, DC: The World Bank.

—— (1990), 'Poverty Risks from Population Displacement in Water Resources Development'. Harvard University, HIID, Development Discussion Paper No. 355. Cambridge, MA: Harvard University.

—— (1991), 'Involuntary resettlement: social research, policy and planning', in Cernea, M. M. (ed.), *Putting People First: Sociological Variables in Rural Development* (2nd edn). Oxford University Press, Washington, DC: The World Bank.

—— (1993), 'The Urban Environment and Population Relocation'. World Bank Discussion Paper No. 152. Washington, DC: The World Bank.

—— (1994), 'Population resettlement and development'. *Finance and Development*. September 1994. Washington, DC: The World Bank.

—— (1995a), 'Understanding and preventing impoverishment from displacement: reflections on the state of knowledge', *Journal of Refugee Studies* 6 (3).

—— (1995b), 'The sociological action-research of development-induced population resettlement', *Romanian Journal of Sociology* 6 (2): 97–120.

—— (1995c), 'Social Organization and Development Anthropology', 1995 Malinowski Award Lecture. Environmentally Sustainable Development Studies and Monographs Series, No. 6. Washington, DC: The World Bank.

—— (1996a), 'Public policy responses to development-induced population displacement', *Economic and Political Weekly* (Mumbai, India) XXXI (24): 515–23.

—— (1996b), 'The Risks and Reconstruction Model for Resettling Displaced Populations'. Keynote Address presented at the International Conference on Reconstructing Livelihoods: Towards New Approaches to Resettlement. Oxford: Refugee Studies Programme, University of Oxford.

—— (1996c), 'Understanding and preventing impoverishment from displacement: reflections on the state of knowledge', in McDowell, C. (ed.), *Understanding Impoverishment – the Consequences of Development-Induced Displacement*. Oxford: Berghahn.

—— (1996d), 'Bridging the research divide: studying refugees and development oustees', in Allen, T. (ed.), *In Search of Cool Ground*. Geneva: United Nations Research Institute for Social Development, in association with London: James Currey and Trenton, NJ: Africa World Press.

Cernea, M. M. and Guggenheim, S. E. (eds) (1993), *Anthropological Approaches to Resettlement: Policy, Practice and Theory*. Boulder, CO: Westview Press.

Chamber of Mines of South Africa Archives, Files 000419–431; 000431.

Chambers, R. (1969), *Settlement Schemes in Tropical Africa: A Study of Organizations and Development*. New York: Praeger.

Champion, A. (1995), 'International migration and demographic change in the developed world', in Paddison, R., Money, J. and Lever, B. (eds) (1995), *International Perspectives in Urban Studies* 3. London: Jessica Kingsley.

Chetty, D. R. (1990), 'The Durban Riots and Popular Memory'. Paper presented at the History Workshop: Structure and Experience in the Making of Apartheid. Johannesburg: University of the Witwatersrand.

Childers, G. W. (1976), *Report on the Survey/Investigation of the Ghanzi Farm Basarwa Situation*. Gaborone: Government Printer.

Christaller, W. (1966), *Central Places in Southern Germany*. Eaglewood Cliffs, NJ: Prentice-Hall.

Christopher, A. J. (1971), 'Land tenure in Rhodesia', *South African Geographical Journal* 53: 39–52.

—— (1982), *South Africa*. London: Longman.

Church, C. (1995), 'Sustainable cities?' *The City Summit*. Newsletter of the Habitat II UK National Council for the UN City Summit 2: 8.

Claassens, A. (1989), *A Toehold on the Land*. Johannesburg: Transvaal Rural Action Committee.

Clarke, J. I. and Kosinksi, L. A. (1982), 'African population redistribution: trends, patterns and policies', in Clarke, J. I. and Kosinski, L. A. (eds), *Redistribution of Population in Africa*. London: Heinemann.

Coetzee, S. F. (1986), 'Regional development in the Southern African Development Area: an assessment of theories, prominent features and the policy framework', *Development Southern Africa* 3 (3): 7–15.

Colson, E. (1971), *The Social Consequences of Resettlement: The Impact of the Kariba Resettlement upon the Gwembe Tonga*. Manchester: Manchester University Press.

—— (1991), 'Coping in Adversity'. Unpublished paper presented at the seminar on Involuntary Migration and Resettlement in Africa. Gainesville: University of Florida.

Comaroff, Jean and Comaroff, John (1993), 'Introduction', in Comaroff, Jean and Comaroff, John (eds)(1993), *Modernity and its Malcontents: Ritual and Power in Postcolonial Africa*. Chicago, IL: University of Chicago Press.

Comaroff, Jean and Comaroff, John (eds) (1993), *Modernity and its Malcontents: Ritual and Power in Postcolonial Africa*. Chicago, IL: University of Chicago Press.

Comissao Nacional de Plano, Direccao Nacional da Estatistica, Unidade de Populaçao e Planificaçao (1993), *Pobreza, Emprego e a Questao Demografica na Cidade de Maputo*. Maputo: CNP.

Compher, V. and Morgan, B. (1991), *Going Home: Building Peace in El Salvador – The Story of Repatriation*. New York: Apex Press.

Cox, D. and Jimenez, J. (1990), 'Achieving social objectives through private transfers: a review', *World Bank Research Observer* 5: 205.

Crankshaw, O. and White, C. (1995), 'Racial desegregation and inner city decay in Johannesburg', *International Journal of Urban and Regional Research* 19 (4): 622–38.

Crisp, J. (1984), 'The politics of repatriation: Ethiopian refugees in Djibouti, 1977–1983', *Review of African Political Economy* 30: 73–82.

—— (1986), 'Ugandan refugees in Sudan and Zaire: the problem of repatriation', *African Affairs*, 85 (339): 163–80.

—— (1996), 'From Social Disarticulation to Social Reconstruction'. Unpublished paper read at the conference on Reconstructing Livelihoods: Towards New Approaches to Resettlement. University of Oxford: Refugee Studies Programme. September, 1996.

Cross, C. (1988a), 'Land Reform in the rural black economy in South Africa', in Cross, C. and Haines, R. (eds), *Towards Freehold? Options for Land and Development in South Africa's Black Rural Areas*. Cape Town: Juta and Co.

—— (1988b), 'Freehold in the homelands: what are the real constraints?' in Cross, C. and Haines, R. (eds), *Towards Freehold? Options for Land and Development in*

South Africa's Black Rural Areas. Cape Town: Juta and Co.

—— (1991), 'Informal tenures against the state: landholding systems in African rural areas', in de Klerk, M. (ed.), *A Harvest of Discontent: the Land Question in South Africa*. Cape Town: IDASA.

—— (1992), 'An alternate legality: the property rights question in relation to South African land reform', *South African Journal on Human Rights* 8 (3).

—— (1994), 'Shack tenure in Durban', in Hindson, D. and McCarthy, J. (eds), *Here to Stay: Informal Settlements in KwaZulu/Natal*. Durban: Indicator Press, University of Natal.

Cross, C. and Evans, J. (1992), 'Interim Progress Report: farmer support programme evolution, KwaMachi Ward, Izingolweni District, Natal'. Rural Urban Studies Unit, Centre for Social and Development Studies, University of Natal: Durban.

Cross, C. and Haines, R. (1988), *Towards Freehold? Options for Land and Development in South Africa's Black Rural Areas*. Cape Town: Juta and Co.

Cross, C. and Preston-Whyte, E. (1989), 'Tenancy on black freehold land: dimensions of history and authority in Natal', *Africa Insight* 19 (1).

Cross, C., Bekker, S. and Clark, C. (1994), 'Migration into the informal settlements of the Durban functional region: an overview of trends', in Hindson, D. and McCarthy, J. (eds), *Here to Stay: Informal Settlements in KwaZulu/Natal*. Durban: Indicator Press, University of Natal.

Cross, C., Clark, C. and Bekker, S. (1994), 'The Informal Population of the Durban Functional Region: an overview'. Report to Town and Regional Planning Commission, Pietermaritzburg. Durban: Rural Urban Studies Unit, Centre for Social and Development Studies, University of Natal.

Cross, C., Evans, J. and Oosthuizen, G. (1993), 'Rise up and Walk: development and the African Independent Churches'. Durban: Rural Urban Studies Unit, Centre for Social and Development Studies, University of Natal.

Cross, C., Luckin, L. and Mzimela, T. (1996), 'Disarming the Borders'. Durban: Rural Urban Studies Programme, for Land and Agriculture Policy Centre. Centre for Social and Development Studies, University of Natal.

Cross, C., Mzimela, T. and Clark, C. (1996), 'Green Rights in the Boundary Lands: land, poverty and resource management in the inner rural districts of KwaZulu-Natal'. Durban: Rural Urban Studies Programme, for Land and Agriculture Policy Centre, Centre for Social and Development Studies, University of Natal.

Cross, C., Bekker, S., Clark, C. and Richards, R. (1992), 'Moving On: migration streams into and out of Inanda'. Pietermaritzburg: Town and Regional Planning Commission, Natal Provincial Administration.

Cross, C., Bekker, S., Clark, C. and Richards, R. (1993), 'New People: the younger informal settlements of Central Durban'. Durban: Rural Urban Studies Unit, Centre for Social and Development Studies, University of Natal.

Cross, C., Bekker, S., Clark, C. and Wilson, C. (1992), 'Searching for Stability: residential migration and community control in Marianhill'. Durban: Rural Urban Studies Unit Working Paper No 23. Centre for Social and Development Studies, University of Natal.

Cross, C., Mngadi, T., Sibanda, S. and Jama, V. (1995), 'The Land is Not Enough: synthesis report for the KwaZulu-Natal District study, Land Reform Pilot Area'. Durban: Rural Urban Studies Programme and Assocation for Rural Advancement, for Land and Agriculture Policy Centre, Centre for Social and Development Studies, University of Natal.

Cross, C., Mlambo, N., Mngadi, T., Pretorius, H., Mbhele, T. and Bekker, S. (1996), 'Locating Productive Small Farmers: population shifts and land reform on the Eastern seaboard'. Development Bank of Southern Africa: Halfway House, Midrand.

Cumming, S. (1990), 'Postcolonial urban residential change in Zimbabwe: a case study', in Potter, R. B. and Salau, A. T. (eds), *Cities and Development in the Third World*. London: Mansell.

Cunliffe, A. (1995), 'The refugee crisis: a study of the United Nations High Commission for Refugees', *Political Studies*, 43: 278–90.

Dachs, A. (ed.) (1975), *Papers of John Mackenzie*. Johannesburg: Witwatersrand University Press.

Daily Dispatch (1992), 23 June. East London.

—— (1994), 4 July. East London.

Daily News (1951), 24 April. Durban.

—— (1979), 5 December. Durban.

—— (1993), 20 October. Durban.

—— (1994a), 22 January. Durban.

—— (1994b), 1 November. Durban.

—— (1995), 3 November, 'Policy on Batswara settlements worries Sebogo', Gaborone.

Davies, R. (1991), 'Durban', in Lemon, A. (ed.), *Homes Apart: South Africa's Segregated Cities*. Cape Town: David Philip.

Davies, R. J. (1963), 'The South African urban hierarchy', *South African Geographical Journal* 45: 15–44.

—— (1967), 'The South African urban hierarchy', *South African Geographical Journal* 49: 9–19.

Davies, R. J. and Cook, G. P. (1968), 'Reappraisal of the South African urban hierarchy', *South African Geographical Journal* 50: 116–32.

Davies, W. (ed.) (1998), *Rights Have No Borders: Worldwide Internal Displacement*. Oslo: Norwegian Refugee Council and Geneva: Global IDP Survey.

de Jongh, M. (1994), 'Field report: Mozambican refugee resettlement: survival strategies of involuntary migrants in South Africa', *Journal of Refugee Studies* 7 (2/3): 220–38.

Desai, A. G. (1986), 'The Origins, Development and Demise of the South African Indian Council: 1964–1983 – a sociological interpretation'. Unpublished Masters Thesis. Grahamstown: Rhodes University.

Desai, S. (1995), 'Nightmare on Tennant Street; yes, but whose land is it?', *Weekend Argus*, 16–17 September. Cape Town.

Devas, N. and Rakodi, C. (eds) (1993), *Managing Fast Growing Cities; New Approaches to Urban Planning and Management in the Developing World*. Harlow: Longman.

de Villiers, R. and Reitzes, M. (eds) (1995), *Southern African migration: domestic and regional policy implications*. Workshop Proceedings No. 14. Johannesburg: Centre for Policy Studies.

Development Bank of Southern Africa, (1991), 'Region E memorandum. Development Bank of Southern Africa'. Midrand: Development Bank of Southern Africa, Halfway House.

Dewar, D. (1994a), 'Reconstructing the South African countryside: the small towns', *Development Southern Africa* 11 (3): 351–62.

—— (1994b), 'Urbanization Patterns and Policies in Southern Africa', in Venter, M. (ed.), *Prospects for Progress: Critical Choices for Southern Africa*. Cape Town: Maskew Miller Longman.

—— (1994c), 'Urban planning, shelter strategies and economic development', in Tomlinson, R. (ed.), *Urban Development Planning: Lessons for the Reconstruction of South Africa's Cities*. Johannesburg: Witwatersrand University Press.

—— (1995a), 'Small towns in development: towards a South African perspective', Johannesburg: Development Bank of Southern Africa.

—— (1995b), 'The urban question in South Africa: the need for a planning paradigm shift', *Third World Planning Review* 17 (4): 407–19.

Dewar, D., Todes, A. and Watson, V. (1983), 'Development from below? Basic needs, rural service centres and the South African Bantustans, with particular reference to the Transkei', *African Urban Studies* n.s. 15: 59–78.

Dewar, D., Todes, A. and Watson, V. (1984a), *Regional Development and Settlement Policy: Premises and Prospects*, London: Allen and Unwin.

Dewar, D., Todes, A. and Watson, V. (1984b), 'Industrial decentralization policy as a mechanism for regional development in South Africa'. Urban Problems Research Unit, Working Paper 30. Cape Town: University of Cape Town.

Dewar, D., Todes, A. and Watson, V. (1986), *Regional Development and Settlement Policy: Premises and Prospects*. London: Allen and Unwin.

Dewar, D. and Uytenbogaardt, R. S. (1991), 'South African cities: a manifesto for change'. Cape Town: Urban Problems Research Unit, University of Cape Town.

de Wet, C. (1988), 'Stress and environmental change in the analysis of community relocation', *Human Organization* 47 (2): 180–7.

—— (1991), 'Some socio-economic consequences of villagisation and the future of betterment villages in the "New South Africa"', *Development Southern Africa* 1 (8): 3–17.

—— (1993a), 'Resettlement as an Aspect of a Land Reform programme in South Africa: some issues and recommendations', unpublished, World Bank-commissioned report.

—— (1993b), 'A spatial analysis of involuntary community relocation: a South African case study', in Cernea, M. M. and Guggenheim, S. E. (eds), *Anthropological Approaches to Resettlement: Policy, Practice and Theory*. Boulder, CO: Westview Press.

—— (1995), *Moving Together, Drifting Apart – Betterment Planning and Villagisation in a South African Homeland*. Johannesburg: Witwatersrand University Press.

Dolan, C. (1995), 'Policy challenges for the New South Africa' in de Villiers, R. and Reitzes, M. (eds), *Southern African Migration: Domestic and Regional Policy Implications*. Workshop Proceedings no. 14. Johannesburg: Centre for Policy Studies.

Dowding, K., John, P. and Briggs, S. (1995), 'Tiebout: a survey of the empirical literature', in Paddison, R. Money, J. and Lever, B. (eds), *International Perspectives in Urban Studies*, 3. London: Jessica Kingsley.

Downing, T. E. (1994), 'Social Geometrics: a theory of social displacement in resettlement'. Paper presented at the International Congress of the Americanists. Stockholm and Uppsala.

—— (1996), 'Mitigating social impoverishment when people are involuntarily displaced', in McDowell, C. (ed.), *Understanding Impoverishment – the Consequences of Development-Induced Displacement*. Oxford: Berghahn.

Drakakis-Smith, D. (1988), Book review of the 'Global report on human settlements', *Journal of Development Studies* 25: 154–5.

Drummond, J. H. and Parnell, S. (1991), 'Mafikeng-Mmabatho' in Lemon, A. (ed.), *Homes Apart: South Africa's Segregated Cities*. London: Paul Chapman.

Drumtra, J. (1993), *'No Place Like Home: Mozambican Refugees Begin Africa's Largest Repatriation'*. Washington, DC: US Committee for Refugees.

D'Souza, V. S. (1990), *Development Planning and Structural Inequalities*. New Delhi/ Newbury Park/London: Sage Publications.

Duggan, W. (1986), *An Economic Analysis of Southern African Agriculture*. New York: Praeger.

Durban Housing Survey (1952), *A Study of Housing in a Multi-racial Community*. Pietermaritzburg: University of Natal Press.

Dwyer, D. and Bruce, J. (1988), *A Home Divided: Women and Income in the Third World*. Stanford, CA: Stanford University Press.

Economic and Social Commission for Asia and the Pacific (1979), *Guidelines for Rural Centre Planning*. New York: United Nations.

—— (1992), Report on the International Seminar on Rural Centre and Settlements Planning, 28 July–4 August 1992, Tehran.

Edwards, I. A. (1983), 'Living on the Smell of an Oilrag: African life in Cato Manor Farm in the late 1940s'. Paper presented at the workshop on African Life in Durban in the Twentieth Century. Durban: University of Natal.

—— (1989), 'Mkhubane Our Home: African shantytown society in Cato Manor Farm, 1946–1960'. Unpublished PhD thesis, Durban: University of Natal.

—— (1994), 'Cato Manor: cruel past, pivotal future'. *Review of African Political Economy* 61: 415–27.

Escobar, A. (1988), 'Power and visibility: development and the invention and management of the Third World', *Cultural Anthropology* 3 (4): 428–43.

Fair, T. J. D. (1965), 'The core-periphery concept and population growth in South Africa, 1911–1960', *South African Geographical Journal* 47: 59–71.

Feeney, P. (1995), *Displacement and the Rights of Women*, Oxford: Oxfam, Policy Department.

Ferguson, J. (1990), *The Anti-Politics Machine: 'Development', Depoliticization and Bureaucratic State Power in Lesotho*. Cape Town: David Philip.

Fernandes, W. (1991), 'Power and powerlessness: development projects and displacement of tribals', *Social Action* 3.

Fernandes, W., Das, J. C. and Rao, S. (1989), 'Displacement and rehabilitation: an estimate of extent and prospects', in Fernandes, W., and Thukral, E. G. (eds), *Development, Displacement and Rehabilitation*. New Delhi: Indian Social Institute.

Fighting Talk (1959), August. Durban.

First, R. (1983), *Black Gold: The Mozambican Miner, Proletarian and Peasant*. Sussex: The Harvester Press.

Fischer, A. (1987), 'Land tenure in Mhala: official wisdom locked up in tradition and people locked up in development', *Development Southern Africa*, 4 (3).

Fisk, R. P., Brown, S. W. and Bitner, M. J., (1993), 'Tracking the evolution of the services marketing literature'. *Journal of Retailing* 69: 61–103.

Floyd, B. N. (1959), 'Changing patterns of African land use in Southern Rhodesia', *Rhodes-Livingstone Journal* 25: 20–39.

—— (1962), 'Land apportionment in Southern Rhodesia', *Geographical Review* 52 (4): 566–82.

Fortmann, L. and Roe, E. (1982), 'Settlement on tap: the role of water in permanent settlements at the lands', in Hitchcock, R. R. and Smith, M. R. (eds), *Settlement in Botswana*. Gaborone: Botswana Society.

Fox, R. C. (1991), 'The use of central place theory in Kenya's development strategies', *Tijdschrift voor Economische en Sociale Geografie* 82 (2): 106–27.

—— (1992), 'The impact of space: land division and urban development in Kenya and South Africa', *International Regional Science Review* 15 (1): 39–49.

Frelimo, (1983a), *Relatório do Comité Central ao IV Congresso*. Maputo: Frelimo.

—— (1983b), 'Moçambique out of Underdevelopment to Socialism: report of the Central Committee, IVth Congress'. Maputo: Frelimo.

Freund, P. J. and Kalumba, K. (1983), 'The Social and Economic Condition of Refugees and Displaced Persons in the Mwinilunga, Zambezi, Kabompo and Solwezi Districts of Zambia's North-Western Province: census of refugees and displaced persons in the four districts'. Community Health Research Reports No. 9. Lusaka: University of Zambia.

—— (1986), 'Spontaneously settled refugees in Northwestern Province, Zambia'. *International Migration Review* 20 (2): 299–312.

Friedmann, J. (1981/2), 'Regional planning for rural mobilization in Africa', *Rural Africana* 12/13: 2–19.

—— (1992), *Empowerment: the Politics of Alternative Development*. Oxford: Blackwell.

Friedmann, I. and Weaver, C. (1979), *Territory and Function*. London: Edward Arnold.

Fujimoto, I. (1992), 'Lessons from abroad in rural community revitalization', *Community Development Journal* 27 (1): 10–20.

Galaty, J. G. and Bonte, P. L. (1991), 'The current realities of African pastoralists', in Galaty, J. G. and Bonte, P. L. (eds), *Herders, Warriors and Traders: Pastoralism in Africa*. Boulder, CO: Westview Press.

Gasper, D. (1988), 'Rural growth points and rural industries in Zimbabwe: ideologies and policies', *Development and Change* 19 (3): 425–66.

Gasper, D., and de Valk, P. (1985), 'Background, Concepts and Issues', paper presented at the Workshop on Rural Industries and Growth Point/Service Centre Policies, Department of Rural and Urban Planning. Harare: University of Zimbabwe.

Gboyega, A. (1981), 'Intergovernmental relations in Nigeria: local government and the 1979 Nigerian Constitution', *Public Administration and Development* 1: 281–90.

—— (1983), 'Nigeria', in Mawhood, P. (ed.), *Local Government in the Third World: The Experience of Tropical Africa*, Chichester: Wiley.

Gelderblom, D. and Kok, P. C. (1994a), *Urbanization: South Africa's challenge*. Volume 1: *Dynamics*. Pretoria: Human Sciences Research Council.

Gelderblom, D. and Kok, P. C. (1994b), *Urbanization: South Africa's challenge*. Volume 2: *Planning*. Pretoria: Human Sciences Research Council.

Gigaba, M. and Maharaj, B. (1996), 'Land invasions during political transition: the Wiggins Saga in Cato Manor', *Development Southern Africa* 13 (2): 217–35.

Giliomee, H. and Schlemmer, L. (eds) (1985), *Up Against the Fences: Poverty, Passes and Privilege in South Africa*. Cape Town: David Philip.

Gillis, M., Perkins, D. H., Roemer, M. and Snodgrass, D. R. (1992), *Economics of Development*. (3rd edn). New York: W. W. Norton and Company.

Ginsburg, N., Koppel, B. and McGee, T. G. (eds) (1991), *The Extended Metropolis; Settlement Transition in Asia*. Hawaii: Hawaii University Press.

Gopal, G. (1992), 'Gender and resettlement in India'. Unpublished manuscript.

Gore, C. (1984), *Regions in Question: Space, Development and Regional Policy*. London: Methuen.

Government of Angola (1996), 'Inquerito Socio-demografico a Populacao Deslocada (relatorio final)'. Luanda: Instituto Nacional de Estatistica (NIS).

Government of Botswana (1966), 'Transitional Plan for Social and Economic Development'. Gaborone: Government Printer.

—— (1968), 'National Development Plan, 1968–1973'. Gaborone: Government Printer.

—— (1970), 'National Development Plan 1970–1975'. Gaborone: Government Printer.

—— (1972), 'Rural Development in Botswana'. Gaborone: Government Printer.

—— (1973), 'National Policy for Rural Development: the Government Decisions on the Report on Rural Development'. Gaborone: Government Printer.

—— (1977), 'National Development Plan, 1976–1981'. Gaborone: Government Printer.

—— (1980), 'National Development Plan 1979–1985'. Gaborone: Government Printer.

—— (1990a), 'Ghanzi District Development Plan 1989–1995'. Ghanzi: Ghanzi District Council.

—— (1990b), 'Kgalagadi District Development Plan 1989–1995'. Tsabong: Kgalagadi District Council.

—— (1990c), 'Southern District Development Plan 1989–1995'. Kanye: Southern District Council.

—— (1990d), 'North East District Development Plan 1989–1995'. Francistown: North East District Council.

—— (1991), 'National Development Plan 7: 1991–1997'. Gaborone: Government Printer.

—— (1992), 'National Settlement Policy'. Gaborone: Department of Town and Regional Planning: Gaborone.

—— (no date), 'National Development Plan 1973–78 Part I', Government Printer: Gaborone.

Government of Lesotho (1987), 'Maseru Development Plan working paper no. 9: Agricultural Land Use'. Maseru: Physical Planning Division.

—— (1992), '1986 Population census analysis report volume IV (Population Dynamics, Prospects and Policies)'. Maseru: Bureau of Statistics.

—— (1994), 'Marketing division border surveys'. Maseru: Ministry of Agriculture.

—— (1995), 'Lesotho Highlands Water Revenue Development Fund: toward a common approach to empowering local communities'. Maseru: Ministry of Planning.

—— (no date), 'Maseru Development Plan Working Paper No. 4: Land Tenure'. Maseru: Physical Planning Division.

Government of Malawi (1971), 'Statement of development policies: 1971–1980'. Zomba: Government Printer.

—— (1978), 'The Malawi 1977 population census: preliminary report'. National Statistical Office. Zomba: Government Printer.

—— (1984), 'Malawi commercial transport project', Unclassified Project Proposal.

—— (1987), 'Statement of development policies: 1987–1996'. Zomba: Government Printer.

—— (1991), 'Malawi population and housing census 1987'. Zomba: Government Printer.

—— (1994), 'Malawi demographic and health survey (1992)'. Zomba: Government Printer.

—— (1995), 'Population statistics for Rumphi district'. Zomba: Government Printer.

Government of Mozambique (1989), 'Forca do trabalho-revista de temática laboral, 3'. Maputo: Ministry of Labour.

—— (1990), 'Forca do trabalho-revista de temática laboral, 4'. Maputo: Ministry of Labour.

Government of Namibia (1995), 'National development plan 1'. Windhoek: National Planning Commission.

Government of South Africa (1949), 'Report of the Commission of Enquiry into riots in Durban (UG 36–1949)'. Pretoria: Government Printer.

—— (1993), 'The Population Development Programme in South Africa and the role of the Chief Directorate Population Development'. Pretoria: Chief Directorate Population Development.

—— (1994a), 'Water supply and sanitation policy: water – an indivisible national asset'. Pretoria: Department of Water Affairs and Forestry.

—— (1994b), 'White Paper: The Reconstruction and Development Programme'. Cape Town: Government Printer.

—— (1995a), 'Urban development strategy of the Government of National Unity', Pretoria: Government Gazette 16679.

—— (1995b), 'Rural development strategy of the Government of National Unity', Pretoria: Government Gazette 16679.

—— (1995c), 'A Green Paper for public discussion: population policy for South Africa'. Pretoria: Ministry for Welfare and Population Development.

—— (1997), 'Green Paper on international migration'. Pretoria: Government Gazette 18033.

Government of Southern Rhodesia (1930), Land Apportionment Act. Salisbury.

—— (1952), Land Husbandry Act. Salisbury.

Government of Zimbabwe (1981a), 'Umfurudzi Intensive Resettlement Area, Shamva District: final project report'. Harare: Department of Conservation and Extension.

—— (1981b), 'Preliminary project report: Chinyika Intensive Resettlement Area'. Department of Conservation and Extension: Harare.

—— (1981c), 'Growth with equity'. Harare: Government Printere.

—— (1981d), 'A programme for the development of service centres in the rural areas of Zimbabwe'. Harare: Ministry of Local Government and Town Planning.

—— (1982), 'Transitional National Development Plan 1982–1982, 1984–1985'. Harare: Government Printer.

—— (1983), 'Resettlement programme'. Harare: Ministry of Lands, Resettlement and Rural Development.

—— (1987), 'Chinyika resettlement scheme: Seventeenth quarterly progress report, January–March 1987'. Harare: Department of Rural Development.

—— (1994), 'Report of the Commission of Inquiry into appropriate agricultural land tenure systems'. Harare: Government Printer.

—— (1995), 'Land Tenure Commission, Vols I and II'. Harare: Government Printer.

Graaff, J. (1987), 'The present state of urbanization in the South African home-lands: rethinking the concept and predicting the future', *Development Southern Africa* 4 (1).

Grest, J. (1995), 'Urban management, local government reform and the democratisation process in Moçambique: Maputo city 1975–1990', *Journal of Southern African Studies* 1 (1): 147–64.

Greyling, D. (1983), 'Die desentralisasie-ideaal en ekonomiese realiteite', *Volkshandel* (February): 6–11.

Groenewald, C. J. (1989), 'Community development'. in Coetzee, J. K. (ed.), *Development is for People*. Johannesburg: Southern.

Guggenheim, S. E. (1994), 'Involuntary Resettlement: an annotated reference bibliography for development research'. Environment Working Paper 64. Washington, DC: World Bank.

HABITAT (1987), 'Global report on human settlements'. Oxford: Oxford University Press.

—— (1990), 'Shelter: from projects to national strategies'. Nairobi: UN Centre for Human Settlements.

—— (1991), 'Rural settlement development in developing countries: selected case studies'. Nairobi: UN Centre for Human Settlements.

—— (undated), 'A new agenda for human settlements'. Nairobi: UN Centre for Human Settlements.

Hampton, J. (ed.) (1998), *Internally Displaced People: a Global Survey*. London: Earthscan Publications, for the Global IDP Survey and the Norwegian Refugee Council.

Hancock, G. (1989), *Lords of Poverty*. London: Macmillan.

Hanlon, J. (1990), *Mozambique: the Revolution Under Fire*. London: Zed books.

Hansen, A. (1977), 'Once the Running Stops: the social and economic incorporation of Angolan refugees into Zambian border villages'. Unpublished PhD thesis. Department of Anthropology, Cornell University.

—— (1979a), 'Once the running stops: assimilation of Angolan refugees into Zambian border villages', *Disasters* 3/4: 369–74.

—— (1979b), 'Managing refugees: Zambia's response to Angolan refugees 1967 to 1977', *Disasters* 3/4: 375–80.

—— (1990), 'Refugee Self-settlement versus Settlement on Government Schemes: the long-term consequences for security integration and economic development of Angolan refugees (1966–1989) in Zambia'. Discussion Paper, Number 17 (November). Geneva: United Nations Research Institute for Social Development.

—— (1991), 'Self-directed versus Government-directed Settlement of African refugees'. Paper read at the conference on Involuntary Migration and Resettlement in Africa, University of Florida, Gainesville. March 1991.

—— (1992), 'Some insights on African refugees', in DeVoe, P. A. (ed.), *Selected Papers on Refugee Issues*. Washington, DC: Committee on Refugee Issues, American Anthropological Association.

—— (1993), 'African refugees: defining and defending their human rights', in Cohen, R., Hayden, G. and Nagan, W. (eds), *Human Rights and Governance in Africa*. Gainesville, FL: University Presses of Florida.

Hardoy, J., Mitlin, D. and Satterthwaite, D. (1993), *Environmental Problems in Third World Cities*. London: Earthscan.

Harrell-Bond, B. (1985), 'Humanitarianism in a straitjacket', *African Affairs* 84 (1): 3–13.

—— (1986), *Imposing Aid: emergency assistance to refugees*. Oxford: Oxford University Press.

—— (1989), 'Repatriation: under what conditions is it the most desirable solution for refugees', *African Studies Review* 32 (1): 41–69.

Harries, P. (1982), 'Kinship, ideology and the nature of pre-colonial labour migration: labour migration from the Delgoa Bay hinterland to South Africa, up to 1895', in Marks, S. and Rathbone, R. (eds), *Industrialization and Social Change in South Africa: Class Formation, Culture and Consciousness*. Harlow, Essex: Longman.

—— (1987), 'A forgotten corner of the Transvaal: reconstructing the history of a relocated community through oral testimony and song' in Bozzoli, B. (ed.), *Class, Community and Conflict: South African Perspectives*. Johannesburg: Ravan Press.

Harris, J. and Todaro, M. (1970), 'Migration, unemployment and development: a two-sector analysis', *American Economic Review* 60.

Harris, M. (1959), 'Labour emigration among the Moçambique Thonga: cultural and political factors', *Africa* 29: 50–66.

Hart, D. M. (1988), 'Political manipulation of urban space: the razing of District Six, Cape Town', *Urban Geography* 9: 603–28.

Hastrup, K. and Olwig, K. F. (1997), 'Introduction', in Olwig, K. F. and Hastrup, K. (eds) (1997), *Siting Culture: the Shifting Anthropological Object*. London/New York: Routledge.

Haughton, G. and Hunter, C. (1994), *Sustainable Cities*. London: Jessica Kingsley.

Hemson, D. (1977), 'Dock Workers, Labour Circulation, and Class Struggles in Durban, 1940–45', *Journal of Southern African Studies* 4: 84–124.

Hermele, K. (1988), *Land Struggles and Social Differentiation in southern Mozambique: A case study of Chokwé, Limpopo, 1950–1987*. Uppsala: Scandinavian Institute of African Studies.

Hindson, D. and Byerley, M. (1993), 'Class, race and settlement in Cato Manor: a report on surveys of African and Indian households in Cato Manor'. Durban: Institute for Social and Economic Research, University of Durban-Westville.

Hindson, D. and Makhathini, M. (1994), 'Community Dynamics and Leadership in Cato Manor'. Durban: Institute for Social and Economic Research, University of Durban-Westville.

Hirschman, A. O. (1958), *The Strategy of Economic Development*. New Haven, CT: Yale University Press.

Hitchcock, R. K. (1978), 'Kalahari Cattleposts'. Gaborone: Ministry of Local Government and Landse.

Holm, M. (1992), 'Macro-level constraints and the growth of the informal sector in

Uganda', in Baker, J. and Pedersen, P. O. (eds), *The Rural–Urban Interface in Africa: Expansion and Adaptation*. Uppsala: Scandinavian Institute of African Studies.

Horn, N. E. (1988), 'The Culture, Urban Context and Economics of Women's Fresh Produce Marketing in Harare, Zimbabwe'. PhD Dissertation. Michigan: Michigan State University.

Houghton, D. H. (1976), *The South African Economy*. London: Oxford University Press.

IDRC (1993), 'Farming in the City: the rise of urban agriculture'. IDRC Reports, 21: 3. Ottawa, Canada.

International Labour Organisation (1978), 'Towards Self Reliance: development, employment and equity issues in Tanzania'. Geneva: ILO.

Jackson, J. (1994), 'Repatriation and reconstruction in Zimbabwe in the 1980s', in Allen, T. and Morsink, H. (eds) (1994), *When Refugees Go Home*. Geneva: United Nations Research Institute for Social Development, in association with London: James Currey and Trenton, NJ: Africa World Press.

Jaeger, D. (1981), *Settlement Patterns and Rural Development: A Human Geographical Study of the Kaonde Kasempa District, Zambia*. Amsterdam: Royal Tropical Institute.

Jaffe, S. M. (1994), 'Contract farming in the shadow of competitive markets: the experience of Kenyan horticulture', in Little, P. D. and Watts, M. D. (eds), *Living under Contract: Contract Farming and Agrarian Transformation in Sub-Saharan Africa*. Madison, WI: University of Wisconsin Press.

Jiggins, J. (1987), 'How poor women earn income in sub-Saharan Africa and what works against them', *World Development* 17 (7): 953–63.

Johnson, E. A. (1970), *The Organization of Space in Developing Countries*. Cambridge, MA: Harvard University Press.

Johnson, S. P. (1994), *World population – Turning the Tide: Three Decades of Progress*. London: Graham and Trotman/Martinus Nijhoff.

Johnston, R. J. (1984), *City and Society*. London: Hutchinson.

Jones, S. (1993), *Assaulting Childhood: Children's Experiences of Migrancy and Hostel Life in South Africa*. Johannesburg: Witwatersrand University Press.

Jordaan, J., Tshabalala, M. and Mfono, Z. (1991), *Population – Our Time Bomb: The Solution to South Africa's Population Problem*. Pretoria: J. L. van Schaik.

Junod, H. (1927), *The Life of a South African Tribe*. New York: Open Books.

Kalipeni, E. (1993), 'Contained Urban Growth in Post Independence Malawi'. Paper presented at the African Association of Political Science Twentieth Anniversary Bi-Annual Congress, Dar es Salaam, Tanzania.

Khama, Sir Seretse, (1970), *His Excellency's speech opening the Ngwaketse Show and Trade Fair Gaborone*. Office of the President.

Khogali, M. M. (1981), 'Sedentarization of nomads: Sudan', in Galaty, J. G. *et al.* (eds), *The Future of Pastoral Peoples*. Ottawa: International Development Research Centre.

Kibreab, G. (1991), *The State of the Art Review of Refugee Studies in Africa*. Uppsala: Department of Economic History, University of Uppsala.

—— (1996), *Ready and Willing ... but Still Waiting – Eritrean Refugees in Sudan and the Dilemmas of Return*. Horn of Africa Series No. 1/96. Uppsala: Life and Peace Institute.

Kinsey, B. H., and Binswanger, H. P. (1993), 'Characteristics and performance of resettlement programs: a review', *World Development* 21 (9): 1477–94.

Klugman, B. (1994), *Population Policy in South Africa: Where to From Here?* Midrand: Development Bank of Southern Africa.

Knox, P. L. and Masilela, C. O. (1989), 'Attitudes to Third World urban planning: practitioners versus outside experts', *Habitat International* 13 (3): 67–79.

Knox, P. L. and Masilela, C. O. (1990), 'Role orientations of Third World urban planners', *Environment and Planning B: Planning and Design* 17 (1): 9–22.

Kockott, F., (1993), 'The Fields of Wrath: cattle impounding in the Weenen area'. Association for Rural Advancement: Pietermaritzburg.

Koenig, D. (1995), 'Women and resettlement', in Gallins, R. and Ferguson, A. (eds), *Women and International Development*, Vol. 4. Boulder, CO: Westview Press.

Kotze, J. C. (1992), 'Children and the family in a rural settlement in Gazankulu'. Unpublished paper presented at the Department of Social Anthropology, University of the Witwatersrand, Friday Seminar Series.

Krog, A. (1998), *Country of my Skull*. Johannesburg: Random House.

Kunz, E. F. (1981), 'Exile and resettlement: refugee theory', *International Migration Review* XV (1–2) Spring–Summer: 42–51.

Kuper, L. (1965), *An African Bourgeoisie*. New Haven, CT: Yale University Press.

Kwele, D. K. (1975), 'A report on consultation with the people of North East District on village regrouping policy initiated by North East District Council'. Unpublished report, North East District Council, Francistown.

Kyle, S. (1991), 'Economic reform and armed conflict in Mozambique', *World Development* 19 (6): 637–49.

Ladlau, L. K. (1975), 'The Cato Manor Riots, 1959–1960'. Unpublished MA Thesis, University of Natal, Durban.

Lassailly-Jacob, V. (1996a), 'Key issues in preventing impoverishment in land-based resettlement programmes', in McDowell, C. (ed.), *Understanding Impoverishment: The Consequences of Development Induced Displacement*. Oxford: Berghan Publishers.

—— (1996b), 'Reconstructing Livelihood Through Land Settlement Schemes'. Unpublished paper read at the conference on Reconstructing Livelihoods: Towards New Approaches to Resettlement, University of Oxford: Refugee Studies Programme. September, 1996.

Leader (1981), 26 July. Durban.

Lemon, A. (1977), 'Urban primacy and regional economic development in the Third World', *Proceedings of the Rhodesian Geographical Association* 10: 3–14.

—— (1989), 'Urban policy options to prevent rural and urban overcrowding: the size and location of urban settlement'. Paper given at the Newick Park Conference, Sussex, 26–29 July 1989.

—— (ed.) (1991), *Homes Apart: South Africa's Segregated Cities*. Cape Town: David Philip.

—— (1995), *The Geography of Change in South Africa*. Chichester: Wiley.

Lemon, A. and Cook, G. P. (1994), 'South Africa', in Tarver, I. T. (ed.), *Urbanization in Africa: a handbook*. Westport, CT: Greenwood Press.

Lerise, F. (1993), *The Management of Rural Service Centres in Tanzania: A Case Study of the Njombe Rural District*. Nairobi: UNCHS (Habitat).

Le Scour, J.-P. (1993), 'Preface' to *Mozambican refugees in South Africa*. Bureau for Refugees, Southern African Catholic Bishop's Conference.

Letsoalo, E. (1987), *Land Reform in South Africa: A Black Perspective*. Johannesburg: Skotaville.

Lipton, M. (1977), *Why Poor People Stay Poor: A Study of Urban Bias in World Development*. London: Temple Smith.

—— (1995), 'Rural financial services (RFS), demography and migration: international experience'. Unpublished report to the Commission of Enquiry into Rural Financial Services, Government of South Africa.

Lipton, M., and Lipton, M. (1993), 'Creating rural livelihoods: some lessons for South Africa from experiences elsewhere', *World Development* 21 (9): 1515–48.

Little, P. D. and Lundin de Coloane, I. B. (1992), 'Petty Trade and Household Survival Strategies: a case study of food and vegetable traders in the peri-urban area of Maputo, Mozambique'. IDA Working Paper No. 90. Binghamton, NY: Institute for Development Anthropology for USAID.

Little, P. D. and Watts, M. J. (eds) (1994), *Living Under Contract: Contract Farming and Agrarian Transformation in Sub-Saharan Africa*. Madison, WI: University of Wisconsin Press.

Lodge, T. (1983), 'The Destruction of Sophiatown', in B. Bozzoli (ed.), *Town and Countryside in the Transvaal*. Johannesburg: Ravan Press.

Logan, M. I. (1972), 'The spatial system and planning strategies in developing countries', *Geographical Review* 62: 229–44.

Lösch, A. (1940), *The Economics of Location*. New Haven, CT.

Louw, L. (1984), 'A critique of decentralization policy', proceedings of a seminar on National and Regional Planning with Special Reference to the State's Decentralization Policy, Institute of Town and Regional Planners, Johannesburg.

Low, S. and Altman, I. (ed.) (1992), *Place Attachment*. New York: Plenum Press.

Lucas, J. (1995), 'Space, Society and Culture: housing and local-level politics in a section of Alexandra Township, 1991–1992'. Unpublished MA thesis. University of the Witwatersrand, Johannesburg.

Lupton, M. and Murphy, S. (1995), 'Housing and urban reconstruction in South Africa', in Lemon, A. (ed.), *The Geography of Change in South Africa*. Chichester: Wiley.

Maasdorp, G. (1985), 'Co-ordinated regional development: hope for the Good Hope proposals?', in Giliomee, H. and Schlemmer, L. (eds), *Up Against the Fences: Poverty, Passes and Privilege in South Africa*. Cape Town: David Philip.

Maasdorp, G. and Humphreys, A. S. B. (1975), *From Shantytown to Township*. Cape Town: Juta.

Mabin, A. (1989), 'Limits of urban transition models in understanding South African urbanization', *Development Southern Africa* 7 (3).

—— (1991), 'The dynamics of urbanization since 1960', in Swilling, M., Humphries, R. and Shubane, K. (eds), *Apartheid City in Transition*. Cape Town: Oxford University Press.

—— (1992), 'Dispossession, exploitation and struggle: an historical overview of South African urbanization', in Smith, D. (ed.), *The Apartheid City and Beyond*. London and New York: Routledge.

Mabogunje, A. L. (1981), *The Development Process: A Spatial Perspective*. London: Hutchinson.

Maema, M. and Reynolds, N. (1995), 'Lesotho Highlands Water Project-induced

Displacement: context, impacts, rehabilitation strategies, implementation experience, and future options', Unpublished paper presented at the Refugee Studies Programme Conference on Development-Induced Displacement and Impoverishment. Wadham College, Oxford University, 3–7 January.

Mahapatra, L. K. (1991), 'Development for Whom? Depriving the Dispossessed Tribals', *Social Action*, 41, (3).

Maharaj, B. (1992), 'The Group Areas Act in Durban: Central – Local Relations'. Unpublished PhD Thesis, University of Natal, Durban.

—— (1994), 'The Group Areas Act and community destruction in South Africa: the Struggle for Cato Manor in Durban', *Urban Forum* 5: 1–25.

—— (1995), 'Residential segregation in South African cities: the Group Areas Act in Durban', in Singh, D. K. (ed.), *Spatial Dimensions of Geography*. Orissa: India: Bhubaneswar.

—— (1996), 'Politics, Community, Displacement and Planning: Cato Manor – past, present and future', paper presented at the IAI/ISER seminar on Understanding Changing Patterns of Settlement and Resettlement in Southern Africa, Rhodes University, Grahamstown, 22–26 January.

Mail and *Guardian* (1995), 1 December 1995. Johannesburg.

Main, H. and Williams, S. W. (eds) (1994), *Environment and Housing in Third World Cities*. Chichester: Wiley.

Makanya, S. T. (1994), 'The desire to return: effects of experiences in exile on refugees repatriating to Zimbabwe in the early 1980s', in Allen, T. and Morsink, H. (eds) (1994), *When Refugees go Home*. Geneva: United Nations Research Institute for Social Development, in association with London: James Currey and Trenton, NJ: Africa World Press.

Makhanya, E., (1996), 'Crucial Issues for Land Reform and Restitution in KwaZulu/ Natal'. Paper presented to the Southern and Eastern African Regional Conference on Perspectives and Strategies on Land Rights and Land Reform in Rural and Urban Settings, Johannesburg, June 1996.

Makhathini, M. (1992), 'Squatting Dynamics: a look from within Cato Manor'. Paper presented at the Twenty-Second Annual Conference of the Association of Sociology in South Africa, Pretoria.

Malkki, L. (1992), 'National Geographic: the rooting of peoples and the territorialization of national identity among scholars and refugees', *Cultural Anthropology* 7 (1): 24–44.

—— (1995), *Purity and Exile: Violence, Memory and National Cosmology among Hutu Refugees in Tanzania*. Chicago, IL: Chicago University Press.

—— (1997), 'News and culture: transitory phenomena and the fieldwork tradition', in Gupta, A. and Ferguson, J. (eds) (1997), *Anthropological Locations – Boundaries and Grounds of a Field Science*. Berkeley, CA and London: University of California Press.

Manona, C., Bank, L. and Higginbottom, K. (1996), 'Informal Settlements in the Eastern Cape Province, South Africa'. Roma: National University of Lesotho, Institute of Southern African Studies, Working Paper No. 10.

Mapetla, M., Phororo, H. and Prasad, G. (1994), 'Gender, Urbanisation and Environment: the role of wild vegetables'. Paper presented at the International Seminar on Gender, Urbanization and the Environment. Nairobi, Kenya.

Mapisa, M. (1993), 'SADF's repatriation of Mozambiçans questionable'. *SACC ECUNEWS: Official Publication of the South Africa Council of Churches*, August.

Marks, S. and Rathbone, R. (eds) (1982), *Industrialization and Social Change in South Africa: Class Formation, Culture and Consciousness*. Essex: Longman.

Maro, P. and Mlay, W. E. I. (1982), 'Population redistribution in Tanzania', in Clarke, J. I. and Kosinski, L. A. (eds), *Redistribution of Population in Africa*. London: Heinemann.

Maryville Indian Ratepayers' Association, (1958), 'Memorandum of objection against the proposal for the zoning of Mayville, Cato Manor, Manor Gardens, Candella and Stella Hill for future European occupation under the Group Areas Act, 1950, as amended', submitted to the Durban City Council by the Mayville Indian Ratepayers' Association, 30 April 1958.

Mascarenhas, A. (1979), 'After villagization – What?', in Pratt, C. and Mwamsasu, B. U. (eds), *Toward Socialism in Tanzania*. Toronto: Toronto University Press.

Matope, J. J. (1993), *Improving Rural-Regional Settlement Systems Management: Case Study of Mkhota Rural Service Centre and Kasungu District in Malawi*. Nairobi: UNCHS (Habitat).

May, J. (1989) 'The push/pull dynamic: rural poverty in urban migration', *Indicator SA* 6.

—— (1996), 'Composition and Persistence of Poverty in Rural South Africa'. Working Paper No. 15. Johannesburg: Land and Agricultural Policy Centre.

May, J. and Trompeter, P. (1992), 'A study of income and expenditure and other socioeconomic patterns in the urban and rural areas of KwaZulu, Vol. 1: overview of results'. Report prepared for the KwaZulu Finance and Investment Corporation, and Department of Economic Affairs, KwaZulu Government. Durban: Data Research Africa.

Mayer, P. (ed.) (1980), *Black Villagers in an Industrial Society*. Oxford: Oxford University Press.

Mayer, P. and Mayer, I. (1961), *Townsmen and Tribesmen: Conservatism and the Process of Urbanization in a South African City*. Cape Town: Oxford University Press.

Mazur, R. E. (1991), 'Self-reliance and future orientations among refugees in southern Africa: alternative conceptions and interests'. Unpublished paper read at the conference on Involuntary Migration and Resettlement in Africa, Gainesville: University of Florida: March 1991.

Mburugu, E. K. (1988), 'A resettlement survey in the Kiambere Hydroelectric Power Project: preliminary report', March 1988.

McAllister, P. (1980), 'Work, homestead and the shades; the ritual interpretation of labour migration among the Gcaleka', in Mayer, P. (ed.), *Black Villagers in an Industrial Society*. Oxford University Press: Oxford.

—— (1991), 'Reversing the effects of "Betterment Planning" in South Africa's rural areas', *Africa Insight* 2 (12): 36–42.

McCall, M. (1985), 'Environment and agricultural impacts of Tanzania's Villagisation Programme', in Clarke, J. I., Khoyate, M. and Kosinski, L. A. (eds), *Population and Development Projects in Africa*, London: Cambridge University Press, 23–5.

McCarthy, C. L. (1985), 'Industrial decentralization and employment creation', in Gilliomee, H. and Schlemmer, L. (ed.), *Up Against the Fences : Poverty, Passes and Privilege in South Africa*. Cape Town: David Philip, 26–32.

McCarthy, J. (1994), 'Durban-Pietermaritzburg Corridor project: draft final report'. Durban: Institute for Social and Economic Research, University of Durban-Westville.

McCarthy, J., Bernstein, A. and Simkins, C. (1995), 'Post Apartheid Population and income trends: a new analysis'. CDE Research, Policy in the Making, vol. 1. Johannesburg: Centre for Development and Enterprise.

McDowell, C. (ed.) (1996), *Understanding Impoverishment – the Consequences of Development-Induced Displacement*. Oxford: Berghahn.

McMillan, D. F. (1995), *Sahel Visions: Planned Settlement and River Blindness Control in Burkina Faso*. Tucson, AZ: University of Arizona Press.

McRobie, G. (1990), 'Increasing technological choice in Third World settlements', in Cadman, D. and Payne, G. (eds), *The Living City; Towards A Sustainable Future*. London: Routledge.

Meer, F. (1969), *Portrait of South African Indians*. Durban: Avon House.

Merton, R. K. (1979), *The Sociology of Science: Theoretical and Empirical Investigations*. Chicago, IL and London: University of Chicago Press.

Middleton, N., O'Keefe, P. and Moyo, S. (1993), *Tears of the Crocodile; From Rio to Reality in the Developing World*. London: Pluto.

Migdal, J. S. (1988), *Strong Societies and Weak States*. Princeton, NJ: Princeton University Press.

Mondlane, E. (1983), *The Struggle for Moçambique*. London: Penguin.

Moore, H. (1994), 'Households and gender in a South African bantustan: a comment', *African Studies* 53 (1): 137–42.

Mosaase, A. (1983), *An Analysis of Existing Land Tenure in Lesotho and Experience in the Implementation of Current Land Policy*. Harare: Commonwealth Association of Surveyors and Land Economists.

Mostert, W. P., Oosthuizen, J. S. and Hofmeyr, B. E. (1991). *Demografie – die studie van menslike bevolkings*. Pretoria: Human Sciences Research Council.

Mougeot, L. J. A. (1988), 'Hydroelectric Development and Involuntary Resettlement in Brazilian Amazonia: planning and evaluation'. Edinburgh: Cobham Resource Consultants.

Moyo, S. (1995), *Land Policy in Zimbabwe*. Harare: Sapes Publications.

Murray, C. (1981), *Families Divided: The Impact of Migrant Labour in Lesotho*. Cambridge: Cambridge University Press.

—— (1987), 'Displaced Urbanisation', in Lonsdale, J. (ed.) (1987), *South Africa in Question*. Cambridge: African Studies Centre; London: James Currey; Portsmouth, NH: Heinemann.

Mutizwa-Mangiza, N. D. (1985), 'Community development in pre-independence Zimbabwe: a study of policy with reference to rural land'. Supplement to *Zambezia*. Harare: University of Zimbabwe.

—— (1992), 'Human settlement policies in Zimbabwe, with special reference to shelter', *Regional Development Dialogue* 13 (4): 138–58.

Mutizwa-Mangiza, N. D. and Helmsing, A. H. J. (eds)(1991), 'Introduction', in Mutizwa-Mangiza, N. D. and Helmsing A. H. J. (eds), *Rural Development and Planning in Zimbabwe*. Aldershot: Avebury.

Mutizwa-Mangiza, N. D. and Helmsing, A. H. J. (1991), *Rural Development in Zimbabwe*. Gower: Avebury Publishing.

Myers, G. W. (1994), 'Competitive rights, competitive claims: land access in postwar Mozambique', *Journal of Southern African Studies* 20 (4): 603–32.

Myrdal, G. (1957), *Rich Lands and Poor: The Road to World Prosperity*. New York: Harper and Row.

Narayana, N. S. S., Parikh, K. S. and Srinivasan, T. N., (1988), 'Rural works programs in India: costs and benefits', *Journal of Development Economics* 29: 131–56.

Natal Mercury (1993), 6 August. Durban.

Nattrass, J. with May, J., Perkins, D. and Peters, A. (1986), 'The Anatomy of Rural black poverty: the challenge to a new economic order',' Rural Urban Studies Working Paper No. 4. Durban: Centre for Social and Development Studies, University of Natal.

Nayak, P. K. (1986), 'Resettlement at Rengali Dam', Orissa, India: Bhubaneshwar,

Nel, E. (1990), 'Mdantsane, East London's homeland township: municipal neglect and apartheid planning 1949–1988', *GeoJournal* 22 (3): 305–13.

—— (1994), 'Local development initiatives and Stutterheim', *Development Southern Africa* 11 (3): 363–77.

Nelson, M. (1973), *The Development of Tropical Lands: Policy Issues in Latin America*. Baltimore, MD: Johns Hopkins Press for Resources for the Future.

Ngaide, T. (1986), 'Socio-economic Implications of Irrigation Systems in Mauritania: the Boghe and Foum-Gleita Irrigation Projects'. Thesis submitted for MSc (Land Resources), University of Wisconsin, Madison, WI.

Niddrie, D. (1974), 'Changing settlement patterns in Angola', *Rural Africana* 23: 47–78.

Notícias (1975), 9 June. Maputo.

—— (1977), 24 January. Maputo.

—— (1977), 14 February. Maputo.

—— (1977), 16 February. Maputo.

—— (1977), 18 February. Maputo.

—— (1977), 19 February. Maputo.

—— (1977), 20 February. Maputo.

—— (1977), 21 February. Maputo.

—— (1977), 23 February. Maputo.

—— (1977), 25 February. Maputo.

—— (1977), 27 February. Maputo.

—— (1995a), 23 June. Maputo.

—— (1995b), 5 October. Maputo.

—— (1995c), 7 November. Maputo.

Ngqaleni, M. (1989), 'A Vertical Systems Analysis of Vegetable Marketing in Lesotho'. Unpublished MSc Thesis, University of Saskatchewen, Canada.

O'Connor, A. C. (1983), *The African City*. London: Hutchinson.

Olowu, D. (1986), 'A decade of local government reform in Nigeria, 1976–1986', *International Review of Administrative Sciences* 52: 387–400.

Opoko, A. K. (1990), 'Migration and rural development: a case study of western region of Ghana', in Union for African Population Studies (ed.), *Spontaneous Papers*. Dakar: Union for African Population Studies.

Padjadjaran University (1989), 'Environmental impact analysis of the Cirata Dam', Institute of Ecology, Padjadjaran University.

Palmer, R. H. (1977), *Land and Racial Domination in Rhodesia*. London: Heinemann.

Parasuraman, A., Zeithaml, V. A. and Berry, L. L. (1985), 'A conceptual model of service quality and its implications for future research', *Journal of Retailing* 49 (Fall): 41–50.

Parnell, S. and Pirie, G. H. (1991), 'Johannesburg', in Lemon, A. (ed.), *Homes Apart: South Africa's segregated cities*. Cape Town: David Philip.

Partridge, W. L., Brown, A. B. and Nugent., J. B. (1982), 'The Papaloapan dam and resettlement project: human ecology and health impacts', in Hansen, A. and Oliver-Smith, A. (eds), *Involuntary Migration and Resettlement: The Problems and Responses of Dislocated People*. Boulder, CO: Westview Press.

Pauw, B. A. (1960), 'Some changes in the social structure of the Tlhaping of the Taung Reserve' *African Studies* 19 (2): 49–76.

—— (1963), *The Second Generation: A Study of the Family Among Urbanized Bantu in East London*. Cape Town: Oxford University Press.

Pearce, D., Barbier, E. and Markandya, A. (1989), *Sustainable Development: Economics and Environment in the Third World*. London: Earthscan.

Phororo, H. (1996), ' Home Gardens in Urban and Rural Areas of Lesotho: income generation, employment opportunities and improved nutrition'. Draft Report prepared for a Regional Project on Gender, Households and Environmental Change. Roma: Institute of Southern African Studies, National University of Lesotho.

Phororo, H. and Prasad, G. (1996), 'Vegetable marketing study'. Working Paper No. 7. Roma: Institute of Southern Africa Studies, National University of Lesotho.

Potts, D. (1995), 'Shall we go home? Increasing urban poverty in African cities and migration processes', *Geographical Journal* 161 (3): 245–64.

Potts, D. and Mutambirwa, C. (1990), 'Rural-urban linkages in contemporary Harare: why migrants need their land', *Journal of Southern African Studies* 16, (4): 677–698.

Preston-Whyte, R. A. and Tyson, P. (1988), *The Atmosphere and Weather of Southern Africa*. Cape Town: Oxford University Press.

Pugh, C. (1987), 'Housing in Singapore; the effective ways of the unorthodox', *Environment and Behaviour* 19 (3): 311–30.

Rakodi, C. (1985), 'Self-reliance or survival? Food production in African cities with particular reference to Zambia', *African Urban Studies* 21: 53–61.

Rakodi, C. (1990a), 'Policies and preoccupations in rural and regional development planning in Tanzania, Zambia, and Zimbabwe', in Simon, D. (ed.), *Third World Regional Development: A Reappraisal*. London: Paul Chapman.

—— (1990b), 'Can Third World cities be managed?', in Cadman, D. and Payne, G. (eds), *The Living City: Towards A Sustainable Urban Future*. London: Routledge.

Rakodi, C. (1995), *Harare: Inheriting a Settler-colonial City: Change or Continuity?* Chichester: Wiley.

Ramphele, M. (1993), *A Bed Called Home: Life in the Migrant Labour Hostels in Cape Town*. Cape Town: David Philip in association with the International African Institute.

Ramphele, M., with Greal, C. (1991), *Restoring the Land; Environment and Change in Post-apartheid South Africa*. London: Panos.

Ranger, T. (1994), 'Studying repatriation as part of African social history', in Allen, T. and Morsink, H. (eds), *When Refugees Go Home*. Geneva: United Nations Research Institute for Social Development, in association with London: James

Currey and Trenton, NJ: Africa World Press.

Redclift, M. and Sage, C. (eds) (1994), *Strategies for Sustainable Development: Local Agendas for the South*. Chichester: Wiley.

Reintges, C. (1992), 'Urban (Mis)management? A case study of the effects of orderly urbanization on Duncan Village', in Smith, D. (ed.), *The Apartheid City and Beyond*. Johannesburg: Witwatersrand University Press.

Reitzes, M. (1995), 'Divided on the "demon": immigration policy since the election'. Centre for Policy Studies, Policy Review Series, No. 8 and No. 9: Johannesburg.

Renaud, B. (1981), *National Urbanization Policy in Developing Countries*. Washington, DC : Oxford University Press for the World Bank.

Reserve Bank of Malawi (1981), 'The Financial and Economic Review'. Blantyre: Blantyre Print & Packaging XIII, (1): 88.

Rew, A. W. and Driver, P. A. (1986), 'Evaluation of the Victoria Dam project in Sri Lanka'. Vol. III. Initial Evaluation of the Social and Environmental Impact of the Victoria Dam project. Annex J Social Analysis. Annex K Environmental Analysis. (Mimeo.)

Reynolds, N. (1981), 'The Design of rural development: proposals for the evolution of a social contract suited to conditions in southern Africa. Parts I and II'. Saldru Working Papers 40 and 41. Cape Town: Southern Africa Labour and Development Research Unit.

—— (1995), 'Rural Development Programme Highlands Trust'. A report for SMEC/Price Waterhouse. Maseru: Lesotho Highlands Development Authority.

Rich, P. (1995), 'Pride of the Ndebele', *Architectural Review* 197: 73–7.

Richardson, H. W. (1976), 'The argument for very large cities reconsidered: a comment', *Urban Studies* 13: 307–10.

—— (1981), 'Development strategies in developing countries', *Urban Studies* 18: 267–83.

—— (1987), 'Spatial strategies, the settlement pattern, and shelter and service policies', in Rodwin, L. (ed.), *Shelter Settlement and Development*. London: Allen and Unwin.

Riddell, R. C. (1978), *The Land Problem in Rhodesia: alternatives for the future*. London: Catholic Institute for International Relations.

Robinson, P. (1994), 'Cato Manor: a legacy of South Africa's past or a model for reconstruction?' Paper presented at the Sixth International Planning History Conference at the University of Hong Kong.

Robinson, P. and Smit, D. (1994), 'Some Early Lessons from Cato Manor Development'. Paper presented at the 1994 Biennial International Conference of the South African Institute of Town and Regional Planners, Cape Town.

Roder, W. (1964), 'The division of land resources in Southern Rhodesia', *Annals, Association of American Geographers* 54 (1): 41–52.

Rodgers, G. (1994), 'Report on Mozambican Refugees' Responses to Repatriation from South Africa', Medecins Sans Frontières, Celula Inter Seccoes, August and September: 75–84.

—— (1996), 'Place to Suffer: an anthropological study of aid to Mozambican refugees in a South African settlement'. Unpublished MA thesis, University of the Witwatersrand, Johannesburg.

Rogerson, C. M. (1989a), 'Managing urban growth in South Africa: learning from the international experience', *South African Geographical Journal* 71: 129–33.

—— (1989b), 'Rethinking national urban policies: lessons for South Africa', *South African Geographical Journal* 71: 134–41.

—— (1991), 'Beyond racial Fordism: restructuring industry in the "new" South Africa', *Tijdschrift voor Economische en Sociale Geografie* 82: 355–66.

—— (1994), 'South Africa: from regional policy to local development initiatives', *Geography* 79: 180–3.

—— (1995), 'The employment challenge in a democratic South Africa' in Lemon, A. (1995), op. cit., 169–94.

Rogerson, C. M. and Kobben, S. M. (1982), 'The locational impact of the Environmental Planning Act on the clothing and textile industry of South Africa', *South African Geographer* 10: 19–32.

Rogge, J. R. (1994), 'Repatriation of refugees', in Allen, T. and Morsink, H. (eds) (1994), *When Refugees Go Home*, Geneva: United Nations Research Institute for Social Development, in association with London: James Currey and Trenton, NJ: Africa World Press.

Rondinelli, D. A. (1981), *Applied Methods of Regional Analysis: The Spatial Dimensions of development policy*. Boulder, CO: Westview Press.

—— (1983a), *Secondary Cities in Developing Countries*. Beverly Hills, CA: Sage.

—— (1983b), *Development Projects as Policy Experiments*. London: Routledge.

Rondinelli, D., McCollough, J. and Johnson, R. (1989), 'Analysing decentralisation policies in developing countries: a political economy framework', *Development and Change*, 20 (1).

Rondinelli, D. A. and Ruddle, K. (1978*)*, *Urbanization and Rural Development: A Spatial Policy for Equitable Growth*. New York: Praeger.

Roux, A. (1991), 'Migration and regional policy', *Urban Forum* 2 (1).

Russell, M. and Russell, M. (1979*)*, *Afrikaners of the Kalahari*. Cambridge: Cambridge University Press.

SABC TV News (1996), News item, 11 July 1996. Johannesburg.

Sachs, W. (ed.) (1992), *The Development Dictionary: A Guide to Knowledge as Power*. Johannesburg: Witwatersrand University Press.

Sahlins, M. (1972), *Stone Age Economics*. London: Tavistock.

Saint-Vil, J. (1993), 'Improving rural-regional settlement systems management: case study of Jacqueville, Côte d'Ivoire'. Nairobi: UNCHS (Habitat.

Samuelson, P. A. (1976), *Economics*. Tokyo: McGraw-Hill Kogakusha.

Sanders, I. T. (1977), *Rural Society*. Englewood Cliffs, NJ: Prentice Hall.

Saugestad, S. (1994), *Research and its relevance: Notes on the History of Research on the Bushmen-San Basarwa-N\oakwe of Botswana*. Paper presented to the conference on Khoisan Studies, Multidisciplinary perspectives, Tutzing, Germany.

Schama, S. (1991), *The Embarrassment of Riches*. Cambridge: Cambridge University Press.

Schapera, I. (1943*)*, *Native Land Tenure in Bechuanaland Protectorate*. Alice, South Africa: Lovedale Press.

—— (1953), *The Tswana*. London: International African Institute.

—— (1955), *A Handbook of Tswana Law and Custom*. London: Frank Cass.

Schmoll, P. G. (1993), 'Black stomachs, beautiful stones: soul-eating among Hausa in Niger', in Comaroff, Jean and Comaroff, John (eds), *Modernity and its Malcontents: Ritual and Power in Postcolonial Africa*. Chicago, IL: University of Chicago Press.

Scudder, T. (1973), 'Ecological bottlenecks and the development of the Kariba Lake Basin', in Farvar, M. T. and Milton, J. P. (eds) (1973), *The Careless Technology*. London: Stacey.

—— (1981a), 'What it means to be dammed: the anthropology of large-scale development projects in the tropics and subtropics', *Engineering and Science* 54 (4): 9–15.

—— (1981b), *The Development Potential of New Lands Settlement in the Tropics and Subtropics: A Global State-of-the-Art Evaluation with Specific Emphasis on Policy Implications*. Binghamton, NY: Institute for Development Anthropology.

—— (1984), 'The Development Potential of New Lands Settlement in the Tropics and Subtropics: a global state-of-the-art evaluation with specific emphasis on policy implications', Executive Summary. US Agency for International Development, Program Evaluation Discussion Paper No. 21. Washington, DC: USAID.

—— (1991), 'A new sociological framework for the analysis of new land settlements', in Cernea, M. M. (ed.), *Putting People First: Sociological Variables in Rural Development* (2nd edn). New York: Oxford University Press for the World Bank.

—— (1993a), 'Development-induced relocation and refugee studies: thirty-seven years of change and continuity among Zambia's Gwembe Tonga', *Journal of Refugee Studies* 6 (2): 123–52.

—— (1993b), 'Monitoring a large-scale resettlement program with repeated household interviews', in Kumar, K. (ed.), *Rapid Appraisal Methods*. Washington, DC: The World Bank

—— (1994), 'Poverty Reduction and Gender Issues'. Paper prepared for the Land and Agriculture Policy Centre and the World Bank.

—— (1997a), 'Social impacts', in Biswas, A. K. (ed.), *Water Resources: Environmental Planning, Management and Development*. New York: McGraw-Hill.

—— (1997b), 'Resettlement', in Biswas, A. K. (ed.), *Water Resources: Environmental Planning, Management and Development*. New York: McGraw-Hill.

—— (1997c), 'Advancing theoretical perspectives on resettlement'. Draft version of a chapter published in McDowell, C. and Cernea, M. M. (eds) *Reconstructing Livelihoods: Towards New Approaches to Resettlement*. Oxford: Berghahn.

Scudder, T. and Colson, E. (1982), 'From welfare to development: a conceptual framework for the analysis of dislocated people', in Hansen, A. and Oliver-Smith, A. (eds) *Involuntary Migration and Resettlement*. Boulder, CO: Westview Press.

—— (in press), 'Long-Term Research in Gwembe Valley, Zambia', in Kemper, R. (ed.), *Long-Term Field Research in Social Anthropology*. New York: University Press of America.

Scudder, T., with Manley, R. E., Coley, R. W., Davis, R. K., Green, J., Howard, G. W., Lawry, S. W., Martz, D., Rogers, P. P., Taylor, A. R. D., Turner, S. D., White, G. F. and Wright, E. P. (1993), 'IUCN Review of the Southern Okavango Integrated Water Development Project. The IUCN Wetlands Programme'. Gland, Switzerland: Samara Publishing Company for IUCN (World Conservation Union).

Sechaba Consultants (1991), 'Poverty in Lesotho: a mapping exercise'. Maseru: Sechaba Consultants.

—— (1994), 'The Situation of Children and Women in Lesotho, 1994'. Maseru: Sechaba, for the Ministry of Planning, Economic and Manpower Development.

—— (1995), *Lesotho's Long Journey: Hard Choices at the Crossroads*. Lesotho: Morija.

Sequeira, D. (1994), 'Gender and Resettlement: an overview of impact and planning issues in bank-assisted projects'. Draft paper prepared for the Bankwide Resettlement Review. Washington, DC: The World Bank.

Serageldin, I. (1995) 'Nurturing Development. Aid and cooperation in today's changing world'. Washington, DC: The World Bank.

Serrano, J. A. M. (1894), 'Exploracões Portuguesas em Lourenco Marques e Imhambane: relatorio da Comissão de limitacão da fronteira de Lourenco Marques', *Boletim da Sociedade de Geografia ds Lisboa (BGSL)* 13 (6).

Setchell, C. A. (1995), 'The growing environmental crisis in the world's mega-cities: the case of Bangkok', *Third World Planning Review* 17 (1): 1–18.

Sharp, J. S. (1982), 'Relocation and the problem of survival in Qwaqwa: a report from the field', *Social Dynamics* 8 (2): 11–29.

Shihata, I. F. I. (1991), 'Involuntary Resettlement in World Bank-Financed Projects', in Tschofen, F. and Parra, A. (eds), *The World Bank in a Changing World*. Dordrecht: Martinus Nijhoff.

Sidaway, J. D. and Power, M. (1995), 'Sociospatial transformations in the "post-socialist" periphery: the case of Maputo, Moçambique', *Environment and Planning A* 27: 1463–91.

Silitshena, R. M. K. (1982a), 'Population movements and settlement patterns in contemporary Botswana', in Hitchcock, R. R. and Smith, M. R. (eds), *Settlement in Botswana*. Gabarone: Botswana Society.

—— (1982b), 'The regrouping policy in the North-East district of Botswana', in Clarke, J. I. and Kosinski, L. A. (eds), *Redistribution of Population in Africa*. London: Heinemann.

—— (1983), *Intra-rural Migration and Settlement changes in Botswana*. Research Reports No. 20. Leiden: African Studies Centre.

—— (1996), 'The Influence of Government Policies on the Development of Rural Settlements in Botswana'. Paper presented at the IAI/ISER seminar on 'Understanding Changing Patterns of Settlement and Resettlement in Southern Africa', Rhodes University, Grahamstown, 22–26 January.

Simkins, C. (1984), 'What has been Happening to Income Distribution and Poverty in the Homelands', Carnegie Conference Paper No. 7, Second Carnegie Enquiry into Poverty and Development in Southern Africa. SALDRU, University of Cape Town.

Simon, D. (1985), 'Independence and social transformation: urban planning problems and priorities for Namibia', *Third World Planning Review* 7 (2): 99–118.

—— (1989a), 'Sustainable development: theoretical construct or attainable goal?', *Environmental Conservation* 16 (1): 41–8.

—— (1989b), 'Colonial cities, postcolonial Africa and the world economy: a reinterpretation', *International Journal of Urban and Regional Research* 13 (1): 68–91.

—— (1989c), 'Rural-urban interaction and development in southern Africa: the implications of reduced labour migration', in Potter, R. and Unwin, T. (eds), *The Geography of Urban-Rural Interaction in Developing Countries*. London: Routledge.

—— (1992a), *Cities, Capital and Development; African cities in the world economy*. Chichester: Belhaven.

—— (1992b), 'Conceptualizing small towns in African development: expansion and adaptation' in Baker, J. and Pederson, P. O., *The Rural–Urban Interface of Africa: Expansion and Adaptation*. Uppsala: Scandinavian Institute of African Studies, 29–50.

—— (1994), *Urbanisation, Globalization and Economic Crisis in Africa*, CEDAR Research Paper 10. Egham, Surrey.

—— (1995), 'Debt, democracy and development: sub-Saharan Africa in the 1990s', in Simon, D., Van Spengen, W., Dixon, C. and Närman, A. (eds) (1995), *Structurally Adjusted Africa: Poverty, Debt and Basic Needs*. London: Pluto.

—— (1996), 'Restructuring the local state in post-apartheid cities: Namibian experience and lessons for South Africa', *African Affairs* 95 (378): 51–84.

Simon, D. (ed.) (1990), *Third World Regional Development: A Reappraisal*. London: Paul Chapman.

Simon, D. and Parnell, S. (1996), 'Postmodernism, Postcolonialism and Post-traditionalism in the Developing World', unpublished manuscript.

Simon, D. and Rakodi, C. (1990), 'Conclusions and prospects: what future for regional planning?', in Simon, D. (ed.), *Third World Regional Development: A Reappraisal*. London: Paul Chapman, 249–60.

Slater, D. (1975), 'Underdevelopment and spatial inequality. Approaches to the problems of regional planning in the Third World', *Progress in Planning* 4: 99–167.

Smith, B. C. (1982), 'The Revenue Position of Local Government in Nigeria', *Public Administration and Development* 2: 1–14.

Smith, B. C. and Owojaiye G. S. (1981), 'Constitutional, Legal and Political Problems of Local Government in Nigeria', *Public Administration and Development* 1 211–24.

Snowy Mountains Engineering Corporation Limited (SMEC)/Price Waterhouse (1995), 'Organization and Manpower Study: rural development programme (RDP)'. The Highlands Trust. SMEC/Price Waterhouse, for Lesotho Highlands Development Authority.

Soeftestad, L. T. (1990), 'On evacuation of people in the Kotmale Hydro Power Project: experience from a socio-economic impact study', *Bistaandsantropologen*, June 1990.

Soja, E. W. and Tobin, R. J. (1975), 'The geography of modernisation: paths, patterns and processes of spatial change in developing countries', in Abu-Lughod, J. and Hay, R., *Third World Urbanisation*. New York: Methuen.

Spalding, N. L. (1990), 'The relevance of basic needs for political and economic development', *Studies in Comparative International Development*, 25 (3): 90–115.

Spiegel, A. (1980), 'Rural differentiation and the diffusion of migrant labour remittances in Lesotho', in Mayer, P. (ed.), *Black Villagers in an Industrial Society*. Oxford: Oxford University Press.

Spiegel, A. D. (1996), 'Migration, urbanisation and domestic fluidity: reviewing some South African examples', *African Anthropology* 2 (2): 90–113.

Stadler, J. (1994), 'Generational Relationships in a Lowveld Village: questions of age, household and tradition', unpublished MA thesis, University of the Witwatersrand, Johannesburg.

Star (1992), 14 May. Johannesburg.

—— (1992), 21 May. Johannesburg.

Stavrou, S. (1987), 'Employment and migration patterns of black farm labourers in the Natal Midlands'. Durban: Centre for Social and Development Studies, University of Natal.

Stohr, W. and Taylor, D. (eds) (1981), *Development From Above or Below? The Dialectics of Regional Planning in Developing Countries*. Chichester: Wiley.

Stoneman, C. (1976), 'Foreign capital and the prospects for Zimbabwe', *World Development* 4 (1): 25–8.

Stren, R. E. and White, R. R. (eds) (1989), *African Cities in Crisis: Managing Rapid Urban Growth*. Boulder, CO: Westview.

Stren, R. E., White, R. R. and Whitney, J. B. (eds) (1992), *Sustainable Cities: Urbanization and the Environment in International Perspective*. Boulder, CO: Westview.

Subramony, K. (1993), 'A History of Chatsworth: impact of the Group Areas Act on the Indian community of Durban (1958–1975)'. Unpublished MA Thesis, University of South Africa, Pretoria.

Sunday Times (1987), 11 January. Johannesburg.

Sunday Tribune (1957), 16 June. Durban

—— (1992), 1 March. Durban.

Surplus People Project (1983), *Forced Removals in South Africa*. 5 vols. Cape Town: Surplus People Project and Pietermaritzburg: Association for Rural Advancement.

Swedeplan (1990), 'Village Upgrading Programme: interim report'. Gabarone: Department of Town and Regional Planning.

—— (1994a), 'District Settlement Strategy: Central District, Vol. I – Survey Report'. Gabarone: Department of Town and Regional Planning.

—— (1994b), 'District Settlement Strategy: Central District, Vol. II – Strategy Proposals'. Gabarone: Department of Town and Regional Planning.

Tevera, D. (1993), 'Waste recycling as a livelihood in the informal sector: the case of Harare's Teviotdale dump scavengers', in Zinyama, L., Tevera, D. and Cumming, S. (eds), *Harare: the growth and problems of the city*. Harare: University of Zimbabwe Publications.

—— (1995), 'The medicine that might kill the patient: structural adjustment and urban poverty in Zimbabwe', in Simon, D., Van Spengen, W., Dixon, C. and Närman, A. (eds), *Structurally Adjusted Africa: Poverty, Debt and Basic Needs*. London: Pluto.

Thangaraj, S. (1996), 'Impoverishment risk analysis: a methodological tool for participatory resettlement planning' in McDowell, C. (ed.), *Understanding Impoverishment: The Consequences of Development-Induced Displacement*. Oxford: Berghan.

Therkildsen, O. (1988), *Watering White Elephants: Lessons from Donor Funded Planning and Implementation of Rural Water Supplies in Tanzania*. Uppsala: Scandinavian Institute of African Studies.

Thornton, R. (1994), 'South Africa: countries, boundaries, enemies and friends', *Anthropology Today* 10 (6): 7–15.

Tiebout, C. (1956), 'A pure theory of local expenditures', *Journal of Political Economy* 64: 416–24.

Tlou, T. (1974), 'The nature of Botswana States: toward a theory of Botswana Traditional Government – The Batswana Case', *Botswana Notes and Records* 6: 57–75.

Todaro, M. P. (1981), *Economic Development in the Third World*. (2nd edn). New York: Longman.

—— (1994), *Economic Development* (5th edn). New York: Longman.

Todes, A. (1993), 'Regional planning in South Africa: an alternative approach', *South African Geographical Journal* 75: 22–8.

Tomlinson, R. (1993a), 'From regional planning to local development planning', *Development Southern Africa* 10, 2: 167–75.

—— (1993b), 'Urban economic development in South Africa', *Development Southern Africa* 10, 3: 335–59.

Tomlinson, R. and Addleson, M. (eds) (1987), *Regional Restructuring Under Apartheid: Urban and Regional Policies in Contemporary South Africa*. Johannesburg: Raven Press.

Torp, J. E. (1989), *Mozambique: Politics, Economics and Society*. London: Pinter.

Tripp, A. M. (1997), *Changing the Rules: The politics of liberalisation and the informal economy in Tanzania*. Berkeley, CA: University of California Press.

TRDC (1995), *Establishment of a Rural Credit Facility for LHDA Projects*. Maseru: Training and Rural Development Consultants (Pty) Ltd.

Turner, J. F. C. (1990), 'Barriers, channels and community control', in Cadman, D. and Payne, G. (eds), *The Living City; Towards a Sustainable Future*. London: Routledge.

Turner, J. R. (1993), *The Handbook of Project-based Management*. London: McGraw-Hill.

Turner, R. K. (ed.) (1988), *Sustainable Environmental Management: Principles and Practice*. London: Belhaven.

United Nations (UN) (1996), *Demographic Yearbook*. New York: United Nations.

UNCHS (United Nations Centre for Human Settlements) (1990a), 'Financing human settlements development and management in developing countries: a comparative overview of case studies', HS/174/98E. Nairobi: UNCHS.

—— (1990b), 'Use of new and renewable energy sources with emphasis on shelter requirements', HS/183/89E. Nairobi: UNCHS.

—— (1991), 'People, settlements, environment and development: improving the living environment for a sustainable future'. Nairobi: UNCHS.

—— (Habitat) (1993), 'Improving rural-regional settlement systems in Africa: with special reference to rural service centres'. Nairobi: UNCHS (Habitat).

—— (1995), *Sustainable City News*, 1 (1). Nairobi: UNCHS.

UNCTAD (1983), 'Malawi country report: transit transport project for the southern African project'. UNDP/UNCTAD Project RAF/77/017.

UNCTAD/UNDP (1990), 'Efficient transport: transit of import cargoes', *Transit Transport Bulletin* 2: 9–11.

UNCTAD/UNDP (1993), 'Malawi's northern transport under MCC Concept'. UNCTAD/UNDP Project RAF/86/046, Issue 7.

United Nations Economic Commission for Africa (1996), 'Report on the state of human settlements in Africa, 1996'. Nairobi: UNCHS.

UNHCR (United Nations High Commissioner for Refugees) (1962), 'Report of the United Nations High Commissioner for Refugees'. New York: United Nations.

—— (1963), 'The Problem of Refugees from Angola in the Congo (Leopoldville)'. New York: United Nations.

—— (1965), 'Summary of information on UNHCR current operations during the period 1 January–31 July 1965 and additional statistical data'. New York: United Nations.

—— (1966a), 'Report on UNHCR current operations in 1965'. New York: United Nations.

—— (1966b), 'Summary of information on UNHCR current operations during the period 1 January–30 June 1966 and additional statistical data'. New York: United Nations.

—— (1966c), 'Note on an allocation from the Emergency fund for Assistance to a

group of Angolan refugees at Shangambo, Zambia'. New York: United Nations.
—— (1967a), 'Report on UNHCR current operations for 1966'. New York: United Nations.
—— (1967b), 'UNHCR programme for 1968'. New York: United Nations.
—— (1968a), 'Report on UNHCR current operations for 1967'. New York: United Nations.
—— (1968b), 'UNHCR programme for 1969'. New York: United Nations.
—— (1968c), 'Summary of information on UNHCR material assistance operations during the period 1 January–30 June 1968 and additional statistical data'. New York: United Nations.
—— (1969), 'UNHCR programme for 1970'. New York: United Nations.
—— (1970a), 'Report on UNHCR current operations for 1969'. New York: United Nations.
—— (1970b), 'Material assistance programme for 1971'. New York: United Nations.
—— (1971), 'Report on UNHCR current operations in 1970'. New York: United Nations.
—— (1972), 'Report on UNHCR current operations in 1971'. New York: United Nations.
—— (1973), 'UNHCR activities in the field of assistance in 1972, 1973 and 1974'. New York: United Nations.
—— (1974), 'Report on UNHCR assistance activities in 1973–1974 and proposed voluntary funds programme and budget for 1975'. New York: United Nations.
—— (1975), 'Report on UNHCR assistance activities in 1974–1975 and proposed voluntary funds programme and budget for 1976'. New York: United Nations.
—— (1976), 'Report on UNHCR assistance activities in 1975–1976 and proposed voluntary funds programme and budget for 1977'. New York: United Nations.
—— (1977), 'Report on UNHCR assistance activities in 1976–1977 and proposed voluntary funds programme and budget for 1978'. New York: United Nations.
—— (1978), 'Report on UNHCR assistance activities in 1977–1978 and proposed voluntary funds programme and budget for 1979'. New York: United Nations.
—— (1979), 'Report on UNHCR assistance activities in 1978–1979 and proposed voluntary funds programme and budget for 1980'. New York: United Nations.
—— (1980), 'Report on UNHCR assistance activities in 1979–1980 and proposed voluntary funds programme and budget for 1981'. New York: United Nations.
—— (1981), 'Report on UNHCR assistance activities in 1980–1981 and proposed voluntary funds programme and budget for 1982'. New York: United Nations.
—— (1982), 'Report on UNHCR assistance activities in 1981–1982 and proposed voluntary funds programme and budget for 1983'. New York: United Nations.
—— (1983), 'Report on UNHCR assistance activities in 1982–1983 and proposed voluntary funds programme and budget for 1984'. New York: United Nations.
—— (1984), 'Report on UNHCR assistance activities in 1983–1984 and proposed voluntary funds programme and budget for 1985'. New York: United Nations.
—— (1986), 'Review of developments in UNHCR activities relating to assistance, durable solutions and refugee aid and development and summary of decisions required'. New York: United Nations.
—— (1987), 'UNHCR activities financed by voluntary funds: report for 1986–1987 and proposed programmes and budget for 1988'. New York: United Nations.

—— (1990), 'UNHCR activities financed by voluntary funds: report for 1989–1990 and proposed programmes and budget for 1991'. New York: United Nations.

—— (1992) 'Report on the UN High Commission for Refugees'. New York: United Nations.

—— (1993a), 'UNHCR activities financed by voluntary funds: report for 1992–1993 and proposed programmes and budget for 1994'. New York: United Nations.

—— (1993b), 'Mission report – reconnaissance mission re Mozambican refugees in RSA: 13–22 August 1993'. N.p.: UNHCR

—— (1994), 'Information Paper 1994'. Geneva: UNHCR Secretariat.

—— (1995), 'Mozambique: back on track – special report'. Maputo: UNHCR Mozambique.

—— (1996a), 'Demographic survey: Meheba settlement'. Unpublished report. Luanda: UNHCR.

—— (1996b), 'Recensement des refugies Angolais au Zaire (1996)'. Unpublished report. Kinshasa: UNHCR.

—— (1998), *The State of the World's Refugees – a Humanitarian Agenda*. Oxford: Oxford University Press.

Unwin, T. (1989), 'Urban-rural interaction in developing countries: a theoretical perspective', in Potter, R. and Unwin, T. (eds), *The Geography of Urban-Rural Interaction in Developing Countries*. London and New York: Routledge.

Urban Foundation (1990), 'Policy Overview: the urban challenge'. Policies for a New Urban Future, No. 2. Urban Foundation: Johannesburg.

Urban Strategies Department (1995), 'Settlement areas and population estimates project: Durban Metropolitan Area'. USD, City of Durban: Durban.

Vance, J. E. (1970), *The Merchant's World: The Geography of Wholesaling*. Englewood Cliffs, NJ: Prentice-Hall.

van den Berg, J. (1987), 'A peasant form of production: wage-dependent agriculture in Southern Mozambique', *Canadian Journal of African Studies* 21 (3): 375–89.

van der Merwe, I. (1990), 'Secondary Cities: a literature survey and implications for an urbanization strategy in South Africa [in Afrikaans]'. Pretoria: Special report for the Department of Planning and Provincial Affairs.

van der Merwe, I. J., van der Merwe, J. H. and de Necker, P. H. (1991), 'A spatial and socioeconomic profile of urbanization in Southern Africa', *Africa Insight* 21: 97–106.

van der Waal, C. (1991), 'District development planning and closer settlement economy in Gazankulu', *Development Southern Africa* 8 (3).

van Hear, N. (1994), 'Migration, Displacement and Social Integration'. Occasional Paper No. 9, World Summit for Social Development. Geneva: United Nations Research Institute for Social Development: Geneva.

Vilakazi, A. (1962), *Zulu Transformations*. Durban: University of Natal Press.

Vincent, V. and Thomas, R. G. (1962), *An Agricultural Survey of Southern Rhodesia*. Salisbury: Government Printer.

Waterhouse, R. and Lauriciano, G. (1994), 'Re-integration of Mozambican Returnees: results from a study of refugees returning to Massingir district, Gaza Province, Southern Mozambique'. Unpublished report, Norwegian Refugee Council.

Webb, N. L. (1996), 'Urban Agriculture: advocacy and practice. A discursive study, with particular reference to three Eastern Cape centres'. Unpublished PhD thesis, Department of Anthropology, Rhodes University, Grahamstown.

Webster, E. (1978), 'The 1949 Durban riots – a case study in race and class', in Bonner, P. (ed.), *Working Papers in Southern African Studies*. Johannesburg: African Studies Institute, University of the Witwatersrand.

Weinrich, A. K. H. (1977), 'Strategic resettlement in Rhodesia', *Journal of Southern African Studies* 3 (2): 207–29.

Wekwete, K. H. (1982), 'Spatial and Structural Analysis of Manufacturing Industries in Zimbabwe and the implications for Regional Planning'. Unpublished PhD thesis, University of London.

—— (1987), 'Growth Centre Policy in Zimbabwe – a Focus on District Centres'. Occasional paper. Rural and Urban Planning Department, University of Zimbabwe.

—— (1988a), 'Rural growth points in Zimbabwe – prospects for the future', *Journal of Social Development in Africa* 3 (2): 5–16.

——(1988b), 'Development of urban planning in Zimbabwe: an overview', *Cities* 5 (1): 57–71.

—— (1989), 'Growth centre policy in Zimbabwe', *Tijdschrift voor Economische en Sociale Geografie* 80,(3): 131–46.

—— (1991), 'Growth centre policy in Zimbabwe: with special reference to district service centres', in Mutizwa-Mangiza, N. D. and Helmsing, A. H. J. (eds), *Rural Development and Planning in Zimbabwe*. Aldershot: Avebury, 187–221.

—— (1992), 'Africa', in Stren, R. E., White, R. R. and Whitney, J. B. (eds), *Sustainable Cities; Urbanization and the Environment in International Perspective*. Boulder, CO: Westview.

Wellings, P. and Black, A. (1986), 'Industrial decentralization under apartheid: the relocation of industry to the South African periphery', *World Development* 1 (14): 1–38.

Wells, B. L. (1991), 'New approaches to community development in the midwest US', *Community Development Journal* 26 (1): 24–7.

Werbner, R. (1993), 'From heartland to hinterland: elites and the geopolitics of land in Botswana', in Bassett, T. and Crummey, D. (eds), *Land in African Agrarian Systems*. Madison, WI: University of Wisconsin Press.

Whitlow, R. and Zinyama, L. (1988), 'Up hill and down vale: farming and settlement patterns in Zimunya communal land', *Geographical Journal of Zimbabwe* 19: 29–45.

Whitsun Foundation (1980), *Rural Service Centre Development Study*. Harare: Whitsun Foundation.

Wilsenach, A. and Lighthelm, A. A. (1993), 'A preliminary evaluation of the new RDP and its impact on regional development in South Africa', *Development Southern Africa* 10 (3): 361–82.

Wilson, K. B. (1994), 'Refugees and returnees as social agents: the case of the Jehovah's Witnesses from Milange District 1988–1991', in Allen, T. and Morsink, H. (eds), *When Refugees Go Home*. Geneva: United Nations Research Institute for Social Development, in association with London: James Currey, and Trenton, NJ: Africa World Press.

Wilson, K. B. and Nunes, J. (1994), 'Repatriation to Mozambique: refugee initiative and agency planning in Milange District 1988–1991' in Allen, T. and Morsink, H. (eds), *When Refugees Go Home*. Geneva: United Nations Research Institute for Social Development, in association with London: James Currey, and Trenton, NJ: Africa World Press.

Wilson, M. (1951), 'Witchcraft and social structure', *American Journal of Sociology* 56: 307–13.

Wily, L. (1979), 'Official Policy towards San (Bushmen) Hunter-gatherers in Modern Botswana: 1966–1978'. Gaborone: National Institute of Development and Cultural Research.

Wisner, B. (1988), *Power and Need in Africa: Basic Human Needs and Development Policies*. London: Earthscan.

Wolfensohn, J. D. (1995), 'Address at the Annual Meeting of the World Bank and IMF', October 1995, Washington, DC.

Wood, A. P. (1982), 'Spontaneous agricultural resettlement in Ethiopia, 1950–1974', in Clarke, J. I. and Kosinski, L. A. (eds), *Redistribution of Population in Africa*. London: Heinemann.

Wood, W. B. (1989), 'Long time coming: the repatriation of Afghan refugees', *Annals of the Association of American Geographers* 79,(3): 345–69.

World Bank (1978), 'Agricultural land settlement. A World Bank issues paper'. Washington, DC: The World Bank.

—— (1985), 'The experience of the World Bank with government-sponsored land settlement'. Report No. 5625. Washington, DC: Operations Evaluation Department, The World Bank.

—— (1990), 'Involuntary resettlement'. Operational Directive 4. 30. Washington, DC: The World Bank.

—— (1992), 'Aide memoire: South Africa urban reconnaissance mission'. Washington, DC: The World Bank.

—— (1994a), *Social Indicators of Development*. Baltimore: John Hopkins University Press: Baltimore.

—— (1994b), 'Resettlement and development: the Bankwide review of projects involving involuntary resettlement 1986–1993'. April. Washington, DC: The Environment Department, World Bank.

—— (1994c), 'World Development Report 1994: infrastructure for development'. New York: Oxford University Press.

—— (1995a), 'Lesotho: Poverty Assessment'. The World Bank: Washington, D. C.

—— (1995b), 'Katse relocation houses'. Maseru: World Bank Supervision Mission to the Lesotho Highlands Water Project.

—— (1995c), 'Data prepared for the World Bank Presentation at the October 1995 South Africa Water Conservation Conference. ' Washington, DC: The World Bank.

World Commission on Environment and Development (1991), *Our Common Future*. Oxford: Oxford University Press.

Yahya, S. S. (1990), 'Residential urban land markets in Kenya', in Amis, P. and Lloyd, P. (eds), *Housing Africa's Urban Poor*. Manchester: Manchester University Press for the International African Institute.

Yudelman, M. (1964), *Africans on the Land*. Cambridge, MA: Harvard University Press.

Yawitch, J. (1981), *Betterment – The Myth of Homeland Agriculture*, Johannesburg: South African Institute of Race Relations.

Zinyama, L. M. (1986), 'Agricultural development policies in the African farming areas of Zimbabwe', *Geography* 71 (2): 105–15.

—— (1988), 'Changes in settlement and land use patterns in a subsistence agricultural economy: a Zimbabwe case study, 1956–1984', *Erdkunde* 42 (1): 49–59.

—— (1990), 'Retail sector response to changing markets in Zimbabwe: some geographical perspectives', *Geographical Journal of Zimbabwe* 21: 32–49.

Zinyama, L. and Whitlow, R. (1986), 'Changing patterns of population distribution in Zimbabwe', *GeoJournal* 13 (4): 365–84.

INDEX